THE WOMEN OF THE CONFEDERACY

IN THE HOSPITAL
From a water color by William L. Shephard. (Courtesy of the Confederate
Museum, Richmond)

The Women of the Confederacy

By

FRANCIS BUTLER SIMKINS

AND

JAMES WELCH PATTON

GARRETT AND MASSIE, INCORPORATED

RICHMOND AND NEW YORK

Republished 1976
Scholarly Press, Inc., 22929 Industrial Drive East
St. Clair Shores, Michigan 48080

Library of Congress Catalog Card Number: 70-145300
ISBN 0-403-01212-0

PREFACE

THIS book describes a significant aspect of the internal history of the Southern Confederacy. It endeavors to evaluate the part played by the women of the South in the inauguration of the Confederate War; their share in sustaining the Confederate armies and in keeping alive the economic life of a war-torn and blockaded country; the several phases of their relations with the Federal invaders; their social pleasures; their anguish and suffering; and their experiences during the final months of the war in which the Confederacy was destroyed. In the treatment of these themes the authors have largely subordinated personalities to general movements, on the theory that eminence in the Confederacy was chiefly confined to political and military leaders, all of whom were naturally men. Varina Howell Davis is practically the only famous woman of the Confederacy, and her distinction rests largely upon the fact that her husband was the President of the Confederate States. Except in a very few instances there were no women in the South who might be compared even remotely with Florence Nightingale, and there is something of the tawdry and the unreal about those who bid for the title of the Southern Joan of Arc; for the prevalence, in an exaggerated form, of the middle nineteenth century conception of feminine duty caused the Confederate women to shun many types of activity that have made the members of their sex conspicuous in later generations. In spite of these facts, however, the women of the Confederacy collectively, if not individually, played as significant a part in the life of their people as that of any other group of women in American history. They labored for the Confederate cause with all the devotion of which women are capable; their hopes for the success of this cause were as fervent as were those of the men whom they sent to battle; and the anxieties and hardships which they suffered when the war took a tragic turn were as great as those of the men who faced the enemy's guns. The fact that the Confederacy, against overwhelming odds, was able to continue its struggle for four long years was in a sense as much due to the courage of its women as it was to the skill and valor of its men; and the fact that the Confederacy collapsed at the end of this period was due to the collapse of the morale of its women as well as to the defeat of its armies.

A few words might be said regarding the methods and the inevitable shortcomings of this study. In the first place, the sources examined reveal the women of the Confederacy as exhibiting the illogical and conflicting behavior which is usually characteristic of human life and society. There were Confederate women who wept at one moment and laughed at another, who were apparently hopeful and full of despair at the same time, and who were both patriotic and disloyal. An attempt is made to give a logical concordance to these complexities, with the hope that the book may be free from glaring contradictions. In the second place, although such would doubtless be the ideal procedure, the work is not based exclusively upon contemporary sources. Letters and diaries both in their published and manuscript forms, as shown by the footnotes and the bibliography, are used extensively, but they are freely supplemented by memoirs, reminiscences, and in some cases secondary sources. The recollections of Confederate women, although in many cases notoriously romantic, are numerous, and from them has been garnered much information that is believed to be truthful, sincere, and naively confessional—qualities largely absent from the more ponderous and sophisticated writings of Confederate men. In all cases, however, memoirs are accepted with critical reservations, and the attempt is made wherever possible to buttress them with contemporary observations and to eliminate the exaggeration and folklore with which some of them abound. And finally, it is hoped that if, as a result of extensive reliance upon their own writings, the Confederate women are here presented through their own eyes, the clouds of romantic illusion are at least cleared away.

Many persons have generously aided the authors in the preparation of this work. Among those who have been of especial assistance in the finding of materials are Professors Albert Ray Newsome and J. G. deRoulhac Hamilton of the University of North Carolina, Professor Lester Cappon of the University of Virginia, Miss Susan Harrison of the Confederate Museum at Richmond, Miss Emma Venable of the Hampden-Sydney College Library, and the various members of the staffs of the Library of Congress, the New York Public Library, and of the libraries of Duke University, the University of North Carolina, and the University of Virginia. Mrs. Martha Cox Wheeler of Burnt Quarter, Dinwiddie County, Virginia, Judge John H. DeWitt of Nashville, Tennessee, and Professor Henry C. Davis of the University of South Carolina have graciously allowed the use of private letters and manuscripts in their possession. The pursuit of the study was greatly facilitated by a grant-in-aid from the Social Science Research Council, and Thomas Moorman Simkins and Annie Augusta Chandler have been of aid in some of the more tedious researches. Professor Frank L. Owsley of Vanderbilt University has made a number of helpful suggestions, and Mr. Elford Chapman Morgan of Converse College has been of invaluable assistance in counselling the authors in the difficult matters of style and composition. Edna Chandler Simkins and Carlotta Petersen Patton have rendered constant and valuable aid, both in the preparation of the manuscript and in reading the proof and making the index.

July, 1936

State Teachers College,
Farmville, Virginia

Converse College,
Spartanburg, South Carolina

Francis Butler Simkins

James Welch Patton

CONTENTS

THE WOMEN OF THE CONFEDERACY

CHAPTER I

CHAMPIONS OF THE SOUTHERN CAUSE

IN the uncertain months that preluded the beginning of the Confederate War the zeal of the Southern women for action was equally as great as that of their masculine associates. United in the belief that the people of the North were in a conspiracy against the basic elements of their civilization and regarding the cause of the secessionists as both supremely righteous and unconquerable, these women were valiant champions of the South. As in the case of the men there were differences of opinion regarding the proper course for the South to pursue. Some women manifested a wise pessimism, and others timidly expressed a desire for caution; but the majority threw aside whatever misgivings they may have entertained, urged secession upon their leaders, and although they lamented war showed little hesitancy in insisting upon this step when they became convinced that it was necessary in order to secure the independence of the Southern States.

FEMININE INTERPRETATIONS OF NORTHERN MOTIVES

The belief that the North was in a conspiracy against the Southern civilization was centered around the conviction that the main purpose of the Northern leaders was to excite servile insurrection. Many women read the pronouncements of the abolitionists with both alarm and disgust, and others were filled with terror and bitterness when the attempt of John Brown to arouse a slave rebellion seemed to indicate that the abolitionist leaders were prepared to translate their pronouncements into actions. "The horrible, horrible time that has come to us," was a typical feminine reaction to the news of the raid at Harpers Ferry; "our world seems topsy-turvy. We feel that we can trust none of the dear black folks who, before this, we relied on at every turn."[1] Many women believed that places "were marked on John Brown's map of blood and massacre, as the first spots for the negro uprising for the extermination of the Southern whites."[2] Brooding over this act and other events of the intersectional struggle, the women found it difficult to believe that the ambitions of John Brown were merely those of a misguided fanatic. In their minds these ambitions represented the desire of the entire North. Union with such a people seemed to them intolerable, and, consequently, when the plans for the coercion of the South took form, the defeat of these plans was held to be more than a mere military or patriotic necessity. The threat of interference in Southern matters involved, in the minds of the women, the menace of servile insurrection, and a servile insurrection meant to them the destruction of a cherished civilization, devastation, and death.

As events progressed, the feminine interpretation of other phases of Northern activity was scarcely less flattering. To some "Lincoln and his crew" were "blasphemous infidels and cowardly fanatics," guilty of "duplicity and cowardly sneaking;"[3] to others "the black administration" at Washington was so bloodthirsty as to entertain the desire "to come down here and sweep us all away."[4] The wife of an important political leader in Alabama expressed the belief that a mad desire for gold on the part of the Northerners had aroused in them an ambition to exploit and plunder the section where gold dollars were supposed to be had merely by shaking a cotton plant;[5] and George Cary Eggleston encountered a woman who firmly believed that in the event of a Northern victory the Negroes and plantations would be confiscated and reassigned to Northern owners.[6]

The assertion on the part of Northern statesmen that their proposal to coerce the South was motivated only by a desire to preserve the Union was drowned in a wave of ridicule and sarcasm. It was useless, said the women, for the Northerners to cry "Union" when the words "Monarchy" and "Tyranny" would be more applicable to their actions. A Northern victory, they believed, would mean disgrace to the South and a type of bondage insufferable to an Anglo-Saxon people.[7]

These attacks upon the motives of the North were accompanied by intolerance and suspicion of strangers and persons who did not share the strong sentiments of the Southern women. Federal sympathizers were designated by unpleasant names and were given to understand in no uncertain terms that their presence was not desired in the South. "Eyes flash, cheeks burn, and tongues clatter," said a Union woman of New Orleans in describing the reaction to her suggestion that the path to victory was not flowery,[8] and when a Philadelphia woman expressed doubts to Mary Boykin Chesnut regarding the possibility of Southern success, the latter diarist "contradicted every word she said, with a sort of indignant protest."[9] Northern governesses, especially, were suspected of disloyalty and dismissed from plantations where they were employed, sometimes on very insignificant pretexts. In Florida one was accused of holding a Negro boy in her lap and kissing and crying over him;[10] another was charged with bursting forth in a tirade of invective and abuse.[11] Other persons suspected of similar misdeeds were threatened with more fearful treatment. At Camden, South Carolina, a mob of women cried for the hanging of a group of strangers who had done nothing more sinister than to walk on a trestle in a swamp.[12] For a Southern woman to marry a Northerner was considered the most dreadful reproach that might come upon her family. "Married to a Yankee!" exclaimed a wealthy North Carolina woman whose niece had thus disgraced herself. "A man against whom her brothers might perhaps be sent. It is terrible to think of."[13]

THE JUSTICE OF THE CONFEDERATE CAUSE

The attacks of the Southern women upon Northern aspirations and activities were inevitably supplemented by fervent proclamations of the justice and righteousness of the Southern cause. A favorite device was to draw parallels between the struggle for American independence and the struggle for Southern independence. It was asserted that the tyranny of the Northern majority over the Southern minority was as oppressive as that of the British crown over the American colonies in 1776; that the right of the Southern states to secede rested upon as secure a foundation as the right of the American colonies to revolt; and that the duty of the Southerners to repel the projected Federal attempt at subjugation was as urgent as had been the duty of the colonists to expel those who sought to reassert the British authority in America. On Washington's Birthday, 1862, a feminine Virginia patriot wrote, "Has there been a day since the Fourth of July, 1776, so full of interest, so fraught with danger, so encompassed by anxiety, so sorrowful, and yet so hopeful, as this 22nd of February, 1862? Our wrongs were then great, and our enemy powerful, but neither can the one nor the other compare with all that we have endured from the oppression, and must meet in the gigantic efforts of the Federal Government."[14]

Realizing that the attack upon slavery was the principal argument of those who condemned the Confederate cause, the women joined their masculine associates in the defense of that institution. Believing it to be "the great dividing line that marks us as a peculiar people,"[15] they justified it on the conventional Southern theory of the inequality of the races.[16] The black man was characterized as scarcely a high animal, an inferior being in whose coarse blood yet moved wild instincts and who could never be taught the wholesome economy and pride which distinguished the white man.[17] Proceeding on this hypothesis, many women confidently felt that only with the Negro as a slave would life in the South be tolerable either to the slaveholders or to that portion of the white population which held no slaves. It was, therefore, expected that all classes of Southern whites should and would unite for the retention of the existing status of the Negro.[18] When approached by outsiders regarding the alleged cruelties of the institution, the women refused to recognize the necessity of abolition, stating that the Negroes' "condition was much improved of late" and that the clergy were "exercising themselves to prevent the ties of matrimony being broken by sale."[19] Still other women, impelled by the same defense mechanism, affirmed that it was the high mission of the South to rescue slavery from the obloquy which a treacherous enemy had imposed upon it and make "the peculiar institution" the basis of the highest civilization.[20]

OPTIMISM AND BRAVADO

It was not difficult for the Southern women, at least in their more confident moods, to allow their belief in the justice of the Southern cause to lead them into an attitude of contempt for the ability of the North, accompanied by an optimistic conviction that the Confederacy was unconquerable. It was said that the Federal government did not possess sufficient stamina to attempt seriously the subjugation of the South; that Northern opinion was disunited; and that threats of occupying the South would disappear as soon as the obstacles in the way of such an accomplishment were apparent. Credence was given to rumors that many Federal officers were disaffected; that the Northern capitalists would not support their government unless a decisive victory was won; that the whole North would gladly avail itself of an opportunity for peace; that "every Irishman's heart was with his Catholic brothers south;" and that the Lincoln government, realizing that it did not have the power, would abandon its attempt to coerce the South.[21] Such reports prepared the women for the acceptance of the wildest rumors of Northern confusion and disaster once the war had gotten under way. That these rumors were exaggerated or without foundation had little effect upon the buoyant optimism of the Southern women. "According to the theory popular with romantic people," wrote one of them, "the real truth underlies the common surface, and it is only by realizing what we feel and cannot see that we reach it."[22]

The character of the Northern troops was unfavorably contrasted with that of the Southern armies. One woman declared that the Northern regiments were being recruited from thieves and cut-throats released from jail;[23] another stated that they were being gathered from "the riffraff, the offscourings of the cities," and that "the scum of Europe" had been induced to come to America by promises of army pay. The Southern regiments, on the other hand, were said to be composed "mainly of gentlemen—the best blood of the South." These gentlemen were believed to be brave, accustomed to riding, shooting, and other outdoor activities and actuated by the holiest of patriotic emotions—the desire to expel an alien invader from their soil.[24] It requires little imagination to infer the result which was expected by the Southern women when armies composed of men of such supposedly contrasting qualities should come in contact with each other.

The belief that the South was unconquerable because of the superior fighting qualities of its armies was more pronounced among the women than among the men. A Virginia woman shed tears for the safety of her soldier-husband, but the idea that the Southern armies could be defeated never entered her mind;[25] another received "with utter scorn" the skepticism of old men concerning the successful outcome of the war.[26] When a wealthy North Carolina planter suggested to his gardener-wife that she might be planting flowers in the conqueror's path, she impatiently retorted, "I plant flowers for our own path! A short time of conflict and the day is ours! . . . They can never overcome us, never conquer us! We fight for our Birthright! Freedom! Let them try their boasted blockade! Who cares? Whom will they hurt most—us? Themselves or England! Not us!"[27]

Among some women this spirit of optimism persisted even when it became apparent that the superior power of the North would make possible invasion and perhaps devastation. "The Federals," they asserted, "may go on invading us and despoiling our land until there are not six men left in the South and still they will gain nothing. . . . They may lay waste our country in ruinous heaps, and exterminate us, but they will not subdue us."[28] And, as will appear later,[29] after heaps of bodies as well as of ashes had actually been created, many women did not despair. They took refuge in fanciful hopes that the great nations of Europe—France or England, or both—would intervene and stay the criminal hand of the North; and when those hopes failed to materialize there remained as a final refuge, Divine Providence, a just and all-powerful force which, it was felt, would not let the seal of final failure be placed upon a cause as just as that of the Southern Confederacy.

Often this confidence in the Confederacy was accompanied by a show of bravado. " 'Hurrah for the rattlesnake bold,' " cried the maidens of Charleston; the younger girls answering, " 'For fearful its wrath to the foe in its path, be he president, peasant, or king.' "[30] "I once thought," wrote a Virginia girl caught in the enthusiasm of the spring of 1861, "how awful civil war would be, but now I feel and see it will be the best for the South, for victory will crown her efforts and God will heap misery on those who seek to destroy the peace of this glorious nation."[31] Other young women, joyously banqueting with newly-mobilized troops, participated in drinking such toasts as: "A short and glorious victory," "South Carolina, the first in the Constellation of the new Republic," and "Missouri, the last but not the least to rise against Tyranny."[32] Still transported in the glow of romantic fervor, one of these banqueting girls wrote some time later, "Visions of glory rise before us, victory, and then peace, with untold prosperity in the wake, to crown with immortality the brow of this fair young Republic."[33]

It is very improbable that the Southern women actually intended to use weapons against the enemy, but their boasts of such intentions were sufficiently emphatic to impress English visitors. Catherine Cooper Hopley saw young ladies firing pistols, "vowing to shoot the first 'Yankee' who comes within sight of their homes," and boasting that "there's not a man, woman, or child who can hold a gun or pull a trigger, who will not fight or die sooner than be any longer under the control of the Yankees."[34] Another English observer believed that "in case Richmond should become invaded a large number of Amazons will be found ready to defend their principles, their property, and their homes by sheer force of arms." " 'You see, Sir,' " he was told, " 'when the Yankees kill all the Southern men, they will have to fight the women—and they'll find them a more formidable foe than they expected.' "[35]

With characteristic lack of foresight thousands of women failed to realize that they were about to become actors in a great tragedy. Caught in the swirling emotions and enthusiasms of a people mobilizing its resources and men for a terrific struggle, during the first half of 1861, they manifested a tendency to associate war only with gold lace and plumes, bands of music, prancing steeds, and handsome officers. Their time was occupied with waving handkerchiefs at passing troops, visiting camps to witness parades, and participating in the presentation of flags. There was gayety at every important center, and the prevailing excitement afforded an outlet for frustrated emotions. "I grew up in a night," wrote a Virginia woman, years later, in describing the effects of participation in the pleasures of the time, adding that "the woods were full of handsome and delightful officers and privates, eager to be entertained and heartened for the fray."[36] At Richmond, where thousands of troops were concentrated, the hotels and boarding houses swarmed with women eager to share the excitement. "Great was the enthusiasm," said Mrs. Gilmer Breckinridge in recalling the situation. "What more stirring than the sound of the drum! What more inspiring than the graceful manoevers of the Zouaves, the Rifles, or the Rangers!"[37]

THE SALT OF REALITY

It should not be assumed, however, that all of the feminine champions of the cause of the South were motivated by the supreme optimism and the arrogant faith which have just been described. The wiser ones tempered their emotions with the salt of reality, philosophized upon the vanity of war, and looked with great apprehension upon the tasks that confronted the South. "All is beautiful but rebellious man whose spirit seems filled with discord," mused a discerning woman amid the calm of a South Carolina spring. "What an unhappy state our country is in. Every young man has entered camp. How many miserable and anxious hearts there are and yet may be. Still more painful, what a sin for thirty millions of people to rush madly into war."[38] The better informed women accepted without complaint the challenge of the North, but they did so without any illusions regarding the long period of tears and privations which lay before them. Varina Howell Davis clearly foresaw the difficulties which faced the government of which her husband was the head, believing that the North would give the South "a hot time."[39] Amid the war enthusiasm of Charleston, Mrs. Louis D. Wigfall, wife of the fiery Texas secessionist, joined with Mary Boykin Chesnut in discussing the possibility of slave insurrections and other horrors of civil war.[40] Mrs. Chesnut herself was too skeptical to share with her South Carolina friends their hopes regarding the alleged benefits of secession. "My companions," she wrote in December, 1860, "breathed fire and fury, but I dare say they were amusing themselves with my dismay, for, talk as I would, that I could not hide."[41]

Indeed there were few Southern women, at least in their quiet and thoughtful moments, who did not experience anxieties concerning the trials which in the past had been the usual lot of women in war times. A Tennessee girl, after joyously bidding godspeed to her favorite regiment, returned to the solitude of her room, prostrated with sorrowful emotion, to write, "I can only shed bitter tears for those poor boys. I know what is before them, and my soul tells me many will never see their homes and their dear ones again. . . . I am crushed. I can only weep and pray."[42] Such feelings of doubt and anxiety, however, were not uttered in loud tones during the months in which secession and war were precipitated; rather did they tend to be stifled by feelings of the opposite character. Moreover, these gloomy thoughts served to give a serious intensity to war emotions rather than to engender hostility to the efforts of the war-makers. Women who shared such thoughts were often as belligerent as those who entertained the rose-tinted notions regarding the glorious future of an independent South.

Sorrowful women united with joyous ones in crying, "Come weal or woe, success or adversity, we will willingly go down with the cause we have embraced."[43]

AGITATION AND PROPAGANDA

Convinced that a continuation of the union with the North was insufferable and that the South was capable of sustaining an independent existence, the Southern women translated their feelings and thoughts into active agitations. They advocated secession, military preparations, and other belligerent activities with a zeal and a conspicuousness hardly in keeping with the restrictions imposed by a Victorian convention regarding the public agitations of their sex. The intense character of this agitation was equalled by the prevalence of its manifestations.

One of the most obvious examples of pro-Southern activity on the part of women was the behavior of the wives of Southern Congressmen and Senators during the crisis which culminated in the withdrawal of these men from the national legislature. Early in the crisis these women drew strict social lines between themselves and former Northern friends, dropping names from calling lists and avoiding social functions where they might meet Republicans. They hailed the secession of South Carolina as "glorious news from the South," and they listened with approval while one of their group explained that South Carolina would not submit to what was interpreted as the North's putting its foot upon that state's neck. They thronged the Congressional galleries, and amid the dramatic scenes which occurred when their respective husbands renounced their allegiance to the United States, they encouraged the speakers with hysterical cries of sympathy and admiration. The final withdrawal of the Southern members awakened in them feelings of triumphant satisfaction, for they believed that the die had been cast in the struggle to preserve cherished virtues of family and state; and they left the Federal capital filled with emotions of self-esteem, fancying that with them departed all the charm and vivacity from the social life of the city. At home in the South, they accepted without question and with a sardonic satisfaction the rumors describing the boorishness and the "shabby economy" of Mrs. Lincoln and the other wives of "Black Republicans."[44]

It was inevitable that feminine enthusiasm should reach its highest point in Charleston, the earliest center of decisive action. On the eve of the secession of South Carolina the atmosphere of that city "rippled and swelled with excitement. . . . The young girls devoted their time to manufacturing every kind of patriotic device in palmetto and silk ribbon. . . . Every young woman was as defiant, as determined, and as ardent as her brother or her sweetheart."[45] Women packed the halls of the secession convention, and when the famous ordinance was signed they greeted it with fluttering handkerchiefs and shouts of impassioned emotion.[46] As the issue over Fort Sumter grew intense, feminine excitement increased. There were regrets over the pending resort to violence, but the women felt that the conduct of their opponents had made such a step necessary. The intentions of Lincoln were assailed, and his acts were interpreted as those of "a treacherous government who, whilst pretending to treat, assuring its own cabinet and the Nation that no reinforcements should be sent, deliberately breaks faith and attempted it."[47]

The belligerent emotions of the Charleston women rose to their highest pitch during the bombardment of Fort Sumter. On the day before that event women rushed out of their homes and mingled with the men with unaccustomed freedom. Some prayed for those in danger; others boasted that the male members of their families were on the islands with Beauregard. Early in the morning of April 12th, when the sound of guns announced that the attack had begun, they sprang from sleepless beds and with strained eyes watched the bombardment from roofs and galleries, alternately cheering the attackers and praying for their safety.[48] There was great rejoicing when the fort was taken by the Confederates. "I hope," wrote a member of the Pettigrew family to a relative, "you have received the glorious news and join with us in feelings of intense thankfulness! To think that our troops are in Sumter, the stronghold that has appeared so menacing for so long."[49] Mary Boykin Chesnut described the groups of women who for days afterwards thronged the Battery as "the very liveliest crowd I think I ever saw, everybody talking at once."[50] Among the better informed this rejoicing was largely due to the fact that neither friend nor enemy had been killed; but one high-strung woman, whose son had enlisted, expressed disappointment to an English traveler because every Yankee in Sumter had not been exterminated.[51]

The women of Virginia participated less demonstratively than those of South Carolina in the events of the spring of 1861, but their belief in the necessity of decisive action was no less pronounced. Assuming, for the first time in their history, a prominent part in political activity, they crowded the hall of the state convention to urge the hesitant delegates to sever the bonds which united the Federal government and the Old Dominion. "Governed by feeling," one of them afterwards confessed, "we thrust judgment in the background, and were for immediate action. We taunted our grand old mother State with her prudence, her slowness—indeed we were so unfilial as to say that she was in her dotage."[52] Observing the presence of the women in such large numbers, and the fact that they were so imprudent as to engage in political discussions in the presence of the assembled delegates, a prominent Virginian stated in disgust that "on one or two occasions some of them have set bad examples to the men in keeping order," and added, with a touch of sarcasm, that within a week "they will set out the night before" in order to get seats in the convention hall.[53] These women beamed with satisfaction when they were assured that secession was inevitable. "Day after tomorrow the vote of Virginia on Secession will be taken," wrote Judith W. McGuire, "and I, who so dearly loved this Union . . ., must now earnestly hope that the voice of Virginia will give no uncertain sound; that she may leave it with a shout."[54]

After these women had done their part in assuring the secession of Virginia, they became enthusiastic over the serious duties which that action involved. "I am ready," ran a typical expression of their sentiments, "to do all in my power for my country; yes, I would gladly lay down my life for my country's sake."[55] Their most immediate duty was to welcome the troops from the South. This obligation they assumed so avidly that, as Mary Boykin Chesnut disdainfully remarked, they were so forgetful of class distinctions as to come for a company of "sandhill tackeys" in carriages. "They fêted them," continued the disgusted South Carolina aristocrat, "waved handkerchiefs to them, brought them dainties with their own hands, in the faith that every Carolinian was a gentleman, and every man south of the Mason and Dixon line a hero."[56]

The women of North Carolina were especially resentful against the politicians and those of their male relatives who resisted the movement to secure the union of that state with the Confederacy. "Oh, that North Carolina would join her Southern sisters, in blood, in soil, in climate, and in institutions the same. Would that those vile party politicians had no lot or part in her fate," wrote Catherine Ann Edmonston as she observed the trend of events from her plantation home in Halifax County. When the male members of her family spoke affectionately of the national flag, she replied, "Who cares for the old striped rag now that the principles it represented are gone? It is but an emblem of past glory."[57] Another North Carolina woman threatened to expatriate herself because her relatives were opposing secession. "In truth," she wrote to her brother, "abuse of that noble little state of South Carolina is the only subject upon which nearly all men agree in this state. If we disgrace ourselves, as I think we will do if we keep on in this way, I intend leaving the state, for I have no part in this shameful policy."[58] These and similar threats were never executed, however, for North Carolina finally seceded.[59] Then delighted women "rushed into each others arms" and with "universality and eagerness" entered the struggle that lay before them.[60]

The same spirit of enthusiasm was in evidence among the women of other sections of the South. An English observer found many men in Savannah who would willingly have shirked the responsibilities of war, "but there was not a woman in this party," he added. "Woe betide the Northern Pyrrhus whose head is within reach of the Southern tile and a Southern woman's hand."[61] " 'Who would be the thrall of the Yankee?' " cried a young woman with flushed cheeks and beaming eyes as she addressed the applauding students of the female seminary at Tallahassee, Florida. " 'Who in this crowd dares blame the noble old state of South Carolina . . . for throwing off the oppressor's yoke? I glory in her pluck.' "[62] At Montgomery, women criticized the Confederate statesmen for harping on the mistakes of the past and the difficulties of the future rather than exulting over the accomplishments of the past and the golden opportunities which the future was thought to hold.[63] At New Orleans, women were jubilant when Louisiana seceded and "blithe and gay" when the state flew to arms.[64] Nor were the women of remote Arkansas to be outdone in martial enthusiasm. "It is very painful to see," wrote a visitor among the feminine secessionists of that state, "lovable and intelligent women rave until blood mounts in face and brain."[65]

WOMEN OF THE BORDER STATES

Some of the most striking examples of women who championed the Southern cause with greater vehemence than the men were to be found in the border states. In Maryland, northern Virginia, Kentucky, and Missouri, women ostentatiously sang rebel airs, waved rebel flags, dressed in rebel colors, and uttered rebel sentiments in the presence of the enemy, with an abandon beyond the courage of their male associates. In addition to this they secretly gathered information and prepared supplies for the men in gray who were encamped to the south of them; and, with these valuable commodities hidden under the hoops of their skirts, they made frequent visits to the territory controlled by the Confederates. That they outshone the men of their communities in pro-Southern activities and expressions of opinion was in part due to the unwillingness of the Federal authorities to deal as summarily with hostile women as with men of similar views, but it was also due to the fact that the Southern sympathies of the more emotional sex were so powerful that they left no room for considerations of prudence.

Certain women of the border states served the Southern cause so notably in the months during which the war was inaugurated that they deserve especial mention. One of these was Virginia B. Moon, a Memphis girl who was attending a school in Ohio. She was so exasperated when a Federal flag was raised over the institution that she shot it down, and when expelled from school for this act she assumed the perilous avocation of smuggling dispatches and contraband goods through the lines.[66] Of similar spirit but more famous were Jennie and Hetty Cary, two charming Baltimore sisters, whose signal act of patriotism concerned the most famous of Confederate war songs. Jennie set James Ryder Randall's "Maryland, My Maryland" to the music of "Lauriger Horatius," and she and Hetty gave the song its first rendition before a group of Baltimore girls. Incurring the disfavor of the Federal authorities in that city, the two sisters fled to Virginia, carrying with them drugs, uniforms, and copies of the song. From the doorway of a tent at Manassas they introduced the stirring lay to a large gathering of soldiers. The soldiers sang it with enthusiasm, and soon its martial strains held the whole South enraptured.[67]

The most conspicuous Southern sympathizers among the women of the border territory were Augusta Heath Morris, Catherine Virginia Baxley, and Rose O'Neal Greenhow. They not only dispatched secret information to the Confederate commanders in northern Virginia, but they were also vigorous in their abuse of the hated Lincoln administration. Rose O'Neal Greenhow, a prominently-connected widow living in Washington, asserted that wherever she went, even in the galleries of the Senate, she poured out the vials of her wrath upon the heads of the Republican leaders, a practice which was by no means stopped by their throwing her into prison.[68]

✓ ✓ ✓ ✓

By such championing of the Confederate cause the women of the South did their share in bringing on one of the greatest wars in American history. They put themselves in an aggressive state of mind by indulging in the belief that the North was in a conspiracy against their happiness and social welfare; by assuming an intransigent attitude toward those who disagreed with them; by fervently proclaiming the justice of slavery and other phases of Southern civilization; by imagining the South to be unconquerable because of the supposedly superior quality of its morale and military forces; and by thoughtlessly boasting of their prowess and by acting as though they were not on the brink of a serious tragedy. That the wiser women did not share with their more credulous sisters in the more roseate phases of this extravagant program detracted little from the aggressive character of the attitude manifested by the Southern women as a whole; for the pessimistic joined with the optimistic in cherishing the grievances of their section. That these women were profoundly stirred and tremendously in earnest will be made clear in the chapters which follow.

CHAPTER II

THE CREATION AND EQUIPMENT OF ARMIES

THE women of the South followed the demonstrations that have been described in the preceding chapter with actions which manifested the serious nature and responsible character of their enthusiasm for the Confederate cause. \They aided in the creation of the Confederate armies by encouraging the willing and goading the reluctant among their neighbors and relatives to enter the military service of the Southern states, and they had scarcely completed the duty of bidding the newly-recruited regiments farewell when they assumed the endless task of supplying these soldiers with many of the material comforts and necessities of army life which the inadequate resources of an impoverished government were unable to secure for its troops. These actions, designed to render the fighting qualities of the Confederate forces as effective as possible, required more than a vapid enthusiasm for the Southern side of a great controversy, more than a mere emotional reaction to the writings of the Northern abolitionists, and more than a romantic attachment for the allegedly superior virtues of the Southern civilization. Sending the men to battle meant tears and anguish, for the women of the South were making the greatest sacrifice known to feminine patriots, risking the lives of those dearest to them in what was going to be a long and bloody war. The assumption of the burden of aiding in the equipment of these soldiers meant painstaking and arduous labor under the most trying conditions and circumstances. Despite their fears and anxieties, however, the women of the Confederacy assumed these two burdens without hesitation or evasion, and in so doing they met with fortitude one of the greatest crises in their history.

THE STIMULATION OF ENLISTMENTS

"All through the war," says a historian of the Confederate women, "the cowards were between two fires, that of the Federals at the front and that of the women in the rear."[1] To all but the brutish and the most abject physical cowards the fire from the rear was undoubtedly the more disconcerting, for the slackers, the "Home Guards," the "bomb-proofs," and the office and hospital "rats" were subjected to discharges of feminine ridicule which were in a sense more discomforting than the fire from the enemy's guns. "All who can go with any propriety, and who are worthy of fighting," according to a feminine analysis of masculine duty in Louisiana, "are off to the seat of war; it is only the trash, and those who are obliged to remain for private reasons, who remain at home."[2] In Charleston, where all classes of women urged their kinsmen to prepare to resist the alleged tyranny of the Washington government by joining military organizations, there were expressions of deep disappointment when some men failed to heed this suggestion. "His family," ran a typical comment on such a non-conformist, "is deeply humiliated by his conduct and never mentions his name without tears of shame."[3]

Feminine resentment at the alleged neglect of military duties was equally pointed in other sections of the South. Henry Jackson, a handsome young man holding a "bomb-proof" position in Florida, imagined that he would get unusual attentions from the young ladies of his community by virtue of the fact that the other young men were absent in the army, but to his surprise and chagrin he was snubbed by the girls at a party which he attended. "His cheek flushed hotly with mortification and anger," wrote one of those present, "and turning abruptly on his heel, he seized his hat and hurried from the house."[4] A detachment of the "Home Guards" marching through the streets of Fayetteville, North Carolina, expected to receive the applause of the women spectators, but instead it evoked cutting sarcasms. " 'Dear me!' " exclaimed one woman, " 'how much fighting can these old men do?' " " 'Do look at old Mr. ———. He looks as though a feather would knock him over!' " observed another. A third added, " 'Lawyer ——— looks as if he thought himself Napoleon; and I'll venture to say he's tired half to death now.' " " 'Don't you think some of them are scared?' " was the undisguised remark of a fourth woman, while a fifth member of the group added with devastating irony, " 'Let's go home; suppose they should send a volley of shells right over here.' "[5] Even an English military observer stationed in the South in 1863 incurred feminine reproach when he declined to accept refreshments, which were offered him on a certain occasion, on the grounds that he was not an active soldier. "The ladies," he commented, "looked at me with great suspicion mingled with contempt, as their looks evidently expressed the words, 'Why are you not a soldier?' "[6]

According to their own assertions, the reproaches which these women inflicted upon men reluctant to enter the army often had the desired effect. Certain young men who were in the habit of passing the doors of patriotic girls in South Carolina were said to have been induced to enlist by the girls singing patriotic songs and waving Confederate flags in their faces.[7] Girl clerks in the government bureaus secured the enlistment of their sweethearts in the same state by pointedly telling them that their places should be taken by wounded men. One day, according to the account of Mary Darby de Treville, five or six men clerks who had been thus upbraided were seen preparing to leave. " 'Where are you going?' " said the girls. " 'To the front,' " was the reply; " 'you have run us off; called us cowards.' "[8]

The women were even more pointed in dealing with members of their own sex who were suspected of encouraging men to remain out of the army. " 'Look at my cheek; it is red with blushing for you. Fie on him! fie on him! for shame! Tell his wife; run him out of the house with a broomstick; send him down to the coast at least,' " cried a South Carolina girl to a woman accused of approving the employment of her son-in-law as a tax collector rather than as a soldier.[9] A similar rebuke was administered by a Vicksburg woman to a wife who looked with favor upon the employment of her husband in an office. " 'The only drawback to the Southern cause,' " this wife was told, " ' are the contemptible men who are staying at home in comfort, when they ought to be in the army if they had a spark of honor.' "[10]

Many women viewed the entrance of their own kin into the army with as much satisfaction as they regarded the enlistment of the husbands, sons, and brothers of other women. It is true that, as will be pointed out later,[11] some women protested bitterly when called upon to make this sacrifice and others suffered silent doubts and misgivings; but the majority, having a sufficient understanding of the gravity of the struggle confronting the South, willingly if sorrowfully let their kinsmen go. Under the stimulus of the exciting scenes that accompanied the first years of the war at least, they felt that a patriotism which did not endorse the military service of their relatives was empty and insipid, and they derived a deeper satisfaction from the knowledge that their men folk were doing their full patriotic duty than would have come from the purchase of physical safety at the cost of what they regarded as the sacrifice of a priceless heritage. When Matthew Fontaine Maury, the distinguished oceanographer, left Washington at great personal and professional sacrifice to offer his services to his native Virginia in 1861, his daughter wrote, "I was proud of my father before, but I am a hundred times prouder of him now. . . . He could not take sides against his own people—against his native state and against the right."[12] On the other hand, General Winfield Scott, a Virginian who did not elect to follow the example of Maury, was characterized by the same writer as "the old humbug, the old crocodile."[13]

Mothers, wives, sisters, and sweethearts assumed this patriotic attitude. Mothers told crowds frightened by the Federal advance in Virginia that, although war was dreadful, they would not by raising a

A FEMALE REBEL IN BALTIMORE
(From *Harper's Weekly*)

finger attempt to prevent their sons from serving their country.[14] Wives wrote their soldier-husbands that, although they loved them and were anxious for their safety, they preferred to be the widows of brave soldiers than the wives of cowards or slackers.[15] Sisters gloried in the belief that their brothers were the bravest of the brave, and wrote that, though Lucifer should dispute their path, they would despise them if they shrank from their duties.[16] Sweethearts refused to pledge their troth to lovers until they had fought the enemy. " 'But suppose I don't come back at all?' " argued one Virginia suitor. " 'Oh,' " replied a Spartan maiden, " 'then I'll acknowledge an engagement and be good to your mother—and wear mourning all the same—provided your wounds are all in the front.' "[17]

MANIFESTATIONS OF SPARTAN MOTHERHOOD

The foregoing examples largely concern the women of the more elegant levels of Southern society. That those of the less favored classes were no less earnest in the encouragement of martial activity on the part of their men folk is demonstrated by a number of instances of exceptional fortitude. When a young widower hesitated about joining the army in Alabama because of a desire to avoid placing the burden of the care of his children upon his aged mother, she replied, " 'Go, Jack, the country must have men, and you must bear your part, and I will take care of the children.' " Responding further to his assertion that in case of his death the children would become a permanent encumbrance upon her, she declared, " 'Jack, I will do a mother's part by them; but you must not talk that way. Why should you get killed more than another? You will be back, and then I shall be happy. God will take care of you.' "[18] Another story concerns the attitude of an humble Virginia woman toward the military services of her sons and husband. When the husband explained his failure to enter the service on the ground that he was too old to march, she said, " 'Old man, I don't think you could; you would break down; but I tell you what you can do—you can drive a wagon in place of a young man that's driving, and the young man can fight.' " When asked if she regretted that her husband and sons were in the army, she replied, " 'Oh, yes, I shall miss my husband mightily; but I ain't never cried about it; I never shed a tear for the old man, nor for the boys neither, and I ain't agwine to. Them Yankees must not come a-nigh to Richmond.' "[19]

The large number of sons given by some women to the Confederate service is strikingly illustrated by a list compiled from the North Carolina muster rolls. Two women from that state, Flora MacDonald

Jones and Lucy Faucett Simpson, each gave eleven sons to the military service of the Confederacy; four gave nine sons; two gave eight; nine gave seven; eighteen gave six; nineteen gave five; thirteen gave four; and twenty-two gave three sons each.[20] The spirit animating these North Carolina mothers is demonstrated in a statement given by one of them to a newspaper reporter in 1863. " 'I have three sons and my husband in the army,' " she said. " 'They are all I have, but if I had more, I would freely give them to my country.' "[21]

The death of sons in the line of duty often stimulated mothers to risk the lives of additional sons in the service of the Confederacy. Among these heroines was a Richmond woman who, after losing three sons in action, "dried up her tears and said, with spirit, that the chief grief of her heart was that she had no more sons to fight for her country."[22] Another Virginia woman, moved by the same spirit, appeared before "Jeb" Stuart after two of her sons had been lost in battle, bringing her only remaining son, a fair-haired youth of fifteen, and telling the general that she was ready to give this boy to the army also.[23] A Tennessee mother, stirred by the loss of three sons, said to General Leonidas Polk regarding her only remaining son, " 'As soon as I can get a few things together, General, you shall have Harry too.' "[24] Exalted suffering and sacrifice demanded an exalted vengeance from these Spartan mothers. The blood of the slain sons called for additional sons to battle for the vindication of those who had fallen.

SOLDIERS' RELIEF

The same stimulus that prompted the Confederate women to the painful duty of yielding friends and kinsmen to the army also impelled them to assume the burden of providing many of the material comforts and necessities that were indispensable to the equipment and efficiency of the Confederate forces. No armed conflict in the previous history of the race had ever witnessed the organization of civilian relief on so vast a scale as was experienced during the War for Southern Independence. The work of the United States Sanitary Commission, the United States Christian Commission and other agencies in the North is well known; and, although not organized to the same extent, the burdens borne by the non-combatant population in the South were even greater than in the free states. It is a tribute to feminine sagacity that the women of the Confederacy understood the significance and the necessity of these labors. From the very beginning of the conflict they realized that, in the face of an imperfect system of transportation, the relative absence of manufacturing industries, and the blockade which the Federal government would likely impose, the resources of the Confederacy would be inadequate to compete with the almost unlimited resources of the North, and that the success of the South depended in large measure upon the counteracting of this disparity between the two sections. Excessive volunteering and conscription depleted the masculine non-combatant population to such an extent that this task fell largely to the women.[25] Upon them devolved the necessity of providing the soldiers with clothing, foodstuffs, flags, tents, gun-cases, cartridges, bandages, and numerous other articles required by men in modern warfare.

The tremendous enthusiasm with which the Southern women assumed these trying obligations is impressive. In addition to its being a patriotic obligation, such work performed the task of securing partial relief from the heartaches caused by the absence of the men.[26] "Many of us," wrote a Virginia woman, "were glad to have our hands kept busy to stop the bleeding of our hearts."[27]

During the spring and summer of 1861, all classes of women devoted themselves to these labors at all hours. School girls abandoned their play and their books to learn the intricacies of sewing from their elders; the devotees of ease and idle enjoyment became busy seamstresses; and the parlors, materials, and sewing machines of the rich were freely put at the disposal of the humblest women workers. Although rich ladies hired the poor to work for them, they did not in this manner relieve themselves of the more burdensome tasks. They labored over heavy tents, overcoats, jackets, and pants, as well as the lighter articles of personal adornment, until their delicate fingers were stiff, swollen, and bloody from overwork. There was no rest for thousands of women until the late hours of the night, and the prevalence of an emergency was considered justification for work on the Sabbath and during the suspense that obtained while great battles were in progress. So great was the preoccupation with these duties that women were observed knitting during visits and as they rode in carriages.[28]

INDIVIDUAL EFFORTS

This zealous enthusiasm inevitably resulted in the accomplishment of large tasks by individuals. "Work was carried on all the time for the boys," said a representative Virginia woman; "gaiters were made for them to march in, havelocks for their caps, not to speak of more prosaic garments."[29] With her own labor supplemented by that of her slaves, a South Carolina woman supplied an entire company of soldiers with all of its necessities, and another woman in the same state was able, through her own efforts, to clothe a company with wool that was grown, carded, and spun on her own plantation.[30] Other women of similar accomplishments included one who knitted 750 pairs of socks in twice that number of days from cotton, grown, carded, and spun on her own farm,[31] and another who, unassisted, made 500 cartridges in a single fall.[32] Mrs. Matthew Fontaine Maury made six pairs of pantaloons, six jackets, and eight shirts and havelocks in three days.[33]

Extracts from their correspondence reveal the attentiveness with which the women regarded the needs of the soldiers. "The thought of what I can do for the soldiers occupies me constantly," wrote the wealthy Catherine Ann Edmonston of North Carolina in her Halifax diary. "I can by using my table covers, scraps of flannel, etc., manage to piece out six flannel shirts. Patrick [her husband] will give cloth from the plantation supplies for six pairs of drawers and woolen cloth for six pairs of pantaloons and six pairs of shoes. . . . I can, I think spare two blankets more, and will take my chintz coverlids and make four comfortables. . . . We will fit out six soldiers."[34] "I can send you," wrote a Texas wife of moderate circumstances to her soldier-husband, "a box by Lt. Fitzpatrick, containing for yourself one pair of pants, two pairs of drawers, five candles, and a little coffee (all I had), a towel which I designed for you to be used in wiping your dishes, and a piece of cloth to wash them with. Lizzie Hargrave asked me to send a vest and two pair of pants for Billie. . . . Your mother sends Norflet [a servant] one pair of pants, two pairs of socks, and a comforter."[35] That the same spirit existed among the less fortunate elements of the population is illustrated in a letter written by a poor woman of North Carolina to the governor of that state. Although she did not have food enough for her large family, she was determined to send supplies to the only surviving one of three sons that she had given to the army. "I have sent them something to eat time and agane," she wrote. "The only one that is left says send him something to eat and so I will as long as I have anything to send."[36]

The relief work of several women was sufficiently notable to find special mention in the chronicles of the times. Mrs. D. W. Brown of Lancaster, South Carolina, for example, dispatched with the aid of her servants numerous boxes to the soldiers on Morris Island and in Virginia, made socks, scarfs, and helmets for them, and attended to the needs of other wives in her community.[37] From the day of the departure of her husband for the army, the entire time of Margaret Tyler McMichael, another South Carolina woman, "was given to the Confederacy." Her days were consumed in preparing delicacies for passing soldiers, knitting socks, and scraping lint, and her nights were often interrupted by rising to receive the sick and wounded into her home.[38] Mary Ann Buie of Wilmington, North Carolina, was one of the most outstanding women of this type. She uniformed a whole company at her own expense and traveled about for the entire length of the war, attending the sick and distressed and soliciting funds for relief work. Writing to Governor Vance in August, 1864, she estimated that she had collected goods and supplies to the value of half a million dollars. Her labors won her the title of "The Soldier's Friend" and the present of a handsome silver service from her admirers.[39] Less spectacular but equally as effective was the work of Mrs. John T. Johnston of Madison County, Mississippi, in whose home spinning wheels, shuttles, and needles were busy all day long. Her silks became banners, her carpets were made into blankets, and her linens and cambrics afforded bandages and gauze; her extensive granaries, smokehouses, and wine cellars gave up their stores. The result of her labors and sacrifices was the maintenance of one company for the length of the war and the furnishing of clothing to two hundred other soldiers.[40]

SOLDIERS' AID SOCIETIES

Essential as were these individual exertions, they were supplanted to a considerable extent, during the early months of the war, by coöperative agencies known as soldiers' aid societies. A number of factors contributed to render the coöperative method of relief more effective than the efforts of individuals. Since the usual problem was to supply companies rather than single soldiers, collective activity afforded an opportunity for the pooling of resources and the division of labor. The inadequate supply of spinning wheels, looms, and sewing machines could be more readily utilized to the limit of their capacities. Moreover, funds and supplies could be more easily solicited and collected from the government and other sources than through individual petitions, and the more efficient distribution of the relief would be facilitated. Finally, a less tangible but equally important accompaniment of group activity was the evolution among the women of an *esprit de corps* to a degree hitherto unknown in the South, a development which furnished an obvious relief from the trials of war.

Consequently, mobilization had scarcely started when women in every section of the South began to assemble in private homes, town halls, courthouses, churches, and schoolhouses—in fact wherever a convenient place of meeting could be found—for the purpose of manufacturing soldiers' supplies. Within a short time these informal gatherings were transformed into permanent societies with appropriate names, formally elected officers, and written rules of procedure. The number of such organizations formed in the South during the war approached a thousand, and the names which they assumed were varied. In Alabama, for example, there was the Grove Hill Military Aid Society, the Scruggsville Soldiers' Aid Society, the Aid Society of Mobile, and the Ladies' Humane Society of Huntsville;[41] in South Carolina, the Baptist Home Society, the Volunteers' Aid Society, the Home Guard Society, the Palmetto Girls' Society, and the Ladies' Clothing Society, to include only a few of the better known ones.[42] Although the formal organization of such societies was usually effected at meetings presided over by clergymen or other male speakers, thus saving the women the embarrassment of appearing before the public, their actual management and labors were accomplished by feminine hands.

The efforts of these societies were almost entirely of a practical nature. "The object of this association," read a statement of the purposes of the Hospital Aid Society of Spartanburg, South Carolina, "shall be to provide garments, hospital stores, and other comforts for our sick and wounded soldiers, and, secondly, to furnish underclothing, socks, and other articles needed for our soldiers in the field—these objects to be carried out by voluntary contributions of money, material, and labor."[43] "We are anxious to do hospital work, and can have cloth if the cotton yarn is furnished," wrote a member of the Ridgeway Soldiers' Aid Society to the governor of North Carolina. "We desire to do our utmost for the brave soldiers, our hearts grieving all the time that our *all* is so little."[44] "In returning thanks to those of our friends who have aided us during the past two years," said the Soldiers' Relief Association of Charleston, typical of the thousands of appeals for private subscriptions made by the societies, "we must entreat them not to forget us in the time of our trouble, but to come to the rescue as in days gone by."[45]

The enthusiasm of the soldiers' aid societies "does not evaporate in words, but shows itself in work, real hard work, steady and constant," wrote a North Carolina diarist in 1862.[46] The truth of this assertion is demonstrated by tangible results. As soon as they were organized, these societies began dispatching boxes at regular intervals to the companies and regiments in which they were respectively interested. The contents of these boxes included pants, shirts, socks, gloves, hats, towels, soap, sheets, mattresses, Bibles, pens, ink, writing paper, and other articles of personal use—approximately everything except shoes that was needed for clothing a soldier or furnishing his tent. In addition to these articles were such nonperishable edibles as hams, bacon, coffee, dried fruits, rice, and flour; and also, as will appear later,[47] bandages and delicacies which were supplied to the hospitals of the Confederacy.

The substantial character of the early efforts of these societies is concretely illustrated by the reports of those who had examined some of the boxes sent to the soldiers. The Soldiers' Friend Association of Lake Orange, Florida, said a local newspaper, has "made thirty pairs of pants for the soldiers at Fernandina, the ladies furnishing the materials from their private stores, besides knitting socks and making other garments."[48] The *Charleston Mercury*, in its capacity as agent of the societies in that city, wrote, "We might enumerate a host of good things we have been the happy instrument of transmitting to worthy recipients—good things of every imaginable kind from mattresses to lint."[49] A box sent by an Alabama society to the Grove Hill Guards was said to have contained sixty pairs of socks, twenty-five blankets, thirteen pairs of gloves, fourteen flannel shirts, sixteen towels, five pairs of trousers, two handkerchiefs, and a bushel of dried apples;[50] and the Methodist and Baptist societies of a South Carolina village had, by July, 1861, shipped to the soldiers from their neighborhood eighty-seven shirts, ninety-seven pairs of socks, eighty sheets, twelve dozen towels, and four dozen handkerchiefs.[51]

The boxes sent during the latter stages of the war were no less substantial in content. During the early months of 1865 the Soldiers' Relief Association of Charleston sent 286 cotton shirts, 233 flannel shirts, 267 pairs of drawers, 189 pairs of socks, 179 pairs of pants, twenty-three pairs of shoes, eighteen blankets, nineteen comforts, and thirty-six scarfs and handkerchiefs.[52] Boxes sent by the women of Arkansas at about the same time contained suits of jeans, blankets made from carpets, bandages made from bed and table linen, goose quills, home-made ink, stationery made from all kinds and colors of wrapping paper, corn-cob pipes with bits of cane for stems, pincushions filled with pins and needles, sewing thread and black balls made of beeswax to color it with, soap to prevent the feet from blistering and red pepper to keep them warm, as well as soap and pepper for conventional uses, and many kinds of nonperishable foodstuffs.[53]

"Were it not for the exertions of the Southern women," wrote an English observer of the work of the soldiers' relief societies, "the volunteers would have been ill provided for."[54] They solicited contributions of money and materials, they held bazaars and fairs, and they ceaselessly strove to transform the supplies at their disposal into articles of immediate use to the soldiers. Their efforts and sacrifices are exemplified in a report of an agent of the governor of North Carolina. "Your patriotic proclamation," wrote this agent to Governor Vance, "has reached the hearts of the ladies and they are determined to use the means which they had designed for the comfort of their families for the use of the brave soldiers. . . . They will continue to divide and fast . . . as long as they hear of a suffering soldier."[55]

The relief societies continued their labors until the end of the war. Compared with the heroic deeds that the men of the South were performing or were about to perform on the battlefields of Virginia and elsewhere, these acts of the women of the South may seem commonplace and inconsequential, but they were one of the necessary bases for the successful pursuit of the drama of war.

✓   ✓   ✓   ✓

In such manner the women of the South took the final steps of their part in giving reality and effectiveness to the martial efforts of the Confederacy. They supplemented their enthusiasm for secession and war by encouraging the men to join the military forces and by assuming the obligation of providing the soldiers with many of their material necessities. These activities, however, were but the beginning of the labors, trials, and enthusiasms of the women for the Southern cause.

CHAPTER III

MARTIAL ENTHUSIASM AND RELIGIOUS FAITH

THE women of the Confederacy had little part in the military events which form the central theme of most accounts of the War for Southern Independence. There were no women among the great heroes of the victories nor among the great martyrs of the defeats. The human traits exalted at that time were physical courage, prowess with sword and gun, and military acumen. These were masculine virtues, and the war produced no women who can be compared even remotely with Joan of Arc. Nor was there even a real Florence Nightingale in the South. Inhibitions against feminine conspicuousness prevented the emergence of any woman sufficiently well known to become a symbol of angelic mercy to the sick and the wounded. Yet the part of the women in sustaining the military fortunes of the Confederacy was vital if inconspicuous. In addition to the physical labors described in the preceding chapter, they exercised a salutary influence upon the morale of the armies. By word and letter they sought to impress upon the men the merits of bravery, contempt for the enemy, and the horror of defeat; by the willingness to sacrifice not only physical conveniences and comforts but also the lives of friends and kinsmen for what was considered a holy cause, they served notice on countrymen and foe alike that they would tolerate no cessation of fighting until victory was won; and by an uncritical faith in the soldiers and a mystical faith in Providence, they inspired confidence in the ultimate success of their cause. When the waves of their hope and zeal finally broke on the rocks of reality, the Confederacy was dead.

PAGEANTRY AND PRODIGALITY

Although the martial enthusiasm of the women of the Confederacy was generally of a serious type, that of the early months of the war frequently manifested itself in a lighter vein, characterized alike by pageantry and prodigality. At New Orleans, for example, the vision of "parties, rides, and walks to grow gayer and more frequent" was for a time realized in what one woman described as "this splendid mimicry of war."[1] Ladies in airy costumes made frequent visits to encampments where they witnessed parades, chatted gaily with men in bright uniforms, and enjoyed lunches of "delicious gumbo, game of all kinds, and fruits only to be found in perfection in the markets of New Orleans."[2]

The passion of women of this type for war is well illustrated by the part which they took in the presentations of flags to military organizations. Dames and maidens considering their phase of these ceremonies a high honor, wrought banners out of the choicest materials in the most elaborate designs. One presented by the ladies of Charleston to Wade Hampton's regiment "was made of a crimson silk dress, the design a wreath of oak leaves encircling 'Hampton Legion.' "[3] Another, presented to a North Carolina company, was of blue silk ornamented with tassels and a heavy fringe; emblazoned on one side with the coat of arms of the state, surrounded with gold stars, and on the other side with a wreath of corn, cotton, and wheat, encircling the words "Scotland Neck Mounted Riflemen" and tied with a ribbon inscribed "Pro Aris et Focis."[4] The presentations of these emblems were attended by elaborate ceremonies. Usually a procession of girls, garlanded with flowers and carrying the heavily ornamented banner, moved through the streets to the town auditorium. There, beneath an arch of flowers, the emblem was presented by a young woman to representatives of the favored military organization, which ceremony was followed by a patriotic address by some local orator and recitations by girls impersonating each of the seceded states.[5]

Another example of the thoughtless zeal of some women for war appears in the manner in which they supplied the physical needs of newly-recruited soldiers. Many of these efforts were characterized by impractical extravagance. Carpets were torn up to cover the floors of tents, and cordials were sent to soldiers to be consumed in the idleness of camp life. The tents of New Orleans officers were equipped with "all the appurtenances of the toilette, in the form of pearl-handled brushes, powder boxes, and plate mirrors;"[6] while "a shimmer of bright ribbons, silk, beads, glossy satin, and downy velvet" featured the "smoking caps, slippers, tobacco pouches, cigar cases, and portfolios stocked with the contents of the women's escritoires" which some of the women of Georgia supplied to their soldier-friends in Atlanta.[7] The luxuries wasted in this manner during the early months of 1861, according to Elizabeth Lyle Saxon, would have been sufficient, had they been properly conserved, to supply the demands of the armies for these articles during the entire period of the war.[8]

DEPRIVATION AND SACRIFICE

The willingness with which the women undertook to sustain the morale of the armies of the Confederacy continued, with certain exceptions to be hereinafter noted,[9] until the end of the conflict, and as the war progressed their attitude assumed a serious reality that stands in decided contrast to the frivolous extravagance that marked the early months. As the available supplies gradually became exhausted in the South, the generosity of the women came to be dispensed at the price of deprivation and sacrifice.

The alacrity with which this sacrifice was performed is exemplified by the manner in which the women met the needs of passing troops. " 'Young ladies,' " said the principal of a Richmond seminary as his students were seating themselves for a meal, " 'several extra trains have arrived, unexpectedly, filled with troops. The committee appointed to attend to them are totally unprepared. What can we do to help our hungry soldiers?' " " 'Give them our dinner,' " cried all the girls in unison, and within five minutes they were on the way to the railroad station with their dinners packed in baskets. "Our dear, dusty, hungry gray coats," wrote the chronicler of this event, "dined to their hearts' content, filled their haversacks, shouted 'Richmond forever!' and went on their way rejoicing."[10] An example of similar conduct occurred when the women of Columbia, South Carolina, heard that there was a destitute Kentucky regiment in town. "Soon the Senate chamber . . . was a scene of activity," wrote Florida Saxon. "All day the ladies stitched away on coats, pants, and shirts. . . . Dainty fingers . . . were busy making coarse yarn into socks. . . . In every pair of socks was placed the name of the donor, together with a verse of poetry, a tract, or a note containing a word of sympathy and cheer."[11]

Many women fell into the habit of volunteering favors to soldiers, regardless of what inconveniences these favors might involve. A wealthly Virginia girl, fortified with a basket of food for the long journey that she was making to a watering place, met some hungry soldiers in Petersburg. Taking no thought of what she would eat on the morrow, she distributed the contents of her basket among the troops.[12] When a passing soldier told a Tennessee girl that his shirt was ragged because he had no other, she immediately retired into another room, divested herself of an undergarment, and made it into a shirt for him.[13] Two young women at Milton, Louisiana, observed a couple of Confederate officers purchasing cloth in a store, whereupon they gleefully volunteered to make it into shirts. "Lilly undertook one of purple merino, and I took a dark blue one," recorded one of these young women in her diary. "All day we worked, and when evening came, continued sewing by the light of these miserable home-made candles. . . . Lilly's was trimmed with folds of blue . . . while mine was pronounced a *chef d'oeuvre*, trimmed with a bias fold of tiny red and blue plaid. With fresh colors and shining pearl buttons, they were really very pretty."[14]

"The armies must be supplied even if the home-folks starve. They must not have our burdens to bear in addition to their own," wrote a Florida woman in 1863.[15] In keeping with this resolution, many women refused to eat meat or drink coffee, after food began to grow scarce, living thenceforth only upon perishable vegetables in order that they might leave the more durable foods for the soldiers. George Cary Eggleston told of a soldier who, while dining at a Virginia table, was mystified by the fact that none of the women present ate any meat. " 'Honestly, I did want the ham,' " one of the women explained to him the next day. " 'I have hungered for meat for months. But we women can't fight, and are trying to feed the fighting men. We have made up our minds not to eat anything that can be sent to the front.' "[16] Luxuries were tolerated on the tables of such women only when soldiers were present. "His plate at the table was different from any other," said a North Carolina woman of a soldier visitor. "Stationed beside it was real coffee, if possible; if not, the best rye with sugar in it, if sugar could be had. Milk, that great boon of the soldier, and everything green, was for him."[17]

Valuables other than food were given up in the same spirit. Women yielded plantation and church bells to be cast into cannon, and preserving kettles to be made into cartridge caps. Underclothing and dresses were transformed into shirts, and woolen mattresses and old garments were torn apart, mixed with cotton, carded, spun, and woven into coverlets or knitted into socks. Jewelry and plate were given to the soldiers' aid societies to be raffled off at fairs. "We do not spare our precious things now," wrote Mary Boykin Chesnut after presenting her pearls and a silver teapot for a raffling;[18] and, in response to the demand of the army for her plantation laborers and supplies, Catherine Ann Edmonston wrote, "Prayerfully do I send them, hoping that their labor *there* will protect us *here*."[19]

Toward the end of the war, when the available supplies appeared to be approaching exhaustion, the women of the Confederacy made sacrifices that resemble those of the women of classic legend. Some were reduced to covering themselves at night with old quilts and shawls because they had sent all their blankets to the army; others deprived themselves of all except one meal of bread and vegetables each day, in order that the provisions saved thereby might be sent to the hungry soldiers.[20] When asked to relieve passing troops, some poor Georgia women, according to Kate Cumming, "brought some cornbread and beans, which, I am certain, they could ill afford. They said they would gladly do without themselves, so our brave defenders had them."[21] To the remonstrance that she was denying herself adequate diet, a Virginia woman replied, " 'There is little that I can do, and I must do that at any cost. . . . I would starve to death cheerfully if I could feed one soldier more by doing so. . . . I think it is a sin to eat anything that can be used for rations.' " Her deprivations, according to the chronicler of this tale, resulted in her death.[22]

A few weeks before the end of the war an orator in Richmond said to his audience, " 'When the women of the South are ready to do as the matrons of Rome did—throw their ornaments of silver and gold in the treasury and redeem the Confederate bonds, the Confederacy will be safe.' " The response was immediate, according to Judith W. McGuire. "Ladies," she wrote with approval in March, 1865, "are offering their jewelry, their plate, everything that can be converted into money, for their country."[23] About the same time a woman signing herself, "A Niece of James Madison," proposed through a Mobile newspaper that the women sell their locks to European hairdressers in exchange for public credit. This suggestion also met with approval. "There is not a woman worthy of the name of Southerner who would not do it, if we could get it out of the country, and bread or meat in return," declared Mrs. McGuire.[24] Some women cut their hair, thinking it could be sold through the blockade, and many others undoubtedly would have done the same, had not the blockade and the early end of the war made the project impracticable.[25]

PATIENCE, DEVOTION, AND DETERMINATION

Along with their physical labors and material sacrifices for the Confederate cause, some women came to manifest a peculiar pride in their destitution. They would show the Yankees, wrote one, that they could do without "their miserable trades-people" with "their wooden nutmegs, paper-soled shoes, etc.," by wearing "good *honest* wooden bottoms" and eating the fruits of the earth which God would give them.[26] Others charged the Northerners, who dared to taunt them over their rags and poverty, with being blinded to true principles by material considerations. There was more glory in the Southerners' rags than in all the gold lace and glitter of the Federals, asserted Kate Cumming.[27] Still others attempted to minimize the gravity of their situation by resorting to a forced optimism. "Courage!" wrote Sarah Morgan in the midst of difficulties of February, 1863. "Better days are coming! And then I'll have a funny tale to tell her [a friend] of the days when the Yankees kept us on the *qui vive,* or made us run for our lives. It will 'tell' merrily; be almost as lively as those running days were."[28]

"Although woe and desolation stare us at every turn," wrote a hospital matron in summarizing the tragic history of 1864, "the heart of the patriot is as firm as ever, and let come what may, he will never fail."[29]

More important than such rationalizations and optimistic platitudes, however, was the patient cheerfulness of the women, which contributed in no small measure to bolster up the courage of the fighting forces. An English observer declared that he was often told on his travels that the women "invariably set an example of patience, devotion, and determination," and that the independence of the country, if won, would be in a large measure due to their efforts.[30] This observation was confirmed by others. "The brave women of the city," wrote T. C. DeLeon of the feminine inhabitants of Richmond, "were a constant reproach in their quiet unmurmuring industry to the not infrequently faint-hearted and despondent men;"[31] and Captain Ham Chamberlayne marvelled at the apparent calmness of the same women during the attack of Grant's forty thousand soldiers upon that city.[32] George Cary Eggleston sweepingly declared, "No complaint from the women ever reminded their soldier-husbands and sons and brothers that there were hardships and privations and terror at home."[33] That such a broad statement was an exaggeration will be hereinafter demonstrated,[34] but it undoubtedly described the intentions and accomplishments of a considerable number of the women of the Confederacy.

The writing of cheerful letters to the soldiers was publicly advocated, and lists of names for this purpose were distributed among the women. "We have plenty to eat, and know that it's only you that's having a hard time," began a model letter written by a Georgia wife to her soldier-husband. "But we are proud that you are fighting for your country. Will be so glad when you get a furlough, but we know that you must and will stick to your post of duty. . . . We never forget to pray for you. If you get killed, darling, God will take care of us, and we'll all meet in heaven."[35] Although less perfect examples of self-abnegation, the letters which a Tennessee woman wrote to her chaplain-husband were equally emphatic in their moral and patriotic fervor. Along with frequent complaints of feeling ill, the infrequency of her husband's letters, war-weariness, lack of funds, and the perils of approaching childbirth, she added, "I must endure these things without complaining. I appreciate my manifold blessings."[36]

It was inevitable that such women should demand a high order of courage from their men. The attitude of intolerance toward men who neglected to enlist in the fighting forces, which has already been described, was extended, as the war progressed, to all forms of masculine weakness, especially cowardice. "I don't enjoy that kind of talk from men; I like dash and flash, and fire in talk, as in action," wrote a Georgia girl after a conversation with a male acquaintance who talked pretty sentiments.[37] The women of Richmond subjected the members of the Confederate Congress "to the most unmerciful twittings" in the fall of 1862, because of "the fleetness of foot" which these statesmen had displayed when McClellan's army threatened the Confederate capital in the preceding spring.[38] Confederate soldiers fleeing through the streets of Vicksburg after a defeat were greeted by the women of that place with cries of, " 'Oh, shame on you! And you running!' " When the men said that it was their general's fault, the women replied, " 'It's all your own fault. Why don't you stand your ground?' "[39] The women of Columbia met soldiers who had come from the front saying that they could not hold Richmond and Charleston, with retorts of, " 'Wretches, beasts! . . . Why don't you stay and fight? Don't you see that you own yourselves cowards by coming away in the very face of battle? If you are not liars as to the danger, you are cowards to run away from it.' "[40]

There was no room for qualified statements in the feminine estimates of those responsible for military or political reverses. Unsuccessful generals were subjected to caustic remarks, with little or no consideration as to whether such strictures were deserved. General Lovell was said to have lost New Orleans because he was frightened or intoxicated.[41] Pemberton, after he had lost Vicksburg, was accused of every conceivable sin and error, not the least among these being that he was a Yankee in whom the government should have put no trust.[42] Because of his misfortune as commander of the western armies, Bragg was declared an incapable misfit.[43] And Jubal A. Early, because of his inability to check the Federal advance upon Charlottesville, was charged with being "the wrong man in the wrong place" and a general who considered his supply of whisky more important than his supply of ammunition.[44] Civil leaders were subjected to even more discriminating criticisms. When William L. Yancey was suggested for a diplomatic mission to England, it was declared absurd to send a man abroad who was more gifted in eloquence than in reticence and who had killed his father-in-law in a street brawl.[45] The President of the Confederacy was almost universally criticized in feminine circles. He was accused of tyranny, of making incompetent appointments, and of manifesting an ill-judged leniency toward deserters. "Now see the result," was a representative feminine reaction when the plans of the chief executive were crumbling. "A noble cause and a free people well nigh sacrificed on the altars of *bad government* and *bad faith in the people.*"[46]

These vigorous assertions were often supplemented by the conviction that the Confederacy was unconquerable. Women stated that they "never had the shadow of a doubt of the final success" of their cause, that they believed that "the last feeble thread of a detested Union was snapped asunder with the first clash of swords," and that the attempt to subjugate the South was "a wild delusion."[47] It was easy for such women to discount the reports of Federal successes and to exaggerate those of Confederate victories. The news of the great Federal triumph at Gettysburg, for example, was interpreted as the invention of "lying newspapers in Yankee pay,"[48] and the accounts of similar successes else-where were characterized as the fabrications of "the miserable news-papers, falsifying one day what they had given out for truth the day previous, filled with impossible schemes and barefaced braggadocio."[49] Fanciful rumors of a victory or deliverance by the Confederate armies, on the other hand, were widely accepted. "The voice which proclaims the daily, hourly coming of the Confederates is swelling louder," wrote Julia LeGrand of the manner in which the women of New Orleans ac-cepted wild stories of the approaching redemption of their city from Federal rule in 1863. "We whisper . . . and tell what Mrs. This One said, or Mrs. The Other One had heard, and feed ourselves with hope that we are soon to take New Orleans back; break our chains; go where we please, and finish the war."[50]

Such delusions frequently led the women to demand that the war be fought to the bitter end, even after the failure of the Confederacy was evident to the more discerning minds. "The prize we fight for is worth every sacrifice," wrote a Virginia woman.[51] Richmond and other cities might fall, said another woman from the same state, but "as long as there is a man to fight and a woman to urge him on, we will contend for our liberties."[52] When there was talk of a negotiated peace in 1863, a South Carolina woman wrote, "Better fight it out until there is not a whole man left in the Confederacy than a slavery like this—no Yankee subjugation."[53] When fortresses and cities were surrendered for reasons better known to soldiers than to women, the latter protested with counsels of further resistance. On the eve of the evacuation of Charleston in January, 1865, the women of that city urged the members of the garrison to remain at their posts. "We implore, as the greatest boon, fight for Charleston!" they cried. "At every point, fight for every inch, and if our men must die, let them die amid the blazing ruins of our homes."[54]

EXCITEMENT ON THE BATTERY AT CHARLESTON
Scene during the bombardment of Fort Sumter. (From *Frank Leslie's Illustrated Newspaper*)

FLORIDA FLAG
Presented to the Florida Independent Blues by the Ladies of St. Augustine.
(Courtesy of the Confederate Museum, Richmond)

When the force of relentless circumstances made the Federal success inevitable, some women clung more tenaciously than ever to their belief in the ultimate success of the Confederacy and gave the most optimistic interpretations to Confederate reverses. The loss of a great city made only the chicken-hearted despondent, said one, adding: "to the true and the brave it gives fresh stimulus for exertion."[55] To others neither the reëlection of Lincoln to the presidency of the United States nor the failure of foreign governments to recognize the Confederacy was regarded as a cause for alarm. The South, it was affirmed, could win its independence without European aid, and Lincoln was characterized as "the greatest and most complete fool of the age," whose retention of power would be advantageous to the Southern cause by virtue of his grotesque and blundering inability.[56] Still others, according to their own accounts, refused to be dismayed even by the approaching spectre of hunger and desolation. "For hungry and shabby as we were," said a Virginia woman in describing the feelings of her associates at the time the fates were closing in on the Confederacy, "we were not in despair. Our faith in Lee and his ragged, freezing, starving army amounted to a superstition."[57] Another woman sweepingly extended this faith to the entire body of Confederate women. "When hope died within the souls of the men," she wrote, "the 'divine spark' was but newly kindled within the hearts of women. When grim despair stalked abroad within the camps of the soldiers, brave cheerfulness sat at an endless feast within the homes of the soldiers' mothers, wives, and daughters."[58] Due allowance must be made for the evident exaggeration and romantic tinge with which the women were prone to describe their emotions, but that their faith in the Confederacy lingered in many cases long after hope had been abandoned by the men is without question.

THE LORD OF HOSTS IS OUR STRENGTH AND SHIELD

Several factors suggest themselves as explanations of this unquestioning faith on the part of the women in the strength and permanency of the Confederacy. For one thing, their unbounded confidence in the prowess of the Confederate soldier left no room for the contemplation of a time when he might surrender to so contemptible a person as the Federal soldier was supposed to be. Furthermore, the romantic tendency to escape reality, always strong among Southern women, was stimulated by the excitement of war times to an extent which made the pondering of so dreadful a calamity as defeat either extremely distasteful or impossible. "We never would listen to the thought that we might fail," wrote an Alabama woman. "We never realized what defeat meant, and dreaded it so much that we were willing to miss our all rather than submit to it."[59] Still another factor was the lack of adequate and accurate information upon which to base practical conclusions regarding the political and military situation in the Confederacy. Agencies of communication were poorly organized, and, moreover, the Confederate government did not hesitate to make use of censorship and propaganda for the purpose of enlisting the support of its citizens.

The most potent factor in stimulating the faith of the women in the Confederacy, however, was their sincere and almost absolute belief in a just and omnipotent Providence. No Aristotelian syllogism of major premise, minor premise, and conclusion was ever utilized with more relentless logic than that with which the Southern women related the expected success of the Confederacy to the Providential ordering of events. A righteous and all-powerful God, who assumed a deciding part in human affairs, would not, it was believed, allow a cause as just as that of the Confederacy to fail. "The Lord of Hosts is the great commander of heaven and earth," according to a typical feminine affirmation of belief. "He it is who directs all conflicts in war; no field is pitched, no battle fought but He worketh the accomplishment of His glory."[60] The manner in which the favors of God would be distributed was stated in a most optimistic fashion by a South Carolina woman. "Well, well," she wrote, "though all nations should be against us, yet will we trust in the Lord Jehovah. He will be our strength and shield."[61] Equally emphatic was the assertion of a native of Virginia: "I thank God for His goodness in giving us brave officers and experienced men. If He is with us, what have we to fear?"[62]

Confederate victories and deliverances from personal peril were interpreted as evidence of the favorable working of Providence. "I do believe the hand of God is in this fight, we are so strangely successful," wrote Judith W. McGuire after an early Southern victory;[63] and Catherine Anne Edmonston explained later successes on the ground that, "He it is who giveth us victory and in His own good time He will grant us peace."[64] The accounts of some women, ascribing to divine intervention their success in escaping personal dangers, resemble those that have come down from an earlier age of faith. When her home was attacked by angry Federals, an Arkansas widow believed that her last hour had come, but she fell on her knees, and her prayers, according to her statement, drove the enemy away.[65] Another woman, whose home was visited by marauders, dispelled the evil intentions of her unwelcome guests, according to her narrative, by saying prayers, reading portions of the Bible which threatened vengeance upon the despoilers of widows, and asking the men to bow their heads in grace. These incidents were recorded in narratives composed at a time remote from the date of their supposed occurrence, and they must be considered in that light. Contemporary statements of faith, however, were no less explicit.

Faith in the God of Victory was unabated on the part of many women even when the shadow of defeat enveloped the land. "My Savior, under Thy care, what need I fear?" wrote a Virginia girl on the gloomy New Year of 1864. "The clouds look dark which hang over my head and shroud my well-beloved country, but lo, the silver lining is there and peace will come I feel ere dawns another New Year's Day."[67] A Tennessee woman wrote some months later that the news of Hood's disasters "somewhat alarmed" her, but added: "I feel confidence in God and our brave army. If He will direct and they do their duty, we must be an independent people."[68] In October of the same unhappy year Varina Howell Davis, although recognizing the seriousness of mounting calamities, wrote, "We hope all things and trust in God as the only one able to resolve the opposite state of feeling into a triumphant, happy whole."[69]

Even the great agony that resulted from the loss of relatives in battle failed to shake the abiding faith of such women. Instead of turning from the God who had apparently failed to answer their prayers for the safety of their kinsmen, some declared that it was impossible to fathom the ways of an inscrutable Providence; others asserted that their losses merely accentuated their belief in the necessity for clinging to the Divine Power. "I know it is the Lord and would fain still all repining," wrote a woman upon hearing of the death of her brother. "God's will be done. It is not for us to question. . . . Brother, sister, and Maggie are sadly afflicted, but glorify in this their day of visitation by their meek submission to His holy will."[70] "In this time of great afflictions upon afflictions," advised a girl who had lost two brothers, "look up to Him who sweetly soothes and gently dries the throbbing heart and streaming eye. Let us remember that He sees *all* our *griefs* and *counts* and *treasures* up all our tears."[71] Still others resorted to the hopeful rationalization that God was taking the dead heroes to the blisses of heaven. "His Christian parents are bowed down but not crushed," wrote Judith W. McGuire after Randolph Fairfax was killed at Fredericksburg; "by faith they see his abundant entrance into the kingdom of heaven, his glorious future, and are comforted."[72] An equally vivid hope was manifested by young Tempie

Person of North Carolina after the death of her two brothers. In a letter to her sister, she wrote, "Oh, how hard it is to give up those dear sweet brothers. My soul is filled with sorrow, but I know we shall not grieve, for they are at rest. . . . We will meet them in heaven."[73]

In a region where a deep religious faith had long been a marked characteristic of the feminine population, it was natural and inevitable that prayer should occupy a prominent part in sustaining the women of the Confederacy against the tragic realities of the war. "It seems to me I never felt the prayers as now," wrote a member of one of the afternoon prayer circles which existed in nearly every Southern community during the conflict.[74] A member of another one of these groups cried, as she heard the Federal guns roaring in the distance, "The Lord reigneth; in that is our trust. The prayers, hymns, psalms, and address were most comforting. God be praised for His goodness, that we are still surrounded by a Christian people, and have the faith and trust of Christians."[75] "Oh, what a privilege," wrote one of the many women who indulged in the comforts of private prayer. "Were it not for this privilege and blessing, I feel that I would be very unhappy indeed under existing circumstances. But, oh, I thank God that there is peace and comfort in believing in Him."[76]

RELIGIOUS OBSERVANCE AND ADMONITION

There was a widespread belief among the women of the Confederacy that their misfortunes were not due to God's neglect of the South but rather to the South's neglect of God. "As a people we have relied too little upon our God and too entirely upon ourselves," asserted Augusta J. Evans in a letter written to Ella King Newsom just after the disastrous military reverses of the summer of 1863. "We have become corrupt, selfish, grasping, and avaricious. We needed chastisement and it has fallen upon us."[77] It followed, therefore, that the chief problem of the South was to secure the exaltation of faith and the extermination of sin. That such tasks demanded feminine leadership was extensively held and frequently stated. "We women of the Confederacy," added the distinguished novelist just mentioned, "are the guardians of the nation's purity, and upon them, in a great degree, must devolve its reformation." In accordance with this purpose, the women engaged in several lines of activity which were designed to maintain the spiritual and moral standards to which they adhered and to superimpose these standards upon the rank and file of the Confederate armies.

The encouragement of Bible reading, prayer, and personal evangelism on the part of the soldiers served as an important means to this end. Societies were organized for the purpose of dispatching Bibles to the camps, and religious journals which made a special appeal to the troops were subsidized. [78] The letters of many women we.e impregnated with pious admonitions to their kinsmen at the front. "I send you this little book," wrote Mrs. Matthew Fontaine Maury to her son; "read its sanctions for my sake; and, oh, that I could hear that you made its petitions your own from a full and earnest heart."[79] Another mother supplemented this hope by requesting her son and other soldiers to join her circle in "offering up our prayers to a merciful God to be with us and grant us victory," and by imploring this son to use his influence in making another son into a moral man and a Christian.[80] When these and similar promptings bore fruit in the numerous manifestations of piety characteristic of the Confederate armies, letters expressing pride and congratulations were written. A Tennessee woman, for example, hearing that "so many brigades are being blessed with gracious revivals," wrote her chaplain-husband, "It encourages me to hear of these things. I pray the work may spread until our soldiers may become a *God-serving* as well as a country-serving army."[81]

Frequent contacts in the hospitals with the ill and the dying gave the women an opportunity to minister directly to the religious needs of the soldiers. Bible reading and the recitation of hymns and prayers were widely practiced by the women in Confederate hospitals, and when deaths were imminent these women made intense efforts to prepare the souls of the dying for the Great Unknown. According to the records and narratives of the women, these last efforts were never unsuccessful. "His death was one of those we can think on with pleasure," read a typical account of these death scenes; "it was that of a soldier of the Cross. He met our great enemy with his armor on, and ready for the conflict. When I told him that his moments were numbered, he said he was perfectly happy, and desired me to write his wife and tell her he hoped to meet her and his child in heaven."[82]

Another act of Christian devotion which enlisted the services of women was the burial of soldiers in those not infrequent instances in which the services of a clergyman could not be had. The most famous and widely publicized act of this character was the interment of Captain William Latané on July 15, 1862, at Westwood, the home of Dr. W. S. R. Brockenbrough in Hanover County, Virginia. When the body of this officer was left on her hands by fleeing Confederates, Mrs. Brockenbrough secured the assistance of other women in the neighborhood together with their slaves and resolved to perform the burial rites. The grave was dug by the slaves, and "in the presence of a few other ladies, a fair-haired little girl, her apron filled with flowers, and a few faithful slaves who stood reverently near," according to the dramatic account that has been preserved, "a pious Virginia matron read the solemn and beautiful burial service. . . . She watched the sods heaped upon the coffin lid; then sinking to her knees, in sight and hearing of the foe, she committed his soul's welfare and the stricken hearts he had left behind to the mercy of the All-Father."[83]

For those who regard the Latané story as being colored by constant repetitions, there are other accounts of similar incidents equally as touching. A description of the burial of a soldier who died in a hospital at Lynchburg, Virginia, is given in the diary of Kate Mason Rowland. "The coffin was brought in the large central hall and laid on the floor and some thirty or forty men assembled," recorded this writer. "I read a part of the Burial Service out of the Prayer Book and mother lined out the hymn and made an appropriate prayer."[84] Less conventional was the part of Phoebe Yates Pember in the burial of Richard Hammond Key, who died in a Richmond hospital during the Battle of Harrison's Landing. She supervised the making of the coffin and set out for Hollywood Cemetery with the body. On the way she met a clergyman and two poor women and impressed their services. While the rattle of musketry from a near-by battlefield paid unconscious tribute to a soldier's burial, she repeated the services with the minister and retired without letting him know her identity.[85]

It was not unusual for women to gather after battles to bury the dead. Under such circumstances "mothers laid out their dead sons with their own hands, and in some instances helped dig their graves."[86] On occasions when there was fear of possible harm from the Federals, women rescued bodies under the friendly cover of night, and with the aid of their children and Negroes dug graves and placed the bodies in them before dawn.[87]

Conscious of their own moral and spiritual superiority, the women admonished the men to act in accordance with the high standards set by a religious people and accentuated by a great struggle. Immorality and religious infidelity or indifference were sharply censored. When it was learned that one of the great military leaders was unfaithful to his wife, feminine admiration for this hero vanished and a feeling of disappointment took its place. "A man is nothing," wrote Julia Le-Grand, "who sins against the purity and divinity which sits by the hearthstone."[88] The sins of other generals were attacked with an equally vigorous spirit. "That men, the highest in office and authority, should be drinking and speculating while the enemy are building fortifications on our own soil and within range of our guns!" exclaimed a South Carolina woman in derision. "What a legacy this sad trouble will be to ages yet unborn. Surely 'tis the Lord's goodness that we are preserved."[89] When an occasional general became notorious for his disbelief in God, he was likely to receive long and flowery letters from the women urging him to forsake the evil of his ways. Ella King Newsom, a distinguished hospital matron, for example, wrote to General Preston Smith, who was suspected of infidelity, that she felt "a bursting and longing of soul" that those subject to the dangers of battle would "yield their sinful natures to the generating influence of the Holy Spirit." Only through religion, she asserted, could the harrowing influences of camp and hospital life be mitigated.[90]

✓   ✓   ✓   ✓

The phases of feminine activity here described—supplying the material needs of the soldiers and attempting to instill a spirit of cheerfulness among them; the belief that the Confederacy was unconquerable; religious faith and the methods adopted to impart it to the soldiers—constitute the more direct labors performed by the women of the Confederacy in their energetic attempts to sustain the morale of the Southern armies. Other measures, if less direct in their purpose and application, contributed to the same end and were equally important. They will be discussed in subsequent chapters.

CHAPTER IV

RECEPTION OF THE INVADERS

THE main objective of the Northern armies was the occupation of the Southern states in order to suppress the movement for Southern independence. The physical superiority of the North and the adoption of a defensive policy by the Confederate military authorities made possible the partial realization of this purpose some two or three years before the final destruction of the Confederacy. During 1861 and 1862 Maryland, Missouri, Kentucky, northern and eastern Virginia, Middle Tennessee, New Orleans, northwestern North Carolina, Port Royal in South Carolina, and portions of northern Florida were occupied or conquered by Federal troops. Before the close of 1863 the Mississippi River had been opened by the invaders, and there was scarcely an unconquered portion of the Confederacy which did not have reason to fear their presence.

The occupation of these vast areas by the enemy created for the women of the Confederacy difficulties which were not experienced by the men of that region. Upon the approach of the hostile forces, the men either enlisted in the Confederate armies, as was expected of them, or fled to the more inaccessible places where they sought safety both from the Federal invaders and the Confederate conscription authorities. In either case, they were sustained by the resources and sympathies of the people by whom they were surrounded, and, whether absorbed in the traditional masculine enthusiasm of fighting for their country or engaged in the less highly respected pursuits of skulking and organizing peace societies, they found in danger and adventure a partial relief from suspense and fear.[1] The women, on the other hand, were confronted with the alternatives of fleeing or remaining at home. Neither of these presented a favorable prospect. To flee meant the surrender of homes and other valuables to the enemy and the seeking of residences among a people unable, and in many cases unwilling, to provide such refugees with adequate support. To remain meant the acceptance of whatever fate a hated invader might wish to inflict upon a helpless non-combatant population. Many women sought a precarious safety by withdrawing to remote places which invasion was little likely to reach,[2] but the majority preferred to face the enemy in familiar surroundings rather than undergo the hardships of living in strange sections of the impoverished and blockaded Confederacy. Without the aid of masculine advice or protection, each woman who remained at home was confronted with difficulties, the solution of which demanded intelligence and tact as well as physical bravery. The emotions, the stratagems, the perils, and the agonies which this situation engendered among the women, and the reaction of the enemy to their behavior, constitute one of the most exciting chapters in the history of the women of the Confederacy.

HATRED AND INVECTIVE

The general attitude of the Southern women toward the men who were invading their states was characterized by an inordinate hatred. An English traveler described this feeling as more violent than it was possible for a European to conceive and added that the women "beat their male relatives hollow in their denunciations and hopes of vengeance."[3] They continued to believe that the ranks of the invaders were filled with "the refuse of Northern prisons and penitentiaries,"[4] and among the horrible fates which they wished visited upon these men and upon Lincoln and his supporters, whether Republicans or Democrats, were deaths by assassination, smallpox, typhoid fever, and other diseases.[5] "Yankee, Yankee, is a detestable word always ringing in Southern ears," wrote a Georgia girl. "If all the words of hatred in every language under the sun were lumped together in one huge epithet they could not convey how I hate the Yankees."[6] "Oh! how I hate the Yankees!" said a pretty Creole woman to an Englishman in Louisiana. "I could trample on their dead bodies and spit on them."[7]

An interesting complement of the hatred which the Southern women expressed toward the Federal soldiers was the hostile attitude with which they regarded the women who were supporting these men. As the Southern women bitterly reflected over the thought that the war was bringing to their Northern sisters only a fraction of the hardships that it was inflicting on them, they came to believe that the Northern women, in supporting the invaders, were as guilty as their men folk of perpetrating the wrongs of the war. This resentment was characterized by the special type of petulance often found in the hatred of one woman for another. Accounts of the activities of Northern women which trickled through the blockade, or were found in letters picked up on the battlefields, were given the most unflattering interpretations in the South. These women were accused of following the Federal troops in the Manassas campaign, not for the purpose of alleviating suffering, but "to pass over the mutilated and mangled corpses of our men, and to go on their way ,oicing to scenes of festivity in the halls of the vanquished, to revel over the blood of the slain, the groans of the dying, and the wails of the widows and fatherless."[8] It was alleged that feminine visitors to Northern hospitals offered delicacies to ill

Federals while to ill Confederates they offered only religious tracts, as if the latter were heathens in need of missionary attentions.[9] The familiarities with Negroes, in which the Northern women were believed to indulge, brought forth hopes of the most horrible fate that a Southern woman could conceive of inflicting upon an enemy of her own sex—that the daughters of the Northern women would select the blackest of these Negroes as their husbands.[10] The greatest resentment on the part of the Southern women, however, was created by the almost universal conviction that one of the principal reasons why Northern women supported the invasion of the South was the desire to have the soldiers send home dresses, jewelry, and other valuables stolen from the homes of the Confederacy. Commenting on this alleged ambition, Kate Cumming wrote, "O shame where is thy blush! What a commentary upon the society of 'the best government the world ever saw'!"[11]

Such hatred of the enemy naturally led to applause of alleged or projected acts of ruthlessness on the part of the Confederates. Some women were delighted when they heard that Confederate sympathizers had fired New York in nine places; that Confederate soldiers had summarily dispatched Federal marauders and sharpshooters left behind by the retreating enemy; and that Stonewall Jackson had hanged prisoners captured in action after having previously been paroled. Others hoped that Lee or Jackson, on invading the North, would reduce every public building in Washington to "a heap of ruins," burn the Pennsylvania towns, tear up the railroads, and destroy New York City.[12] Upon hearing of the alleged ruthlessness of Stonewall Jackson, Louisa Susanna McCord, a prominent writer and a devoted Christian, exclaimed, "They say he wants to hoist the black flag, have a short, sharp, decisive war and end it. He is a Christian soldier."[13]

The prevalence of this extreme rancor toward the Federals on the part of the women of the Confederacy is amply confirmed by the testimony of the Federals themselves. Almost every Northerner who spoke or wrote on the subject, as a matter of fact, believed that the animus of the Southern women was far greater than that of the Southern men. Among those who expressed this opinion was a newspaper writer accompanying McClellan on the Peninsula, who wrote, "The women were, by all odds, far worse rebels than the men," wishing "that the rain would come down ever so fast thar on the swamp" so that the Federals could not move, or that "General McClellan would fall ill, get shot, or the Yankees get beaten."[14] A Federal general at New Orleans asserted that the men of Louisiana were "as brave as any the world contains," fighting splendidly and treating their prisoners nobly, but that the women of that state "were so very bitter, so uncompromising, that they would not give an enemy a civil word."[15] A similar report came from Florida. The Union officer who captured St. Augustine affirmed that the men of that town acquiesced in the occupation, but the women displayed no such spirit. "They seem to mistake treason for courage," angrily added this officer, "and seem to have a theatrical desire to figure as heroines."[16]

Some women went to such extremes in their expression of malignant feelings against the invaders that at least one Confederate woman of unquestioned patriotism felt constrained to protest. "O, what unutterable horror that remark causes me as often as I hear it," wrote Sarah Morgan of Louisiana when her associates expressed the wish that the enemy would die of yellow fever and other plagues. "O, women! into what loathsome violence have you debased your holy mission. God will punish us for our hardheartedness."[17]

THE YANKEES ARE COMING

It was not difficult for women who cherished such hatred toward the invaders to believe that these men were capable of extreme acts of cruelty and outrage. Some women asserted that Federal soldiers had been induced to enlist by the promise of being allowed to seize lands and ravish women; that Federal officers permitted their prostitute friends to insult decent women; that the Negroes of invaded territories were allowed "to rove through the country and seize from the defenseless inhabitants what they list;" and that "murder and outrage at which the heart sickens and the blood boils" featured the approach of the Federal armies.[18] Others asserted that their blood was congealed and sleep driven from their eyes by the recital of the horrible details of the Federal advance, and that they anticipated being subdued by starvation and devastation or "being blown up with shot and shell, finished with cold steel, or whisked off to some Northern prison camp."[19] That such rumors were in practically all cases great exaggerations of Federal intentions detracted little from the alarm of the highly emotional and nervously distraught women who believed in them.

Anticipating the worst from such intruders as the Federal soldiers were supposed to be, some women prepared to repel with violence expected attacks upon their persons. They armed themselves with knives and pistols which their male relatives had given them, and displaying these weapons proudly, resolved to die rather than face dishonor.[20] "What more significant fact of the change in our country

than when a husband gives his wife the parting present of a pistol!"
observed a North Carolina woman upon whom such a gift had been
bestowed. "Yes, I will learn to use it," she added, "and should the
occasion arise, God will give me strength and nerve to use it aright."[21]
Such arrogant demonstrations seldom bore fruit in active defense, however. In the majority of cases the wildest consternation reigned among
the women when it was actually learned that the enemy would shortly
descend upon them. There were excited farewells to fleeing men, the
closing of doors and windows, and much weeping and wailing over the
"indescribable horrors" which were expected. "They are coming! The
Yankees are coming at last!" wrote Sarah Morgan as the Federals occupied Linwood, Louisiana. "For four or five hours the sound of their
cannon has assailed our ears. There! that one shook our bed! Oh,
they are coming!"[22]

Although there was little systematic destruction and burning during
the first years of the war, the Federal soldiers frequently, though by no
means always, followed their entry into settlements of women by resorting to pillage. In some cases they were actuated by the greed for
plunder; in others they were merely impelled by hunger and need for
forage. The women, however, observed no distinction between these
respective motives. "This morning they came in earnest," wrote a
Virginia woman regarding a Federal entry into her plantation settlement. "They took our carriage horses and two others, in spite of our
remonstrances; demanded the key of the meat-house, and took as many
of our sugar-cured hams as they wanted; tonight they broke open our
barn, and fed their horses, and even now are prowling around the
servants' houses in search of eggs, poultry, etc. . . . The officers are
polite enough, but they are determined to steal everything they
fancy."[23]

Similar depredations are described in accounts from other sections of
the Confederacy. "The Yankees swarmed like devils, yelling, whoop-
ing, and screaming," said a North Carolina woman in describing the
Federal invasion of her plantation. Her house was sacked, her furniture chopped to pieces, her hogs and cattle killed and their carcasses
thrown into a fire, and her carriages and horses taken away.[24] According to a Mississippi woman, the Federal marauders looted the store-
rooms of her plantation, carried away such of their contents as could be
placed in a carriage impressed for the purpose, and rendered the rest
useless by pouring molasses and vinegar upon them.[25] A Louisiana
woman, returning to her home in the northern part of that state on
Christmas Day, 1862, discovered that Federal raiders and their Negro

allies had broken open trunks, pillaged drawers, turned furniture over, robbed storerooms of butter, milk, Christmas cake and forty freshly-killed hogs, and were in the act of hunting for money and jewelry.[26] When one of the Morgan sisters returned to her home at Baton Rouge after the Federal occupation of that place, she was reduced to tears by the discovery that the soldiers had made her home into "one scene of ruins." Downstairs she found "libraries emptied, china smashed, side-boards split open with axes, three cedar chests cut open, plundered, and set up on end; all the parlor ornaments carried off—even the alabaster Apollo and Diana." Upstairs the glass of the mahogany armoire was broken, its shelves split, and their contents scattered. The floors were littered with rags, and the bric-a-brac pulverized by the use of rods pulled from the beds. "The debris filled my basin and ornamented my bed," concluded the narrative of the dismayed owner. "My desk was broken open. Over it was spread all my letters and private papers, a diary I kept when twelve years old, and sundry tokens of dried roses, etc."[27]

No group of Southern women experienced more trying hardships than did those of Confederate sympathies in Missouri during the first year of the war. In that state neighbor was arrayed against neighbor, and the struggle was characterized by all the horrors of civil strife.[28] Although Confederate bushwhackers were not averse to dark deeds, Northern marauders had a freer hand because they were usually pre-ponderant.[29] Jennison and his Kansas Redlegs descended upon pros-perous plantations, and, while helpless women looked on, took off Negroes and carted away silver plate, jewelry, bedding, clothes, plows, and even toys. "Our home was raided and robbed," wrote one of the many victims of these outrages; "a box of old family silver was un-earthed and taken, keepsakes were appropriated, and even a locket con-taining a dead child's hair, amid the piteous entreaties of a mother to spare her one small treasure."[30] These marauders seized patchwork quilts from Negro cabins as eagerly as they took silk comforts from the mansions. One woman reported that she witnessed the smoke going up from twenty-seven houses and barns at one time,[31] and another asserted that her premises were ransacked seven times by men who threatened her and the other members of her family with death if they gave aid and comfort to the bushwhackers.[32]

FEMININE ARROGANCE AND AUDACITY

In some cases the Federals were greeted with deathly silence as they marched for the first time through the streets of captured towns. The women hid behind closed shutters and figuratively rained tears and imprecations upon the heads of those whom they feared and despised. "I never saw such a desolate looking place," wrote a visitor to Alexandria, Virginia, shortly after its occupation; "not a lady on the streets, nearly all have left, and those who remain never go out at all. Nothing to be seen but soldiers."[33] In other cases the hardships and alleged insults which the invaders inflicted upon them often made the women defiant. If their own narratives are to be accepted, even after making allowances for inevitable exaggerations, many women proclaimed their feelings directly and openly to the enemy and rebuked the invaders for their destructiveness. The display of bold tactics, it is asserted, often made these women victors in encounters with the Federals, and they occasionally made effective use of weapons which they held in their hands or hid beneath the folds of their dresses.

The manner in which the more defiant among the women of the Confederacy proclaimed their feelings to the Northern intruders is well illustrated by a number of accounts selected from the state of Virginia. When Mrs. Gilmer Breckenridge ironically suggested to a group of Federal soldiers who had invaded her home that they read her private letters, they replied that they would not be guilty of such an act. To this she hotly rejoined, " 'Indeed, I should think gentlemen who would steal towels, wouldn't hesitate to examine private correspondence.' " One of the invaders, angered by her sarcasm, said, " 'If you were a man I would put my sword through your body.' " In no wise abashed by this suggestion of blood, she yelled, " 'I am only a woman, but if you choose to use your weapons, you will find me equal to the occasion.' "[34] When another Virginia woman refused to play her piano for the pleasure of the invaders of her home, one of them seated himself at the instrument. He had scarcely begun to play, however, when the owner, raising the piano top, severed nearly all the strings of the instrument with a hatchet and shouted to the astonished performer, " 'That's my piano, and it shall not give you a moment's pleasure.' "[35] Another Virginia woman knocked in the heads of several casks of wine when Federal officers had expressed their intentions of imbibing a portion of her treasure.[36] When a sentinel asked an Alexandria girl to show her pass in order to enter her town, she became so indignant that she knocked him down, scratched him severely, and ended by taking his gun from him.[37]

Many stories are related whereby these women saved themselves and their property from the violence of the invaders by bold tactics. A striking example of this was the behavior of a certain Mrs. Dixon who lived near Berryville, Virginia. A band of soldiers bearing torches surrounded her house and told her that they had orders to burn it. Suspecting that no such orders had been given, she summoned firmness of voice and manners to her assistance and ordered the men off with such force that they obeyed her.[38] Similar conduct was said to have saved the five Stroud sisters, who lived alone with their father at Milliken's Bend on the Mississippi, when a band of marauders threatened to hang their father if the hiding place of alleged treasure were not revealed. Instead of beseeching their father to yield what treasure he may have had, these sisters silently surrounded him on the moon-lit piazza of their home, resolving to face whatever consequences their obduracy might involve. The marauders left without doing any harm, in the opinion of Emma Stroud, because "our white garments in the moonlight made us such a 'phantom party' that the raiders were overawed and conscience-stricken."[39] When a Missouri woman ordered her Negro cook to prepare a meal for the Federals who had invaded her home, an insolent member of the party cried, " 'You have got to cook; we have set the niggers free!' " The housewife calmly replied that the freeing of the Negroes caused her no worry. " 'Who will do the work?' " burst out an insolent fellow. " 'Oh, I will send North and hire your wives, sweethearts, and sisters and make slaves of them,' " she retorted. Furious over this sally, the men pointed their guns at "the damned rebel," but, instead of whimpering before her tormenters, she boldly threatened them with the vengeance of the bushwhackers. No guns were fired and the men left.[40]

SELF-DEFENSE AND RETALIATION

According to their assertions, women occasionally prepared to use the weapons with which they had armed themselves to forestall real or imaginary threats against their persons. An outstanding case of this type was that of a North Carolina woman who often wondered if the stiletto which she kept hidden in the folds of her dress would ever serve any useful purpose. She almost lived to prove that it did, for one day she found herself locked in a room with a stalwart intruder whose breath was hot with brandy and who seemed ready for any atrocity. Frightened almost to petrification, she pressed her hand to her weapon and exclaimed in a vibrant voice, " 'What do you mean, sir? Open that door.' " For a moment the eyes of the intruder retained their fiendish brightness; then dropped to the floor, as the soldier turned, unlocked the door, and left.[41] A similar account is given by a young girl of Yazoo County, Mississippi, who was captured by a party of Negro troops and threatend with being carried away on a transport. "Backing up against a huge cypress tree," said the girl, "I took my little revolver from the pocket of my underskirt and cocked it, and placing the muzzle against my breast, I declared that only my dead body should be taken on that boat." Consternation struck her captors, according to her account, and she was released.[42] Such accounts as these, even if accurate, are not numerous, however; for the Federal soldiers, in spite of their frequently bad conduct in other respects, did not often attempt to put their hands on Southern women. *BULLSHIT!*

There were, however, numerous trying situations which, although not involving threats to their persons, impelled the women to demonstrate their willingness to use the weapons which they possessed. When Sallie Whitley of Aberdeen, Mississippi, sat with the head of a murdered uncle on her lap, his assassins, Federal soldiers, stood by and mocked her tears. Under this ordeal her tears turned to rage, and drawing a pistol from her breast she threatened to kill her tormentors. Several guns were leveled at her head, but she persisted in her threat, and the men, finally moved by her bravery, left her unharmed.[43] Similar courage was manifested by Linnie Hutchinson, a girl who lived near Memphis, when a party of fifty Federal plunderers began shooting her chickens. Raising a gun, she threatened to shoot the soldier who fired the next shot, whereupon the men vacated her premises without more ado.[44] When a Negro was ordered by a Federal soldier to enter and burn the home of Winnie Scruggs at Kinston, North Carolina, she replied, " 'That Negro knows better than to come in. If he comes in I shall kill him.' " Then she seized the rifle which the soldier had carelessly laid down, and, pointing it with deadly aim, forced both the soldier and the Negro to leave her house.[45] At Winchester, Virginia, two girls were asked to submit to the humiliation of being searched for contraband by a Negress appointed for this purpose by Federal officers. Boldly exposing pistols, they said to the Negress, " 'Well, auntie, you will have to take our word for it, because we won't submit to your searching us.' " Needless to say, according to the version of the story that has been preserved, the purpose of the Negress was not carried out.[46]

In some cases, if the chronicles of the time are to be accepted, the women demonstrated that their threats were not idle by putting them into actual execution. When a soldier indecently exposed his person in the presence of a woman at Benton, Arkansas, she put him to flight by firing twice.[47] Similar determination was manifested by Mat Barrington of Fayetteville in the same state. After a band of Federals had

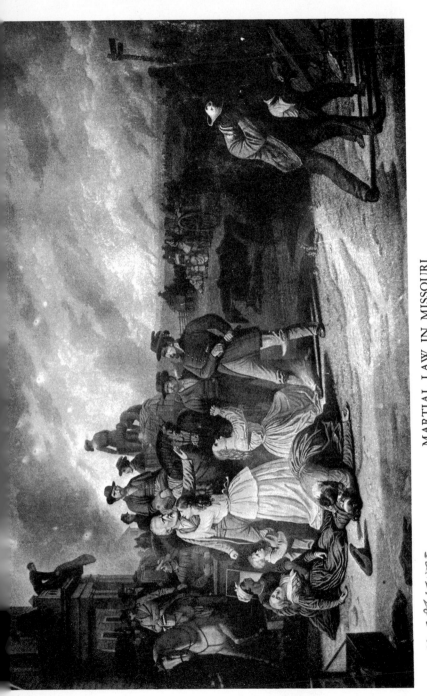

A TRUE PICTURE

MARTIAL LAW IN MISSOURI

An artist's conception of the execution of General Ewing's famous Order No. 11. (From an engraving in the Confederate Museum, Richmond)

swept her home clean of all food except a precious bag of coffee, she ordered them not to touch that article. When one of the men showed a tendency not to heed her request, she felled him with an iron poker, and after he had recovered sufficiently from this blow to arise he limped away without the contested bag.[48] A more violent demonstration was that of a girl named Bailey of Crooked Creek, also in Arkansas. Believing her mother dead from blows delivered by a Unionist, she rushed to the edge of her porch and dealt the supposed assassin such a blow with a candle mold that he had to be carried away by his comrades.[49] Even more extreme violence is exemplified in other cases that have been recorded. On March 5, 1864, a band of Federals entered the home of a young woman named Morris in Fannin County, Georgia, and wounded her brother in an attempt to arrest him. The irate sister grabbed a bowie knife and stabbed the assailant to death.[50] Marina Gunter of Putnam County, Tennessee, distinguished herself by conduct equally as violent. When three bushwhackers were torturing her father one night, she killed two of them with an axe and put the third to flight after breaking his arm.[51]

⚹ ⚹ ⚹ ⚹

It must again be observed that these accounts are taken in large measure from the narratives written by the women themselves, in many cases long after the events occurred. That such accounts abound in exaggerations may be assumed, but they are still of value as indications of the general feeling that prevailed among the women when the invaders were entering the South. The hatred of the women for these invaders created the gravest apprehensions concerning the evil deeds of which such intruders were thought to be capable. These apprehensions were in part justified by the actual turbulence and pillaging that characterized the entrance of the enemy into many localities. On the other hand, if their assertions are to be accepted as valid, the women often reacted defiantly to the acts of their conquerors. They claim that they did not hesitate to lecture the enemy for alleged misdeeds and in some instances they used or threatened to use weapons in the defense of their persons, property, and peace of mind. The shock of receiving the enemy for the first time was, however, but the beginning of their troubles with these soldiers, for in vast areas the occupation of the Confederacy by the enemy lasted for the duration of the war.

CHAPTER V

RELATIONS WITH THE ENEMY

THE initial contacts with the invaders, which have just been described, constituted only the first phase of the relations between the women of the Confederacy and the enemy. These relations, continuing in many localities until the end of the war, were complex and oftentimes contradictory. In the greater portion of the occupied areas the majority of the women continued to assume, until the close of the conflict, the hostile attitude which they had displayed when the enemy first came into their midst. This was largely due to the fact that the general conduct of the Federals, at least in the opinion of the women, was not such as to soften preconceived hatreds. On the other hand, the women of certain areas, in which the attachment of the population to the principles of the Confederate cause was not so pronounced, were willing to exhibit cordial tendencies toward the invaders. Two circumstances fostered these tendencies. One was the fact that the invaders did not always turn out to be such brutes as they were expected to be; the other was the prevalence, among the women, of the human inclination to seek a convenient solution for unhappy situations. Such a solution was often found in compromise and cordiality toward the men who dominated the territory in which these women lived. Still other women were Unionists and regarded the Federals as deliverers. At the same time, these more or less territorial categories were complicated by the fact that some women of unquestioned devotion to the Confederacy were inflexible in their obduracy at one moment while manifesting a conciliatory disposition at another.

HARDSHIPS OF THE OCCUPATION

Although there were numerous instances in which the Federals refrained from rude or unkind conduct, the hardships attendant upon their occupation of the South were extremely inconvenient and irritating to the sensitive Southern women. Indeed many women felt that the privations which they suffered were almost beyond their powers of endurance. Their homes were liable to be entered at any time of the day or night by plundering soldiers, or seized to make room for Federal officers and their families. Passes were often required for women to enter and leave their premises. "There must be," said a woman exasperated by this requirement, "a pass for the cow to go to the pasture, another for the horse to be shod, a third to go to the post office, a fourth to go to church, another for town."[1] The absence of male support and the interruption of normal economic life often reduced the

women to such a degree of want that they were forced to undergo the
humiliation of applying to the Federal commissaries for rations. When
they applied to these agencies, they were frequently told that no food
would be forthcoming unless they would undergo the additional humi-
ation of taking the hated oath of loyalty to the United States government. Sometimes they were treated rudely, deported, or imprisoned for
refusing to take the oath or for other conduct deemed improper by
Federal officers. And if they escaped such physical inconveniences,
there was still the annoyance of frequent parades and other demonstrations of hostile troops to offend their petulant natures. Most of the
acts to which the Southern women took exception were nothing more
than the unavoidable consequences of the invasion of a hostile country,
and during the first two or three years of the war these acts were
certainly not as severe as they might have been. This fact, however,
did not prevent the women from suffering from many vexatious discomforts or from attempting to retaliate for what they regarded as the
insolence of the enemy.

The most costly of the hardships imposed by the invaders were their
visits to seize supplies. The fear of such visits often compelled women
to pass nights in terror behind barricades of pianos, chairs, tables, and
wardrobes. The Federals, wrote Judith W. McGuire, in describing the
nature of these raids in their worst form, "will ride bravely up to a
house, where they will find only women and children; order meals to
be prepared; search the house; take the valuables; feed their horses at
the barns; take off the horses from the stables; shoot the pigs, sheep
and other stock, and leave them dead in the fields; rob the poultry-
yards; then, after regaling themselves on the meals which have been
prepared by force, with the threats of bayonets and pistols, they ride
off, having pocketed the silver spoons and forks, which may have been
unwittingly left in their way."[2]

While the foregoing description is obviously of a composite character, its substantial accuracy is demonstrated by the experiences of
women who actually suffered from such depredations. One Virginia
woman asserted that she was forced to stand by helpless while raiders
caught her sheep, broke through the walls of her barn to get horse
feed, and robbed her storehouses of enough corn, pork, linen, and
breadstuffs to fill six wagons.[3] The house of another woman in the
same state was surrounded by soldiers who reminded her "more of
raving wolves than anything human." They stole her turkeys, most of
her chickens and hogs, and a goodly portion of her corn. Due to the
intervention of an officer she was able, for a time, to save her sheep,

but one morning she awoke to see the skins of these animals dotting her fields.[4] A similar experience occurred to a group of Mississippi women whose house had been occupied by the Federals. Awakened one night by the noise of a hammer, they looked through an opening in a partition to see an officer packing china, silver, and other valuables for shipment to the North.[5] In other sections of the Confederacy, these foraging days, when Federal soldiers walked about plantations deliberately breaking open storerooms and appropriating their contents, were described as being "as much dreaded as the plagues of Egypt."[6]

Nothing angered the women more than being evicted from their residences in order to make room for Federal generals and their families. "I did hate him, the vulgar-minded official who imagined that place would make him a gentleman," wrote Julia LeGrand of an officer who had seized a friend's house in New Orleans.[7] The rage of the Southern women was even greater when the Federal officers installed their own women folk in the houses they had occupied. When General Milroy impressed a Winchester home for the use of his wife, the women of that Virginia town retaliated by characterizing him as "a low Western Yankee" and his wife as a woman "not above but below the stamp of a servant."[8] "Yankees do inhabit it, a Yankee colonel and his wife," cried Sarah Morgan when she heard what had happened to her home at Baton Rouge. "A stranger and a Yankee occupies father's place at the table, and mother's bed belongs now to a Yankee woman."[9] When a daughter of the general who had seized the Clement C. Clay house in Huntsville, Alabama, rode about the streets of the town on Mrs. Clay's horse, women subjected her to insults. One girl indignantly cried after her, " 'Hey! Git off 'Ginie Clay's mare. Git—off—'Ginie Clay's ma-are!' "[10]

The Federal authorities occasionally dealt harshly with women whom they considered refractory. Some, suspected of having pistols or other contraband articles about their persons, were searched while their arms were pinioned behind them or rifles leveled at their heads.[11] Others were told when they protested against their hardships, " 'None but you damned women put the men up to fighting, and you are the ones to blame for this fuss.' "[12] As in the case of Rose O'Neal Greenhow, whose experience in this respect has already mentioned[13] a few of the more flagrant violators of the Federal sense of propriety were arrested and thrown into prison. Madame Tochman, the wife of a Polish subject who had raised a Confederate regiment at New Orleans, was made a prisoner in her Washington home and her correspondence seized.[14] Elizabeth Waring Duckett was arrested at her father's home in Maryland on the charge of sedition, remanded to the Old Capitol Prison in Washington, released, and then reimprisoned when she refused to take the oath of allegiance to the Federal government.[15] Ellen Roan, a girl who had been within the Confederate lines, was ordered by Benjamin F. Butler, the Federal commander at Norfolk, to reveal whatever information that might have come to her attention. Upon her refusal she was incarcerated incognito in Fortress Monroe and later transferred to "the pestilential casements of Fort McHenry."[16]

As it was an easier and more practical method of getting rid of them, the deportation of undesirable women was more frequently practiced than imprisonment. A signal example of this treatment was that of Margaret A. E. McClure, a prominent inhabitant of St. Louis. Accused of concealing Confederate soldiers and mail in her large house, she was at first arrested and, along with several other women accused of similar activities, imprisoned in her own residence; but on May 12, 1863, she was banished into the Confederate lines south of Memphis.[17] Another prominent case of this type was that of Mary Tucker of Winchester, Virginia. When a letter of hers, describing in caustic terms the eviction of the Tucker family from their home to make room for General Milroy, was intercepted by that general, she was given the alternatives of apologizing or suffering banishment. Accepting the latter fate, she was seized without ceremony and dumped into the country near Winchester, from whence she was forced to take refuge within the Confederate lines.[18] An example of wholesale deportation was witnessed at New Orleans on May 15, 1863, when a large number of women were sent away from that city for refusing to take the oath of loyalty to the United States. "Such dismal faces one meets everywhere," said a commentator on the fate of these women. "Each looks brokenhearted. Homeless, friendless beggars, is written on every face."[19] Even worse troubles were caused by the famous Order No. 11 of General Thomas Ewing, compelling the inhabitants of Confederate sympathies in the western counties of Missouri to migrate. "The road from Independence to Lexington," wrote one who witnessed the execution of this order, "was crowded with women and children, women walking with babies in their arms, packs on their backs, and four or five children following them—some crying for bread, some crying to be taken back home."[20]

NORTHERN OSTENTATION AND SOUTHERN SECLUSION

Although less burdensome from a physical standpoint than the hardships described above, the parades and martial demonstrations of the Federal soldiers were equally effective in arousing feminine resentment. "The drums and trumpets by day and the hideous yells by night strike our hearts like the knell of dear ones," wrote Betty Herndon Maury.[21] Another woman asserted that the parades of hostile regiments, with starry banners floating and what was formerly the national music playing, filled her with a sort of excited melancholy which she had never felt before.[22] Still others were moved to rage and contempt by such demonstrations. As Sarah Morgan watched the parade at New Orleans on July 10, 1863, celebrating the fall of Vicksburg, she disdainfully observed that the lines of march were composed of "a motley crew of thousands of low people of all colors"—workingmen in soiled clothes, newsboys, ragged children, swarms of Negroes and low white women elbowing each other. "To see such creatures exulting over our misfortunes," she added, "was enough to make one scream with rage. . . . As they passed they raised the yell of 'Down with the rebels!' that made us gnash our teeth in silence. The Devil possessed me. 'O Miriam, help me pray the dear Lord that their flags may burn!' I whispered as the torches danced around."[23]

Intense as were these feelings of disgust, however, they were slight in comparison with the violent emotions that were aroused by the demonstrations of former slaves. Dressed in the uniforms and inspired by the enthusiasm of a nation that was thought to be bringing ruin to the South, these Negro troops were regarded with horror and alarm by the women of many sections of the Confederacy. The mere fact that ex-slaves bore "the once honored Stars and Stripes" and were "armed and equipped, wearing the leather belt which other soldiers wear, having the letters 'U.S.' in brass upon it," brought consternation to the women of New Orleans.[24] In other localities the demonstrations of these troops seemed a brutal and grotesque carnival, rendered "awful by the devilish mirth of the black wretches racing horses up and down the streets," some arrayed in ladies' dresses and fancy bedquilts and uttering drunken songs or blood-curdling yells, intermingled with obscene jests and blasphemy.[25]

The resentment which the women felt toward these and other acts of the invaders in most of the occupied areas led the majority of them to reject the social attentions which the Federals frequently attempted to bestow upon them. Such advances were usually interpreted as the insufferable insolence of men who were the destroyers of cherished institutions and the murderers of fond relatives. "I met him on the street but did not speak to him," wrote Betty Herndon Maury of her conduct at Fredericksburg toward a relative who was in the uniform of a

Federal general. "I could not shake hands with a man who came as an invader, to desolate our homes and kill our brothers and husbands."[26] When a soldier later asked to be allowed to purchase some candy for this same woman's little girl, the child replied, " 'No, I thank you. Yankee candy would choke me.' "[27] In passing the hated Yankees on the streets some women even averted their faces and swept aside their skirts, on the theory that all contact with creatures adjudged so vile should be eschewed. "I crossed the street to avoid meeting a squad of them," said Eliza Frances Andrews of the bluecoats who had occupied Washington, Georgia; "but as I heard some of them make remarks on my action, and didn't wish to do anything that would attract their notice, I bulged right through the midst of the next crowd I met, keeping my veil down and my parasol raised, and it wouldn't have broken my heart if the point had punched some of their eyes out."[28]

It was suggested by some that since the women of the American Revolution had received British officers in their homes it was proper for Southern women to extend the same courtesy to Federal officers, but this analogy was generally rejected. "It is scarcely decorous," wrote a New Orleans woman, "to take a hand in friendship which is red with Confederate blood. . . . No woman's smiles should cheer these invaders. There is a latent disrespect of us when they force their way into our houses, and we make tacit acknowledgement of want of self-respect when we receive them."[29] A similar reaction was that of a Georgia girl to the kindly offer on the part of a Federal officer to drive her into Atlanta. "If the blood within me had overflowed its proper channels, and rushed to the surface," she wrote in describing her rejection of the offer, "I could not have flushed more. . . . The indignation and contempt I felt for the man! That one who was aiding and abetting in the devastation of my country and the spoliation of my home, should ask me to take a seat with him in a buggy which he doubtless had taken, without leave or license, from my countrymen, was presumptuous indeed, and deserved rebuke."[30]

The thought of Northerners' becoming suitors for the hands of Southern girls created extreme disgust. "I would not let the upstart think, even in jest, that a Southern woman *would* marry him," said Julia LeGrand, when it was suggested that a Federal officer change his politics so as to be able to woo a New Orleans heiress. "He is good natured, but to my certain knowledge he is not honest. He lives in a 'captured house,' and broke open the trunks which Mrs. Brown left there, in search of sheets and table cloths."[31] When a Virginia woman heard Federal officers, who were quartered in her home, express inter-

est in a certain girl, she was surprised to learn that the object of their
solicitude was a Southerner. "I hardly suppose," she wrote, "a Yankee
even would have the presumption to suppose that, after robbing us,
insulting us . . . ., we would for an instant forget our wrongs and let
them step into places they made vacant. The idea of a Southern lady
receiving or looking upon the enemy of her country in the light of an
admirer!"[32]

This feeling of repugnance was so strong in many communities that
even those who were tempted to exchange favors with the more gracious among the Federal officers were restrained from doing so by the
opinions of other women. After she had neglected the opportunity to
flirt with some handsome officers at Baton Rouge, in the first week of
June, 1862, Sarah Morgan wrote with evident wistfulness, "Dear me,
why wasn't I born old and ugly? Suppose I should unconsciously en-
trap some magnificent Yankee! What an awful thing it would be!"[33]
Regarding the action of a kindly officer who called at the Morgan home
a few days later, offering protection and food to its owners, she wrote
in a similar spirit, "I like him, and was sorry I could not ask him to re-
peat the visit. We are unaccustomed to treat gentlemen that way; but
it won't do in the present state to act as we please. Mob governs."[34]
And when the Morgan sisters returned the salute of a polite officer
who had bowed to them after church, they did so at the danger of
losing their social standing in Baton Rouge. "By tomorrow," wrote
Sarah, "those he did not bow to will cry treason against us. . . . All
the loudest gossips have been frightened into the country, but enough
remain to keep them well supplied with town talk."[35]

THE "LADIES" OF NEW ORLEANS

At no place was the tendency of Southern women to snub the Federals carried to greater extremes than in New Orleans. The women of
that city, according to James Parton, a Northern historian, "by no
means confined themselves to the display of minute rebel flags on their
persons. They were insolently and vulgarly demonstrative." With noses
upturned and skirts drawn they walked in the middle of the streets to
avoid contacts with the Northerners; with expressions of disgust on
their faces they left street cars and churches upon the entrance of the
bluecoats; and when from their balconies they saw these men approaching they rushed to their pianos and played "The Bonnie Blue Flag."
The climax of these insults, added Parton, occurred when "a beast of a
woman" spat in the faces of two officers.[36] These observations were
confirmed by Sarah Morgan, a girl of unquestioned devotion to the Con-

federate cause, who described "the Billingsgate oratory and demon-strations of some of these 'ladies' of New Orleans," stating further that a Federal officer could "not pass a street in New Orleans without being grossly insulted by *ladies.*" Greatly indignant over the spitting incident, she declared, "Do I consider the female who could spit in a gentleman's face, merely because he wore the United States buttons, as a fit associate for me?"[37]

At first the soldiers regarded these exhibitions of feminine spleen good humoredly and did nothing in retaliation. They lost patience when they heard of the spitting incident, however; and their com-mander, General Benjamin F. Butler, himself a coarse egotist, came to their aid with his notorious Order No. 23 of May 15, 1862. Since the women of New Orleans had answered the scrupulous non-interference and courtesy of the soldiers with repeated insults, affirmed this decree, "it is ordered that hereafter when any female shall by word, gesture or movement, insult or show contempt for any officer of the United States, she shall be regarded and held liable to be treated as a woman of the town plying her avocation."[38]

This was by no means the worst act against Southern womanhood of which a Northern soldier was guilty, and it was not followed by any direful deeds on the part of Butler's soldiers. The general explicitly warned his men that he would punish any of them who interpreted the order as an opportunity for license, and undoubtedly the order had the salutary effect of restraining the rudeness of the women. The worst acts of which Butler himself was guilty while in New Orleans centered around unproved accusations of financial irregularities, popularly characterized by the tradition that he pocketed the silver spoons from the house which he occupied, and his main energies were directed toward acts no less humanitarian than feeding the poor and restoring the business activities of the city.[39]

Nevertheless, there was no act of any Federal commander in the South which created more indignation and was subjected to more sinister interpretations than Butler's Order No. 23. The governor of Louisiana described it as an invitation to the soldiers "to quicken the impulses of their sensual instincts by the suggestion of transparent excuses for their gratification;" the mayor of New Orleans character-ized it as "a reproach to the civilization, not to say Christianity of the age;" and a group of women signing themselves "The Daughters of New Orleans" declared that it would "have been better for New Orleans to have been laid in ruins and buried beneath the moss than that we should be subjected of such untold sufferings."[40] The letters

and diaries of the Southern women of the times, and for years there-
after, were filled with unmeasured denunciations of "Spoons Butler"
and "The Beast of New Orleans," the unflattering sobriquets under
which the general became familiar to thousands. To save the womanhood of the South from the horrible implications of his threat was considered ample reason why the Confederates should fight to the last drop
of blood.

VACILLATION AND CORDIALITY

In addition to these unpleasant relations with the enemy, there were,
however, many social contacts between the Federal soldiers and the
women of the Confederacy which did not result in such uncompromising attitudes as those which have just been described. The invaded
regions were large, and they were inhabited by women of varied
opinions. If the women as a whole tended to be recalcitrant, there
were some who found themselves able to be friendly with the enemy
without difficulty, and there were others who exhibited the human
weakness of vacillating between attitudes of hostility and cordiality.

As previously intimated, the fact that the invaders did not always
develop into such inhuman monsters as they were expected to be, prepared the way for the manifestation of kind feelings between them and
the women of many localities. In the early years of the war at least,
the Federals seldom forgot completely the restraints which the conventions of civilized war provided for the protection of non-combatants
in invaded regions. Systematic pillaging and burning was not the rule,
and many of the destructive acts which have been described were committed during the excitement of occupying positions, or by independent
bands without, and in many cases distinctly contrary to, the authority
of commanding officers. If the soldiers generally stole from the women
whatever attracted their fancy, they seldom struck women or attempted
suggestive familiarities; and they did not commit rape. In fact, generally speaking, the persons of the women were almost as safe from
violence, during the early part of the war, as they would have been had
the invading regiments been friendly troops visiting the cities and
towns of the South for gala occasions.

That they were agreeably surprised by the good conduct of the invaders was frequently admitted by the women of certain localities.
Many found time in the recording of their fury over the invasion to say
that the invaders were personally harmless. Harriette Cary of Wil-
liamsburg, Virginia, for example, said that the officer detailed to search
her house, instead of breaking in, subjected it only to a nominal inspection, and that the sentinel sent to guard it was so affable that she

felt disposed to laugh and talk with him.[41] Another woman, residing in Hanover County, Virginia, wrote that the invaders of her community "took nothing but what was considered contraband. . . . No houses were burned and not much fencing. The ladies' rooms were not entered except when a house was searched; but I do not think much was stolen from them."[42] A resident of Fairfax County, in the same state, described a Michigan trooper who visited her home as saying "he expected to beat the 'hull' out of us etc.," but she added that "on the whole he was candid and good-natured."[43] When a Federal officer, detailed to search a mansion near Winchester, Virginia, returned the furious censure of the mistress of the house by politely hiding her provisions from his comrades, her wrath melted into admiration. " 'I owe you an apology,' " she said. " ' I have often said that there were no gentlemen in the Yankee army, but I must except one.' "[44]

The accounts of many other women make grateful acknowledgment of the protection given them by individual Federals from the less kindly disposed members of the invading armies. The mistress of Oakley Plantation at Upperville, Virginia, according to her diary, found the hiding of her money and silver to be unnecessary, because a colonel of Swiss extraction, shocked at her recital of the depredations of other Federals, gave her the protection of a guard of two men.[45] A similar incident is described as occurring at Lynchburg during Hunter's raid upon that place. While soldiers were ransacking the home of Elizabeth Ann Obenchain, an officer appeared and, claiming relationship with the owner, cleared her house of marauders and sent a surgeon to attend her sick child.[46] Still another instance of this type of conduct concerned a Federal soldier who was known by the sinister title of "Butch." He visited the premises of a Mrs. Booth at Bovina, Mississippi, to secure plunder, but his evil intentions were changed to compassion when he heard the members of the Booth household bemoaning the destruction which other Federals had inflicted upon them. He returned the stolen family silver to its closet and asserted that he would do anything in his power to protect the family from his associates.[47] It was even admitted that officers of the hated Negro regiments could be kind to distressed women. One of these officers, after rescuing a box of French china from some soldiers, is recorded as saying to its grateful owner, a Virginia woman, " 'I will do what I can, for I cannot be too thankful that my wife is not in an invaded country.' "[48]

A few women, after experiencing good treatment at the hands of the enemy, regretted that they had previously made hostile demonstrations in their presence. "Fine, noble-looking men they were," wrote Sarah

Morgan in expressing her misgivings for having waved a Confederate flag in front of the invaders of her Louisiana retreat. "One cannot help but admire such foes! . . . They came as visitors without either pretensions to superiority, or the insolence of conquerors; they walked quietly on their way, offering no annoyance to the citizens, though they themselves were stared at most unmercifully."[49] Other women were extravagant in their praise of Federal gallantry. An escort of Union cavalry, taking three Virginia women through the lines, "treated us as if we were queens," according to one of these women. "Not one profane word did we hear—not a syllable but breathed respect and kindly feeling."[50] Still others went so far at times as to contrast the Confederates unfavorably with their adversaries. "I was much struck by the superior discipline of the Yankee troops over ours," wrote Betty Herndon Maury, after observing the behavior of the Federal soldiers at Fredericksburg. "I have not seen a drunken man since they have been here."[51] The members of the Confederate garrison at Baton Rouge—"gentlemen all"—so exasperated Sarah Morgan by their attempts at flirtation that, according to her own statement, she would have liked to have used daggers on them. She found their Northern successors, on the other hand, to be more polite; no more flirtatious than to take off their hats to the ladies and to give them simple glances.[52]

THE WOMEN OF THE DEBATABLE LAND

Such acts of kindness and heroism on the part of the Federal soldiers as have just been described caused many patriotic Southern women to show respect and even sympathy for the enemy. These women acknowledged the fact that the Federals had "exhibited a bravery and determination worthy of a better cause," and they felt a certain pride in the fact that the Confederates were meeting brave contestants in hard-fought engagements.[53] Likewise, as will presently be shown,[54] there were many patriotic women who sympathized with the sad plight of the thousands of Federal soldiers who found their way into Confederate prisons and hospitals. And there were some women of the same type who sympathized with women of the North who had sufferings and sorrows like their own. "It is dreadful to think of the dead and the dying, the widows and orphans," wrote Judith W. McGuire in considering the heavy losses of the invaders. "They have no business here on such an errand; but who, with a human heart, does not feel a pang at the thought that each one has somebody to grieve for him?"[55] This same diarist later refused to join with her associates in hoping that the Southern invaders of the North would take vengeance for the wrongs of the South. "We don't want the Northern women and children to suffer," she wrote on the eve of the Gettysburg campaign; "nor that our men should follow their example, and break through and steal. I want our warfare carried on in a more honorable way."[56]

The fact that such women occasionally found themselves able to applaud a gallant foe or to sympathize with an enemy in distress did not in any way lessen the intensity of their devotion to the Confederate cause. In certain regions, on the other hand, there were women who assumed attitudes toward the Federals which did not meet with the approval of their more patriotic associates. As previously indicated, there were many women who possessed the human tendency to seek a convenient solution of unfortunate situations by making the best of whatever opportunities which might present themselves. To escape deportation, therefore, a considerable number of these opportunists, especially in Norfolk and New Orleans, took the oath of loyalty to the Federal government.[57] Others accepted offers of friendship from the bluecoats. "These Virginia girls," wrote Alexander Hunter of the young women of Fauquier County, "did not turn up their noses, or sweep aside their skirts as if contamination dwelt in a Federal soldier, especially if the man in blue was a gentleman. . . . The kindly overtures were not met with superciliousness or insult." Some of these girls, according to Hunter's account, even reciprocated romantic advances. A beautiful maiden named Nannie Dixon, for example, "fell madly in love with a Federal captain of cavalry."[58] Nor were other romances lacking, both to the amusement and infuriation of those who observed them. The passengers on board a flag-of-truce boat, operating between Washington and Richmond, were pleasantly diverted by "a sudden and desperate love affair between a Southern girl and a Federal officer,"[59] and the women of Louisiana were outraged when a beautiful Creole maiden consented "to marry one who had spent months in command of soldiers desolating her country."[60] A North Carolina girl was provoked with her friends "for letting the nasty things [the Federals] build 'air castles.' "[61] Indeed the practice of Southern girls falling in love with Northern officers was sufficiently widespread to become one of the conventions of Southern novels.[62]

Some of the most striking examples of cordiality between Southern women and the Federal soldiers occurred in Nashville and its vicinity. The occupiers of Middle Tennessee were noted for their unusually good conduct, and they were stationed in that region for a long period. Likewise, the devotion of the inhabitants of that area to the Confederate cause was less intense than that of the people of the lower South.[63] It is not surprising, therefore, that the relations between the women of this locality and the enemy are probably without parallel in any of the seceded states. " 'What shall I say to General Buell for you?' " said a member of a committee appointed to meet the conqueror of Nashville to Sarah Childress Polk. " 'Tell him I am at home,' " calmly replied the widow of a President of the United States. As a matter of fact, Buell, Sherman, and other Federal officers called upon her, and she entertained them graciously.[64] Following the example of Mrs. Polk, many other Nashville women entertained Union officers in their homes, and a considerable number, with no high degree of reluctance, took the oath of loyalty. "I have been true to my oath, voluntarily and freely given, and prompted by no motive but to submit to the government of the United States," wrote the daughter of a member of the Confederate Senate to General Rousseau.[65]

The facility with which certain young women of Nashville accepted the attentions of Federal officers is well illustrated in a letter written by a girl of that city. "You will be surprised to hear that your friends of the female denomination," she wrote to her brother, "are dropping off every day—yes, dropping off—as willing victims into the arms of the ruthless invaders. Just think of it! Mollie the unconquerable, who used to parade with a large Beauregard breastpin, and who sang 'Maryland, My Maryland' with so much pathos, was married some four months ago to a Federal with one bar on his shoulder. Sallie, who used to sleep with the 'Bonnie Blue Flag' under her pillow . . . ., is married to one with two bars, and so on." Similar hospitality was extended in many instances by the inhabitants of the small towns of Middle Tennessee. "He visited Mrs. McLean, Mrs. Perry, Mrs. Mattell, Annie Parks and Sarah Andrews and the Hughes as a matter of course," wrote a resident of Columbia in describing the characteristic manner in which the ladies of her community entertained a Federal officer.[67] According to this same correspondent, "one of the loud-mouthed secesh" of this town "went voluntarily into the jaws of the lion" by going to Nashville, where she took the oath of allegiance.[68] Irritation at the existence of this state of affairs in Middle Tennessee impelled a native of that section, in exile because of her loyalty to the Confederacy, to write, "I hope the army will get up in the Summer and clear it out of those who have been remaining so easily and quietly at home enjoying themselves under Lincoln's rule, while their brothers and friends have been suffering and fighting for their independence. How I blush to think that there are such in my country—and that some of them are my own relations."[69]

In East Tennessee, where the conflict assumed the character of a bitter civil struggle as well as a political and military contest, a large proportion of the women were Unionists and regarded the Federals as deliverers.[70] A Southern sympathizer wrote to Jefferson Davis in November, 1861, that these people "look for the establishment of the Federal authority with as much confidence as the Jews look for the coming of the Messiah, and I am quite sure when I assert that no event or circumstance can change or modify their hope."[71] A Confederate officer stationed at Loudon observed the inhabitants of that place "actually manufacturing Union flags to welcome the refugee Tennesseans when they return,"[72] while William Blount Carter, a Unionist, wrote from Kingston that "women weep for joy when I merely hint to them that the day of our deliverance is at hand."[73] "Although the government, which owed them protection, did not protect them," these women, according to a memorial presented to Congress in 1864, "broke their last biscuit, and gave them [the Federals] the biggest half, out of the mouths of hungry children. They gave up the last horse, mule, cow, sheep, hog, everything they had to the soldiers that needed them, because they were Union soldiers, or were plundered out of them by the enemy."[74]

There were some women in other sections of the South who embraced the Federal cause as soon as such a policy became advantageous. Reference has already been made to the "low white women," who participated in the New Orleans parade celebrating the fall of Vicksburg,[75] and, according to the account of a Northern observer, there were some white women who applauded when Sherman's men tramped through the streets of Columbia.[76] When this general left the South Carolina capital, he carried with him several families who claimed that they had succored Federal prisoners.[77] Among this group was the golden-haired Mary Boozer, a young woman of marvelous beauty, wit, and charm, who had espoused the Union cause early in the war.[78] Her interest in Federal prisoners had caused her to be socially ostracized and placed under military surveillance, but she effected the escape of a young Ohio officer and kept him concealed in her house until the arrival of the Union forces. She was observed leaving Columbia in the grandest equipage available in the city, engaged "in a lively conversation with a gay looking officer riding by the carriage,"[79] and she is said to have ruled as a veritable Cleopatra, in the Oriental splendor of her retinue, as the army of Sherman paid tribute to her beauty and the romance of her career.[80] Similar conduct was exhibited by women in Richmond, who, upon hearing of the triumph of the Federals, gleefully proclaimed their allegiance to the national government.[81]

THE TREATMENT OF FEDERAL PRISONERS

No account of the relations between the women of the Confederacy and the invaders of that section would be complete without some reference being made to the treatment of Federal prisoners. In this respect, as in the other phases of their relations with the enemy, the women exhibited various attitudes. In general they were not deliberately cruel or vindictive toward these unfortunates; many women sympathized with them in their sufferings; and there were cases of women doing relief work among prisoners in hospitals and even condemning the alleged cruelty or neglect on the part of the Confederate prison service. On the other hand, it must be admitted that the women as a whole often neglected golden opportunities to minister to captives in distress. Their main energies were absorbed in the titanic task of alleviating distress among their own kith and kin, and as a rule they were unable to rise above the passions of the time to a degree sufficient to have allowed the disregarding of distinctions between friends and enemies in acts of charity. Moreover, whatever condemnation the impartial historian may now bestow upon the Confederate authorities for their treatment of prisoners, such criticism was largely absent from the thoughts of the Southern women during the war. They defended the prison policies of the Confederate government far more often than they condemned them. They firmly believed that Confederates in Northern prisons received worse treatment than Federals in Southern prisons; that the South was doing for its prisoners all that its limited resources would allow; and that the Lincoln government, because of its hesitation in adopting a liberal policy of exchanges, was responsible for most of the sufferings of men in the prisons of the Confederacy.

When brought face to face with the sufferings of individual prisoners, however, many women exhibited tender emotions in spite of the general hate which they entertained for the nation that was waging a relentless war against the South. "Seeing an enemy wounded and helpless is a different thing from seeing him in health and power," wrote a hospital matron after the battle of Corinth.[82] "They were half-naked, and such a poor, miserable, starved-looking set of wretches that we couldn't help feeling sorry for them, in spite of their wicked war against our country," said a fiery young Georgia patriot of some prisoners who had the impudence to kiss their hands at her.[83] Indeed

BUTLER, THE BEAST, AT WORK
A contemporary caricature. (From *The Southern Illustrated News*)

it may be said that in some instances the women were able to make their sympathies for prisoners into fresh causes for vindictiveness against the Northern government. Among such women was Judith W. McGuire, who applauded Mosby's policy of showing no quarter to invaders caught burning houses, and at the same time expressed a deep sympathy for captives who pled for mercy. "Two came to us, the most pitiful objects you ever beheld," she wrote of such unfortunates, "and we did what we could for them; for, after all, the men are not to blame half as much as the officers."[84] Kate Cumming, a devoted hospital matron, showed the same attitude toward prisoners put in her charge. "On looking at these poor creatures," she wrote, "I thought what a pity it was that men in Washington could not be made to take their places."[85] And Sarah Morgan, making the same contrast between the hard lot of the prisoners and the alleged wickedness of the leaders who sent them into the South, wrote, "I wish these poor men were safe in their own land! It is heartbreaking to see them die like dogs, with no one to say Godspeed."[86]

Expressions of sympathy for prisoners of war were occasionally accompanied by acts of charity on the part of the Southern women. Varina Howell Davis set a worthy example in this respect by treating a prisoner with so much kindness that he asserted long afterwards that he could never forget it.[87] " 'Feed my prisoners if all the rest of us lose our breakfast,' " said Roger A. Pryor as he brought a party of captured Federals into his camp, whereupon his wife and family agreed to sacrifice the only food they had, a small pail of meal.[88] A similar response was made by the Black Oak Soldiers' Relief Association to a request that they aid the starving men in the Confederate prison camp at Florence, South Carolina. "Five thousand men starving, dying of disease, though they were the enemy, appealed strongly to the hearts of our women," said a member of this South Carolina organization, and large boxes were filled with food and sent to Florence.[89] In response to similar humanitarian impulses, there were times when women even rushed out of their homes to feed passing prisoners with something of the same spirit in which they performed this service for the men of their own armies. "My sister says that she had every drop of milk and clabber in her dairy brought out and given to the poor fellows," wrote Eliza Frances Andrews regarding the treatment accorded by a Georgia plantation mistress to some men being taken to Andersonville, "and she begged the officer to let them wait until she could have what food she could spare cooked for them. This, however, being impossible, she had potatoes and turnips and whatever could be eaten raw, hastily collected by the servants and strewn on the road before them."[90]

Although the women who condemned alleged acts of inhumanity inflicted upon the prisoners were few in number, they spoke with emphasis. The sentiment of this group was well expressed by Kate Cumming when she heard that a Confederate officer had shot a prisoner committed to his charge. "Such men ought not to be allowed to bring dishonor on a brave people, and deserve punishment," she wrote. "There might be some excuse for a man in the heat of battle refusing to take a prisoner . . . but this captain had no such excuse. He has been guilty of murder, and of the most cowardly kind."[91] Likewise, Eliza Frances Andrews, although believing that the principal blame for the sufferings of prisoners rested upon the Federal government's refusal to effect exchanges, roundly condemned the horrors of Andersonville. "It is a horrible blot upon the fair name of our Confederacy," she declared with considerable disgust after observing the famous prison. "I shuddered as I passed the place on the cars, with its tall gibbet full of horrible suggestiveness before the gate, and its seething mass of humanity inside, like a swarm of blue flies crawling over a grave."[92]

It must be admitted, however, as has already been suggested, that the Southern women did not do all that they might have done for the relief of the distressed enemy in their midst. There was naturally much neglect, due to factors over which they had no control, but there was also a tendency manifested on the part of some women to oppose the inclinations of other women to relieve human distress without regard to distinctions between friends and enemies. "Whilst every attention was given our sick and wounded by the inhabitants," said Colonel Bela Estvan of the women of Richmond, "the unfortunate prisoners were allowed to rot." This Confederate officer asserted that, after the Battle of Seven Pines, he observed ladies from the Southern capital and their black servants distributing hot drinks to wounded Confederates without taking any notice of wounded prisoners. In the hope of relieving a particular Federal, Colonel Estvan secured a cup of coffee from a woman, but as he was stooping to give the beverage to the man someone plucked him by the sleeve. It was a woman remonstrating with him for helping a miserable Yankee. According to the conclusions of this writer, the passions of war time were so violent as to lead to much feminine brutality and a consequent vanishing of pity altogether.[93]

Although such sweeping assertions are contradicted by evidence already cited, there is a limited amount of evidence from the pens of Southern women themselves supporting Estvan's contention. Sarah Morgan, for instance, declared that the women of her family were characterized as "traitors and Yankees" by certain of their associates in Baton Rouge because they had aided a dying Federal colonel. "I am threatened with Coventry," she continued, "because I sent a custard to a sick man who is in the army, and with anathema of society because I said if I could possibly do anything for Mr. Biddle—at a distance— (he is sick) I would like to very much." She believed that God would punish her feminine associates for these "wicked, malignant feelings" and the "loathsome violence" of their passions, and she regarded their acts of omission with equal disgust. "Not a square off, in the new theater," she wrote, "lie more than a hundred sick soldiers. What woman has stretched forth her hand to save them, to give them a cup of water? Where is the charity which should ignore nations and creeds, and administer help to Indian and heathen indifferently?"[94]

It is very likely that there were few women in the Confederacy with a philosophy of human sympathy as broad as that of Sarah Morgan. While many of them were willing to minister to the needs of such of the enemy as the fortunes of war threw upon their mercy, the majority neglected this service, succumbing to the human tendency to let charity begin and end at home. Moreover, to expect that the Southern women should have accorded to a deadly foe the same treatment given to friends and relatives involves the ignoring of the violent passions unloosed by civil war. It seldom occurred, even to those women who recognized the sad plight of the prisoners, that, in refusing aid to these men, they were neglecting a humanitarian and a Christian duty. Rather was there a tendency to reason that the prisoners were cruel and meddlesome invaders who were the authors of their own miseries, as well as the sufferings and hardships of the Southern population. Likewise, it is perhaps unreasonable to expect that the women should share with prisoners the resources which were in no sense sufficient to satisfy the needs of their own armies.

There were two other factors which also served to provide a convenient feminine rationalization and to aid in stifling whatever qualms of conscience that might arise over the sufferings of prisoners. One of these was the belief, almost universally cherished by the women of the South, that Southerners in Northern prisons were worse treated than Northerners in Southern prisons.[95] "How hard it is to suppress feelings of hatred for our enemy!" exclaimed Kate Cumming, when she heard some of the lurid tales from Northern prisons that were being circulated in the South. "I feel confident as I am living, that God, in His own good time, will avenge our wrongs. When I think of the kind treatment which our people have bestowed on our prisoners here, bad off for food as we were, did I think otherwise, it would be contrary to the faith I have in the justice of God."[96] The other factor which served to salve the feminine conscience and to arouse the anger of the women was the belief, also widely held in the South, that upon Lincoln and his government, and not upon the Southern women and the Confederate authorities, rested the entire responsibility for the terrors of the Southern prisons. This convenient excuse was based upon the refusal of Lincoln to adopt a liberal policy regarding exchanges.[97] That the Federal government was less anxious than the Confederate government to effect a general method of exchange is well known, but the women ignored completely the Federal President's contention that his policy was actuated by a desire to prevent the prolonging of the war by adding exchanged prisoners to the fighting forces of the Confederacy. To them he was a Moloch indifferent to sufferings of his many fellow-countrymen whom the Confederate authorities would have willingly released in exchange for their own men in similar plight in the North. This feminine viewpoint was likewise expressed forcefully by Kate Cumming. "O, how I thought of him who is the cause of all this woe to his fellow-countrymen—Abraham Lincoln," she cried as she meditated over the horrors of Andersonville. "What kind of heart can he have, to leave these poor wretches here? It is truly awful to think about. But, as sure as there is a just God, his day of reckoning will come for the crimes he has been guilty against his own countrymen alone."[98]

⁂

By way of summary it may be concluded from the foregoing account that the majority of the Southern women regarded the objectionable acts of the Federals as sufficient grounds to justify their rejection of all proffers of cordiality from the invaders. It is likely that the attitude of this group would not have been more compromising had the enemy always been the very soul of kindness, however; for the fact that these men were the invaders of the South, menacing the institutions of a cherished civilization, made them abhorrent to the women of that section. On the other hand, there were exceptions to this unbending patriotism, for there were some women who reconciled cordiality toward the invaders with devotion to the Confederacy; others who were Unionists without the bother of Southern sentiment to stand in the way of their making friends; and a few who thoughtlessly or selfishly accepted whatever favors the Federals offered them. Similar variety characterized the relations of the women with prisoners of war, and additional illustrations of the manifestation of their always varied and sometimes inconsistent attitude toward the enemy will appear later.

CHAPTER VI

INSTANCES OF HEROISM

IT has already been observed that the prevalence of middle nineteenth century inhibitions upon feminine conspicuousness militated against the appearance of a Southern Joan of Arc. There were, however, certain phases of the activity of the women of the Confederacy, in playing their part in sustaining the causes for which the men of the South were fighting, which may be truly characterized as heroic. In the majority of cases this heroism manifested itself along lines already described—in taking pride in privations, being hopeful in the face of disaster, and assuming an uncompromising attitude both in their relations with the hostile invaders from the North and with the complacent slackers and peace advocates at home. In a somewhat smaller number of cases the women displayed a heroic attitude by enduring with fortitude the hazards of being under Federal fire and the perils of living in besieged places. The heroism of a small and more or less unconventional group of women expressed itself in chafing under the prohibitions against active military service on the part of their sex, in becoming camp followers, in spying, and engaging in other auxiliary military services. And in a very few bizarre instances women are reputed to have served as soldiers.

THE HAZARDS OF FEDERAL FIRE

It was only natural that many women should have been dreadfully frightened when they were compelled for the first time to observe the bullets and shells of the enemy entering their towns and cities. In the buoyant enthusiasm with which they had entered the war, these women had never contemplated a time when the invaders should attain such proximity, or when the "splendid mimicry of war" should assume such a tragic reality. Now they were faced with a situation in which the flash of every gun spelled possible death. Mrs. Roger A. Pryor wrote that it was impossible to describe "the terror and demoralization" which overtook the women of Petersburg when the Federals first opened fire upon that city, adding that she herself "literally 'went all to pieces,' trembling as though I had a chill," when she had fled beyond the range of the attacking guns.[1] The first shells thrown into Charleston were said to have sent "a quiver of terror" through the nerves of the women of that place. "One such night completely demoralized us," wrote one of them afterwards, "though up to this time we had thought ourselves brave soldiers."[2]

As the war progressed, however, such testimonials of timidity grew less numerous, being replaced in many instances by accounts of the manifestation of a coolness on the part of the women that was in decided contrast to their earlier action. "I now hear of acres of dead and cities of wounded with less sensibility than was at first occasioned by hearing of the loss of half a dozen men in a skirmish," wrote a Virginia woman in 1862.[3] Two years later at Richmond, Mary Boykin Chesnut asked herself, "Am I the poor soul who fell on her knees and prayed, and wept, and fainted, as the first guns boomed from Sumter?" She felt constrained to answer in the negative, for she now found herself absorbed in the reading of a novel while the cannon of the enemy were thundering in her ears.[4] Nor were the women of the Confederate capital more excited than their South Carolina visitor. During the Seven Days fighting around Richmond, Judith W. McGuire wrote that the inhabitants of that city were so "unmoved by these terrible demonstrations of our powerful foe," that "when the battle was over, the crowd dispersed and retired to their respective homes with the seeming tranquility of persons who had been witnessing a panorama in a far-off country."[5] And if the women of Petersburg and Charleston were frightened by their first experiences with hostile shells, they soon recovered their composure. George Cary Eggleston asserted that the women of the former city eventually reached the point where they did their shopping and went about their duties under a most uncomfortable bombardment, without evincing the slightest fear or showing any nervousness whatever;[6] and the women of Charleston, after refugeeing in what were considered to be safe portions of that city, were said to have become accustomed to the dropping of shells, while their children even clapped their hands and laughed at the flying missiles.[7]

In addition to the women who from necessity learned to display a calmness under fire, there were others who deliberately endured such hazards from patriotic or sentimental motives. While the Federals were discharging a hailstorm of bullets at a Southern company advancing through the streets of Gainesville, Florida, the women of that town, undismayed, brought buckets of water to the heated Confederates and joined their captain in lustily repeating the command, "Charge, Charge!"[8] When a small body of Mountjoy's men, hotly pursued by Federals, passed the home of two Virginia girls, these girls mounted a fence and, amid a shower of bullets, directed the men to a safe retreat over a ford. Upon the arrival of the enemy, the girls pointedly refused to show them the direction which the fleeing Confederates had taken.[9] During the Battle of Nashville a contingent of the Confederate army was forced to retreat, whereupon Mary Bradford, a young woman of the neighborhood, thinking the men in cowardly flight, rushed from her home and, braving a storm of hostile missiles, attempted to turn the retreating soldiers upon the enemy.[10] When General Wickham's brigade was driven back toward his own home at Hanover Junction, Virginia, his mother and her two granddaughters stood on the porch under a heavy fire. The general, fearing for the safety of his relatives, sent an officer to order their retirement. " 'Go and tell General Wickham,' " said the mother of the officer, " 'that he can command the men of the South, but he does not command the women of the South, and we will stand here and die with you until you whip those Yankees. Go and do it.' "[11]

Women at times underwent the hazards of Federal fire in order to rescue victims from the battlefields. Among these was a woman of Howard County, Missouri, who rescued a Confederate wounded by Federal raiders and concealed him in underbrush near her home until he was well enough to resume active service.[12] Another woman of this type was Allie McPeek, an humble Georgian upon whose farm the Battle of Jonesboro was fought. Exposing herself during the battle to the fire of both armies, she moved fearlessly about relieving both friend and foe. General Schofield, the Federal commander, touched by her heroism, sent her provisions and caused his adjutant to write her a letter of thanks.[13] The most famous of these heroines, however, was Lenie Russell, who volunteered to attend Randolph Ridgely, a beardless youth of Ramseur's command, who was so severely wounded in the Battle of Winchester that a surgeon said his life would be endangered were he removed from the field. "All through the anxious night," said General D. H. Maury, "the brave girl sat sustaining the head of the wounded youth and carefully guarding him against anything that could disturb his rest."[14]

CAVE LIFE IN VICKSBURG

The women of Vicksburg had the worst trials of any group of Confederate women in a city under siege. Although Pemberton, the general in command of this town, ordered all non-combatants to leave before their departure was blocked by the investment, many women failed to obey his injunction, feeling that life in Vicksburg was safer than in the surrounding rural districts; and, with warnings regarding the possible consequences, they were allowed to remain. The result was that, for a period of several months, they found themselves bottled up in a city that was threatened with famine and whose entire area was within the range of the attacking guns.

RECEPTION OF GENERAL BURNSIDE BY THE UNIONISTS OF
KNOXVILLE

(From *Harper's Weekly*)

Underground habitations were constructed to protect the women and children from the shells. "Caves were the fashion—the rage—over besieged Vicksburg," according to Mary Ann Loughborough, whose intimate account forms the chief source of information on the gnome-like existence of the inhabitants of these subterranean recesses. "On every side we could see, thickly strewn among the earthy cliffs, large caves and little caves—some cut out substantially roomy and comfortable, while others were only large enough for one person to stand." In one suburb they were so numerous that this writer was reminded of "the numberless holes that swallows make in the summer."[15] The digging of such holes became a profession with certain Negroes, from ten to fifty dollars being charged for each excavation. Some were commodious, containing several rooms. One was described as being well-boarded, well-ventilated, and equipped with niches for flowers.[16] Another was said to have branched six feet from the entrance, forming an excavation in the shape of a T; in one wing was the bedroom, in the other a dressing room, and standing room was secured by cutting a hole in the floor. "Our quarters were close, indeed," added the owner of this singular abode, "but I was far more comfortable than I expected I could ever be under earth in that fashion."[17]

It should not be assumed, however, that life among the cave-dwellers of Vicksburg was generally comfortable. Not even the deepest excavations were sufficient to protect their inhabitant against the possibility of death. One authority listed thirteen women and children who were killed or seriously wounded during the siege.[18] While sitting in her cave, Mary Ann Loughborough heard heartrending screams on two occasions. At one time these screams came from a mother who had just seen her child killed by a shell which burst through the roof of her cave; at the other time they came from a child who was hit by a shell as she ventured out of the close atmosphere of her cave in search of fresh air. "One wild scream," said the account of the latter incident, "and she ran into her mother's presence, sinking like a wounded dove, the life blood flowing over the light summer dress in crimson ripples."[19] It was inevitable that such a prevalent danger of sudden death should produce intense fright on the part of many women. "Every night I had lain down expecting death, and every morning rose with the same prospect without being unnerved," wrote one woman of her struggle against the dominant fear, but after a shell had broken through her roof she was forced to add, "A horrible day. The most horrible yet to me, because I have lost my nerve."[20]

Likewise, there was much suffering in Vicksburg from weariness and privations. The women were reduced to a diet of coffee made of parched corn meal, musty bacon, and bread made without soda or yeast. Many ate rats and mule steak, as beef could be spared only when the shells killed a cow.[21] "I am told that I am looking pale and wan, and frequently asked if I am weary of my cave life," wrote one of the chroniclers of these events. "I *am* tired and weary," she added, "ah so weary! I never was made to exist under ground; and when I am obliged to, what wonder that I vegetate like other unfortunate plants—grow weary, spindling and white."[22] And yet a considerable number of the women of Vicksburg endured this unusual life with a fortitude that is amazing, counselling resistance to the bitter end, and fondly clinging to hopes that the siege would be raised. "Tomorrow and the next day," wrote one hopeful patriot, "we will listen eagerly for the sound of the battle which can save us."[23]

AUXILIARY MILITARY SERVICES

The intensity of their martial enthusiasm caused some women to chafe under the social conventions which made fighting the monopoly of the stronger sex. They felt that these restrictions deprived them of the most direct means of expressing their patriotism and of securing relief from the terrible strain of comparative inaction. "We are leading the lives which women have led since Troy fell," wrote Julia LeGrand, as she bitterly reflected upon the position to which she and her feminine associates were consigned; "wearing away time with memories, regrets and fears; alternating fits of suppression with flights, imaginary, to the red fields where great principles are contended for, lost and won; while men, more privileged, are abroad and astir, making name and fortune and helping to make a nation. . . . We are like pent-up volcanos. . . . Now that there is better work to do, real tragedy, real romance and history weaving every day, we suffer, suffer, leading the life I do."[24] At least one maiden accompanied the display of this resentment with the manifestation of a thirst for carnage. "I talk of killing them! For what else do I wear a pistol and a carving knife?" said Sarah Morgan as the Federals were entering Louisiana. "Oh! if I were only a man. Then I could don the breeches, and slay them with a will! If some few Southern women were in the ranks, they could set the men an example they would not blush to follow. Pshaw! There are no women here! We are all men!"[25]

The services of women in activities auxiliary to military service were, however, more frequent and more generally approved than actual fighting. Some women lived in camps in order to minister to the varied wants of the men, while others, whose homes were on or near battlefields, waited on the combatants and cheered them to the charge. The most important auxiliary service of the women, however, was the furnishing of military intelligence. Often this information was derived from casual contacts with the happenings in the women's communities; at other times it was wheedled from Federal officers; and in a few cases women acted as professional spies.

The women who lived in camps usually did so in order that they might be near a soldier-son or a soldier-husband. Among their many activities, conventional and unconventional to women, were rescuing the wounded, nursing the sick, praying for the dying, cooking delicacies, and mending worn clothes. Outstanding among the numerous women of humble station who performed this type of service was Rose Rooney, an Irish woman who attached herself to a Louisiana regiment. "In everything but the actual fighting," says an account of her services, "she was as useful as any of the boys . . . and served with undaunted bravery which led her to risk the dangers of every battlefield where the regiment was engaged, unheeding havoc made by shot and shell, so that she might give timely aid and succor to the wounded or comfort to the dying."[26] Another outstanding camp follower was Betty Sullivan, also an Irish woman attached to a Louisiana regiment. With canteens and bandages suspended from her shoulders, she stood near the soldiers during battles in order to stanch their wounds and moisten their lips. Often she slept on the frozen ground, a blanket her sole covering and a knapsack her only pillow. She was so beloved by the men of her regiment that they affectionately named her "Mother Sullivan,"and it was said that there was not a man among them who would not have shed his blood for her.[27] The most distinguished woman of this type was Jane Claudia Johnson, the wife of General Bradley T. Johnson of Maryland and a daughter of Romulus M. Saunders of North Carolina. Discovering that her husband's command at Point of Rocks on the Potomac was without proper equipment, she hastened to North Carolina, where she secured the necessary supplies from Governor Ellis and others. She then undertook ministration to the physical and religious needs of the men, services as useful if not as spectacular as her earlier activities.[28] The services of such women were so well appreciated that the *Charlottesville Chronicle* suggested that forty thousand women be conscripted to act as cooks, nurses, seamstresses, clerks, and washerwomen for the army.[29]

Frequently women gave timely aid or encouragement to Confederates engaged in battle. That the men appreciated such assistance is illustrated by an incident in the career of Nathan Bedford Forrest. As that general was drawing up his men for what was expected to be a sharp encounter, some women rushed from a house in front of the line and cried, " 'What shall we do, General, what shall we do?' " Firm in the faith that they meant to help him, Forrest replied, " 'I really don't see what you can do much, except stand on the stumps, wave your bonnets, and shout "Hurrah boys!" ' "[30] That the women could act as well as shout is demonstrated by another incident in Forrest's career. While trying to intercept the Federal commander Streight, who was attempting to sever Confederate communications between Chattanooga and near-by towns in the spring of 1863, the Confederate cavalry leader found his progress blocked by a burning bridge over Black Creek in northern Alabama. At this juncture, Emma Sanson, a girl familiar with the stream, came forward and offered to show him a "lost ford." " 'She's going to show me where I can get my men over in time to catch these Yankees before they get to Rome,' " said the general to the girl's mother as the young heroine climbed behind his saddle. The mission was successful, for the girl showed him the ford, and he crossed in time to frustrate the enemy's advance.[31]

In giving intelligence to Confederates operating near their homes the women performed a more valuable service than the one just mentioned. Indeed it is asserted that in many cases the success of Confederate military activities was due to knowledge supplied in this manner.[32] Often better acquainted with their own localities than were the Confederate scouts, and not subject to arrest by the Federals unless under positive suspicion, many women gained valuable military secrets, which they eagerly communicated to the Southern commanders. Such services frequently necessitated long and perilous trips on foot or on horseback and called for extraordinary resourcefulness and fortitude.

Some idea of the accomplishments of these women informers is gained from an examination of several incidents gleaned from the literature on the subject. One day at Columbia, Tennessee, Antoinette Polk observed the Federals mustering to go in pursuit of a group of Forrest's scouts quartered near by at her father's mansion, Ashwood. Feeling instinctively that there was danger, this maiden, a splendid figure mounted on a thoroughbred, dashed by a short route to Ashwood just in time to save the scouts from capture.[33] In Loudoun County, Virginia, a Miss Porterfield walked five miles at night to warn the Confederates that the enemy were about to cross the Potomac, an act which saved a considerable contingent of the Southern army from capture.[34] Equally clever was Laura Radcliffe of Fauquier County,

Virginia, whose principal exploit concerned Mosby, the Confederate partisan leader. She heard from a garrulous Federal officer that the Unionists had set a trap for Mosby at a church they knew he was going to pass. The officer told her that this information could be given her without prejudice to the Federal cause since she had no horse on which she could ride to forewarn the Confederate leader; but her resourcefulness was greater than the foolhardy Federal imagined, for she managed to secure a horse and reach Mosby in time to warn him against the trap.[35]

Certain stories from northern Virginia indicate that a few women at least were capable of capturing Federals. During the First Battle of Manassas a party of half a dozen Union soldiers visited the near-by home of a girl to seek refreshments. "When the martial visitors manifested a disposition to depart," according to the chronicler of this event, "their fair captor assumed a rather defiant attitude, naïvely assured them that they were her prisoners; and pointing a revolver towards her surprised victims, informed them that she would put a ball through the first man that moved." She immediately turned them over to a Confederate guard.[36] Another story concerns a young woman who lived in the neighborhood of Camp Pickens. She willingly fell into the plans of a group of Confederate guerrillas who expressed a desire to capture a party of Federals known to be at a near-by farmhouse. She paid this house a social call and, upon leaving, eagerly accepted the invitation of one of the Federals present to escort her home. At a prearranged point on the journey of the couple, two of the guerrillas sprang upon the luckless male and carried him away to Centreville.[37] The most famous woman of this type, however, was Nancy Hart, a Virginia mountaineer, whose practice of leading Jackson's cavalry upon Federal outposts caused the Northerners to offer a reward for her capture. She was bagged at Summerville in July, 1862, by Colonel Starr of a West Virginia regiment. After a brief imprisonment, however, she shot her guard and escaped on Starr's horse to the nearest Confederate outpost. A few days later she surprised Summerville, at the head of a body of two hundred Confederates, and carried Starr and his West Virginians away as captives.[38]

WOMEN SPIES

Aside from those women who gained information for the Confederates through casual contacts with the Federals, there were others who circulated among the enemy specifically for this purpose. In other words, they became spies. Examples of minor work of this type were furnished by the conduct of certain women of New Bern, North Carolina, after the capture of that place by the Federals. One of these women was Elizabeth Carraway Harland, who sent to the Confederate authorities the specifications of the New Bern fortifications concealed in the bone of a ham which her daughter carried out of the town. Another was Mrs. A. M. Meekins, who entered New Bern disguised as a country woman with a bale of cotton for sale. Her purpose was to ascertain for General Lee the strength of the Federal garrison. A third example of this type was Emmeline Piggott, who rendered valuable services by carrying packets between New Bern and Beaufort concealed in the ample folds of her skirts. When she was finally seized by the Federals, she destroyed her incriminating evidence by chewing it into fragments.[39]

Among the more romantic type of spies were two women in the services of "Jeb" Stuart, the celebrated Virginia cavalry leader. We catch a glimpse of one of these agents as she was "captured" by Stuart's pickets near Washington. Riding a superb chestnut mare, she was "a Juno in appearance, with a wealth of raven hair twisted carelessly in a loose knot under the jockey cap she wore." Stuart received her cordially; she gave him papers taken from her hair and was then, by his orders, returned to the Federal lines.[40] The other agent of Stuart was a certain Miss Antonia Ford of Fairfax Courthouse, Virginia. Good-looking, pleasing in manners, and fluent in the expression of Unionist sentiments, she gained information from Federal officers boarding in her father's house. The communication of these secrets to Colonel Mosby is believed to have made possible several of his surprise attacks upon Federal outposts and the capture of Colonel Stoughton at Fairfax Courthouse on the night of March 8, 1863. On one occasion she was said to have entertained Mosby in disguise at her home. "Miss Ford," said the Federal agent who uncovered her machinations, "was accustomed to go out at night to meet Mosby, the famous guerrilla, and impart whatever information that might be of service to the enemy. Indeed one day she was invited by a staff officer to take a horseback ride into the country, and met Mosby, whom she introduced to her escort under an assumed name, and passed along with loyal words on her traitorous lips."[41]

Another woman famous for her work as a spy was Rose O'Neal Greenhow, whose imprisonment has already been mentioned.[42] In 1861 she furnished to the Confederates information concerning the movement of Federal troops out of Washington, a service which some believe to have been an important factor in winning the Battle of First Manassas. After her release from prison, she was deported to Richmond where she was cordially received by President Davis. She continued to furnish information to the Confederate authorities until September, 1864, when, running the blockade out of Wilmington on an official mission, she was drowned off the coast of North Carolina. Her body and dispatches, however, were recovered. Aside from hospital workers, she bears the distinction of being the only woman who died while performing official duties for the Confederate government.[43]

The most noted of all the women spies was Belle Boyd, a seventeen-year-old girl in 1861, living in her native town of Martinsburg in the Shenandoah Valley. Stirred to action by the outrages committed by the Federal garrison in that town, she found, in collecting the secrets of the very approachable Union officers, a fruitful means of serving her country. She communicated the information thus secured to the Confederates, sometimes at the risk of her life. When one of her notes to Stuart was intercepted, she became a suspect, but the negligence or courtesy of the Union officers forestalled summary treatment. After the second capture of Martinsburg by the enemy, she went to Front Royal where she found General Shields occupying her aunt's house. She returned the courtesy with which this officer treated her by listening, through a hole in the ceiling of his chamber, to one of his councils of war. Jotting down what she had heard, she rode fifteen miles after midnight to an agent of Colonel Ashby, communicated her discoveries to him, and was back in bed before dawn. Her most important service was informing Jackson's men at Front Royal that, by advancing rapidly, they could save the bridges that were necessary for their attack on Banks. Unable to secure a man from a group of Confederate sympathizers, to whom she had appealed, to carry her message, she ran down the streets of Front Royal through a throng of Federals and reached the open fields beyond. There the conspicuous contrast between her blue dress and white bonnet and apron made her a target for the guns of the Federal pickets. Bullets pierced her dress, but she continued to run and was rewarded with cheers from the advance guard of the Confederates. Then she waved her bonnet as the sign for them to advance. "Miss Belle Boyd," said Jackson in a note to her, "I thank you, for myself, and for the army, for the immense service you have rendered your country today."

When the Federals reoccupied Front Royal in July, 1862, she was arrested and, under a guard of four hundred soldiers, was carried to Washington and thrown into the old Capitol Prison. After a month's confinement, however, she was released for want of sufficient evidence and allowed to return South, where, in a triumphal tour of the Confederacy, she was received as a heroine. In 1863 she was again arrested while nursing Confederates at Martinsburg, but after several months' incarceration in Carroll Prison at Washington was again permitted to return to the South.[24] In May, 1864, she sailed from Wilmington, North Carolina, for England, bearing dispatches from the President of the Confederacy. Captured at sea by a Federal cruiser, and carried to Boston, she was released for the third time by lenient captors. She then went to Europe in order to pursue a romance that had developed between her and an officer of the ship which had effected her capture, Sam Wylde Hardinge, to whom she was married in London on August 24, 1864.[45]

That such a career as that of Belle Boyd was possible is doubtless explained by the fact that she was endowed to a high degree with the feminine virtues and frailties that appealed to the men whose favor and indulgence she courted. She was handsome, charming, and possessed of a deep and tender devotion to the Southern cause. "She was a brilliant talker and soon everybody in the room was attracted to her, especially the men," wrote a feminine contemporary. This writer asserted that Belle Boyd took the shoes from her feet at Winchester and gave them to a barefooted Confederate, and that at Culpeper she flung her shawl over the shoulders of a ragged officer.[46] Her frailties were mendacity, lack of principle, and a flare for the romantic and spectacular. If these qualities prevented her from becoming the model heroine of the South, they at least made possible the beguiling of many a man and the calling of her melodramatic career to the attention of both friend and enemy.

CONFEDERATE AMAZONS

Although their services were not impressive, a few women are reputed to have assumed the attire of men, joined military organizations, and participated in battles. Among these was Mrs. L. M. Blalock, who is said to have enlisted in the Twenty-sixth North Carolina Regiment along with her husband in May, 1862, representing herself as his younger brother. She neither resumed feminine dress nor retired from the army until after she had participated in three major engagements.[47] A similar case was that of Mrs. Amy Clarke, who is said to have enlisted along with her husband and to have fought at Shiloh. After that battle she followed Bragg into Kentucky, where two wounds and capture put an end to her military services.[48] Travelers occasionally encountered women soldiers. Lieutenant Colonel Fremantle had pointed out to him, on a train between Chattanooga and Atlanta in 1863, a

GROUP OF UNION PRISONERS BEING ESCORTED THROUGH A SOUTHERN TOWN

(From *Harper's Weekly*)

girlish-looking woman with the reputation of having served in the Battles of Perryville and Murfreesboro,[49] and Fitzgerald Ross, another Englishman, met, on the train between Augusta and Atlanta, a woman captain whom he described as having taken an active part in the war.[50]

The most ambitious woman of this type was Loreta Janeta Velasquez, a New Orleans girl of Cuban extraction. According to her confessions, the war gave her an opportunity to gratify a youthful desire to emulate the great heroines of history. She effaced the feminine lines of her body with wire shields and braces, put on a uniform, assumed the *nom de guerre* of Lieutenant Harry T. Buford, and proceeded to Arkansas to raise a battalion of troops. There her success in winning recruits was, according to her assertions, only surpassed by her conquests of feminine hearts. Tiring of inaction in the far South, she abandoned her command and went to Virginia, where, independent of any command, she took part in the battles of Ball's Bluff and Manassas. After further adventures as a spy and mock gallant, she joined the Western armies, participated in the defense of Forts Donelson and Pillow, and received a wound on the field of Shiloh.[51]

It should not be assumed, however, that these Confederate Amazons were taken seriously. They were regarded as eccentrics, and if not always morally loose, they were so considered by the public. Lieutenant Colonel Fremantle said that the women soldiers whom he observed had been discharged because of "bad and immoral conduct," and a Lynchburg officer characterized the women attached to a Louisiana regiment as "disgusting looking creatures."[52] The only person impressed with the valor and worth of Loreta Janeta Velasquez was that woman herself. Her services on the field, according to her own admissions, were spasmodic, and the stories of her adventures have an air of the tawdry and the unreal.

↗   ↗   ↗   ↗

Had the women of the Confederacy lived in a more heroic age, in which their sex put on armor and went forth to battle with dignity, it is possible that they would have produced real Amazons and Joans of Arc. Such conditions, however, did not exist in the middle of the nineteenth century, and the Southern women had to express the most of their heroism in less spectacular forms.

CHAPTER VII

TREATMENT OF THE SICK AND WOUNDED

WHEN mobilization and the first battles had brought into existence that inevitable result of the vicissitudes of war, the problem of the disabled soldier, the women of the Confederacy responded with promptness to meet the emergency thus created. Volunteers rushed to the Virginia camps and battlefields to nurse the sick and wounded, and hospitals supported by the soldiers' relief societies soon made their appearance. When the Richmond government later assumed the task of directing these and similar hospitals, the women retained a large portion of the burden of supplying their needs, and a considerable number of women entered these institutions as volunteer nurses, matrons, and supervisors, thereby performing useful functions that might otherwise have been neglected. In addition to these more or less formally organized services, the women established stations known as wayside homes along all lines of travel, where men stranded by the inefficient railroads of the Confederacy were doctored and cared for; and women in every section of the South, the mistresses of cottages as well as of mansions, flung open their doors to receive those for whom the hospitals had no room.

There was little of the spectacular in these services. The prevailing conception of feminine propriety prevented the creation of hospital heroines through newspaper publicity, published notices of the labors of such women being limited to what was considered necessary to enlist popular support. There was little opportunity for the development of the hospital romances so popular in the literature of later wars, for the wounded veteran was not given the privilege of being nursed by a maiden possessed of the modern combination of beauty and scientific training. The Confederate woman was usually untrained when she entered the hospital services, and she would have been scandalized had her activities been given a romantic motivation. Indeed the hospital activities of women, especially the young, were so circumscribed that many believed they were not allowed to do their full duty. In spite of these obstacles, however, the women of the South did much for the disabled soldiers that was useful and satisfying; and if their services were not lit by the glow of romance, they were illuminated by a more substantial light, a deep urge of Christian compassion.

HOSPITAL RELIEF SOCIETIES

Stories of sick and wounded men constituted one of the first impressions which the South received concerning the actualities of the war.

Many were wounded in the first battles, and in addition there was the larger number ill with measles, typhoid fever, and the other diseases which usually develop among soldiers experiencing the contacts of camp life for the first time. The Confederate government, burdened with a multitude of other labors, was unequal to the necessity of caring for this large mass of casualties, and it soon became evident that thousands were suffering for want of medical attention and nursing.[1] "Many of the soldiers," said an observer of this neglect at Fredericksburg, "are laid on the floor and are not touched, or their cases looked into for twenty-four hours. One or two died when there was no one near them."[2]

When this situation was brought to the attention of the women, they assumed with alacrity a large portion of the burden of remedying such conditions. Hospital relief societies sprang into existence in all the states of the lower South, and appeals made to them for supplies met with hearty responses. "The express," said an account of the manner in which these appeals were answered, "quickly brought us lots upon lots of valuable boxes, containing sheets, pillow cases, towels, wines, brandies, gelatine, knives, forks, plates and spoons—every comfort for the sick room."[3] In addition to furnishing supplies, these societies frequently sent members of their organizations to Virginia to do hospital work. The effectiveness of the work of such agents is well illustrated by an account of the ministrations of Catherine Gibbon of North Carolina to the soldiers from that state who were ill at Yorktown. Finding the men miserable because of neglect, she improvised comfortable quarters for them and established much-needed rules of order and discipline. Even more gratifying than such practical services was the cheerful manner in which she sought to revive the nostalgic spirits of these unfortunate sufferers. "Ah! how happy some of these poor fellows were to offer their fevered hands and greet the familiar face from their distant home," wrote Catherine Cooper Hopley, an Englishwoman, who was a witness of these touching scenes.[4]

Nor did the women of Virginia neglect to join their feminine compatriots from the more southernly states in ministering to the disabled. Partially throwing aside scruples against acts considered indelicate to women, they rushed into hospitals to assist the physicians and male nurses. Women who had previously fainted at witnessing a bleeding wound, according to an acute observer of Richmond life, grew strong under the painful tuition of the scenes in newly established military hospitals and became able to work upon and dress even the most ghastly wounds.[5] After the Battle of First Manassas an English visitor noticed the women of the Confederate capital bringing delicacies to the hospitals and standing by the bedsides of the wounded to fan away the flies,[6] while at the same time Judith W. McGuire was pleased to note the manner in which the women of Winchester cared for the men who had been removed from the camp at Harpers Ferry. "It rejoices my heart," wrote this Virginia patriot, "to see how much everybody is willing to do for the poor fellows. . . . Nice food for the sick is constantly being prepared by old and young. Those who are very sick are taken to private houses and the best chambers in town are occupied by them. The poorest privates and officers of the highest rank meet with the same treatment."[7]

The generosity of these Virginia women is especially well illustrated by the conduct of the feminine inhabitants of Charlottesville toward the hospitals located in that town. The Confederate government provided these hospitals with such staples as flour, meat, lard, sugar, and fuel, but for milk, butter, fruit, vegetables, and other fresh foods and delicacies the institutions had to depend upon the munificence of the women of the community. One of these, Mrs. William Hart, made a daily contribution of ten gallons of milk for a period of three years, in addition to liberal quantities of eggs, poultry, fruits, and vegetables. In order to assure the proper preparation of the supplies they had furnished, the women divided themselves into committees and took turns in working in the hospital kitchens. There they were so successful in making teas, soups, and other concoctions suitable for invalids that some believed the disabled men enjoyed greater comforts under the care of the Charlottesville women than they would have experienced in their own impoverished homes.[8]

As in the case of other aspects of soldiers' relief already mentioned,[9] the hospital relief societies continued their services for the entire duration of the war. One of the greatest concerns of the women throughout the South was to see that the hospitals, both large and small, had the necessities as well as the comforts which would aid in the alleviation of suffering. Under the more fortunate circumstances this meant the supplementing of staples provided by the government with luxuries and delicacies from private kitchens; under unfavorable conditions, which frequently existed, it meant the supplying of staples as well as luxuries. In their efforts to achieve these objectives, women scoured the countryside for supplies; they yielded the luxuries of their tables; they established hospital kitchens; and in the folds of their skirts, as will later be described,[10] they smuggled quantities of precious quinine and morphine from beyond the lines. The contemplation of these features of their activity impelled an English woman observer to remark, "Heaven only knows what the soldiers of the South would have done without the exertions of the women in their behalf."[11]

THE INAUGURATION AND MANAGEMENT OF HOSPITALS

The mounting of casualties led women in all sections of the Confederacy to found hospitals. Useful work along this line was accomplished by the Southern Mothers' Society of Memphis. The members of this organization, moved by the sad plight of the large number of wounded men in their midst, established the Southern Mothers' Hospital in rooms lent for the purpose by a public spirited citizen of the town. Beginning with thirty, the number of patients in this institution soon rose to several hundred. Everything was said to have been provided for the comfort of the men, including a warm breakfast each morning.[12] Equally successful was the Ladies' Hospital at Montgomery, which was established in buildings lent by a philanthropic woman to meet the needs of sick and wounded soldiers. The actual conduct of this institution was in the hands of a German and his wife hired for the purpose, but the women of Montgomery, in their daily visits, were of much service to the patients. When the rooms which had been used at first became inadequate for the increasing number of men who sought admission, toward the end of 1861, these women secured larger quarters and called their new venture the Soldiers' Home of Montgomery. As many as five hundred men at one time were cared for in the larger undertaking, and so widespread was the recognition of its services that people from all over Alabama made substantial contributions to its upkeep.[13]

Although these and similar ventures were both valuable and meritorious, it soon became evident that the resources of the women were inadequate for such a gigantic endeavor as the treatment of all the disabled of the Confederate armies. Except for a few Roman Catholic sisters, there were no trained nurses among the Southern women, and moreover the hospitals needed the discipline of skilled experts with the authority of the state behind them. During the last months of 1861 and the first months of the following year, therefore, the Confederate Government assumed the control and partial support of all soldiers' hospitals in the South. This change from voluntary to official management, however, did not result in eliminating the women from the hospital scene. They continued to supply these institutions with food and clothing, as has already been indicated; the Catholic sisters continued their work as nurses; an important and able group of lay women

found work as matrons; and a few women of exceptional ability remained as managers of hospitals. In fact, the services of the women to
the disabled soldiers continued, until the end of the war, to be so varied
and sacrificial that the luster attached to these efforts was in no sense
dimmed by the fact that the managerial phases of hospital work
largely passed into masculine hands.

Among the few women of exceptional ability who remained as
managers or superintendents of hospitals was Sally L. Tompkins. After
the Battle of First Manassas she had devoted her means and talents to
the establishment and management of a hospital in an old Richmond
mansion, and her services were considered so valuable and efficient that
she was not removed from this position when the government assumed
control of the hospital service. To remove the irregularity of having
a person without official title in her position, President Davis com-
missioned her a captain of cavalry, unassigned. She thereby enjoyed the
distinction of being the only woman who was ever regularly commis-
sioned by the Confederate government. She remained in her position
until the end of the war, treating a grand total of thirteen hundred
soldiers.[14]

Another hospital executive noted for her devotion and efficiency was
Ella King Newsom, a wealthy Arkansas widow who, at the outbreak
of the war, abandoned the task of directing the education of her
younger sisters to undertake the relief of disabled soldiers. Unlike
other Southern women who followed this course, however, she appreciated the need of specific training and secured instruction in the Memphis City Hospital under the direction of a physician and the Sisters
of Mercy. In December, 1861, she began her career among the sick
soldiers at Bowling Green, Kentucky, where she found the men suffering from cold, lack of supplies, and administrative inefficiency. Working with tireless energy every day from four in the morning until midnight, she established an orderly routine and was rewarded by being
made superintendent of the Bowling Green hospitals. Upon the retreat
of the Confederates from Kentucky, she established herself in Nashville, where she organized a hospital in the buildings of the Howard
High School. After the fall of Nashville she dexterously supervised the
removal of her patients to Winchester in the same state, organizing in
the latter town a hospital of such excellence that it acquired the name
of "The Soldiers' Paradise." Her talents for organization were effectively displayed later at Chattanooga, Atlanta, Corinth, Mississippi, and
Abingdon, Virginia, and she won among her friends the title of "the
Florence Nightingale of the Southern Army."[15]

HOSPITAL MATRONS

More numerous than the women who remained as superintendents were those who entered the hospital service in the capacity of professional matrons. To give these latter positions official status, the Confederate Congress, by Act of September 27, 1862, defined the functions of chief matron, assistant matron, and ward matron and fixed their salaries at forty dollars, thirty-five dollars, and thirty dollars a month, respectively. The matron was charged with the duties of seeing that the orders of the surgeons were executed, supervising the sanitary and commissary arrangements of the hospital, and satisfying the needs of individual patients.[16] The actual implication of this last mentioned duty was described in detail by an experienced matron, Mrs. S. E. D. Smith. "The matron," she wrote, "will call on the steward for whatever diet the patient's appetite calls for, see that it is prepared to suit his taste, feed him herself if he is too feeble to do so; bathe his fevered brow; comb his hair." Other duties enumerated by this same writer included the dressing of wounds considered too delicate for the hands of male nurses; the placing of pads and pillows so as to relieve the wounds of the patients from the pressure of the mattress; the making of slings and the padding of crutches; the visiting of the wards at every spare moment to join in the conversations of the men, to read and sing to them, write letters for them, and to encourage their religious inclinations; and the filling of haversacks when the soldiers returned to the army, or the saying of prayers when death was imminent.[17]

A noble group of women performed with signal success the duties thus delegated to hospital matrons. Outstanding among these was Kate Cumming whose detailed and authoritative *Journal of Hospital Life* has already been referred to. A woman of Scotch birth, living in Mobile at the outbreak of the war, she possessed a combination of practical skill and intense devotion to the Confederate cause without being fettered by the contemporary Southern feeling that nursing was a profession indelicate to women. She entered the hospital service of the Army of Tennessee after the Battle of Shiloh and served with distinguished ability in this capacity until the end of the war. Another heroic matron was Louisa Susanna McCord, a daughter of Langdon Cheves and the widow of David J. McCord, a distinguished lawyer of South Carolina. The mistress of Lang Syne Plantation, a writer on political and economic subjects, and a poet of some ability, she was, at the outbreak of the war, regarded as the foremost woman of Columbia in executive efficiency. After serving as president of the Soldiers' Relief Association and the Ladies' Clothing Association, she resigned these duties in 1862 in order to give her whole time to the military hospital established in the buildings of the South Carolina College. In the midst of this activity there came the news that her son had been killed at Second Manassas, but her work continued "patient and cheerful and tender in its ministrations in the hospital; it was also capably executive. She managed the scheduling of the assistant nurses, planned the provisioning of the larder, that was often meager and largely dependent on gratuitous contributions. She regulated the convalescents, she wrote letters for them, talked with them, soothed the restless, gave Christian comfort to the dying."[18]

Still other matrons noted for their devotion and efficiency included Sallie Chapman Gordon Law, Mary Joyner, Annie E. Johns, Kate Mason Rowland, Fannie A. Beers, Juliet Opie Hopkins, Emily V. Mason, Margaret Walker Weber, and Phoebe Yates Pember.[19] What Mary Boykin Chesnut wrote of Louisa Susanna McCord might have been written, with individual modifications, for each of these women. "She is dedicating her grief to her son," wrote the South Carolina diarist, "sanctifying it, one might say, by giving up her soul and body, her days and nights, to the wounded soldiers in her hospital. Every moment of her time is surrendered to their needs."[20]

In the discharge of their numerous duties, these matrons had to overcome many obstacles. For one thing, they had to contend with the vagaries of the volunteer nurses and woman visitors. An experienced matron went so far as to say that the visiting and nursing of these women did more harm than good. She affirmed that none of them appreciated the need of training in nursing practices; that they visited the hospitals at hours inconvenient to the patients and the hospital authorities; and that, with pugnacious insistence, they gave the patients food that often had disastrous effects.[21] Another authoritative observer asserted that the visiting ladies were so imprudent in their ideas regarding the proper care and remedies "that the poor doctors were forever beset with applications to take unadvisable measures for their patients."[22] The following anecdote which went the rounds of the Confederacy illustrates the misdirection which it was possible for feminine zeal to assume in behalf of the welfare of the patients. " 'How do you do? Is there anything you want?' " said a lady visitor at the bedside of a sick soldier. " 'No, I believe not,' " curtly replied the man. " 'Is there nothing I can do?' " insisted the visitor. The impatient victim repeated, " 'I believe not.' " " 'Oh,' " cried his persecutor, " 'I do want to do something for you! Can't I wash your hands and face?' "

ROSE O'NEAL GREENHOW WITH HER DAUGHTER
Taken in Old Capitol Prison, Washington. (From *Photographic History of the Civil War*. Copyright by Review of Reviews Company and reproduced by permission)

With resignation the soldier said, " 'Well, if you want to right bad, I reckon you can; but if you do, you will be the fourteenth lady who has done so this morning.' "[23]

Another obstacle was the inefficiency of the assistants who were assigned to the matrons. The male nurses under their direction were usually convalescing soldiers, selected more often because they were not strong enough for field duty than because of aptitude or experience in the care of the sick. And moreover, as soon as they grew well enough to be of real help to the matrons, they were usually whisked off to the army. Women substitutes for the male assistants often proved to be equally unsatisfactory. Some turned out to be drunkards or flirts; others, whose real motive for entering the hospital service was merely to be near their husbands, proved to be incompetent and unwilling to perform the duties assigned them. At Richmond, Phoebe Yates Pember had to contend with a hard featured North Carolinian, who had to be dismissed because she refused to circulate among the men in wards, and with an Englishwoman who arrived at the hospital with seven trunks, complained that the quarters assigned her were inferior to those of Miss Pember, boxed off a part of a ward for her own private use, and got so drunk that she had to be removed from the hospital by physical force.[24]

A more serious handicap was the widespread public prejudice against women serving in hospitals. It was generally held in the South that an occupation involving such intimate contacts with strange men was unfit for self-respecting women to pursue. There was no tolerance whatever of young, unmarried women in these positions. Older women drove them away from the hospital doors, saying that the duties were "irksome and strongly discordant; and relatives prevailed upon ladies to give up their intentions of entering hospitals."[25] "The simple truth is," wrote a distinguished Southern novelist, in withdrawing her application for a matron's position, "that my family is much opposed to my doing so, *especially my brothers. . . .* The boys have heard so much about ladies being in the hospitals that they cannot bear for me to go."[26] A concession was grudgingly made in favor of women of maturity, but even they were hounded by criticism. "There is scarcely a day passes," wrote Kate Cumming, "that I do not hear some derogatory remarks about the ladies who are in the hospitals, until I think, if there is any credit due them at all, it is for the moral courage they have in braving public opinion."[27]

Strange as it may seem to modern ears, the majority of the surgeons shared the contemporary prejudice against the service of women in the hospitals. Most women ascribed this attitude to professional jealousy. Surgeons were accused of being snobbish toward matrons, refusing to sit in the same room with them, "envious of or impatient toward them," and disinclined to respect the act of Congress involving "the advent of female supervision" and other aspects of "petticoat government."[28] On the other hand, the surgeons themselves, as well as a great many of the more efficient matrons, justified their position on the ground that the majority of the women who wished to become matrons were woefully lacking in the elements of hospital administration and in the proper professional attitude. Kate Cumming, whose observations may be taken as authoritative in this respect, wrote, "I know many women will say that the surgeons will not have them, nor do I blame the surgeons if the stories are true which I have heard about the ladies."[29] Nevertheless, the fact remains that the surgeons were not exempt from the popular belief that attending the needs of wounded men was a function too indelicate for women of character to perform. "His principal objection," added Kate Cumming regarding a representative surgeon, "was that the accommodations were not fit for ladies."[30]

Regardless of whose fault it was, the Southern prejudice against women in the hospitals had evil effects. It reduced the number of women who were willing to ignore or flaunt public opinion to a level far below the actual needs of the hospital service, and it tended to drive the better class of women away from the hospitals and to throw the positions open to women of indifferent character and training. Matrons complained bitterly but vainly against the women who neglected their Christian duty because of this prejudice. "I have no patience," wrote the noncomforming Kate Cumming, "with women whom I hear telling what wonders they would do if they were only men, when I see much of their legitimate work left undone." Why, she asked, did not the women come forward to make bandages for the wounded as these men came in from the battlefields? Why were so many men allowed to die without a word of Christian cheer from women who knew not what to do with their time?[31] In the meantime, wealthy and cultivated women, who were wasting their time, suffered compunctions of conscience because they were not doing the type of work which women like Kate Cumming said they should do. "O that I could do something for them," wrote Catherine Ann Edmonston, "instead of sitting down at ease and comfort at home and giving the soldiers wishes that cost me nothing."[32] But the pressure of public opinion was too much for her, and, devoted as she was to the cause of the Confederacy, Mrs. Edmonston joined the others of her class in refusing to translate her patriotic sentiments into unconventional activity. Phoebe Yates Pember said in 1862 that "very few ladies and a great many inefficient and uneducated women hardly above the laboring class" constituted the feminine portion of the hospital forces. She later found women of education and refinement filling these positions in Virginia, but such was not the case in other states, where the men continued to suffer from lack of intelligent attentions until the end of the war.[33]

Still other obstacles in the way of efficient service on the part of the matrons included the inadequate and uncomfortable quarters to which they were frequently assigned. These quarters were often of such a character as to lead their occupants to suspect the truth of the prediction that their finer sensibilities would be blunted by hospital service. Sometimes their dormitories were furnished only with boxes and shelves and their living quarters were separated from those of the men merely by obstructions composed of the women's baggage.[34] At other times they lived in rude structures in the midst of arid wastes, encircled by trenches which stank with the refuse of camps.[35] Even more discouraging than their unpleasant quarters were the perplexities which the matrons experienced, especially toward the end of the war, in attempting to secure adequate supplies for their charges. Often there was not even enough dry corn bread to satisfy the hunger of the patients, and the only delicacies at their command were dried apples for the convalescent and herbs and arrowroot for the desperately ill.[36]

And yet, as already indicated, a number of women overcame these numerous obstacles successfully enough to achieve enduring reputations. One of the factors which contributed to this success was their ability to marshal an invincible logic against the views of those who claimed that hospitals were not decent places for women. "Christians," said one, "should not mind what the world says so they are conscientiously striving to do their duty to their God." When certain so-called "Christian, high-toned, and educated women" criticized Kate Cumming's activities, she replied that it seemed strange for women in America to consider it a disgrace to do what Florence Nightingale and other aristocratic women of Great Britain had done with honor.[37] In answer to the argument that women in hospitals were not treated with respect, the matrons asserted that the bearing of the patients toward them was usually faultless. But their most satisfying argument was that the needy and suffering champions of the cause of the Confederacy had the right to demand all the services which the women were capable of giving. "Are we willing," said Kate Cumming, "to nurse these brave heroes who are sacrificing so much for us? What in the name of common sense are we to do? Sit calmly down, knowing that there is many a parched lip which would bless us for a drop of water, and many a wound to be bound up?"[38]

Another reason for their success was the confident spirit in which these matrons faced the obstacles which confronted them. Although their physical surroundings might be imperfect, they did not sink to pessimism. One matron told Kate Cumming, as a joke, that the rain poured into her room in torrents, and optimistically added that unless there were drawbacks there was no credit to be derived from staying in hospitals. When the matrons of a Chattanooga hospital were confronted with the disconcerting intelligence that their cooking stove smoked and that there was not a change of clothing for their patients, they were not baffled. Instead they secured a good stove by appealing to friends in Mobile, and they made the required garments by sitting up all night and sewing.[39] The complaints of the patients against unsavory or insufficient food were met by the matrons in similar fashion. One secured quiet in her hospital by telling the men that they should be satisfied with dried peas, since that was all the food they possessed. " 'It is food for fighters,' " she said as she put a portion of the unpleasant dish in her mouth.[40] Others stretched the scant supplies at their command in such a way as to forestall dissatisfaction. "There was really a great deal of heroism displayed," said Phoebe Yates Pember, as she recalled "the calm courage with which I learned to count the number of mouths to be fed, and then contemplating the food, calculated not how much but how little each man could be satisfied with."[41]

If the testimony of the matrons is authentic, one of their most significant services was performed in correcting the neglect and stupidity of their masculine co-workers. These women protested vigorously against the "total disregard of human life" which was manifested by the male attendants in allowing wounded men to remain unattended on railroad platforms and in preparing for these unfortunates food which they could not eat. At times, against the orders of their masculine superiors, they even received into their hospitals freshly-wounded men for whom there was supposed to be no room, and when the patients from certain regiments were discriminated against by the hospital authorities, the women fitted out special quarters for these men and entertained them at their own tables.[42] One matron in a Richmond hospital was called "The Great Eastern" by the hospital officials and "Miss Sally" by the patients. She was pleased with this contrast in nicknames, however, since the one was caused by her reporting of official neglect, the other by her ministering unselfishly to the patients.[43]

Signal service was also rendered by the hospital matrons in their treatment of sick and wounded prisoners. The regulations of the Confederate government provided that these men should be given the same care as the wounded Southerners received, and the matrons as a rule experienced little difficulty in carrying out these orders. "The Federal prisoners are receiving the same attention as our own men; they are lying side by side," reported Kate Cumming at Corinth, Mississippi, after the Battle of Shiloh.[44] The dressing of wounds, the bathing of hands and feet, the feeding of the desperately ill, and the saying of prayers and other comforting words for them were some of the numerous favors which the matrons bestowed upon these unfortunates. In fact an English visitor was so impressed with the care given to the wounded enemy in the hospitals of the Confederacy that he spoke of it as "the exuberance of Christian charity" and "the exercise of a lofty magnanimity."[45] Outstanding among those who distinguished themselves for their charity toward the wounded prisoners was Annie E. Johns, a matron in a Danville, Virginia, hospital. She refused to follow the example of the other matrons in resigning when the removal of the Confederates to Richmond left only Federals in the Danville hospitals, and the quality of the service which she rendered is indicated by the gratitude which it won. "Strange as it may seem," she wrote with regard to the attitude of the prisoners toward her, "I felt, in standing among these men, if danger assailed me, they would defend me as soon as our own soldiers."[46]

Some matrons, it is true, manifested a tendency to interlard their attentions to the captives with reproaches for the alleged crimes of the Federal armies, and many were unable to offer them the same warm sympathy which they gave to the Confederate patients, but, as in the case of the attitude of the Southern women toward Federal prisoners generally, the majority of the matrons responded generously with their services in cases of individual suffering. Ella King Newsom, for example, nursed a Federal who had fallen into her hands after the Battle of Shiloh so faithfully that he begged to be carried with her when she left with the retreating Confederates.[47] Similar tenderness was manifested by a Mississippi woman in her attentions to a dying Ohio soldier. "I entered the ward," she said in describing this pathetic scene; "his eyes sought mine, with a wistful look; and brightened as I came near his bed. I smoothed the hair from his forehead, moistened his lips, and then, taking the fly brush, resolved to stay near him until the last. Oh, dear Jesus! those wistful eyes that followed every motion of mine!—those wistful dying eyes."[48]

The greatest compensation that came to the matrons for their labors and tribulations was the love and gratitude of the men whom they served. They were pleased when their appearance in the wards was a signal for the patients to look up in the hope of attracting their attention, and when men, whom they had overlooked on their tours of inspection, recalled them to the wards.[49] Sometimes they even changed the plans which they had made to quit the hospital service, in the long and discouraging hours of the night, into resolutions to remain until the end of the war, after they had observed the smiles with which the unfortunate sufferers greeted their return to the bedsides the next morning.[50] Another source of comfort to the matrons was the large number of grateful letters which they received from former patients and their relatives. "The many acts and kindnesses you have shown me," read a typical letter of this sort, "are indelibly stamped upon my heart, and words cannot express the gratitude I feel toward you."[51]

NUNS OF THE BATTLEFIELD

Doubtless the most skillful and devoted of all the women who nursed disabled Confederates were the members of the various Roman Catholic sisterhoods. They constituted the only class of women in the South possessed of formal training in nursing and hospital management, and they worked among the sick and wounded in camp, in hospital, and on the battlefield with the calculated self-abnegation and efficiency that was traditional among such orders of holy women. Largely Northern or else foreign in origin, wearing habits strange to Protestant soldiers, and observing no distinctions of race or nationality in their ministrations, they were naturally received with suspicion at first, but when they proved by silent deed that their aim was to relieve suffering humanity, they won the confidence and admiration of both the soldiers and the people of the South generally.

That the bravery of the sisters was no less unswerving than their devotion was demonstrated by incidents that occurred on many battlefields. " 'My God! Look at those women. What are they doing down there? They'll be killed,' " cried a soldier as he observed the conduct of the Sisters of St. Ursula during the Battle of Galveston. " 'Oh,' " replied another soldier, " 'those are the Sisters. They are looking for the wounded. They are not afraid of anything.' " Significant services were also performed by the Sisters of Charity of the convent at Emmitsburg, Maryland. The members of this order began their work in June, 1861, at Harpers Ferry, where, in spite of the suspicion of local women, they nursed many ill soldiers back to health. Later they served in hospitals at Richmond, Lynchburg, Gordonsville, and Danville, bringing order out of chaos in institutions suffering from the mismanagement of incompetent and inexperienced officials. The hooded forms of these Emmitsburg sisters were seen on numerous battlefields. At Gettysburg, for instance, they were observed picking up the disabled and stanching their wounds with bandages torn from their own garments.

Other sisters served with similar distinction. The Sisters of St. Dominic took charge of the Memphis City Hospital, where according to a local newspaper, "the soldiers received the best attention and the kindest and most efficient nursing." In Kentucky the Sisters of Charity of Nazareth won the admiration of both armies by their services on the battlefields and in the chain of hospitals they established. The Sisters of Mercy of Vicksburg refused the opportunity to return to their mother house in Baltimore and remained in the besieged city, where they converted their school into a hospital for the accommodation of the wounded. Some of these sisters followed the Confederates in their retreat across Mississippi, doing noble work in the hospitals at Oxford, Mississippi Springs, and Jackson. With thirty years of experience in the care of the sick behind them, the Sisters of Our Lady of Mercy in Charleston performed signal service in the hospitals of that city. "Since the beginning of the siege of our city," said a newspaper of that place, "their presence has diffused its blessings in every hospital and their unmarred attentions to the soldiers have done incalculable good." In fact it may be said that the only drawback to the services of the sisters in the South was their scarcity, less than two hundred being in service.[52]

WAYSIDE AND TRANSIENT SERVICES

More extensive if less efficient than the services of the hospital matrons and the nuns were those of the women who organized and maintained the wayside homes. These institutions were small hospitals or rest rooms which sprang into existence at almost every railroad junction in the Confederacy to care for the numerous sick and wounded men who were dumped off or left stranded by the inefficient railroad service. The first wayside home was established at Columbia, South Carolina, in March, 1862, when a clergyman called the attention of the Young Ladies' Hospital Association of that city to the fact that there were many ill and needy men stranded at the local railway station. These young women immediately equipped a room at the station which they called "The Soldiers' Rest." When this room became inadequate to accommodate the number of soldiers who desired to make use of its facilities, the women of Columbia secured larger quarters, capable of housing one hundred men and feeding three hundred. At the same time the services of older women and men ward masters and nurses were impressed in order to relieve the supposedly more sensitive young women of "the grim work to be done" and "the ghastly sights to be seen."[53] The extent of the activities of these women is illustrated by Mrs. Thomas Taylor's account of their work during an emergency created by the arrival of a large number of men from a recently fought battle. This writer recalled "seeing Mrs. Bryce with a huge coffee pot in her hand, standing in the Wayside kitchen; Mrs. Fisher, with a large spoon, stirring something on the stove; the invaluable Dinah Collins, making up something and turning a portly figure and kindly face to one and any who spoke to her, and at the same time giving directions which kettle to get warm water from."[54]

The wayside homes established at other places had histories similar to the one at Columbia. The one at Macon, Georgia, was described by a hospital matron as "one of the most useful institutions we have;"[55] the one at High Point, North Carolina, from its foundation in September, 1863, until the end of the war, supplied the needs of no less than 5,795 men;[56] and the one at Millen, Georgia, not only fed the passing soldiers bountifully but forced them to forget the terrors of war for a time by providing bevies of fair maidens for their entertainment.[57] Such stories were related of wayside homes in every section of the Confederacy.

The wayside homes furnished relief to the disabled soldiers who were on board the trains as well as to those who were stranded at the stations. Whenever a train stopped at a town, it was customary for a committee of women to board it in order to bind up wounds and supply the passing soldiers with food and medicines. "A committee of ladies met every afternoon train" at Anderson, South Carolina. "With pitchers of buttermilk and bottles of whisky they would go through the cars, and if sick soldiers were on board they ministered to their wants."[58] It was not unusual, when trains loaded with the wounded passed through a town after a battle, for the entire feminine population to turn out. "Every lady, every child, every servant in the village," wrote Judith W. McGuire of such an occasion at Ashland, Virginia, "has been engaged in preparing and carrying food to the wounded as the cars stopped at the depot—coffee, tea, soup, milk, and everything we could obtain. . . . The cars passed on, and we filled our pitchers, bowls and baskets, to be ready for others."[59] Some women

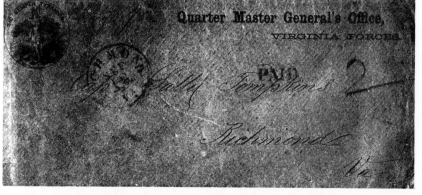

Confederate States of America,
WAR DEPARTMENT.

Richmond Sep 9th 1861.

Sir:

You are hereby informed that the President has appointed you

Captain

IN THE ARMY OF THE CONFEDERATE STATES. You are requested to signify your acceptance or non-acceptance of said appointment: and should you accept you will sign before a magistrate, the oath of office herewith, and forward the same with your letter of acceptance to this Department.

L. P. Walker
Secretary of War.

Capn Sally Tompkins
Richmond
Va

I accepted the above commission as Captain in the C.S.A. when it was issued. But I would not allow my name to be placed upon the pay roll of the army.

Sally L. Tompkins

Quarter Master General's Office,
VIRGINIA FORCES.

PAID

Sally Tompkins

Richmond

Va

COMMISSION ISSUED TO SALLY L. TOMPKINS
(Courtesy of the Confederate Museum, Richmond)

devoted their entire time to this type of work. Sarah K. Rowe of Orangeburg, South Carolina, for example, met the train each day and rode with it to the near-by village of Kingville. Loaded with boxes of medicine, bandages, and food, she went up and down the cars, giving food and words of comfort to the well, delicacies and medicine to the sick, and cordials and fresh bandages to the wounded.[60]

EMERGENCY AND CONVALESCENT RELIEF

When the regular hospital facilities of a town were crowded by the arrival of large bodies of wounded men after a great battle, the women frequently came forward to assist in the emergency. After the Seven Days fighting around Richmond, for example, all the married women in the city were said to have formed themselves into bands for the purpose of aiding the hard-pressed surgeons and nurses. Their services included the establishing of hospitals in their homes, bathing bleeding wounds, washing the stiffened mud and gore from the hair and beards of the soldiers, and the administering of restoratives to the dying.[61] Another example of this type of conduct was that of the women of Greensboro, North Carolina, after the Battle of Bentonville. "All else was forgotten," says an account of these Greensboro women, "as with tender hearts and eager hands they sought to make the poor fellows comfortable in their hastily improvised beds and comfortless quarters. . . . The town was divided into districts and the women of each neighborhood fed from their tables the body of soldiers nearest them. Daily their waiters threaded the town, and daily their interest in the boys grew."[62]

In performing such acts of mercy the women occasionally created scenes sufficiently dramatic to be memorialized in the literature of the period. "There was scarcely a murmur in the crowded car," began a South Carolina writer in describing a touching incident that occurred on a railroad train in that state. A young girl sat patiently beside a soldier prostrated by injuries and the heat, bathing his wounds and fanning his face. Sympathetic observers handed her money, but instead of keeping it she put it in the invalid's pocket.[63] A similar scene was described by T. C. DeLeon as occurring in Richmond. One day in 1863 this writer saw an old man, ragged and dirty, being conveyed through the streets of the city in a springless cart, his bare feet protruding and his open wounds dripping blood. At his side walked one of the city's most beautiful young women, wiping the damp sweat from the old man's forehead and attempting to smooth his rough journey with comforting words. There was no romance in this scene, said DeLeon. The wounded man "could not be conjured into a fair, young knight—old, dirty, and vulgar as he was. But he had fought for her—for the fair city she loved better than life—and the gayest rider in all that band was not more a hero to her."[64]

Women of all sections of the South generously received the disabled soldiers into their homes. So widespread was this practice, asserted George Cary Eggleston, that at one time almost every home within a hundred miles of Richmond held one or more wounded men as especially honored guests.[65] At times, overcrowded hospitals were relieved of their excess of recent casualties in this manner, but the more usual practice was not to remove the men to private homes until they had begun to show signs of convalescence. It was currently believed that the patients in private homes secured better treatment than those in the public hospitals, the superiority of domestic over institutional care being ascribed to the motherly attentions which the women bestowed upon their disabled guests.[66]

As a rule such women did not allow distinctions of breeding and class to stand in the way of their receiving disabled men into their homes. Indeed it may be said that the wearing of the gray was usually the only passport that was required for entrance even into the most aristocratic houses. When certain women in Mississippi were asked why they tolerated the presence of convalescents whose ill manners extended to the point of rudeness, they casually replied that their own soldier-sons might be committing similar indiscretions in the homes of other people.[67] In some cases the women were so eager to avoid the appearance of discrimination that they wrote to the hospital authorities requesting that only wounded privates be sent to them, feeling that the officers would get all the attention they needed anyway.[68] The substantial and unselfish character of the work of the women in this respect is well illustrated by the numerous glowing accounts written by convalescents regarding the treatment which they received in the cottages as well as in the mansions of the Confederacy. "I take my place three times a day at a beautifully appointed table," wrote a Texan from Virginia, "sleep in a feather bed between clean white sheets; hear the clatter and laughter of little children; and may, when I choose, listen to the low, sweet voices of refined and cultured women, or the music evoked by skillful fingers from a melodious piano."[69]

✓   ✓   ✓   ✓

When the war was over many of the women of the South were able to recall with a high degree of satisfaction a variety of services which they had rendered to thousands of disabled Confederates. It is true that there had been numerous mistakes of omission and commission, as a result of inexperience, inefficiency, and prudishness, but these mistakes were largely counteracted by the devoted manner in which many women discharged their duties toward the sick and wounded. Without the wayside homes, the work of the Catholic sisters, the activities of the matrons, the furnishing of hospital supplies, the receiving of convalescents into private homes, and the numerous other services of the women, it is difficult to believe that the fate of the incapacitated Confederate soldier would not have been far worse than it actually was.

CHAPTER VIII

THE REFUGEES

AS the waves of war rolled back and forth, rendering life precarious in the districts near the seats of hostilities, thousands of women and children fled to the more remote regions of the South in the hope of escaping from the ever-advancing enemy. The refugees, as these helpless families were called, were confronted with peculiar hardships in addition to those shared by the Southern women in general. They were forced to leave the familiar surroundings of their homes to live in a beleaguered territory, sometimes among strangers, who had few of the comforts of life to share with them. Consequently, they were able to secure at times only primitive shelter, frequently the crudest diet, and at intervals no food at all. It was seldom possible for them to remain with safety in the places to which they had fled, for the constant shrinkage of the defensive lines threatened them with the necessity of moving for a second or third time and gradually confined them to smaller and smaller areas. For the more fortunate refugees, travel was by uncomfortable and crowded trains; for the less fortunate, it was an Odyssey of flights on foot or in private conveyances, over the desolate and unoccupied spaces so characteristic of the Southern countryside, through forests and across rivers, where the arm of the law was now powerless to protect them. On reaching their remote and insecure destinations, they frequently found themselves in despair, helpless and unhappy among strange surroundings, unprotected by their own fighting men, and in many cases inadequately cared for by such agencies of relief as were at their disposal. Only their resolute courage, their powers of adaptability, the mild climate of the South, and the kindness of the people upon whose mercy they were thrown saved the precarious existence of these distressed classes from being attended by even more tragic consequences.

THE PERILS OF CONFEDERATE TRAVEL

It was inevitable that the women who undertook, either by choice or from necessity, the hardships of refugee life should have been frequently filled with emotions bordering upon despair when they contemplated the apparently hopeless future that lay before them. It seemed as though they were in the grip of some malevolent destiny which, without rhyme or reason, impelled them to become homeless and purposeless wanderers, knowing not one day what perils the next might bring. Some women, it is true, made initial efforts to cover their real feelings with smiles and jests, but in many cases this forced optimism gave way to loud lamentations as they thought of the comfortable homes they had left to the mercy of a relentless foe; while they roamed shelterless over the countryside, took up habitations in crowded city tenements, or experienced the loneliness of rough cottages remote from civilization. The belief that friends and relatives left behind were suffering worse fates than theirs added to the sorrowful emotions of the refugees, and when the greatly exaggerated reports of the brutality of the invaders seemed to confirm these fears, their drooping spirits sank lower.[1] And finally, when the early hopes that the Confederate offensives would make possible the speedy return to their homes were supplanted by the realization that the hold of the enemy was too firm to be shaken off, these women felt that their cup of sorrow had been filled to the brim. "I begin to feel," wrote a prominent Virginia refugee, "that we may all hang our harps on the willows; and though we do not sit by the waters of a strange land . . . our 'vine and fig tree' is wanting . . . and while shut out from it and its many objects of interest, there will be a feeling of desolation."[2]

The hardships attendant upon their departures from home and the journeys which they were consequently forced to undergo immediately demonstrated to the refugees that their apprehensions had not been imaginary. Sometimes sudden bombardments by the enemy caused hasty exits from towns. Under these circumstances women often ran hatless and half-dressed from their houses, leaving behind necessities in their frantic eagerness to carry articles of no immediate use. Children cried because they had lost their mothers, and mothers wandered about hysterically looking for lost children, amid shrieks over the terrors experienced and moans over the terrors contemplated. Such a flight, from Baton Rouge in May, 1862, was graphically described by an eyewitness. "These are not sheep but human beings, running pell-mell . . . panting, rushing tumultuously down the hot dusty road, hatless, bonnetless, some with slippers and no stockings, some with wrappers hastily thrown over nightgowns," wrote Eliza McHatton-Ripley of the women of the Louisiana capital who had just seen their homes riddled with bullets. Once in the open road, added this observer, these terrified creatures "ran as though the very demons pursued them, never turning back or branching off." They moved "through yards and over fences and down narrow dusty lanes—everywhere to get away from the clash of steel and the bursting of countless bombs."[3] When they had reached a safe distance, such women gathered in groups along roadsides, often without shelter, food, or known destination, their feelings of excitement giving way to those of desolation.[4]

When departures were more leisurely they were usually made by railroads. Travel by this means was naturally less difficult than on foot, but, under the conditions which prevailed among the railways of the Confederacy, it was sufficiently discomforting to be undertaken with eagerness only under impelling circumstances. The trains were so crowded that all the dexterity at the command of a woman was required to get aboard one. Conductors had to be cajoled in the most unfeminine fashion, and often the only accommodations that could be secured were in congested baggage or freight cars.[5] Within the cars the conditions were calculated to sicken even the stoutest feminine hearts. There were crowds of wounded men exhibiting their infirmities with the ghastly unconcern that was frequently characteristic of patients in Confederate hospitals. One refugee saw a soldier bathing his wounded arm in the water bucket and a woman passenger carrying the remains of her dead husband on the seat beside her.[6] Many men felt that the frequent movement of women on the crowded trains was unnecessary and consequently were rude to them. " 'Women had better stay at home; they have no business to be running about in such times,' " cried one man in refusing to give up his seat to a feminine passenger.[7] In addition to the occasional examples of masculine rudeness, there were frequent instances in which masculine crudeness was demonstrated. Male travelers were often boisterous and unwashed. One scattered fragments of his hair upon a woman passenger as he combed it, and another offered the same woman plums from a greasy hat.[8]

Every refugee who traveled by train suffered from the mechanical imperfections for which the Confederate railroads were notorious. In winter broken panes and the absence of stoves which burned made travel a test of endurance, while in the summer the stifling atmosphere of the cars prompted desperate struggles to get near the windows. Some passengers even preferred riding in freight cars.[9] To these discomforts were added the risks of jolting over uneven rails and rickety bridges and the chronic delays necessitated by frequent stops in order to patch up worn-out engines and running gears. "We crawled along, stopping almost every hour, to tinker up some part of the car or road, getting out at times when the conductor announced that the travelers must walk 'a spell or two,' " wrote Phoebe Yates Pember in describing her experience on one of these journeys.[10] In fact, such travel was so tiresome that the stopping of trains as a result of accidents was often welcomed by the passengers as a relief from bouncing on the rickety tracks of the Confederate railroads, even though the delay thus occasioned might necessitate spending the night in a wilderness.

In areas where railroads had never existed or where they had been destroyed, carriages, buggies, and wagons were used, when they could be secured, as a means of travel. These private conveyances were preferred by many of the refugees, since they were free from some of the more irritating inconveniences of the railroads, but journeying in them had its own special perils. It often meant moving, with few attendants, through desolate regions where the refugees were subject to possible harm from outlaws, Federal raiders, and other lawless elements who frequented the great unoccupied spaces of the Confederacy. Moreover, highways were bad, and horses and vehicles were scarce, dilapidated, and inordinately expensive. The roads were usually of mud, cut deep with ruts, and in areas which had been traversed by the armies they were often blocked with fallen trees and the carcasses of horses and mules. Streams and swamps could frequently be forded only with the travelers and their baggage perched high on the seats or tops of the vehicles to avoid the high waters. A typical Confederate vehicle was described by Eliza Frances Andrews. "It was," said the Georgia woman, "only a shabby little covered cart, with the bows so short that if we attempted to sit upright the cover rested on our heads and the sun baked our brains through it."[11] The teams were frequently so wretched that the male escorts of the refugees, when there were any, were compelled to walk beside the animals for the entire journey, while the women had to walk up the hills and over other difficult portions of the roads.

HIGH RENTS AND HUNGER

The chronic delays of travel made it necessary for the refugees to make use of hotels on those frequent occasions when they could not secure accommodations in private homes. The rural South had never been distinguished for the quality of its hotels and inns, and under the stress of war these institutions were reduced to the lowest grades imaginable. The refugees found them dirty, expensive, and overcrowded. The room assigned to three women at Mandeville, Louisiana, according to a representative observation, was furnished with one narrow bed, a decrepit table on which stood a broken mirror, a broken lounge, and a pine armoire filled with corn. In the center of this room stood its most prominent object, a pile of dirt. The mosquitoes were said to swarm "like pandemonium on a spree," and the supper consisted of one egg and a spoonful of rice for each guest. "A feast, you see," concluded one of the disgusted guests, "price, one dollar each, besides the dollar paid for the privilege of sleeping among dirt, dogs, and fleas."[12]

The accommodations secured by the refugees in private homes were likewise often of the most inadequate character. Judith W. McGuire did not think it a hardship to live crowded in a small cottage with several families totaling from sixteen to twenty persons, and she saw other establishments so congested with refugees that every couch and sofa was occupied and pallets had to be spread on the floor.[13] So prominent a woman as Mrs. Roger A. Pryor was compelled, after being unable to secure quarters in Petersburg in the fall of 1863, to settle in the vicinity of that city in a little house which she described as "hardly better than a hovel," with a kitchen that was windowless, blackened with smoke, and possessed of a floor through the cracks of which the naked earth could be seen.[14] The rents extracted from refugees for the use of these and similar quarters were extortionate. At Charlottesville, in 1863, the daughter of a Confederate Senator was charged three hundred dollars a month "for poor accommodations and wretched fare,"[15] and such high rents were demanded at other places that some women were compelled to reside in abandoned box cars.[16]

Because of the unusually crowded conditions prevailing there, the large number of women who went to Richmond experienced especially trying hardships in this respect. Often they walked the streets of the city for days vainly trying to secure rooms within the limits of their pocketbooks. "Spent this day in walking from one boarding-house to another and have returned fatigued and hopeless. I do not believe there is a vacant spot in the city," reads an entry in the diary of Judith W. McGuire which could have been duplicated in the records of hundreds of other strangers in the Confederate capital.[17] Those fortunate enough to effect rentals were frequently unable to pay the extortionate prices demanded by the Richmond landlords for separate houses and consequently had to resort to what was known as "room-keeping." This was a practice whereby five or six families rented a single house in which one or two rooms were assigned to each family. Usually there was a common parlor in which all the families in the house received their guests, and some houses had a common kitchen presided over by a single Negro cook who, by the exercise of an uncommon sagacity, seems to have been able to keep the food of her numerous employers separate. The less fortunate tenants of these houses were forced to do their cooking and washing in single rooms cluttered with fuel, trunks, and other baggage.[18] "Such living," gloomily remarked a Mississippi woman residing in Richmond, "was never known before on earth. The poorest hut in the Tennessee mountains was a palace in comparison."[19]

POULTRY FOR THE TIMES

A contemporary lampoon upon high prices at boarding houses. (From *The Southern Illustrated News*)

REFUGEES CAMPING IN THE WOODS NEAR VICKSBURG

(From *The Illustrated London News*)

More discomforting to the Richmond refugees than unsatisfactory housing conditions was the scarcity of food that prevailed among them. That so refined a woman as Judith W. McGuire should have frequently interspersed her otherwise lively diary with references to such a prosaic subject as the price of provisions, indicates that the normally simple problems of getting something to eat had become a major difficulty in the most aristocratic of Richmond refugee circles. "Potatoes are twelve dollars per bushel, pork and bacon two dollars and fifty cents per pound, good tea at twenty-five dollars per pound," reads one of her records during the third year of the war.[20] Toward the close of the next year, she affirmed that a reduction of the daily number of meals to two had become a necessity among the refugees in the Confederate capital, adding that she herself had not tasted milk more than twice in eighteen months.[21] Among some of these women meals consisted only of potatoes and a small quantity of meat and bread, and even this limited diet had to be apportioned with miserly care.[22] Among the typical sufferers was a fragile woman who, on applying to T. C. DeLeon for work, said that she had eaten nothing that day and that for weeks she and her three children had lived on three pints of rice.[23] The young Malvina Gist, although no suffering could dampen her ardent spirits, experienced a lively hunger. "I'm hungry," she confided in her Richmond diary on March 6, 1865. "I want some chicken salad, and some charlotte russe, and some ox palate, and corn muffins! These are the things I want, but I'll eat anything I can get. Honestly, our cuisine has become a burning question." Apparently her wishes did her no good, for two days later she went to bed in the fond hope that sleep would satisfy her craving for food.[24] Many refugees in Richmond were forced to sell cherished valuables as a means of obtaining supplies. Their jewelry, watches, plate, books, and other articles were displayed in the shops of the city, and it was not unusual to see Negro servants peddling them on the streets.[25]

Although the hardships of the Richmond refugees were, for reasons already pointed out, especially distressing, they were by no means unique. The fact that the refugees were cut off from their homes and from the incomes which they had previously enjoyed meant that food was generally scarce among them. Compelled to purchase their foodstuffs at war prices, they frequently lived "on the plainest corn bread and cowpeas for breakfast, dinner, and supper, with only water to drink."[26] Judith W. McGuire wrote of a refugee friend, residing in an inland place where nothing could be bought, who was forced to hire a skillet from a servant for one dollar a month as a means of preparing food with which to prevent starvation; also of another friend, whose health demanded that she have a hot beverage at night, resorting to plain water because she had neither tea, sugar, nor milk.[27] "A wretchedly dressed woman of miserable appearance," who had fled along with many others from Fredericksburg, told this same writer that she was forced to feed herself and her three small children on turnip tops. When asked if this diet was satisfying, she replied, " 'It is something to go on for a while, but they do not stick by us as bread does, and then we gets hungry again. . . . Sometimes the woman in the next room will bring the children her leavings, but she is monstrous poor.' "[28]

The hardships of the refugees were at times accentuated by the fact that they were not always kindly treated by the people among whom they sojourned. In Georgia, according to Kate Cumming, strangers were referred to as "mean old refugees" and great hostility was shown toward them.[29] "We cannot understand," said the *Wilmington Journal* in commenting upon a similar situation in North Carolina, "the feeling manifested by the people in some parts of the Confederacy which prompts them to acts of unkindness to refugees."[30] Certain hints given by contemporaries, however, throw some light upon the causes of this hostility. Kate Cumming was told at Marietta, Georgia, that the refugees, especially those from New Orleans, "behaved very badly," regarded the citizens as social inferiors, and did little else than to give balls and parties.[31] Martha B. Washington, a South Carolina refugee, noted that the poorer classes of farmers in that state looked upon the members of her group as aristocrats who were responsible for the war and its privations, and that they manifested this dislike by refusing to sell the refugees food except through barter.[32] In other words, a considerable number of ordinary people seem to have regarded the refugees as aristocratic snobs who had brought their own troubles upon themselves and who consequently deserved little sympathy or favor. On the other hand, certain contemporaries noted that exactly the opposite reasons for this hostility prevailed in some sections—that the refugees were rebuffed by the rich because they were poor. When, for example, Judith W. McGuire applied to a wealthy Richmond woman for the rental of a room, the latter, according to the applicant's account of the incident, looked "lofty and cold and meant to make me feel that she was far too rich to take roomers."[33] In all probability, however, the most important cause of this hostility was nothing more or less than the fact that many Southern people, naturally provincial and suspicious of strangers, were oppressed with their own privations and consequently were reluctant to share their meager resources with outsiders.

BRIGHTER PHASES OF REFUGEE LIFE

Life among the refugees, however, was not without its bright spots. With the exceptions already mentioned, it may be said that they were generally received warmly and generously by those among whom they settled. Many of them showed a great sagacity in adjusting themselves to trying difficult conditions, making the most of their scant opportunities for comfort and happiness, and great numbers of them were generously endowed with the remarkable ability of the Confederate woman to face hopefully situations which might have appeared altogether irremediable to persons of less courage. These favorable conditions were especially prevalent among the refugees who belonged to the aristocracy, a class having wide social and family connections upon which to rely throughout the South, and a class which seems to have been the most adequately equipped with the imagination necessary to withstand successfully the vicissitudes of unaccustomed circumstances.

The accounts of the refugees contain many references to acts of good will that were displayed toward them; so many, as a matter of fact, that the records of the opposite tendency seem to sink into insignificance in comparison. "From our neighbors we received unflagging acts of kindness," wrote one of the many women who recognized these services. "We had no horse, but we drove to church every Sunday. We kept no cows, but our children always had milk. We had no gardens, but our tables were supplied with vegetables. . . . We had only to say or pray 'Give us this day our daily bread,' and it came."[34] Refugees in cities were frequently touched by the generosity of their country friends who, in spite of the depredations of the enemy, sent presents of beef, dried fruits, turkeys, and other provisions to them.[35] Some communities provided systematic relief for the refugees, assigning them quarters and regular allotments of food.[36] Nor were all landlords as extortionate as those mentioned in the preceding pages; at times they delicately refrained from pressing upon importunate refugees the necessity of paying rent. "Mrs. Randolph, whose husband owes us for a few months' rent, offered to raise it for me," said an account of such behavior, "but times are so hard for people out of business, and who came here as strangers as they did, and who are cut off from friends who might aid them, that we told her that we would not take it from her, even should she get it for us."[37]

The refugees who needed aid most acutely were those in flight and on journeys, and from the records available they seem to have been well treated in many instances. Upon reaching Scotsborough, a town in the path of Sherman's sweep through Georgia, Eliza Frances Andrews and her sister went to the village inn. "When Mrs. Palmer, the landlady, learned who Metta and I were," wrote this young refugee, "she fairly hugged us off our feet and declared that Mrs. Troup Butler's sisters were welcome to her house and everything in it."[38] A similar reception was given to a party of government clerks, in flight from Richmond, by a country woman in Fairfield District, South Carolina. This hostess gave the travelers her only spare room and a dinner consisting of chicken stew, vegetables, bread, and blackberry preserves—truly a prodigious feast for a community supposedly swept clean by Sherman. The only compensation she would accept for her hospitality was the writing of the guests' names in her daughter's album.[39] Still another example of kindness to such travelers was the treatment accorded to the daughters of Judge A. P. Aldrich in their seven-day flight through that portion of South Carolina which had been ravaged by the Union army. Only once were they refused a share of the meager resources of the people they met. The first night they were given the freedom of a log cabin, the use of a large fire, and a share of the host's small supply of sweet potatoes and "straw tea." On the second night they were able to secure shelter only by the use of threats, but on the following day they stopped at a house where they were given milk and corn bread. The third night was passed under the roof of a host who compensated for his inability to offer food to his guests by accompanying them the next day on a part of their journey. The fourth night was spent with a family who gave the girls corn bread, fried pork, and sorghum. Fearing the wrath of hostile dogs, the party approached the house in which they desired to spend the fifth night with misgivings, but when they cried out that they had come from a long distance, a welcoming voice said, " 'Come right enn, for Lord knows you must be putty well dun up.' " The master of this house accommodated the girls as best he could, and refusing all compensation, gave them "a grand meal" of hominy, corn bread, sorghum, and beef stew. The last two nights were spent with friends who naturally did all they could for their guests.[40]

The facility with which some of the refugees managed to adjust themselves to the turbulent conditions under which they were often forced to live is little short of remarkable. Dilapidated country houses, equipped with only a few pieces of furniture, were given a homelike appearance by bright fires and the lively conversation of their occupants, and in cases where several families dwelt under one roof friction was forestalled by the careful division of domestic labors.[41] "I look back on my life in Louisburg as a bright spot in memory," afterward declared a woman who had experienced the rude comfort which had been thus evolved in an isolated North Carolina town.[42] Even those women who engaged in "room-keeping" in Richmond worked out systems of domestic harmony for their close quarters and were able to get some pleasure out of their dismal situations. Nor were those who lived in box cars to be denied the privilege of making themselves comfortable. Some of these residences, according to a South Carolina woman, were nicely and even handsomely furnished with articles brought from former homes. Sometimes a family would furnish one car as a sitting room with Brussels carpets, easy chairs, books, and a piano, while a second car would serve as a bedroom, and a third as a kitchen and servants' quarters.[43]

Some refugees were even able to turn the inconveniences of Confederate travel into pleasant diversions. "You should have seen us last night," wrote Mary Darby de Treville, a member of a party of fleeing government clerks who had established their camp in a church, "all sitting around one big camp fire, a great many soldiers with us, all singing 'The Bonnie Blue Flag,' 'Dixie,' 'My Maryland,' and many other songs."[44] Another party of travelers was enthusiastic over the novelties of outdoor life—coarse meals eaten from tin plates, songs in the woodlands, and the shelter formed by wagon tents.[45] At least one girl waxed romantic over the wonders of sleeping on the ground with the sky as a canopy. "Oh! night of night we camped out," exclaimed Malvina Gist. "Vividly do I recall the minutest detail connected with that night in the woods—the pink line that flushed the western sky, the slowly descending twilight, the soft curve of the hills. . . . I lay with face upturned and eyes opened to the tender benediction of the stars."[46]

Nor did the refugees, whatever may have been the discomforts which they encountered, always interpret their experiences as being filled with despair. Even from box car dwellings issued the sounds of the violin and piano, indicating that there were some whose spirits had not been broken by their difficult living conditions. Their recitals of hardships often ended with optimistic assertions that such privations were inevitable and that they should be cheerfully borne as a part of the cost of the ultimate success of the Confederacy. Likewise there was a tendency to assume toward hardships and inconveniences the attitude of "shut-your-mouth-and-go-it-blindly."[47] Many refugees also took prominent parts in the social diversions which will be described later.[48]

They danced, picnicked, received soldiers on furlough, and acted in plays with a spirit that gave little hint of the fact that theirs was a full share of the burdens of the world.[49]

It may be concluded that the women who were uprooted from their homes by the fortunes of war suffered peculiar hardships in addition to those which were the lot of the women of the Confederacy in general, and that these trials were such as to cause many of the refugees to sink into despair. On the other hand, there were many who experienced good treatment at the hands of the inhabitants of the regions to which they had fled and many others who possessed the ability to adjust themselves to the turbulent conditions of refugee life, being thereby fortified with a hopeful courage that prevented despair. In either case, however, the record of the adventures of those unfortunate classes constitutes one of the saddest chapters in the annals of the women of the Confederacy.

CHAPTER IX

THE PROBLEM OF SELF-SUPPORT

SCARCELY less trying than the hardships of the refugees were those of the women who, in the absence of their men folk in the army, were faced with the problem of supporting themselves and their families by performing duties which had previously been almost exclusively the function of the stronger sex. Thousands of women were forced to become managers of plantations, farms, and other undertakings; and many others, for whom such opportunities to work for themselves were not available, were compelled to seek profitable employment outside the home. The task of assuming these duties in normal times would have involved difficulties for a sex whose economic activities had been definitely limited and prescribed by custom and tradition; under the disordered conditions of war times the difficulties were more numerous and acute. In addition to those women who were fortunate enough to secure remunerative employment there were many others who, through lack of ability or opportunity, could get no positions and as a consequence were forced to live on the charity of neighbors or their state governments. It was obviously impossible for such agencies to provide adequately for all of those who made demands upon their resources, and as the war progressed physical distress increased. The result was discontent and serious disorder, but there was little or no actual starvation.

THE MANAGEMENT OF PLANTATIONS AND FARMS

The more fortunate among the women solved the problem of self-support by assuming the duties which the men had abandoned upon entering the army. In hundreds of cases they became the operators of plantations, and in a vastly greater number of instances they undertook the management of small farms. For the burden of plantation management they were not wholly unprepared, for Southern wives, even those of wealth and social position, had been accustomed to share with their husbands many of the duties of plantation life. They were familiar with the tasks of feeding and clothing their families and slaves, nursing the sick, seeding the flower beds, and numerous other household and yard activities. Such experiences served to prepare them for the more extensive activities in field and forest which the necessities of war imposed upon them. They were also well acquainted, in most instances, with the slaves, upon whom devolved the execution of the details of plantation labor; and throughout the war, as will appear later, they retained the loyalty of these laborers.[1] Moreover, the plantation mistresses, when successful in their endeavors, had the satisfaction of knowing that their families and slaves would have most of the necessities of life. The Southern plantations had long supplied much of their own food as well as many of the materials used in housing and clothing, and war conditions accentuated this self-sufficiency, thus making it easier to carry on planting operations without purchases from the outside.

Many women approached the problem of plantation management with energetic determination, and at times with sagacious optimism. "She gave her personal attention to the details of plantation work," said an account of the manner in which one representative woman of this class discharged her duties. "She was up at daylight, attended to the feeding of the horses and cattle, rode over the fields to see that the work was done there as it should be, looked after plantation supplies and sick negroes; in short displayed such energy that the whole neighborhood talked of her extraordinary management."[2] Mrs. Robert F. W. Allston, the wife of a wealthy planter of the South Carolina low country, seemed crushed when the exigencies of war forced upon her the management of several plantations and six hundred Negroes, but, according to her daughter's account, "it was perfectly wonderful to see how she rose to the requirements of the moment, and was perfectly equal to her new position."[3] Caroline Pettigrew, in the same state, expressed the wish that she might have the assistance of her male relatives in directing her multiform activities, but she rose with spirit to the necessities of the occasion. "I am a planter for the first time," she wrote to her brother in 1862. "I *insist* upon myself being very energetic, and make an appearance of knowing more than I really do."[4] Ida Dulany, a Virginia woman who was forced to assume the duties of plantation management, sweetened her heavy obligations by the exercise of native charm, wit, and industry. She had the assistance of efficient overseers and faithful slaves, but she traveled over her plantation each day on horseback, with her riding habit almost sweeping the ground, a feather in her hat, and gauntlets reaching to her elbows.[5]

The courage of women of this type bore fruit in the successful management of many plantations. With the assistance of the slaves, the kindly advice of the old men of their communities, and occasional letters of instructions from their husbands at the front, they supervised the planting, the cultivation, and the harvesting of the crops, and the countless other duties of agricultural life. As a result of such labors, they were able to supply the plantation communities with the necessities of a simple rural existence, to satisfy the oppressive demands of the

SEARCHING THE BAGGAGE
(From *Frank Leslie's Illustrated Newspaper*)

Confederate taxes in kind, and to send, as has already been shown,[6] numerous boxes of clothes and victuals to the men at the front. "I managed the farm with a great deal of worry," said a typical account of such activity. "We made not only an abundance of food for ourselves, negroes, and stock, but at the close of the war had $1,800.00 worth of cotton."[7]

The manner in which a Mississippi woman overcame the numerous difficulties which beset her efforts at plantation management is intimately revealed in a letter that she wrote to her husband in February, 1863. Her troubles included the fear of both Federal and Confederate intruders, the prevalence of excessive rains and floods, the delay of an agent in dispatching some Negroes that belonged to her, the stealing of her cattle and hogs by neighbors, the failure of a cobbler, to whom she had sent leather, to furnish the shoes he had promised to make, and the impressment of fifteen of her best slaves by the Confederate government. In spite of these obstacles, however, she pursued her duties with a firm optimism, reporting that she was producing homespun for clothing her slaves; that she had been able to sell enough corn to satisfy her needs for cash while reserving enough to feed her numerous hogs; and that she had perfected plans for building rail pens to protect the hogs against thieves. She had prepared hides from which the next winter's shoes for her Negroes were to be made, and she had begun the preparation of two hundred acres for the planting of cotton. Moreover, she asserted that her equanimity had not been disturbed by the Confederate government's taking some of her Negroes nor by the prospect of the Confederate soldiers' eating some of her supplies, for she considered that submitting to such sacrifices was a part of the duty of a patriot.[8]

The experiences of the ladies of the Elmore family in managing their varied and extensive planting interests in York and Lexington Districts, South Carolina, afford a further illustration of the successful operation of plantations by women. During the first years of the war they enjoyed the services of competent overseers, and they were not harassed by the presence of predatory troops, but these fortunate conditions did not relieve them of the necessity of carefully supervising their interests. When the call of the army later removed their overseers, they assumed full control of their plantations, the mother and her three daughters carefully dividing their labors. "My main energies during the four years," wrote one of the daughters, "were concentrated on the matter of supplies, and to secure these, the mill and plantation affairs required the most consideration and a large amount of foresight." She was able, however, to keep the spectre of want away from the doors of both the family and the slaves. She supervised the manufacture of clothes, syrup, salt, and other foods; she supplied the Confederate army with heavy timbers; and she gave large quantities of vegetables to the hospitals and the refugees and sold some in the Columbia market. Toward the end of the war the devastations of Sherman's army made the problem of providing food for the family and slaves a serious matter, but she was equal to the emergency. She secured corn for them by making long expeditions on horseback, accompanied only by faithful Negroes, and on one occasion her search for this precious commodity led her to cross a swollen river at the risk of her life.[9]

Unlike the Elmore ladies, Ida Dulany of Oakley Plantation, Upperville, Virginia, had the constant presence of hostile troops in her neighborhood added to the other perplexities that beset the women plantation managers. Nevertheless, her strategy and perseverance enabled her to overcome many of these difficulties and to conduct her plantation with a considerable measure of success. When the Federals were planning to confiscate her live stock in June, 1862, she checkmated their predatory intentions by selling the animals. Shortly afterwards she found that her wheat was in danger of being lost before it could be harvested because the Federals had seized her overseer and several of her Negroes had fallen ill, but, equal to the emergency, she hired a substitute overseer and nursed the sick slaves back to health. As a result her grain was successfully harvested, and she was able to carry some of it to the near-by Middleburg market and to give another portion of it to Stonewall Jackson's men as they passed her home on one of their forced marches. In the spring of 1863 she complained of a lack of clothing for her family and servants, of a monotonous diet that consisted largely of salt pork and hominy, the strictness of the Federal blockade across the Potomac, the lateness of the seasons, and of having "no toys, no bonbons, no parties for the children," but she went to Baltimore where she purchased the necessary clothing, and when favorable weather arrived, toward the end of May, she assured herself a plentiful harvest by energetically pushing her planting operations. Of the approval which one aspect of these activities excited, she wrote, "I took Uncle John over my garden today. It is in beautiful order, and I received warm commendation from him for my good management."[10]

The wives of small farmers were confronted with certain difficulties that were not experienced to the same degree by the wives of large farmers and planters. One of these was the high-handed impressment policy of the Confederate government. This policy, legalized by the Impressment Act of March, 1863, and amended by successive acts, enabled the government to impress slaves, wagons, live stock, and provisions needed for the army, and compelled the farmers to accept prices fixed by government commissioners, always below the market price.[11] The act was bitterly assailed throughout the Confederacy on the ground that it was discriminatory and therefore unconstitutional,[12] and the provision relating to slaves was especially resented by the women who had been left in charge of small farms. This class of women had few or no slaves to aid them in their agricultural operations, and when those which they did possess were taken by the impressment commissioners many women had only the assistance of young white boys in the performance of even the heavier tasks of the farm. Naturally they did not accept their responsibilities as cheerfully as did the more fortunate plantation mistresses who had many Negroes at their disposal. Their dissatisfaction was most clearly manifested in the thousands of letters which they wrote to public officials protesting against the impressment of the blacks. "I have only one man left who is my field hand," said a typical protest of this nature. "He is my only dependence for ploughing and doing the heavy work. My husband is in the service, and I have a large family both white and black to support, and I don't see how it is possible for me to feed them if the only field hand I have is taken from me."[13]

Another source of great irritation among the wives of small farmers was the oppressive Confederate tax in kind. This tax, advised by C. G. Memminger, the Secretary of the Treasury, and approved by the Confederate Congress in April, 1863, attempted to provide revenues which should not be paid in depreciated currency by falling back on the ancient system of tithes and direct contributions of produce. The law demanded one tenth of the produce of all farmers, and since land and slaves were not directly taxed, there was a widespread feeling that the government was discriminating in favor of the large planters and the capitalists. Moreover, this was the first general tax that the common people of the South had ever been conscious of paying, and when the tax-gatherer "suddenly appeared like a malevolent creature who swept off ruthlessly a tenth of their produce," the act was denounced as "unconstitutional, anti-republican, and oppressive" by the class who had no resources except their crops.[14]

Under such conditions the wives of small farmers frequently assumed the burden of field work. Some did it from a patriotic zeal similar to that of the planters' wives; others did it because it was the only alternative to destitution. "In the fields the women were ploughing, for their husbands have gone to the army," observed an English traveler in the South in the summer of 1863,[15] and during the following year another traveler noted that the mothers, wives, sisters, and daughters of soldiers were aiding "in preparing and getting in a great grain crop to which we have been looking with anxious expectations."[16] Such women, according to their own testimony, tilled crops, built houses, slaughtered hogs and beeves, and killed game when these animals were not available. In Arkansas one woman plowed and hoed all day and wove and spun until late in the night in order to support her family; another trudged early and late behind a yoke of steers, cultivating enough corn for her family and her neighbors; and still another "was mother, wife, and landlord; had to chop wood, make fires, cook, plow, hoe, card, spin, and weave, running the whole gauntlet."[17] At Dardanelle, Arkansas, women were observed going in groups of forty, sometimes for a distance of as many miles, to a mill where they exchanged the grain which they had produced for meal and flour. Most of them drove steers hitched to queer looking carts which they themselves had constructed. "Two women," wrote a miller whose establishment they visited, "would get two wagon wheels, sometimes one would belong to the front and the other to the hind part of the wagon." With two yearling steers hitched to the contrivance thus effected, and with one woman walking on either side of the team, they made their painful journeys to and from the mill.[18]

REMUNERATIVE EMPLOYMENT

The plight of the women who lived in cities and towns, or who had been driven from their farms by the enemy, was much more serious than that of the classes just described. These women had no farms or plantations from which to extract the means of subsistence, nor could they look to the soldiers in active service for support, as the pay of these men was usually not sufficient to satisfy their own personal needs. At the outbreak of the war the salary of a private or corporal was eleven dollars a month; that of a sergeant twenty dollars; that of a captain $130.00; that of a colonel $195.00; and that of a brigadier general only $210.00.[19] Although the rates of pay increased as the war continued, these increases were not in proportion to the great rise in the prices of the necessities of life. In 1863 the *Raleigh Standard* declared that the wages of the common soldiers "will no more than suffice to half-sole their shoes and buy them a pair of socks,"[20] while

Richard Maury observed about the same time in Virginia that his salary as a major was hardly sufficient to provide him with bread, meat, and a room. "Buying clothes," added Major Maury, "is out of the question. If breadstuffs rise higher I don't know what to do."[21] Nor did these conditions improve in the months which followed. A writer on the internal history of the Confederacy asserted that the monthly pay of a foot-soldier "would, for many months preceding Lee's surrender, have barely sufficed, in Richmond, to buy a pound of bacon to eke out his pitiful rations, or a swallow of poor whiskey to induce momentary forgetfulness of hunger, although, perchance, in Raleigh, at times that amount would have put him in possession of both."[22]

Where conditions of this nature prevailed, many women were forced to seek remunerative employment outside their homes, in domestic service, in the war industries, and in positions made vacant by the absence of the men in the army. Many of the humbler type were employed by wealthier women in spinning, weaving, sewing, and other domestic activities given impetus by the war, while others of this class made hats, bonnets, and baskets, for which there was a ready market, or were employed by the government as cutters and seamstresses and as makers of cartridges and other munitions. Women of the upper levels of society secured work as teachers, hospital matrons, and clerks in the government bureaus, and when necessity prompted they often supported themselves by doing handiwork.

An outstanding example of the success of a woman in solving the problem of self-support was that of Madge Brown of Vicksburg. Left by her soldier-husband with a family to provide for, she was too proud to accept the public charity offered her. At first she was able to meet her obligations by teaching in the mornings and taking in sewing at night. Her students paid her in pumpkins, potatoes, and other country products, and she was able to get plenty of rough sewing from the army. When, however, her burdens were increased by the return of her husband blinded in the war, she was forced to seek more profitable employment. This she found in making hats from palmetto leaves gathered in the near-by Louisiana swamps, but she was soon thrown out of this work by the exhaustion of her supply of leaves. Undiscouraged, she then turned to baking, in which her labors were so remunerative that she was able not only to provide for her family, but also to support her invalid husband in comfort without his having to call on public charity for relief.[23]

The spirit in which women of the upper classes took up handiwork as a profession, when reduced in circumstances by the war, is revealed by several passages in the diary of Judith W. McGuire. "Some young ladies," wrote this Virginia matron, "plait straw hats for sale; I saw one sold this morning for twenty dollars—and their fair fingers, which have not been accustomed to work for a living, plait on merrily; they can dispose of them easily; and, so far from being ashamed of it, they take pride in their handiwork." A woman who belonged to a wealthy Maryland family, added this chronicler, "took in sewing, and spoke of it very cheerfully. . . . She began by sewing for brothers and cousins, then for neighbors, and now for anybody who will give it to her. She laughingly added that she thought she would hang out her sign, 'Plain sewing done here.' "[24]

Many women of education and refinement eagerly sought positions in the clerical service of the Confederate government, enlisting the assistance of men of influence in their behalf. Congressmen, military leaders, and even clergymen were asked to write or speak to the employing officials concerning the applicants' social positions, alleged qualifications, and need of remunerative employment.[25] At first women clerks were allowed only in the Treasury Department, notably in the Note Signing Bureau, but eventually they were taken into the various offices of the War and Post Office Departments and finally into virtually every branch of the Confederate civil service. The employment of large numbers of women in this capacity was a novelty, but under the unusual conditions of war time they were welcomed into the government service by the male officials. Such an arrangement performed the double function of releasing male clerks for military duty and at the same time relieving the public authorities of the necessity of providing for women who would otherwise have been destitute. Although most Southern women had no previous experience in clerical work, their services proved generally satisfactory—in fact more satisfactory than those of the men whom they displaced, according to the account of one observer.[26] The women who were able to secure such positions regarded themselves as peculiarly fortunate, and they were extremely grateful to those whose services had been enlisted in their behalf.[27]

THE RELIEF OF SOLDIERS' FAMILIES

Neither the operation of farms and plantations nor the other classes of employment that have been described were sufficient to provide a livelihood for all the women who were deprived of male support by the war. Consequently, there were thousands of women who experienced serious physical deprivation, and public and private agencies had to be created for the alleviation of their sufferings. Plantation masters and mistresses, and to a certain extent the merchants of the cities and towns, readily listened to the cries of their distressed neighbors, and numerous relief societies were organized in every state for the specific purpose of preventing destitution among soldiers' families. Municipalities frequently established markets where supplies were given away or sold at cost, and the county governments in many instances supplemented the liberal appropriations of the state legislatures for those in need.

Some of the most effective efforts on the part of individuals and volunteer organizations to relieve women in distress were those which were manifested in North Carolina. There the railroads graciously volunteered to transport supplies for this purpose free of charge, and many individuals generously contributed supplies as well as money for the purchase of these commodities. Outstanding among such individuals were a citizen of Haywood County who refused three dollars a bushel for his corn in order to sell it to women for one fourth of that amount; a merchant of Stanly County who refused thirty dollars a barrel for his flour in order to sell it to women for ten dollars; a citizen of Salem who stored his barns and smoke houses with flour, corn, and bacon for the use of the destitute women in his community; a miller in Robeson County who offered to grind without charge the corn of soldiers' wives; and President Braxton Craven of Trinity College who assumed the responsibility of providing thirty or forty families with corn. Other notable examples of relief work in this state included that of the citizens of Cumberland County who, in November, 1862, subscribed $41,355.00 for the benefit of destitute soldiers' families, and that of the citizens of Caldwell County who, a year later, subscribed $4,000.00 for the same purpose.[28]

Perhaps the most effective work accomplished by the collective efforts of a North Carolina community along this line was that of the Wilmington Relief Association. This organization was formed in order "to distribute gratuitous relief to persons unable to purchase" and to sell commodities at prices below the market quotations to those whose incomes had been curtailed as a result of the war. During one week alone, in 1864, it distributed free of charge food valued at $2,424.00 to 181 families consisting of 630 individuals, and sold at cost articles valued at $3,375.00 to 265 families consisting of 915 individuals. A local newspaper declared at the time that the sales of the association did as much good as its gifts and estimated that the organization had up to that date saved persons of limited means fifty or sixty thousand dollars in the making of purchases.[29]

Although the slaves and overseers were generally opposed to sharing with others the products of their labors, the plantation masters and mistresses usually gave freely of their substance to the destitute women of the poorer classes. The planters of Alachua County, Florida, for example, pledged themselves to furnish the produce of their estates to families able to pay for it, at prices fixed by state commissioners; and to supply these commodities without cost to those who were unable to pay. The first of these promises, asserted the planters in question, was made because of "the fabulous prices which the necessities of life have attained"; the second, they added, was "not an act of charity, but a debt due to our brave soldiers."[30] Another example of this type of generosity was the conduct of certain plantation mistresses in southern Alabama toward the women who came from the northern counties of that state with certificates from the judges of probate asserting that the bearers were destitute. These women, according to an observer, came in parties of twenty or thirty and scoured the country for miles around, never failing to have their sacks filled and sent to the railroad depots or boat landings for them. One woman was seen with several sacks, each of which was two yards long and one yard wide and capable of holding two bushels of corn. When the plantation mistresses had no corn to spare, they often gave the supplicants money. "I saw a party of these women on the steamboat counting their money," concluded the narrator of these occurrences. "They had hundreds of dollars and quantities of corn."[31]

The conduct of Catherine Ann Edmonston, a wealthy plantation mistress of Halifax County, North Carolina, affords still a further illustration of the manner in which women of her class frequently rendered assistance to their poorer neighbors. She conferred untold benefits upon the small farmers of her community in 1861 by exchanging eight hundred bushels of salt for their home-made socks at hog killing time. She built a comfortable cabin for a poor family whom she discovered living in a leaky hovel, and she gave a shoeless and shelterless girl employment in her home as a spinner.[32] Even more sustained and beneficent were the services of Sadie Curry of Edgefield District, South Carolina. This woman fell into the habit of visiting the homes of the destitute in her vicinity each day, relieving their wants out of her own private means, and reporting cases of illness among them to a local physician.[33]

The larger cities of the South, especially Charleston, New Orleans, Mobile, and Richmond, maintained "free markets" for the benefit of the poor. Such institutions were supported by gifts of money and provisions made by the citizens of these respective cities and by neighboring planters. The market at Mobile, according to a contemporary observer, "is supported wholly by donations of money and provisions. Many of the planters send all kinds of vegetables to it."[34] Richmond citizens gave their institution $130,000.00 at one time; at another time they gave it $70,000.00; and for a while the market supported four hundred persons.[35] The Charleston market announced in November, 1862, that it was supporting entirely the families of six hundred soldiers, and six months later this number had increased to eight hundred.[36]

STATE RELIEF MEASURE

The most thoroughgoing and persistent efforts to relieve distress among soldiers' families were not those of individuals and voluntary organizations, however, but those made by the state governments. These agencies, possessing the power to appropriate forcibly the resources of the community through taxation, were consequently in a better position to look after the wants of the needy than were organizations which had to depend upon voluntary contributions from persons who, in those parlous times, had usually suffered radical reductions in income. Adequate studies of the relief activities of the governments of North Carolina, Florida, and Alabama have been made,[37] and what was done by these states may be regarded as fairly typical of the other states of the Confederacy.

During the war North Carolina appropriated, by legislative enactment, a total of $6,020,000.00 for the relief of soldiers' families, in addition to numerous special grants, estimated at something like $20,-000,000.00, made by the counties with or without the authorization of the legislature. A relief agent was appointed for each county; there was a similar official for the entire state; and it is doubtful if there was any one in the whole Confederacy who was more zealously interested in the welfare of the soldiers' wives and families than the celebrated war governor, Zebulon B. Vance. Examples of county relief work in this state include that of Guilford County, in giving twenty dollars a month to each soldier's wife and ten dollars to each child, and that of Wake County, in issuing a monthly allowance of five pounds of bacon and a half bushel of meal to each wife and a peck of meal to each child of this class. Of Cumberland County the *Fayetteville Observer* asserted, early in 1864, "The provision made in this county for assisting the families of the soldiers was so liberal that the poor by their own confession 'had never been so well provided for as since the war.' "[38]

State relief activities in North Carolina generally took the form of distributing carefully the salt, cards, and other necessities which were purchased by the governor through the thriving blockade trade running out of Wilmington and through other means. These efforts resulted in substantial benefits to thousands of poor women and children. "The indigent families of soldiers," wrote a typical relief agent to the governor, "are well provided for. With the amount of money which has been furnished me I have done all that any man can do."[39] Although the sums appropriated were in depreciated currency, they were nevertheless instrumental, according to the conclusions of the historian of war relief in North Carolina, "in alleviating a vast amount of suffering on the part of the poor families of the state."[40] That the recipients of such relief were grateful for what was done for them in this respect is indicated by the esteem with which these classes regarded the governor. "I have seen tears of thankfulness running down cheeks of soldiers' wives on receiving a pair of these cards, by which they were alone able to clothe and procure bread for their families," wrote Cornelia Phillips Spencer of the spirit in which one of Vance's most valuable gifts was received. "And they never failed to express their sense of what they owed their Governor. 'God bless him!' they would cry, 'for thinking of it.' And God will bless him."[41]

The relief measures of Florida, although confined to a more limited area, were as intensive as those of North Carolina. As soon as the army removed the men from productive activities, the civil authorities of that state undertook the relief of the families who were thus deprived of their normal means of support. In 1862 the justices of the peace were enjoined to make lists of the indigent soldiers' families in their respective districts, and immediately after these lists had been made available, the governor, acting either through the boards of county commissioners or the judges of probate, began the distribution of clothing, salt, wool-cards, spinning wheels, and other necessities among the poverty-stricken women. This work was made possible during the years 1862, 1863, and 1864 by legislative appropriations totalling $1,-200,000.00. During the winter of 1862-1863, 3,431 families comprising 11,744 persons received state aid in Florida; during the following winter these figures increased to 3,633 and 13,248, respectively. Since that state sent less than 13,000 men to the army, it was in 1864 contributing to the support of at least one non-combatant for every soldier in the field.[42]

In Alabama the relief measures were largely confined to the predominantly white counties in the northern portions of the state, since the southern counties were largely free from the ravages of the enemy and were assured a rude plenty by the faithful labors of numerous slaves. To relieve the distress in the northern part of the state, the legislature in 1862 devoted twenty-five per cent of the income from the regular taxes of the entire commonwealth. In the following year a relief tax equal to the taxes of the state for all other purposes was levied, in addition to a special appropriation of $2,000,000.00. Sixty thousand dollars of this special appropriation was used to facilitate the distribution of cotton and woolen yarn at cost, and the state also took charge of the distribution of salt, selling it at cost or giving it away in cases of great need. In 1864 the special relief appropriation was increased to $3,000,000.00 and the county commissioners were authorized to impress supplies for the benefit of the poor when these unfortunates were unable to purchase them. In 1865 the relief appropriation was further increased to $5,000,000.00, and a special grant of $180,000.00 was made for the relief of counties which had been overrun by the enemy. It has been estimated that from late in 1862 to the end of the war at least one fourth of the white population of Alabama was supported out of the public funds of the state.[43]

EFFICACY OF THE RELIEF MEASURES

It is difficult to estimate the degree of success that was achieved by the relief measures of the various private and public agencies of the Confederacy. It should be borne in mind that the South, although blockaded, was never threatened with a general deficiency in the basic necessities of life. The gaunt spectre of famine raised its head only in limited areas and under special circumstances. The great privations which the people of the Confederacy endured were largely due to inadequate transportation, an unjust distribution of the burden of poverty, and a fantastic fiscal policy, rather than to an actual breakdown of the processes of production. Two of these evils—the unjust distribution of the burden of poverty and the inflation of prices—were remedied to a certain degree by state action. The first of these two evils was met by high taxation, summary impressments of goods, and the partial distribution of the proceeds of these actions among the poor; the second was met by taxes in kind, barter, and the forced sale of commodities at what were considered reasonable prices. With only the problem of transportation not effectively tackled, the state authorities may be said to have made considerable progress in rectifying the most glaring irregularities that led to distress among their people.

There were indeed certain discerning contemporaries who regarded the poor as being adequately provided for. Sallie A. Putnam believed that the so-called pauper classes of Richmond were not the worst sufferers among the population of that city, since they were supplied, at public expense, with sufficient food. "They had furnished them," asserted this critical observer, "rations of corn-meal, sorghum syrup, and small quantities of bacon and flour. Starvation to them was not imminent, and the pauper class was indeed in more comfortable circumstances than persons who lived on salaries, or depended on moderate incomes for support."[44] A similar observation was made in Mobile toward the end of the war. "With all the rumors of starvation," wrote Kate Cumming, "people look well. I am told that there is less dyspepsia than ever known before. The poor do not suffer as much as one would think. Work of all kinds seems to be plentiful, and the Supply Association is still in operation."[45]

Moreover, the manifestations of discontent, so numerous among women of the poorer classes during the war, cannot be ascribed altogether to the privations which they experienced. This class of Southern women had always been hard to satisfy and strident in their complaints. In many instances the liberal charities of the period, instead of producing gratitude and contentment, were pretexts for the neglect of normal duties and provocative of cries for aid beyond the capacity of the relief agencies to satisfy. A semi-illiterate North Carolina woman said in 1864 that there were "easy wimin" in her neighborhood who expected to live off the public funds and who sold their "meet" in order to get money with which to have their spinning done. "Thay never did work neither do thay now," concluded this observer; "their men never kept them up as mutch as thay get now."[46] Many of the "corn women" who descended upon the plantations of the Alabama black belt were said to be truly needy, but others, thinking begging an easy livelihood, neglected to plant crops and returned home to share the returns of their excursions with husbands who were evading army service.[47] Nor did the liberal donations of the "free markets" always satisfy the beneficiaries. "The poor, it seems, are quite fastidious," wrote Julia Le-Grand at New Orleans in 1862. "Some of the women, if told they cannot gratify some particular taste, refuse all that is offered; for instance, one became angry a few days ago because presented with black tea instead of green, and another finding no coffee turned up her nose at all other comfortable items which the market contains. Some women curse their benefactors heartily when disappointed."[48]

On the other hand, there were numerous cases of genuine destitution in many communities of the Confederacy which were not taken into account by the writers of the upper classes which have just been cited.

Under the trying conditions of the times, it was obviously impossible
for the public agencies to provide adequately for all the families deprived of their male supports by the army. Glimpses of the privations
which such families suffered were caught by the discerning eyes of
foreign travelers. Eliza McHatton-Ripley, for example, in her journey
through Texas in 1863, stopped at "a miserable country house" near
Beaumont where she found two forlorn women whose husbands had
gone "to fight Lincoln." These women made their appearance with a
handkerchief full of "borrowed" cornmeal for their dinner, "for except
for a pound or two of rusty bacon, they had nothing whatever in the
house to eat." When asked for milk, they pointed to their "old one-
eyed mare, stretching her long, skinny neck over the fence, as the
'onlyest she-critter' they had."[49] In the same year Lieutenant Colonel
Fremantle, another traveler, found similar conditions among the wives
of Alabama farmers who had gone to war. "It is impossible," he said,
"to exaggerate the unfortunate condition of the women left behind in
these farm houses; they have scarcely any clothes, and nothing but the
coarsest bacon to eat, and are in miserable uncertainty as to the fate of
their relations, whom they scarcely ever communicate with."[50] A staff
officer who accompanied Sherman on the march through South Carolina
in 1865 found conditions among certain classes of women in that state
even more harrowing. "It would be difficult," he wrote of the Saluda
River cotton mill village, "to find elsewhere than at this place a collection of two hundred and fifty women so unkempt, frowsy, ragged,
dirty, and altogether ignorant and wretched." The homes of these
women, he added, were wooden shanties "where doors hung shabbily
by a single hinge, or were destitute of panels; where rotten steps led
to foul and close passage-ways, filled with broken crockery, dirty pots
and pans, and other accumulations of rubbish . . .; where old women
and ragged children lolled lazily in the sunshine; where even the
gaunt fowls that went disconsolately about the premises partook of
the prevailing character of misery and dirt."[51]

The impressions of these travelers were confirmed by many Confederate women in their own writings. The thoughts of such women
are perhaps most sharply revealed in the numerous letters of complaint
written to the sympathetic war governors of Virginia and North Carolina, William Smith and Zebulon B. Vance, respectively. "I have fore
children and myself and all I get to eat is a little corn bread," said a
Virginia woman, in a letter that was typical of many which the governor of that state received. "I am knot allowed the privilege of a
negrow. Because I rased foore shoats the County refuses to find me eny

meet. It is indeed hard for when the County found me meet they found me only fifteen pound for me and fore children and that is anuf to last too weeks. . . . It is two weeks that me and my children has bin living on corn bread and water and the cort says they can do nothing for me."[52] "Times is hard hear now," wrote another woman from that state. "Provisions is scarce and high. All the men hear is all in the armmy and all kild nearly. You can't tell how Bad I suffer both in Boddy and mind."[53] Still another Virginia woman, attempting to describe the general conditions that prevailed among the women of her neighborhood, wrote that "the poor soldiers' wives are in the most distressing situation without the necessitys of live, and everything in the way of provisions and clothing are so high that we can't get them." "How can I buy," she pointedly concluded, "a barrel of corn or flour or a pound of bacon at the present price, and my Husband in service at eighteen dollars a month?"[34]

In North Carolina there was a concerted attack made upon the adequacy of the public relief measures of that state by the wives of soldiers. Some said that these measures did not reach them. "We have not Drawn nothing but want in three months an without help we must starv," declared a group of Wayne County women. "How can our husbands surporte ther famileys at a Leven Dollars amounth when we have to give to the Speculator 2 Dollars a bushel for Bred and fifty sent a pound for our meet? We have seen the time when we cod call our Littel children and our Husban to our tabel and hav a plenty, an now wee have Becom Beggars and Starvers an now way to help our Selves."[55] Others asserted that unless the allowances made by the public authorities were increased, or their husbands permitted to return home from the army, they would starve. One woman declared that the ten dollars a month allotted her and her child was not sufficient for their survival, since grain was selling at from twenty to thirty dollars a bushel and bacon at from three to five dollars a pound.[56] Another, a war widow with five children and unable to work, wrote, "There is plenty to eat about here but we cant get it; the farmers wont take the money for it and they sell it so high we cant get anything worthwhile with the little money we git."[57]

THE BREAD RIOTS

The anger engendered by such conditions as have just been described was an important factor in precipitating the most notable civil disturbances in the Confederacy, the Bread Riots of 1863 and 1864. Although it would be inaccurate to say that actual hunger was the sole cause of these disturbances, the women were nettled by privations and high prices to such an extent that they were induced to make demonstrations which vividly impressed the entire Confederacy with their plight. Among the demonstrations of this nature occurring in 1863 were those at Salisbury, North Carolina, where two hundred women armed with hatchets forced the keepers of stores and warehouses to yield quantities of flour, salt, and molasses to them, and at Boon Hill in the same state where a large group of women gathered to demand that corn, for which three dollars a bushel was asked, be sold to them for one dollar a bushel.[58] Similar outbreaks occurred in 1864, including one at Bladenboro, North Carolina, when a group of women broke into a warehouse and seized sacks of grain,[59] and another at Mobile where the fire department had to be called out to disperse a great throng of women who had gathered in Dauphin Street to protest against high prices and to demand food for themselves.[60]

These and similar disturbances occurring in other sections of the Confederacy were overshadowed, however, by the great Bread Riot at Richmond on April 2, 1863. On that day a large crowd of women led by Mary Jackson, a huckster in the city market, moved through the streets of the city brandishing weapons and crying for bread. As the mob advanced it was augmented by a motley group of both sexes. Moving into Cary Street it emptied the grocery stores, and passing next into Main Street it looted the shops of jewelry, brooms, millinery, shoes, glassware, and other objects, thus belying the assertions of some of the members of the mob that its only purpose was to satisfy hunger. Stalwart women, crying that they were starving, were seen bent under heavy loads of shoes or dragging cavalry boots after them. The interpretation put upon this disorder was of such a serious character that troops were called out, the mayor of the city read the riot act, and the governor warned the disturbers that they would be fired upon unless they dispersed in five minutes. This bloody threat would probably have been executed but for the timely arrival of President Davis who spoke to the women with such sympathetic kindness that, taking their loot with them, they quietly returned to their homes. The next day there was another gathering of women, but it was easily dispersed without bloodshed by a battalion of troops.[61]

As already indicated, physical distress was not the only cause of such riots, but it is not fair to assert, as some contemporaries did,[62] that the Richmond women were underworld viragoes bent solely on unholy profit. Doubtless, as in most mobs, there were many who were actuated by such motives, but there were others who could claim with justice that they were rising against cruel privations aggravated by the machinations of war profiteers. An outstanding example of the latter group was a young girl of delicate features, but emaciated by hunger, whom a friend of Mrs. Roger A. Pryor met among the mob. " 'I could stand it no longer,' " said this girl in describing her desire for food. " 'We celebrate our right to live. We are starving; as soon as enough of us get together we are going to the bakeries and each of us will take a loaf of bread. This is little enough for the government to give us after it has taken our men.' "[63]

﹅﹅﹅﹅

In solving the problem of self-support, during the absence of the men in the army, the women of the Confederacy were surprisingly successful. A large number of them managed plantations and farms or accepted remunerative employment. Through such efforts they were able, in many instances, not only to support themselves, their families, and their slaves but also, as is shown in another chapter, to furnish the absent men with many necessities. When the soldiers' wives were unable to support themselves and their families, various public and private charitable agencies made generous attempts to come to their rescue. These agencies were not as successful as they might have been under more favorable conditions, and many privations and complaints resulted from their acts of omission; but they husbanded well the scant resources of the Confederacy and made it possible for many women who were unable or unwilling to support themselves to keep body and soul together.

CRINOLINE AND QUININE: A Delicate Investigation
(From *Frank Leslie's Illustrated Newspaper*)

CHAPTER X

INFLATION, THE BLOCKADE, AND SMUGGLING

IN addition to the absence of vast numbers of the able-bodied white men in the army, there were many other circumstances arising out of the war which combined to bring about a radical alteration in the living habits of the Southern women. Of especial importance in this respect were the reckless policies of inflation to which the Confederate government resorted in the administration of its finances and the vigilant blockade with which the Federal government surrounded the Southern ports. These two factors caused many articles of consumption, more or less plentiful in normal times, to became so scarce that it was difficult to find them or so expensive that it was frequently impossible to purchase them when they existed. Such a state of affairs evoked intense dissatisfaction and criticism on the part of the Confederate women, but their protests were not successful in abrogating the economic laws which had thus been brought into operation. Eventually it became necessary to abandon the ordinary channels of trade, and those women who were not satisfied with the crude plenty which their plantations afforded were forced to resort either to substitutes or to the precarious practice of smuggling through the Federal lines in order to secure the articles which they had been accustomed to purchase from the outside.

THE EVILS OF INFLATION

The great rise in prices which produced such severe economic dislocations and wrought such violent consternation among the Southern women was intimately connected with the history of Confederate finance. The principal supplies of specie in the South were in the Southern branch of the United States Mint and in the various Southern banks. The former was seized by the Confederacy and converted to its own use at the beginning of the war, and a large proportion of the latter was drawn into the hands of the government by the so-called "fifteen million loan," an issue of eight per cent bonds authorized in February, 1861. The most of this specie was taken out of the country by the purchase of European commodities, and although there was still some gold at home when the Confederacy fell, the amount of this medium available for domestic circulation after the first year of the war was exceedingly small. Having thus impounded and spent the greater portion of the specie reserves of the South, the Confederate Treasury began to have recourse to the perilous device of paper money, the gold value of which was not guaranteed. Beginning in March,

1861, it issued under successive acts enormous quantities of paper notes, some of them bearing interest, some not. The purchasing value of these notes soon started on a disastrous downward course, hastened by the fact that the government itself avoided accepting them, and in 1864 the gold dollar was worth thirty paper dollars. In the meantime the Confederacy had partially solved the problem of its own self-preservation by resorting to the system of tithes and impressments, already referred to,[1] but the depreciation of its notes sent prices rocketing upward and left thousands of soldiers and other persons who lived on salaries without adequate means of providing for their families.[2]

Not understanding the economic laws which were brought into operation by these circumstances, the women complained of those who demanded high prices of them. They argued that it was outrageous to be asked to pay two dollars for a pound of butter, twenty dollars a pound for tea, four dollars for coffee, fifteen dollars a barrel for corn, and six to eight dollars for a muslin dress,[3] and denounced the merchants as speculators exacting unprincipled gains out of their country's woes. "We, poor fools, who are patriotically ruining ourselves," wrote Mary Boykin Chesnut with bitter fatalism, "will see our children in the gutter while treacherous dogs of millionaires go rolling by in their coaches—coaches which were acquired by taking advantage of our necessities."[4] Others called the speculators murderers in the eyes of God and advocated that some means be devised to disgorge them of their unholy gains.[5]

Protests brought no remedy, however, for prices climbed to dizzier and dizzier heights. A typical complaint of 1862 spoke of calico and blue twill at forty cents a yard, the coarsest domestic cotton at seventy-five cents a yard, and baking soda at seventy-five cents a pound. Such prices, concluded the author of this complaint, "will do to wonder at after a while."[6] This time for wonder, in which the pleasure of looking back upon the period of high prices was anticipated, had to be postponed indefinitely, however, for there was no abatement in the upward movement of commodities as long as the war lasted. In 1863 a North Carolina woman complained that prices were "almost fabulous." Meal was eighteen dollars a bushel; sugar was $750.00 a barrel; butter was selling at from four to five dollars a pound; and a pair of French boots cost sixty dollars.[7] In the spring of the following year Mary Boykin Chesnut paid thirty dollars for a pair of gloves at Richmond, fifty dollars for a pair of slippers, twenty-four dollars for six spools of thread, and thirty-two dollars for "five miserable, shabby little pocket handkerchiefs."[8] A few months later, at the same place, Judith W.

McGuire wrote, "Just been on a shopping expedition for my sisters and niece, and spent $1,500.00 in about an hour. I gave $110.00 for ladies' morocco boots; $22.00 per yard for linen; $5.00 a piece for spools of cotton; $5.00 for a paper of pins, etc. It would be utterly absurd, except that it is melancholy, to see our currency depreciating so."[9]

The evils of inflation eventually reached such a point that the merchants and farmers refused to accept Confederate currency as a medium of exchange, and the women were forced to resort to barter. In 1864 a North Carolina woman reported that this method of trading had "become the order of the day." Two pounds of lard was paid for the weaving of two yards of coarse cloth; and tallow, beeswax, leather, wool, vegetables, and other products of the farms were exchanged at the cotton mills for thread, yarn, and cloth.[10] Board could be had at many hotels and inns only in return for lard, bacon, and other substantial victuals, and travelers frequently moved about encumbered with quantities of these commodities.[11] Still more grievous was the fact that the Confederate currency was discredited by the government itself. "I saw a widow lady, a few days since, offer to pay her taxes of $1,-271.31 with a certificate of $1,300.00," said the author of an official report early in 1865. "The taxgatherer refused to give her the change of $28.69. She then offered the whole certificate for the taxes. This was refused. This apparent injustice touched her far more than the amount of the taxes."[12]

THE EFFECTS OF THE BLOCKADE

Long before the worst evils of paper money were realized, however, the North, moving with devastating swiftness, had concentrated its naval forces in such a way as to dominate the Southern ports which had trade relations with Europe. Although the South was never threatened with a general deficiency in the basic necessities of life, the blockade was a severe blow at the economic structure of the Confederacy. The women as the maintainers of the domestic establishments were most directly affected. They had scarcely recovered from the shock caused by the entrance of hostile troops into their territory when they were confronted with the equally disconcerting intelligence that a naval wall had been erected around them which prevented the importation of numerous articles hard to relinquish—not only such luxuries as tea and coffee but also such utter necessities as medicines. This condition aroused a spirit of resistance among the women similar to that aroused by the invasion, for many of them knew that the frustration of the attempt to cut off their supplies was as necessary for the survival of the

Confederacy as was the repulse of the Federal invaders. If the struggle against the blockade was not as spectacular as that against the invasion, it required as much inventiveness and more labor.

The blockade aggravated the hardships attendant upon the rise in prices by producing a scarcity which prevented the purchase of many necessities at any price. It was rare for a store to stay open regularly. The merchant who could find anything to sell opened his shop for a few hours at occasional intervals and quickly disposed of what he had to the eager crowds that scrambled in.[13] Shops of this type, according to an English observer, "had the most mixed lot of goods I ever saw— odds and ends, in fact, of their used up neighbours' stocks—medicines, dry goods, books, hardware and tobacco being a common assortment."[14] Many shops closed permanently, not because their owners had failed but because their sold-out stocks could not be replaced. A visiting Englishwoman was impressed with the great number of these abandoned stores which she saw, their doors and windows broken out and their shelves cluttered with dirty bottles and other rubbish.[15]

The extent to which the effects of this scarcity were experienced by the women of the Confederacy is revealed in numerous contemporary accounts. "I mean to ask some clerk, out of curiosity, what they do sell in Clinton," wrote the irate Sarah Morgan after a visit to that Louisiana town in 1862. "The following," she added, "is a list of a few of the articles that shopkeepers actually laugh at if asked for: Glasses, flour, soap, starch, coffee, candles, matches, shoes, combs, guitar-strings, bird-seed—in short, everything that I have heretofore considered as necessary to existence."[16] A similar experience was recorded by a boarding-school teacher who accompanied three of her charges on a shopping expedition in Warrenton, Virginia. One of the three druggists to whom they applied for a certain medicine reported that he was "sold out"; another had just disposed of his last ounce of the desired article to a hospital; and the third offered to send to Nashville "next week" for it. A visit to the shoemaker produced results no more satisfactory. "Poor man!" exclaimed the teacher. "What with his workmen all enlisted, and his materials so scarce, it was a slow process to get shoes, or even to have them repaired. He said he has been waiting, I forget how long, for the shoe thread."[17] During the course of an address at Cincinnati, shortly after his expulsion from Tennessee as a Unionist in 1862, William G. Brownlow asserted: "They are nearly 'out of soap' down South. They lack guns, clothing, boots, and shoes. The boots I have on cost me fifteen dollars in Knoxville. They are out of hats, too. In Knoxville there is not a bolt of bleached domestic or calico to be had, nor a spool of Coates's thread. . . . Sewing-needles and pins are not to be had. The blockade is breaking up the whole South. It has been remarked on the streets of Knoxville that no such thing as a fine-toothed comb was to be had, and all the little Secession heads were full of squatter sovereigns hunting for their rights in the territories."[18]

So scarce did some articles become that the announcement of the arrival of a blockade runner at a seaport, or the appearance of a stray merchant at an interior point, usually brought women together in great numbers. Some came merely to gaze upon the articles exhibited; others to make purchases if they possessed the huge amounts of Confederate money necessary to strike a bargain. In the interest of fair play the number of purchases allowed to a single buyer was often limited. One "blockade store" was reported so crowded that women fainted and had to be laid on counters to avoid being trampled on;[19] another was said to have been so crammed with animated faces that the women wedged against each other and tried to peep over the sea of heads by standing on chairs.[20] "How vividly do I recall the sensation the event created," wrote a Georgia woman who had witnessed the sale of a small stock of goods by a merchant in the interior of the state. "We scarcely waited for him to unpack ere we besieged his door. The place was so crowded that we could not get in at once, so we went in 'squads,' and when we left he was 'out of business,' for we took the whole stock."[21]

In some cities, notably Richmond, where population congestion, inadequate transportation facilities, and the pressure of the enemy were added to the rigors of the blockade, the women often returned from market with little or nothing of even the great food staples in which the South specialized. During Grant's assault upon the Confederate capital in the spring of 1865, the city market contained only a few potatoes and vegetables and beef of the poorest quality. Servants sent there by Sallie A. Putnam returned empty handed or with "something of so miserable an appearance that the stomach revolted."[22] At that time breakfast among the upper classes in Richmond consisted of corn bread, the drippings of fried bacon, and coffee made of dried beans or peanuts without milk or sugar; luncheon of bacon, rice, and dried apples sweetened with sorghum; the evening meal of cakes made of corn meal and water, eaten with sorghum molasses and the coffee substitute just described.[23] Other sections of the South were more fortunate, but there was a general deficiency in certain commodities as a result of the blockade. Among breadstuffs the Confederacy was plentifully supplied only with Indian corn. Wheaten bread could scarcely be secured, and soda grew to be a thing of the past. Tea, coffee, sugar, chocolate, lemons, oranges, and ice became delicacies of the favored few; salt and vinegar grew very scarce; and the lack of many medical supplies, especially quinine and morphine, created trying difficulties among all classes.

It should not be assumed, however, that this scarcity meant starvation, or even general undernourishment. Wheaten bread was a traditional necessity only among the upper classes, the middle and poorer classes being accustomed to corn bread as a basic diet. The South was a rich agricultural empire, unable, it is true, to supply the varied diet to which many of its inhabitants were accustomed, but amply able to provide its basic food necessities. By deliberately increasing its food crops at the expense of cotton, tobacco, and other export commodities, it achieved this aim even under blockade conditions. Only those communities subject to military violence, difficult transportation problems, or a depletion of the labor supply suffered for want of the simple foods.

More than one traveler found comparative plenty in the Carolinas, Georgia, southern Alabama, and central Mississippi, regions enjoying an ample labor supply and untouched by the hand of the invader until late in the war. The crops of war-time plantations in certain sections of Mississippi were reported as bountiful, and the corncribs were said to be bursting with their heaped up treasures.[24] Mrs. Clement C. Clay, tiring of the privations of Richmond, retreated to Buxton Place, a North Carolina plantation, where she found the best meats and bread, "pyramids of the richest butter, bowls of thick cream, and a marvelous plentitude of incomparable clabber."[25] Catherine Cooper Hopley, an English traveler, was so impressed with the profusion of the Charleston market that she believed there was not much chance of South Carolina being "starved out." She discovered an abundance of eggs, poultry, and vegetables common to the English markets, as well as many Southern products which she recognized neither by sight nor name.[26]

Even during those months in which the Confederacy was undergoing its last agonies, women travelers were able to report an abundance of the fundamental necessities of life in certain sections of the lower South. "There is no appearance of poverty among the people of this town," wrote Kate Cumming at Newnan, Georgia, in March, 1864. Raising an abundance of necessities on their plantations, many of these people lacked only tea, coffee, and fresh beef.[27] A year later this same observer noted that the table of a hotel at Columbus, Georgia, "actually groaned under the weight of the feast." On it she found turkey, sausage, roast pork, biscuits, hot rolls, corn bread, and, to her great surprise, cake.[28] About the same time another observer reported that a family at Washington, in the same state, was able to serve "such a dinner as good old Methodist ladies know how to get up for their preachers."[29]

THE AVOCATION OF SMUGGLING

There were numerous women in the Confederacy, however, who were not satisfied with the crude plenty which their plantations afforded. They sought to find ways of securing those articles which they had formerly been accustomed to purchase from outside sources; and smuggling became an avocation with many of those who lived within or near the ever-shifting lines of the invading armies. Allowed to pass with relative freedom from the well supplied regions under Northern control into the impoverished areas of the South, these women took advantage of the opportunity to carry valuables with them. Sometimes they concealed such necessities as quinine, morphine, tea, coffee, and silk thread under the hoop skirts or other ample garments of the period. At other times they hid these articles in trunks, and wore several heavy dresses which might later be used by friends or relatives. It is even asserted that such heavy articles as muskets, revolvers, and cooking utensils were successfully hidden beneath hoop skirts and smuggled in.

The smugglers employed various stratagems. Mattie McSweeney, an eighteen-year-old Arkansas girl who wished to smuggle goods to the Confederates, made frequent trips from Fort Smith with contraband articles attached to her person. On one occasion she fastened tin cups and frying pans to her underclothing, and, thus encumbered, had herself placed in a buggy while friends distracted the attention of the officer appointed to watch her by treating him to lemonade.[30] Among the numerous tricks of a Nashville woman was that of carrying a coffin packed with valuables through the lines.[31] A New Orleans woman stuffed an elaborately dressed doll with quinine, and when her trunk was opened by Federal inspectors, forestalled examination of her precious toy by declaring, tearfully, that it was for a poor, crippled child.[32] Mrs. Roger A. Pryor discovered beneath the hoop skirts of a woman who came riding into the Confederate camp on Blackwater River, in Virginia, "a roll of army cloth, several pairs of cavalry boots, a roll of crimson flannel, packages of gilt braid and sewing thread, cans of preserved meats, a bag of coffee."[33] Perhaps the most successful smuggler was Mrs. William Kirby, the wife of a Louisiana wheelwright. She took clothing, medicine, and other supplies through the lines at Baton Rouge, and, emboldened by her success in this respect, she began transporting arms and ammunition through areas closely guarded by the enemy. Traveling by difficult and rarely used routes, she often succeeded in delivering her valuable freight to Confederate scouts who came out to meet her.[34]

Impatient with the demands that they submit to being searched before entering their own localities, some feminine smugglers displayed a sullen arrogance. "The searchers found it a troublesome business," said a typical account of the reaction of such women to these inspections; "not the least assistance did they get from the searched. The ladies would take their seats, and put out first one foot and then the other to the Yankee women, who would pull off the shoes and stockings—not a pin would they remove, not a string untie."[35] Other women met these embarrassing impediments with tact and cleverness; and, especially where there was no "Yankee woman" to do the searching, they were frequently allowed to pass through the lines without examination. Federal officers as a rule were not inclined to put their hands on Southern women and were usually willing to temporize if the latter showed good manners.

At times, however, the smugglers were treated rudely. This was especially true when the Federal officers had the assistance of women searchers at their disposal. At Richmond in 1862 Mary Boykin Chesnut wrote of hoop skirts being "ruthlessly torn off" by ubiquitous females looking for "not legs but arms,"[36] and at New Orleans in the following year Julia LeGrand heard of such inquisitors searching the hair and even the more intimate parts of the bodies of women suspects. "Even babies," said the Louisiana diarist, "were searched and left shivering in the cold without their clothes. Flannels were taken from all, and a little bag of flour which a very poor woman . . . had taken to thicken her baby's milk was cruelly thrown into water."[37] The vigilance with which the Federal sleuths could act at times is illustrated by an incident that occurred in northern Virginia. "I closely watched the fair traveler as she walked down the narrow, springy plank to the boat," wrote the chief of the Federal secret service in describing this incident, "and saw that the footbridge yielded to her step too much for her natural weight." This woman was searched and divested of forty pounds of sewing silk.[38] Some women were arrested carrying contraband goods, and a few of them died from the rigors of Northern prisons.[39]

✓   ✓   ✓   ✓

Such were the effects of Confederate inflation and the Federal blockade upon the South. The blockade was an important factor in bringing about the destruction of the Confederacy, but the women made desperate efforts to nullify its force. In small measure this was accomplished by smuggling through the Federal lines articles which had formerly been secured from outside sources. Far more effective, however, were the efforts to create substitutes for these articles out of domestic resources.

CHAPTER XI

THE ECONOMY OF SCARCITY

THE women of the Confederacy undertook with energetic courage the difficult task of manufacturing substitutes for those commodities of which they were deprived by the blockade. For aid in this endeavor they were confined largely to the assistance of the Negroes, as the white men were usually too preoccupied with military matters to be of much service in this respect. In spite of this and other handicaps, however, the women displayed an intelligent resourcefulness, and they were keenly aware of the advantages to be derived from the successful achievement of their efforts. Moreover, the South was essentially a rural section, abounding in vast quantities of native raw materials which readily lent themselves to conversion into articles of food and clothing, and the great majority of the Southern women were not so far removed from the experiences of frontier life as to be entirely unfamiliar with many of these processes. The makeshifts which they devised were generally crude and unpalatable reflections of real drugs and articles of food or imperfect attempts to imitate genuine household supplies and articles of clothing, but they were better than doing without the opiates, hot beverages, sweetening substances, condiments, toilet articles, and numerous types of wearing apparel for which the people of the South had a need.

DRUGS AND MEDICINES

"The woods . . . were our drug stores," said an Alabama woman in describing the ingenious methods which were used in supplying the medical deficiencies of the Confederacy. Whiskey, the basic ingredient of most Confederate medicines, was secured without difficulty from the backwoodsmen who had long been accustomed to its manufacture. The principal substitute for quinine, a medicine of primary importance in a malarial climate, was the dogwood berry, which, when boiled into a paste, was found to contain the alkaloid properties of Peruvian bark. Other remedies for malaria were cotton-seed tea, the bark of the willow, cherry, and Spanish oak, and the bark and root of the chestnut and the chinquapin. A syrup made from the leaves and roots of the globe flower and the mullein plant, or from the bark of the wild cherry, was thought to be efficacious in the treatment of coughs and lung diseases. Turpentine, an extractive substance plentiful in the South, had a variety of uses. It was employed in the treatment of fevers, colds, throat troubles, bruises, sprains, and many other aches and injuries. Local applications of mustard seed or leaves, of hickory leaves, and of pepper were used for pneumonia and pleurisy, while remedies for rheumatism, neuralgia, and scrofula were found in sassafras, alder, the prickly ash, sumac, and pokeroots and berries. A soothing cordial for dysentery and similar ailments was made from the root of the blackberry. Other cordials were made from blackberries, huckleberries, tomatoes, and persimmons, and brandies were made from watermelons and other fruits. The dandelion, the pleurisy root, and the butterfly weed took the place of calomel; sassafras tea served as a blood medicine; black haw roots and partridge berries were used for hemorrhage; snakeroot and peach leaves were employed as a treatment for dyspepsia; and a salve made from the Jimson weed mixed with spirits was described as healing and soothing.[1]

The medical department of the Confederate government appealed to the women to engage in the culture of opium, and through its instrumentality quantities of poppy seeds were distributed for that purpose. As a consequence, many women planted rows of poppies in their gardens, and when the buds of these plants were ripe, they were pierced with needles and the opium gum allowed to exude and become inspissated by evaporation. The product thus secured was collected and used in its raw state or made into laudanum.[2] The women also cultivated small patches of palma Christi, the plant from which castor oil is obtained. Since no rollers were available, rude mortars were used in crushing the beans of this plant and in extracting the oil. The oil extracted in this manner was mixed with water and boiled in order that the impurities might rise to the top and be skimmed off.[3]

This falling back on nature, old ladies' simples, and crude domestic concoctions was not an adequate solution of the pharmaceutical problems of a people at war. One woman said that these home-made medicines were "only a make-out" and that the castor oil produced, "with all the refining we were capable of, was a terrible dose and only used in extreme cases."[4] Despite their imperfections, however, such remedies were certainly better than no medicines at all, and in many cases they doubtless relieved or lessened pains that would otherwise have been unendurable. At least one woman spoke in terms of positive praise for the medicines that she made, asserting that the soporific influence of her laudanum "was not excelled by that of the imported article" and that her castor oil, contrary to the assertion of the other contemporary just cited, was "as thick and transparent as that sold by the druggists."[5]

BEVERAGES, SWEETS, AND CONDIMENTS

No deprivation of the blockade caused greater discomfort than the cutting off of the supply of coffee. By 1860 this Brazilian product had become almost the sole table beverage of the South; thousands were accustomed to drinking it three times a day, and when deprived of it they suffered from nervousness and headaches. Hence the providing of substitutes for this article became a crying need. No other subject among household problems was more widely discussed, and recipes for making "coffee without coffee" were extensively advertised. Substitutes were found in many substances; "in short anything in the vegetable kingdom," said a contemporary with pardonable exaggeration.[6] Rye, wheat, Indian corn, sweet potatoes, and peanuts, as well as okra, persimmon, and watermelon seeds, after being parched, all found their way into the coffeepot. An Alabama authority believed that okra seed, "when mature and nicely browned, came nearer in flavor to real coffee than any other substitute." The next best substitute, in her opinion, was sweet potatoes dried and parched after being cut into small squares, although she conceded that browned wheat meal and burnt corn made passable beverages.[7] Mrs. Roger A. Pryor favored parched corn or meal, which, she said, made "a very nourishing drink, not unlike the postum of today."[8]

Many patriotic Southerners tried to pretend that these beverages were delicious. In Virginia, said Mrs. Gilmer Breckinridge, they were swallowed amid jests and witticisms, "some declaring that after all there was little difference between ri-o and ry-e."[9] "Let South America keep her Rio and the antipodes its Java," exclaimed an enthusiastic newspaper writer. "It is discovered to be true beyond peradventure," he asserted, "that as a beverage the seed of the sea-island cotton cannot be distinguished from the best Java, unless by its superiority; while the seed of the ordinary variety is found to be not a whit behind the best Rio."[10] Most contemporaries, on the other hand, affirmed that such zealous effusions were arrant nonsense. Imitation coffee, said a traveler in Texas, was "a hot sickening drink, entirely devoid of the stimulating effects of the genuine article,"[11] and a Mississippi woman declared that most coffee substitutes were vile and the others not much better.[12] Moreover, the high value placed upon the small quantity of real coffee which found its way through the blockade belies the popularity of the substitutes. Such coffee was cautiously used as a flavor for the imitations, and a cup of the unadulterated liquid was, in the opinion of many blockaded Southerners, an extravagance akin to Cleopatra's famous draught.[13]

The absence of tea did not cause as much concern as that of coffee, as it was not widely used in the South. The roots of the sassafras and the leaves of the sage, the holly, the cassena, the blackberry, and the orange were tried as substitutes for this product of the Orient, but they gave little satisfaction. Eliza McHatton-Ripley asserted that the "weak decoctations of sage and orange leaves served by those dependent on the cheering cup . . . could only be taken in moderation,"[14] while Mrs. Gilmer Breckinridge declared that the tea made from raspberry leaves "was taken with an aversion which nothing but patriotism could have alleviated."[15]

Early in the war granulated sugar became a rare delicacy, and after the fall of Vicksburg even brown sugar became very scarce. In sorghum, however, was found a sweetening substitute which was more satisfactory than the majority of the makeshifts of the period. This plant had been introduced into the South a few years before the war, and its cultivation was so extensive after 1862 that its syrup became one of the few commodities which could be used without stint. Sorghum-boiling was added to corn-shucking and hog-killing as one of the great festivities of the rural South. On going home for the Christmas holidays in 1863, a Virginia woman was surprised to find her relatives "completely 'submerged' in sorghum; it seemed to absorb the whole family and to give occupation to numberless darkies."[16] What was true of sorghum on this plantation was true throughout the South. "It sweetened the coffee, tea, and all the desserts of the time," said David Dodge; "sorghum candy was the national confection. . . . The strange creaking hum of the cane-mills pervaded the land. Every place was redolent of it; everything was sticking with it."[17]

As a substitute for sugar, however, sorghum had certain drawbacks. When boiled by unskilled hands in vessels of every variety and shape, its syrups were as varied as the vessels in which they were extracted. Some were as hard as candy; others were as sour as vinegar; those boiled in iron pots made the teeth black, and even the best had an acrid taste. For these reasons many persons took advantage of their limited opportunities to secure other sweetening substances. Maple sugar was available in some areas, and the sweetening properties of honey were used to the limit of the supply. Some used cornstalks and watermelons for making syrups and sugar. Parthenia Antoinette Hague who experimented with the boiling of watermelon juice was rewarded with a syrup which she characterized as being "of a flavor as fine, or even finer, than that made from the sugar-cane."[18]

The lack of baking soda was supplied by the discovery that the ashes of the corncob possessed the alkaline properties essential for leavening dough. The cobs were burned in a clean fireplace or in a

Dutch oven and the ashes placed in a jar, covered with water, and allowed to stand until clear. One part of this solution mixed with two parts of sour milk and added to cakes or the various Southern breads produced the requisite lightness.[19]

Since the typical Southerner was said to be satisfied with "plenty of Indian corn, salt pork, sweet potatoes, and whiskey,"[20] the scarcity of salt was a handicap of major importance. There was only one saline deposit of any consequence in the Confederacy, that at Saltville in southwest Virginia, and the probability that this supply might be cut off by exhaustion or capture was a source of ever-deepening anxiety. Almost every community suffered from a deficiency in salt. Many persons were willing to sacrifice their preference for salt pork by eating fresh meats, but the benefits derived from this procedure were limited. A warm climate, combined with the necessity of shipping much of the meat to the army, made a preservative necessary, and salt was the only known substance which could be used for this purpose.[21]

The means of preventing a salt famine became a topic of conversation as common among feminine circles of the South as the weather. The Confederate and state governments came partly to the rescue by appropriating the available salt works and distributing their products among the people at non-speculative prices. Women who lived near the seacoast were able to supervise the extraction of considerable quantities of salt by the boiling of sea water, and children learned how to roll and pulverize the resulting substance into the fine articles suitable for the table. These expedients were limited in scope, however, and the majority of the women, especially those who lived in the remote sections of the interior, were forced to resort to cruder and less satisfactory methods. During the early months of the war the brine scraped from old barrels and troughs was carefully reboiled into salt, and when this supply was exhausted, the earthen floors of smokehouses were dug up for the purpose of extracting the small quantities of the precious substance which had been deposited by the dripping of meat. The earth thus collected was placed in hoppers, water poured over it, and the brine allowed to percolate into vessels placed underneath. The brine was then boiled and skimmed several times and the residue placed in the sun to dry. The product of this difficult process was limited in quantity, and it was a brownish substance which would not have been tolerated on many tables in normal times; but the emergency was acute, and the procuring of salt in this manner was widespread. There was scarcely a smokehouse in the entire South having an earthen floor that did not undergo a thorough scraping in the effort to secure the precious grains deposited there.[22]

In addition to devising substitutes for the basic articles of food, the Confederate housewives learned to supply the minor deficiencies of the family larder with numerous substitutes and imitations. Peanuts were roasted and pounded to make an imitation chocolate. When this substance was blended with milk and sugar, according to Mrs. Clement C. Clay, "the drink was ready for serving, and we found it delightful to our palates."[23] Beer was made from persimmons, corn, potatoes, and sassafras, and a pseudo-lemonade was concocted from maypops and pomegranates. Mustard seeds were raised in gardens and manufactured by young girls, using old muslin dresses for bolting cloths, into a table preparation equal to the article of commerce. Red peppers grown in gardens were said to make a healthful substitute for imported black pepper. When apples could not be had, as was often the case in the South, a "very weak and mawkish" vinegar was made from persimmons; and "an excellent quality of vinegar from honey." Persimmons dried in brown sugar replaced figs and dates. As a result of the scarcity of sugar, dried fruits largely took the place of preserves; while okra and other dried vegetables were held in high favor. When flour could not be obtained, many women requested the bolting of a portion of the corn meal which they secured from the mills. This process was effected by passing the meal successively through a wire sieve, a piece of tarlatan, and a piece of ordinary muslin. The resulting substance, mixed with water to make it viscid and adhesive, was as easily moulded into pie crust as real flour, and it was said to have been excellent for muffins, cakes, and waffles.[24]

In their attempts to devise substitutes for the foods of which they were deprived, the women made every effort to publicize the results of their experiments as widely as possible. To this end, information was freely circulated in newspapers, in private letters, and in pamphlets of Confederate recipes. The last named, in bindings of coarse paper, were quite popular and contained not a few useful hints to distressed housewives. Likewise, culinary knowledge was eagerly transmitted orally whenever willing listeners could be found. "Every old lady," said a South Carolina woman, "had some pet receipt of her own invention for some peculiar need which she would confide in the most earnest manner, as if she thought your eternal welfare depended upon your going home and concocting it at once."[25]

HOUSEHOLD AND TOILET ARTICLES

The blockade created deficiencies in household and toilet articles as trying as those in foodstuffs. Soap became as scarce as salt, and the exhaustion of the supply of lamp oil and candles, or the breakdown of the gas works of cities, reduced many homes to darkness. The breaking of china and glassware became a household calamity, since these articles could not be replaced. Through such misfortunes many families were reduced to "a motley assemblage of dilapidated tableware, broken-nosed teapots, cups minus handles, ill assorted plates, and miscellaneous knives and forks."[26] Added to these deficiencies was the exhaustion of the supply of stationery and ink; while needles, pins, hairpins, tooth brushes, and other small articles of this nature rapidly became very scarce or vanished altogether. "A needle dropped or misplaced," said a contemporary, "was searched for for hours; if one was broken its irreparable loss was lamented."[27] Often one comb did service for a whole family, while the use of a hairbrush was entirely dispensed with.

The women showed the same zeal in attempting to overcome the shortage in household articles that they exhibited in dealing with the shortage in the food supply. The making of laundry soap, an old plantation industry, was continued with much success, despite the fact that salt for hardening purposes was usually unavailable. In the absence of fats a splendid soap was said to result from placing the berries of the China tree in lye,[28] and an excellent lather was secured from boiling the root of the buckeye in flannel.[29] Ropes were made from bear grass, sunflower stalks, and cotton; a paste which hardened into a durable putty was secured from roasted Spanish potatoes mixed with flour; and mucilage was manufactured from peach-tree gum mixed with potatoes, flour, or starch from ripening corn. Mattresses were stuffed with Spanish moss, leaves, or cat-tails.

Old paper had a variety of uses. It served to cover broken blinds and windowpanes, to cover walls, and fill quilts and comforts; it was also spread underneath carpets and rugs. Broken chairs, stools, and tables were replaced by homemade articles, while improvised wooden boxes draped with muslin took the place of commodes. Willow work was introduced into many sections of the South for the first time. The switches were gathered while the willows were flowering and immediately woven into baskets or placed in warm water to be used later for that purpose. The growing scarcity of chinaware was met by several expedients. Some women made practical use of pots without tops or handles and of chipped cups, saucers, and plates. Others learned to broil sausage and steaks on coals and to bake bread on a johnny-cake board, on a worn plow share, or in ashes. A more energetic group resorted to the manufacture of pottery. The products of their labors were rough, coarse, and crudely enameled, but the cups, saucers, plates, pitchers, washbowls, and milk crocks which resulted therefrom were exceedingly useful in the prevailing emergency.[30]

Since many women desired to sit up late at night to pursue knitting, weaving, and other tasks which the war had imposed upon them, the need of artificial illumination was keenly felt. Consequently, the providing of lights became one of the most pressing among the domestic problems of the period, and various devices were resorted to in the effort to supply this need. When molds were available, substitutes for candles were devised by mixing powdered alum and lard with beeswax or the juice of the prickly pear. When molds could not be obtained, strands of thread were passed through a mixture of rosin and melted wax or tallow until they had grown to the size of a man's finger and then given rigidity by being wound around some upright object fastened to a block. Some of these improvised candles were said to have been bleached as white as sperm candles and to have been as transparent as the candles of commerce. There were likewise various substitutes for imported oil lamps. Bottles, gourds, and old tumblers served as lamp bowls, small rolls of cotton as wicks, and cottonseed or peanut oil mixed with lard as fuel. Sweet-gum bolls floating around in shallow vessels of oil or melted lard "gave a fairy-like light," according to Parthenia Antoinette Hague;[31] while the *Charleston Mercury* announced that "spirits of turpentine, in a lamp lately invented, make a beautiful gas light, very brilliant, very safe, costing about three cents per night."[32] When the supply of candles and oils was exhausted, a last resort was found in torches made from the wood of the resinous pine. These "lightwood knots," to use the conventional Southern expression, gave a ruddy and picturesque glow, but they made a flickering light that was a severe strain on the eyes, and they filled the room with a stifling smoke unless they were set in the fireplace.[33]

The problem of overcoming the scarcity of writing materials was also a matter of major consequence, since the absence of thousands of men in the army stimulated the desire to write letters to a degree never before known in the South. In place of the ink of commerce, the women devised almost as many substitutes as they did for coffee, among the more important ones being the juices of the pokeberry, the green persimmon, the sumac, green walnut hulls, and the parasitic ink balls that grew on certain kinds of oak trees. In the absence of copperas, rusty nails were used to deepen the color of these substances. Substitutes for stationery included wrapping paper, blank pages from books and ledgers, and the reverse side of wall paper. Old envelopes were turned and used again, and a favorite evening's occupation for young ladies was the making of these indispensable articles, gluing them together with peach-tree gum, from paper considered too coarse to be used in the bodies of letters. Although such ink on such paper often "blotted at every turn of the pen," these crude writing materials were the means of conveying the messages of cheer or grief which thousands of Southern women were constantly inditing to absent husbands, sons, and brothers.[34]

The necessity of giving a second life to so many old garments, and the desire to create pleasing colors for the homespuns and other fabrics of domestic manufacture, combined to give dyeing a position in the industrial life of the South which it had never occupied before. The setting up of the dye pot on the plantation was of an importance second only to bringing out the spinning wheel and the loom in the attempt to deal with the deficiency in clothing that accompanied the war. "Dyeing old clothes," said a diarist of the period, "is about the most fashionable thing done,"[35] while another contemporary went so far as to declare that the women were more anxious to learn a new process of dyeing than they were to learn a new stitch in crochet or worsted work.[36] Indeed it may be safely stated that they were as much interested in discovering the coloring properties of all available substances as they were in any other industrial endeavor.

Since commercial dyestuffs, which had formerly been used for this purpose, were entirely lacking, it was necessary to improvise substitutes for these highly prized preparations. Therefore, as soon as old clothes had lost their gloss or new homespuns had come from the looms, the women began eager searches for coloring substances in the fields and forests, returning with a varied supply of berries, barks, roots, leaves, and nuts. "We used to pull our way," said Parthenia Antoinette Hague, "through broad fields, and return richly laden with the riches of the Southern forest!"[37] These women were delighted when they discovered that "a beautiful shade of 'solferino' pink" resulted from placing yarn saturated with pokeberry juice inside a pumpkin. They were also pleased when they found that "a beautiful dark brown" came from walnut hulls; that the root of the pine produced "a beautiful dye, approximating very closely to garnet"; that the juice of the pokeberry produced "a red as bright as aniline"; and the blue was secured from indigo, a plant long known in the South both in its wild and domestic state. A scarce and precious weed known as the queen's delight mixed with willow bark, or the roots of the black walnut, produced a satisfactory black; swamp maple gave a clear purple; and common browns were extracted from the barks of the maple, the red walnut, and the red oak. Various shades of gray came from the barks of the myrtle, the pine, the willow, the white oak, and the sweet gum, and also from guinea-seed corn; yellow was extracted from peach leaves and sassafras; and the bark of the hickory yielded a bright green.

The principal mordant, a substance used for brightening and making durable the colors, was copperas. It was made by casting pieces of useless iron—old nails, horseshoes, old plowshares, and chains—into a cask of water to which a small quantity of vinegar had been added. Other mordants were alum, blue vitriol, wheat bran, lye, and lime water; and when none of these substances could be had, the water of springs strongly impregnated with iron was found to be effective.[38]

Other makeshifts in the way of household and toilet articles included the use of thorns for pins, and a hair oil made by placing a mixture of rose petals and lard in the sun and later straining the compound through muslin.[39] Soot mixed with cottonseed or peanut oil made an excellent shoe blacking, while a paste made of flour, bolted corn meal, or starch "gave the shoe as bright and glossy an appearance as if 'shined' by the best of boot blacks."[40] The juice of the elderberry boiled, strained, and mixed with molasses was also said to produce "a beautiful, glossy blacking."[41]

THE SHORTAGE OF CLOTHING

The scarcity of clothing was even more keenly felt than that of foodstuffs and household supplies, since the satisfying of this need involved not only the protection of the bodies of the women against exposure but also conforming to the elaborate feminine styles of the middle nineteenth century. This problem also involved basic difficulties not encountered in dealing with the food supply. Many of the basic articles of food—flour, meal, pork, and vegetables—could be produced in the blockaded areas without a radical modification of economic habits, and substitutes had to be provided only for fancy groceries and a few of the basic essentials. On the other hand, cloth, the basic commodity in clothing, could not be produced in sufficient quantities to satisfy more than a fraction of the demand by means existing in the Confederacy at the outbreak of the war. Consequently, the women were confronted with the necessity of devising substitutes for cloth, as well as for the less essential features of feminine attire.

The first efforts in meeting the war-time shortage of clothing was the salvaging of garments which had been cast aside in better days. Dress goods, hats, and bonnets which had been laid away in trunks and drawers, and which in normal times would have been given to servants, now became hoarded treasures. The work of remodeling, of turning and twisting, of piecing and pacing, and of trimming off the worn parts of garments and replacing them with something better, became a major industry. Hats were ripped and turned so often that no vestiges of the original articles seem to have been left, and old stockings were unravelled and knitted into new ones or into gloves. Silk dresses were cut up to supply the need for handkerchiefs; stray bits of ribbon were made into rosettes; and jackets were fashioned from the overcoats of men and from the cloaks which girls had outgrown. Twin girls were known to have covered up the deficiencies of two well-worn garments by converting them into one dress.[42]

By similar devices household furnishings were made into clothing. Curtains became heavy dresses, and sheets and pillow shams were made into waists and underclothing. So widespread was the latter practice that an Alabama authority declared, "I doubt very much if a fine sheet could be found in our settlement when the war closed. Perhaps there was not one in the blockaded South."[43] Even so coarse a fabric as bedticking was utilized by the women of some communities; if striped it was carefully ripped so as to preserve the blue thread for embroidering collars, cuffs, and the fronts of waists.

Another means adopted by the women in overcoming the scarcity in clothing was the practice of the most rigid economy. "The gentlemen talk a great deal about the ladies dressing extravagantly," said Kate Cumming, "but I do not think they do. We have learned the art of making 'auld claes look amaist as well's the new.' . . . And everything is the fashion; nothing is lost." This diarist even asserted that toward the close of the war it was considered "a kind of disgrace to have plenty of clothes."[44] Although the latter assertion was most certainly not true of all women, many of them were proud of their feats of economy. A Kentucky girl, for example, boasted of the fact that four calico dresses lasted her for the four years of the war and that one velvet jacket, passed around among five girls for festive occasions, triumphantly survived the surrender of Lee.[45] Children and servants were constantly warned against inroads upon soles and insteps, so as to conserve shoes. In fact, in the far South, children learned to save shoes by going barefooted all twelve months of the year, remaining indoors in winter, while many grown persons adopted this expedient for the summer months. [46]

SPINNING, WEAVING, AND KNITTING

Ingenious as were the makeshifts which have just been described, they were in no wise sufficient to satisfy all the textile demands of the Southern women, their children, and the slaves. If dire need were to be forestalled, therefore, it became necessary to devise some means of providing substitutes for at least a portion of the cloth which had formerly been imported from outside the bounds of the Confederacy. This was done by the revival of domestic spinning and weaving, industries which had been largely supplanted by textile factories some fifty or more years before the war. On nearly every plantation a few spinning wheels and in some cases looms had survived from the pre-factory period, and there were old women, both in the slave quarters and among certain classes of the whites, who knew how to operate these implements. As soon as the effects of the blockade began to be felt, carpenters were called in to model new spinning wheels and looms after the old ones, and the old women were impressed to teach the young the intricacies of the textile arts. "A special house was dedicated to the purpose and a spinning wheel was procured," wrote Claudine Rhett in describing the revival of this industry on a South Carolina plantation. "Old Mark and Cinda were detained to card the wool. . . . Sappho and Phoebe spun, and our cook Rosetta, who was a thrifty soul, was appointed dyer of the yarn. . . . But the worst part of the operation was yet to come—a hand-loom had to be obtained. . . . We at last heard of one, which belonged to an old Indian woman. So we forthwith dispatched Lymus, our head carpenter, to inspect it, and in a few months' time he had constructed a similar one for us; then Keziah, the Indian, was sent for to teach Rhyna how to work it, and oh! triumph, our jeans were woven, and the negroes had strong, warm clothing."[47]

By the second year of the war the hum of the spinning wheel and the clang of the batten of the loom could be heard everywhere in the South. Thousands of plantation mistresses became the supervisors of black spinners and weavers, who went about their work for long hours in great rooms set aside for this purpose. "The great spinning wheels," said a Mississippi account of these operations, "stand at the other end of the room, and Mrs. W. and her black satellites, the elderly women with their heads in bright bandanas, are hard at work. Slender and auburn-haired, she steps back and forth out of shadow into shine following the thread with graceful movements."[48] The unremitting character of these labors was the cause for frequent comment. "It keeps me so busy," wrote a North Carolina woman to her sister, "that

I find little time for reading and writing. When I tell you that I have cut out and wove and spun about six hundred yards of cloth since last fall you will overlook my not writing."[49]

Many women pursued this labor with enthusiasm, since it seemed to provide a means of demonstrating the ability of the South to combat the enemy. "Hurrah for domestic manufactures and a fig for the Yankees. We can do without them," triumphantly exclaimed a patriotic Virginia girl.[50] Absorption in cloth-making was also said to afford a relief from the cares of the times. "I have entertained myself at work since you left," wrote a Texas woman to her husband who was absent in the army. "I get much cotton spun now. Employment drives dull care away. I am more content when I work busily than at any other time."[51] Among such women a spirit of wholesome rivalry frequently existed, each one trying to surpass the efforts of the others in turning out homespun. "Mrs. Murrah is so busy," wrote the Texas correspondent just mentioned in commenting on these strivings; "she makes her negroes spin until ten or twelve o'clock at night. Your mother is making 90 yards of cloth a week—two looms going all the time. Aunt Betsy is as busy as she can be warping and drawing it for them. She stays with the looms all the time."[52] There were some women who even went so far as to claim that the making of cloth was a pleasure in itself. Sallie A. Putnam thought it "delightful to watch the magic shuttle shoot to and fro under the thread of the warp and to hear the strange music of the almost obsolete loom, and to see the stout fabric grow under ingenious hands."[53]

These enthusiastic labors were greatly facilitated by the fact that the production of wool on a large scale was introduced for the first time in the history of the South to supplement the traditional quantity of cotton. The result was the manufacture of fabrics of varied designs and weaves. An Alabama woman wrote of making "cloth in stripes broad and narrow, and in checks wide and small," "plain cloth, twilled cloth, jeans, and salt-and-pepper cloth," plaids woven both of wool and cotton thread, and "dice-woven home-spuns, or 'basket plait.'"[54] Other types of textiles mentioned in the literature of the period included coarse osnaburgs, sheetings, coverlets, towels, flannels, and balmorals; also plow lines and other varieties of rope. Tired of wearing the heavy homespuns to which they were not accustomed, the more venturesome spirits succeeded in making muslin. "Our muslins," said the Alabama authority quoted above, "reminded me of 'Swiss muslins,' with their raised flowers of silk or fine wool thread. When we first appeared in them, they were mistaken for the genuine imported muslins."[55]

It should not be assumed, however, that the making of cloth in the home was always attended with happiness and success. At the best it was a slow process which had to be pressed continuously if sufficient textiles were to be produced for families and slaves. The inevitable long hours often evoked complaints. Many women spoke of the trials of both spinning and weaving—how these tasks exhausted the patience and caused pains in the arms.[56] "Oh, how I did hate it," wrote a typical despiser of spinning; "I detested the very sight of the spinning wheel; but it had to be done or I go without dresses, so of the two evils—I spun." This woman found weaving no more attractive. "Just a thread at a time," she wrote. "Oh, how slow it was, and how long it took one thread in a place to make a yard."[57] A Virginia woman was exasperated when a man remarked to her that the sound of the loom was sweeter than that of the piano; she reminded him that the work was hard and that he should regret its having to be done.[58]

Certain obstacles of a more serious nature also hindered the making of homespun clothing. Of especial importance in this respect was the scarcity of cards, frail implements necessary in preparing the lint for spinning. Attempts were made to supply the deficiency in these articles by their distribution at cost by the state governments, by the establishment of factories for their manufacture, and by importing them on blockade runners; but it was not until near the end of the war that a good pair of cards was easily secured in the South. Another obstacle experienced by the garment makers was their inability to make a satisfactory sewing thread, a difficulty only partly overcome by bartering with the cotton mills. These difficulties, coupled with the inevitable slowness of domestic manufacture, meant that the women would not have been able to secure enough clothing for their needs had not homespuns been supplemented by occasional accretions from outside the home. Now and then a planter was able to lighten the domestic problems of his wife by securing a bale of cloth from a factory, and occasionally a soldier was able to send, from territory covered by the army, a bolt of calico to his family.[59]

Weaving was supplemented by knitting, an occupation which was followed by the women throughout the war with the same enthusiasm as that already described as being characteristic of this activity during the early months.[60] They continued to knit while riding in carriages and railroad cars, while visiting, while directing servants, and at night when there was not enough light for spinning, weaving, and sewing. Since this task required little physical or mental exertion, it served to occupy moments of rest from heavier duties and periods which had formerly been given to social pleasures. Traditionally the occupation of the old, it commanded the efforts of all ages under the stress of war, and many a young woman was able to boast of the skill with which she turned out numerous socks and sacks. "I became a veritable knitting machine," wrote a representative young woman of this class. "I knitted a sock a day, long and large, and not coarse, many days in succession. At the midnight hour the wierd click of the knitting needles . . . was no unusual sound."[61]

Knitting appears to have been the most fascinating of all the domestic arts. "It was delightful," wrote the enthusiastic Sallie A. Putnam, "to watch the busy fingers of our dear old matrons, as they deftly wove the yarn through the shining steel needles, making cheerful music by the winter evening's fireside. . . . It was amusing to behold the patient industry with which the young girl who had 'never thought to knit,' caught the manipulations from dear old hands."[62] This art also provided a satisfactory occupation for many of those who were unable or unwilling to pursue the more intricate tasks of spinning and weaving. "It is a great blessing," wrote one such woman, "to be able to work so—to see the work grow under your hands! It is heartsome and encouraging and it is all a matter of habit. After all, anyone can do it who gets the sling of moving her fingers rapidly."[63]

The knitting activities of the women bore fruit in the creation of many garments both useful and pleasing in appearance. Socks for the soldiers were the principal result of these efforts, but gloves, mittens, shawls, shirts, hoods, and the uppers of shoes and slippers were also produced in large quantities. In order to secure the smoothest and prettiest thread for such articles, lamb's wool or cotton that was unstained by the action of the weather was often carded and spun fine by hand and then dyed in the brightest colors. Corn shucks were sometimes wrapped tightly around certain portions of the hanks of thread when they were placed in the dyes, so that the encased parts would absorb less of the liquid and thus enable the garments to be given a clouded or dappled appearance. The pleasing effect of these garments was further enhanced in some instances by borders of vines and decorative devices of green leaves, roses, and other bright colored flowers skillfully knitted into the fabric.[64]

MILLINERY, SHOES, AND OTHER PERSONAL NEEDS

The attempts of the women to make hats can scarcely be regarded as successful if the products of their efforts are to be measured by objective standards. The milliner's craft was a complicated art in the sixties, and the Confederate amateur had neither the deftness of touch nor the basic materials necessary for the designing of hats that would approximate the prevailing fashions. The limited resources of the period compelled her to rely upon pine needles, oat or wheat straw, corn shucks, bulrushes, the inner coating of the "bonnet squash," and the feathers of common barnyard fowls. Hats made from such materials were often characterized as grotesque or fantastic and either too flimsy or too heavy. One woman declared that her hat of corn shucks was light and tasteful, but that it lacked durability and came to pieces in the first shower of rain; while another asserted that hats made of palmetto leaves were both durable and pleasing in appearance, but that they were not light enough for comfort.[65] Still another woman stated that the only reason why men wore the hats made by women was to avoid hurting the feelings of the fair laborers, and that her taste had to be satisfied by a "coal-skuttle hat of the loftiest dimensions," an absurd creation with foundations of pasteboard.[66] Among the most ridiculous of all Confederate hats were those made of guinea feathers. "I saw one once," said a Georgia woman, "completely covered with them, which gave the beholder temporary vertigo from the innumerable spots. The front of this marvel was filled in with twenty camellias made of dyed goose feathers."[67]

The Confederate women succeeded in being hopeful under worse trials than unsightly hats, however, and although strangers might smile at such headgear, many women were able to ignore these smiles and feel proud of whatever hats they were able to fabricate. "Ladies' hats," wrote a Virginia woman with a deep faith in everything Southern, "are shaped so becomingly that though a Parisian milliner might pronounce them old-fashioned and laugh them to scorn, yet our Confederate girls look fresh and lovely in them with their gentle countenances and bright enthusiastic eyes."[68] Palmetto hats, in spite of the defects mentioned above, were said to be "very pretty . . . and beautifully white;"[69] bonnets woven from rushes, lined with tarlatan and dyed with willow bark, were declared equal to those purchased before the war; and frames covered with brightly dyed feathers and down were said to make hats by no means rustic in appearance.[70] Mrs. Roger A. Pryor described the so-called Alpine hats worn by the Petersburg beauties as triumphs of the milliner's art. They were decorated with artificial flowers made by sticking feathers into balls of wax suspended on the ends of wires; the incurving feathers made apple blossoms and half-open roses, and the outcurving feathers formed camellias. "Neatly trimmed and suitable tinted," concluded Mrs.

Pryor, "these flowers were handsome enough for almost anybody."[71]

No phase of the shortage of clothing was more acutely felt than the deficiency in shoes, for these necessities became as scarce as any commodity in the Confederacy. The first recourse of the women in their attempts to overcome this deficiency was to assign to the shoemaker every bit of leather which had previously served less useful purposes. To this end, furniture was deprived of its upholstery; saddles, belts, bags, trunks, and buggy tops were utilized; and even needle books and other small articles were carefully stripped of their coverings. When, for example, a chance piece of bronze morocco fell into the hands of Mrs. Roger A. Pryor, she had it converted into a pair of boots for her little daughter, while an old leather pocketbook and two or three leather bags served the same purpose for her two boys.[72] With the exhaustion of their supply of pre-war leather, many women fitted knitted or woven uppers of their own manufacture to leather soles prepared in plantation tanneries that were forced into existence by the necessities of the period. When these leather soles outlasted the cloth uppers, as was usually the case, the shoes were ripped apart, the stitches picked out of the soles, and new uppers fitted to them. The more fortunate among the women were able to secure shoes made entirely from home-tanned leather. Many kinds of hides, including those of mules, squirrels, and dogs, were used in this process, and the tanners, mostly unskilled Negroes, usually produced only the roughest type of leather; but despite their crudeness, the shoes made from it were serviceable enough to protect the feet from the elements.[73]

Those who were unable to secure leather soles had recourse to wooden substitutes. In certain localities wooden bottoms had long been worn by slaves to a limited degree, and one of the first patents issued by the Confederate Government was for a wooden shoe. Some of these shoes were nothing more than rude receptacles dug out of blocks of wood, a travesty on the *sabot* of the French peasant, but the more serviceable ones had soles of willow, ash, or some other light wood, to which leather uppers were attached. In order to secure durability, the soles were made so thick at first that they added noticeably to the height of the wearer, but this difficulty was later solved by protecting thinner soles with iron reënforcements. Such shoes were always clumsy, noisy, and liable to damage anything they touched, but they had their compensations. Wood was plentiful and waterproof; there were few carpets left in the Confederacy to injure; and if one had scruples against entering houses in such rough shoes, they could easily be removed at the threshold.[74]

Generally speaking, the women expected the village shoemaker to do the actual making of their shoes. This individual was usually an old Negro or a white man unfit for military duty because of age or some other infirmity. Such shoemakers, however, were often found to be most unsatisfactory; their charges were considered excessive, and they were frequently so overloaded with work that their services could not be secured at any price.[75] As a consequence, many women were forced to become their own shoemakers. While this was a difficult endeavor, some were able to report success in its prosecution. "I was often surprised," wrote Parthenia Antoinette Hague, "at the dexterity with which we could join soles and uppers together. . . . We used to hold our self-made soles at arm's length and say, 'What is the blockade to us, so far as shoes are concerned, when we can not only knit the uppers, but cut the soles and sew them? Each girl and woman her own shoemaker; away with bought shoes; we want none of them!' "[76] A certain Mrs. McMeekin of Fairfield District, South Carolina, not only made all the shoes necessary for herself and five children but also produced a pair of such excellence that they were considered worthy of being exhibited among Confederate sympathizers in England.[77]

Various expedients were used in supplying minor feminine needs of a personal nature. Gloves were knitted or made out of spare bits of cloth. The parasol problem was solved at times by re-covering old ones, although the majority of the women had to dispense with the use of this luxury altogether. Fans for ordinary purposes were made from palmetto leaves and woven rushes; while finer ones, with handles fashioned from cedar or pine, were made from the wing feathers of geese and peafowls. The scarcity of buttons was relieved by a number of substitutes. Those carved from wood and polished were considered strong and lasting, as were those made of pieces of gourd and covered with strong homespun. Persimmon seeds and also scraps of paper or cloth pasted together in a sufficient number of layers were regarded as satisfactory, while buttons made of pine bark were excellent for garments which were not washed.[78]

THE UTILITY OF THE CONFEDERATE TOILETTE

The expedients just described resulted in the creation of wearing apparel which the Confederate women were able to regard with a considerable degree of satisfaction. Most certainly they refuted with indignation the rumors from the outside world that they were not adequately clothed. When, for example, a sympathetic article appeared in a Northern journal to the effect that the women of Richmond were lacking in shoes and hose and that they perambulated about the streets with their feet "wrapped in rags," these women entered an emphatic denial. On the other hand, favorable outside opinion was eagerly recorded and widely publicized. In 1863, as an illustration, Judith W. McGuire reported a friend who had lately arrived in the Confederate capital from Washington as saying to a group of women arrayed for church, " 'Why, how genteel you look! I had no idea of it. We all thought of you as suffering in every respect.' "[79]

Regardless of whether friends from the outside were able to praise their dresses, however, the women of the Confederacy were able to wear these garments without losing self-confidence and self-respect. "Many a girl," wrote a Georgia woman, "who in ante-bellum times would have scorned a calico dress, now wore homespun dresses; aye wore them with an air of pride."[80] A Charleston girl acquired a dress which she knew to be a misfit and poorly dyed. "But fortunately," she remarked with confidence, "the cheval glass is not here, and I can see only a small portion of myself at a time . . . and I fancy it is a trim fit."[81] Indeed there were many women who were able to persuade themselves that they looked well in any attire. They felt that their supposedly statuesque figures, their small feet, their beauty of face, and their alternating moods of languor and vivacity gave them a radiance not marred by even the crudest of homespuns. It should also be remembered that dressing well, or creating the illusion of so doing, was a vital part of their patriotism. They felt that they were compelled to indulge in the "very little things of dress" to prove that the South was self-sufficient and to bolster up the morale of the soldiers on furlough.[82]

Nor was this admiration of the women for their apparel always based on imaginary excellences. Many of them took full and effective advantage of the variety and beauty possible in homespuns and homemade dyes, and the ever-changing idiosyncrasies in style were not neglected. The latest mode occasionally struggled through the blockade to the centers of population in *Godey's Lady's Book, Frank Leslie's Weekly,* or *Le Bon Ton,* and articles written by European authorities on fashions appeared now and then in the newspapers. One of these articles directed the women to wear short dresses in place of the long ones to which they had been accustomed. These short dresses, they were gravely advised, "are scolloped round the edge of the skirt and worn with balmoral jupons short enough to display the boot, or else the skirt is looped up at every seam nearly to the knees, showing the colored petticoat of mohair or other material, trimmed either to match the dress or in contrast and corresponding with hat and mantle."[83] That many women gave ample attention to such advice is evident from the fact that they adopted such innovations as the Garibaldi waist and the "waterfall" and Watteau hats, at the same time clinging to such traditional conventions as the hoop skirt. A feature of romance, said a commentator on Confederate styles, was given to unpretentious toilettes by hats "bent in a deep curve back and front and wreathed around with natural roses."[84] Another writer of the period told of women appearing at entertainments in stylish homespuns made *en train* and trimmed in palmetto buttons *à la militaire* and in long and close fitting wraps with scarfs of colored wool.[85]

A few women even dressed superbly. Girls appearing at dances were said to have worn gowns which fitted their statuesque figures and showed their pretty feet to advantage. One such girl wore palmetto earrings, pins, and bracelets "cut in lacelike fibres and so prepared and cured as to be cream-tinted and very becoming to her dark complexion," while "the rosy fairness" of another girl was set off by gleaming pearl-like flowers made from fish scales into "a fairy-like necklace and spray for her long, curling hair."[86] Late in the war a Georgia girl entering a Macon hotel was certain she looked nice because several people inquired who she was. She wore a flowered merino skirt which had been freshened up with black silk rushings and a made-over waist set off with Elizabethan sleeves.[87]

Nevertheless, it would be extravagant to claim that the average Confederate wardrobe came near to fulfilling the intricate demands of the fashions of the middle of the nineteenth century. This fact was rudely evident when an occasional woman entered the Confederacy from the outside world and spoke frankly of the contrast between what she had seen and what she was seeing. One such visitor to Jackson, Mississippi, in the summer of 1862 wrote of seeing in single suits "sleeves of one color, the waist of another, the skirt of another; scarlet jackets and gray skirts; black waists and blue skirts; black skirts and gray waists; the trimming chiefly of gold braid and buttons, to give a military air."[88] A woman entering Georgia from Europe noted "how queerly everything looked to her in point of costume, each form seeming a comic picture and appearing almost as if there had been a rivalry in each to excel the other in these effects."[89] At the same time, women accustomed to the costumes of the Confederacy confessed their lack of faith in what they were wearing by bestowing unconcealed admiration upon the clothes of those who had come from beyond the blockade. A Tennessee bride-elect, for example, looked upon the wardrobe of a friend who had come from the North "with tears in her eyes" because she had no such garments in her trousseau;[90] and when a bride appeared in Georgia from beyond the blockade, "her beautiful dresses" were said to be a revelation to "dowdy Confederates," making them "feel like plucked peacocks."[91]

Another evidence of the lack of faith in the clothes they were able to make was the eagerness with which the Confederate women sought the few bolts of factory-made cloth that came in through the blockade. "Their firm faith in their home-made clothes collapsed in sight of these treasures," said Parthenia Antoinette Hague of a group of women who had traveled a long distance to purchase some English prints.[92] Mrs. Burton Harrison said that she was delighted to get imported clothes, since the chamois gloves made by her and her friends were "dreadful looking"; while others declared that they preferred to go barefooted than to appear in shoes made at home.[93]

Still other women despaired of keeping in style. Unable to secure style books or suitable materials, they threw fashion to the winds and appeared in bizarre and fantastic makeshifts. Some idea of the extremes to which such costumes could go is given by the following description of the "full dress toilette" in which a Richmond woman appeared before the Federal authorities after the fall of that city. "I was dressed," said Phoebe Yates Pember, "in boots of untanned leather tied with thongs; a Georgia woven homespun dress in black and white blocks—the white, cotton yarn; the black, an old silk, washed, scraped with broken glass into pulp, and then carded and spun; . . . a hat plaited of rye straw picked from the field back of us, dyed black with walnut juice, a shoe-string for ribbon to encircle it; and knitted worsted gloves of three shades of green—the darkest bottle shade being around the wrist, while the color tapered to the loveliest blossom of pea at the finger-tips."[94]

✓   ✓   ✓   ✓

In spite of the numerous imperfections it may be concluded that the Confederate woman was reasonably successful in overcoming the serious deficiency in domestic supplies which the blockade imposed upon the South. Her teas and coffees may have been unpalatable; her drugs may have been crude; her home-made dresses and shoes unstylish and awkward; and her stationery, buttons, pins, and other small articles poor substitutes for the factory-made originals; but these creations of hers filled a void in the domestic economy of the period which had to be filled in order to prevent a relapse into semibarbarism.

The Confederacy might have survived its allotted span of four years solely on the crude staples which its fields plentifully afforded, but its existence would have been much more difficult had not its women been able to supplement these basic necessities with articles necessary for existence on a level of civilization in keeping with traditional standards.

CHAPTER XII

RELATIONS WITH THE SLAVES

NO aspect of the history of the Confederacy is more remarkable than the behavior of the three and one-half million slaves, upon whose proper discipline the social and economic welfare of the South had long depended. Early in the war it was recognized by both the enemies and the friends of the Confederacy that the conduct of these slaves would be an important factor in determining the outcome of the struggle. "A thousand torches would have disbanded the Southern army," and had there been a general servile revolt, the Confederacy would have fallen more suddenly and more violently than it did fall as the result of Union victories. Consequently, the Northerners dangled before the slaves, with ever-increasing frequency as the war progressed, the bait of freedom through insurrection, and the fear that the Negroes would accept this allurement haunted the thoughtful moments of every defender of the Southern cause. And yet, despite the absence of great numbers of the white men at the front, these patient blacks generally remained submissive and faithful to their owners, and their labors produced the food that was needed for the armies and the cotton with which it was possible to secure the supplies and loans that came from abroad. That this situation prevailed was due largely to the temperament of the Negroes and to the precautions taken by the Southern white men; but it was also due in part to the efforts of the Southern white women. Willingly staying behind on the plantations while the men went to war, these women continued to exercise their accustomed supervision over the slaves and sought in various ways to meet the new problems that were created in this respect by the war emergency.

RESTLESSNESS AND DISAFFECTION AMONG THE SLAVES

In considering the possible conduct of the blacks, the Southern women professed faith in the loyalty of their slaves, but not to the same extent as they regarded that of the other elements of Southern population. The fidelity of the slave, in the opinion of great numbers of women, was merely the ox-like submissiveness of an inferior being which could be maintained in emergencies only by the use of force.[1] Shrewder feminine observers, crediting the blacks with more intelligence, regarded their show of loyalty as but a mask behind which was hidden wise but sinister ambitions. "Not by word or look," wrote Mary Boykin Chesnut during the bombardment of Fort Sumter, "can we detect any change in the demeanor of these negro servants. . . . Are they stolidly stupid? or wiser than we are: silent and strong, biding their time?"[2] Likewise, there were many women who shared with the enemy the belief that there was a conflict of interest between the two races of the South and viewed with alarm the desire of the North to make this conflict the basis of internal disturbances. Try as they would, they could not forget the ominous words uttered by a Northerner on the eve of the war. " 'You cannot fight!' " this man had said. " 'Your worst enemy is in your midst. Let us but sound the tocsin of war and your slaves will rise! Why, you will have murder and the cutting of throats in every house.' "[3] The public authorities were also alarmed over the possible conduct of the slaves to such an extent that they took measures for strengthening the citizen patrols, and in some cases detailed detachments of light cavalry to guard plantations.[4]

Although the apprehensions of the whites were not followed by any slave revolts, there were many instances in which the blacks failed to serve their owners with a whole-souled loyalty. Slaves who had worked with apparent zeal for the Southern cause under the influence of their mistresses, worked with the same zeal for the Northern cause when they fell under the influence of the Federals. While serving their masters in plantation labor, many slaves kept the Northerners posted regarding Southern conditions through the "grape-vine telegraph," and when the enemy arrived, they willingly worked on Federal fortifications and heeded the suggestion that they enlist in the Union army. Likewise, thousands of Negroes became restless when the enemy was near and in many cases fled to his lines. This was especially true of Richmond where, during 1863 and 1864, there were frequent thefts from wardrobes and pantries and, while these occurrences were being investigated, flights of the suspected servants to the easily accessible lines of the Federals. Not even the residence of President Davis was exempt from such annoyances;[5] thefts, attempts at incendiarism, dangerous propaganda, and flights occurring so often among the servants of the Executive Mansion that Mary Boykin Chesnut feared for the safety of the President and his family.[6] And paradoxical as it may seem, the servants who fled from Southern mistresses were often the ones previously considered the most faithful. "The first news which greeted us this morning before we were out of bed," said a typical account of such desertions, "was that Uncle Billy, the servant we trusted most, had gone off to the Yankees. . . . We always looked on him as a faithful servant."[7]

Women frequently complained that the absence of the men from their plantations produced an alarming demoralization among the slaves. A governess on the plantation of Governor Milton in Florida noted that the Negroes had become thievish and slovenly in the absence of their master. These slaves, she wrote, "thought proper to make high charges for the fish they caught in their leisure time. . . . The hen-houses were left open or broken, the hens lay astray in the woods, and we scarcely got one egg without buying it. The garden fence was down, and the calves got all the milk from the cows; butter became a luxury."[8] A Virginia woman declared that in the absence of her husband "the slaves are trying themselves to see what amount of thieving they can commit,"[9] and a North Carolina woman, laboring under this same handicap, asserted that her slaves had become "awkward, inefficient, and even lazy."[10]

That the absence of white men from the plantations could tempt the Negroes to conduct which was interpreted as being even worse than laziness and slovenliness was demonstrated in a number of letters written by the feminine members of the Pettigrew family of Abbeville District, South Carolina. Margaret Pettigrew sounded the alarm in 1862, complaining that "no authority scarcely" existed among her slaves and expressing doubts that "things will ever be or seem quite the same again."[11] Similar alarm was expressed by Caroline Pettigrew later in the same year. "I feel no confidence in them," she wrote to her husband regarding the Negroes. "You will find that they have all changed in their manner, not offensive but slack." Aroused during the following year by "an atrocious article" in a Northern newspaper counseling servile insurrection, she prayed that this advice would not be taken by her slaves, but she sorrowfully noted that "there is a great and increasing disaffection among the negroes."[12] Some months later a third member of the family was panic-stricken when she heard that the home guard was to be called away. "If the men are going," she wrote, "then awful things are coming, and I don't want to stay. My God, the women and children, it will be murder and ruin. There are many among the black people and they only want a chance."[13]

The disaffection that existed among the slaves was especially evident in the delight with which they received the Federal conquerors of Southern settlements. With these conquerors came bands of music playing martial airs, whisky flowing freely, commissary stores, the offer of freedom, a chance to enlist in the United States army, and the promise of social and economic opportunities. Abolition preachers collected crowds of slaves, harangued them on the cruelty of the servitude which had been imposed upon the Negro race, and announced that Abraham Lincoln was the Moses sent by God to deliver them "from the land of Egypt and house of bondage" and carry them into the Promised Land.[14] "The poor servants," wrote a woman of northern Virginia who had witnessed such a scene, "could not resist these intoxicating influences. . . . Scarcely a representative of the sons and daughters of Africa remained in that whole section of the country; they have all gone to Canaan, by way of the York River, Chesapeake Bay, and the Potomac."[15]

LOYALTY AND DEVOTION OF THE SLAVES

It should be emphasized, however, that the disaffection which has just been described was very limited until the actual arrival of the enemy; and that, when manifested before that event, it was characterized by a minimum of violence. Flight to the Federals was the most flagrant manner in which the blacks showed their sympathy for the enemy, and for the thousands who fled there were tens of thousands who remained behind to labor for masters and mistresses in the traditional fashion. The conflict of interest between masters and servants, which has been mentioned, did not take an active form as long as the Southern whites remained in control of plantations and towns, and in no instance did a slave raise an insurrectionary hand. In fact, for all practical purposes, the Negroes were so loyal to those who were waging a war to keep them in bondage that their conduct has excited the wonder of historians and evoked the lasting gratitude of those who cherished the cause of the Confederacy.

To later generations of Southern women it may seem strange that the women of the Civil War period should have possessed such a strong faith in the loyalty and devotion of their servants and that, generally speaking, the conduct of the blacks was such as to justify this faith. Yet, according to the overwhelming mass of contemporary evidence, thousands of plantation mistresses were able to sleep, alone with their children behind unbolted doors, without apprehending or experiencing harm from the slaves who surrounded them. Among those who gave testimony to this effect was an English clergyman on a visit in 1862 to a plantation of two hundred slaves in South Carolina. "Here was an English lady with her little English maid," wrote this visitor, " 'dwelling among her own people, the sable descendants of Canaan, as safely as if in their native land—yea, safer; for they slept with their doors and windows unbolted."[16] Margaret Junkin Preston spoke with similar emphasis. "One thing which surprises me very much in the progress of this war," she wrote at Lexington, Virginia, in 1862, "is the entire quietness and subordination of the negroes.

We have slept all winter with the doors of our house, outside and inside, all unlocked. . . . It is more remarkable, this quietness and sense of security, because there are no men left in town, except old men and boys. . . . There is not, and never has been, a particle of anything like insurrectionary movements."[17] Likewise, Catherine Ann Edmonston, a North Carolina plantation mistress whose extensive diaries show that she was aware of every current of thought and action in the Confederacy, professed to have no fear of a servile insurrection. "It would astonish our Northern brethren and England also," she wrote in 1862, "did they know how little we regard it." Although surrounded by hundreds of slaves, she was able to write, less than two months before the end of the war, "I am on an island—a kind of Anglo-Saxon Robinson Crusoe with Ethiopians only for companions— think of it! I sit here the only white person for miles and they cut off from me by an angry sea—and have not a single tremor."[18]

In some cases the Negroes, sensing the trouble which the war had brought to their mistresses, are reported to have been more dutiful in their services than they had previously been. "The servants," wrote Susan Dabney Smedes of the conduct of the slaves on the Dabney plantation in Mississippi, "went about their duties, we thought, more conscientiously than before. They seemed to do better when there was trouble in the white family, and they knew that there was trouble enough when all the young men in the family were off at the wars."[19] Another woman asserted that her slaves "took pride in feeling themselves the only protectors of the mistress at home deprived of her natural support and guidance from the stronger sex."[20] Negroes were reported to have stood guard over their mistresses at night and to have willingly performed many other duties which would have caused the women great perplexity.[21]

That the Negroes were capable of acts of gallantry and heroism in the interest of their mistresses is illustrated in numerous accounts. Such conduct included the guarding of women imperiled by the enemy and the rebuking of Federal pillagers. During the siege of Vicksburg a slave standing before the cave of his mistress gallantly cried to her as a shell took his life, " 'Don't stay here, mistress. I said the Lord wanted me.' " Another protector of this same woman saved her life twice; once by tossing a shell out of her cave before it exploded, and a second time by forestalling the attack of a Negro intruder by brandishing a carving knife in the latter's face.[22] When the Federals took possession of a hospital at Covington, Georgia, all the attendants except one colored woman fled. This dusky heroine, according to one who was present, "didn't see what made all de fool niggers an' wimmin run for, no how; de Yankees didn' want dem. She wan't 'fraid of dem; she was gwine to stay right dar, and stan' her ground, so she was."[23] A striking example of a Negro rebuking marauding Federals was the action of a servant of the Morgan family at Baton Rouge. " 'Ain't you 'shamed,' " he cried as he observed the Federals sacking the Morgan home, " 'to destroy all dis here, that belongs to a poor widow lady who's got two daughters to support?' "[24] Another example of this type of conduct, no less striking, was that of Aunt Betty, one of the Toombs servants at Washington, Georgia. When the Federals, appearing on the premises in search of General Robert Toombs, asked where her master was, she replied, " 'Ef I knowed, I wouldn't tell you' "; and when the intruders ordered her to prepare a meal for them, she turned her broad back and said, " 'I won't do no sech a thing; I'se a gwineter help my mistress pack up her clo'es.' "[25]

Contemporary chronicles relate many instances of servants making sacrifices for their white people during the war. Often in boxes prepared for the soldiers there were articles contributed by Negro women and children. Eight of the two hundred dollars raised at a raffle in Charleston for the benefit of the garrison at Fort Sumter came from the sale of toys given by two black children; "a lot of vegetables" was the gift of one colored woman to the troops of that city; and a box for the Charleston soldiers from the village of Helena was found to contain substantial contributions from slaves.[26] During flights or conflagrations servants were known to have saved the belongings of their mistresses in preference to their own, and when the devastation of the enemy brought the women face to face with destitution, it was often the faithful blacks who prevented the realization of that calamity. Hundreds of Negroes were observed in the Confederate retreat from Baton Rouge in 1862, carrying the bundles and babies of their white owners. When asked what they had saved for themselves, they almost invariably replied, " 'Bless your heart, honey, I was glad to get away with the mistress's things; I didn't think 'bout mine.' "[27] One of the Elmore servants in South Carolina secured salt and a hog, which he cut up and stored in Columbia for Grace Elmore and her mother; then, "weighting himself with all sorts of things," he made his way to the plantation in York District to look after the members of the family who had remained there. "I shall never forget," wrote Ellen Elmore, "his happiness as he emptied his pockets of his gifts—a pound of coffee to one, sugar for the children, a candle to another, and a lot of preserves from Miss Grace to all—not one was forgotten."[28]

With such experiences as these in mind, great numbers of the Southern women received with scorn and ridicule Lincoln's bid for the slaves to rise and assert their freedom. The Emancipation Proclamation was compared with the Chinese waving their flags and beating their drums in the face of the enemy.[29] The author of this document, it was asserted, would go "down marked with the finger of scorn to the latest posterity—for an act alike weak and wicked."[30] A Louisiana girl, observing the joyous manner in which the Negroes continued to work in spite of the Emancipator's offer, was moved to exclaim, "And to think, old Abe, wants to deprive us of all our fun! No more cotton, sugar cane, or rice! No more old black aunties and uncles! No more rides on mule teams, no more songs in the cane fields, no more steaming kettles, no more black and shining faces around the furnace fires! If Lincoln could see the grinding season on the plantation, he would recall his proclamation. As it is, he has only proved himself a fool, without injury to us."[31]

STRENGTHENING THE BONDS OF AFFECTION

Throughout the war the women strove actively to maintain the good discipline of the slaves, an objective the importance of which has already been noted. Among the various measures which they adopted to this end were stimulating and reciprocating the affections which the blacks felt for the whites; promoting contentment by taking an active part in the religious and recreational functions of their wards; and striving to stifle grounds of discontent by maintaining to the best of their ability the standards of material comfort and well-being to which the slaves had been accustomed. They also sought to promote distrust of the Northerners among the slaves, and when the occasion demanded, they used moral persuasion and even force to supplement the efforts of the men in suppressing disobedient influences.

The intimate bonds of affection which frequently served to prevent antagonism between mistress and slave are revealed by many phrases dropped here and there in the letters of the times. "Remember me kindly to all," wrote Anne E. Hume, a South Carolina refugee, in closing a communication to one of the slaves who had remained at her home in Charleston. "I often think of and pray for you all, and trust, God willing, we may all meet in peace in our beloved home once more, but if not, that we may meet in Heaven."[32] A South Carolina slave, writing to his mistress from Winnsboro, closed his letter with, "I hope, dear Mistress, I hope to hear from you very soon. No more at present. I am your faithful servant."[33]

The sincerity of these expressions of affection is demonstrated by the numerous acts of kindness which the women performed for their slaves in times of illness and other adversity. "No clergyman's wife in England," wrote a visitor from that country to the Confederate States in 1862, "can be more conscientious in visiting the sick and aged amongst her husband's parishioners, reading the Bible to them, and furnishing them with medicine and little comforts, than are the ladies of the South in administering to the wants of the helpless amongst their own people."[34] Although this statement may be too sweeping in some of its details to inspire full confidence, its substantial accuracy is verified by many other records of the period. On an Alabama plantation, according to Parthenia Antoinette Hague, a sick Negro boy was not only taken into the plantation house but was also given medicines and gruels at regular intervals as well as hot bricks for his feet.[35] Catherrine Ann Edmonston prepared a bottle for a Negro baby prematurely weaned by its mother on her plantation in North Carolina, and when the home of one of her slaves was burned, she utilized her private stores to give him household supplies which could not otherwise be secured. Her diary reveals that she also labored diligently to provide substitutes for the medicines which she was unable to purchase for her slaves through the blockade.[36]

The extent to which solicitude for the welfare of ill servants could go is further illustrated by two instances occurring in South Carolina and Florida, respectively. On hearing that one of her servants was mortally ill, a Charleston woman wrote to her husband, "About poor Catherine I have thought ever since reading of her suffering and danger. Although luxuries are so high-priced, let the poor thing have as much tea, etc., etc., that she wants, and tell her that her absent mistress thinks of her and will pray that she may be prepared for her great change."[37] The mistress of Sylvania, the plantation of Governor Milton in Florida, was intensely provoked by the refusal of an English governess to give a sick slave her last bottle of brandy. " 'You thought brandy too good to give a nigger,' " said the governor's wife. " 'We don't consider anything too good for our niggers, and give them whatever we may have ourselves when they are sick and need it.' "[38]

The women also retained the good will of their slaves by intervening to protect them against the tyranny of the white men, especially against that of the members of the non-slaveholding class. Their soft hearts were often troubled when the blacks were punished for misconduct, even when they knew that such punishment was necessary in order to maintain discipline, and they frequently exerted themselves to see that the penalties were lightened. A striking illustration of this attitude is found in Eliza Frances Andrews' account of the return of a slave who had absconded four times from her sister's plantation in Georgia. "He implored me to beg 'missis' to forgive him," she wrote, "and I couldn't help taking his part. . . . A soldier caught him and brought him back this morning with his hands tied behind him. Such sights sicken me, and I couldn't help crying when I saw the poor wretch." Her sister sent the truant to jail more as an example than as a punishment, giving orders to the sheriff not to be severe. "But there is no telling," sorrowfully concluded the kind-hearted diarist, "what brutal men who never had any negroes of their own will do; they don't know how to feel for the poor creatures."[39]

The bonds of affection existing between mistress and slave were so strengthened by such acts of kindness that in some localities the planters' wives felt that they had less to fear from the blacks than from the poorer classes of Southern whites.[40] "We are surrounded," said a typical account of the behavior of these "poor whites," "by a lot of low-born country people—'home-made Yankees!' . . . We live daily and hourly in expectation of being reported, robbed, burned out, or murdered by these vultures in human form."[41] Another planter's wife reported that the burning of her house was threatened by a woman of this class. When the granddaughter of the would-be incendiary was asked why this threat was made, the girl replied, " 'Oh, because she don't like you and the Secesh, and wants the Yanks to come in and take off the niggers, so that poor white folks can get work.' "[42]

ENCOURAGEMENT OF RELIGION AND RECREATION

It was only natural that the women of the Confederacy should have played a vital part in the promotion of Negro religion. Intensely religious themselves, they would have been odd creatures had they not mixed spiritual sympathies and activities with the other sympathies and activities which characterized their relations with the slaves. Moreover, religion had long been regarded as an important factor in the maintenance of slave discipline in the South, and it continued to be so regarded during the war. It taught the virtues of humility and obedience, and it offered an other-worldly realization for ambitions which might else have found expression in discontent with the lot of this world. Consequently, the Southern women viewed with satisfaction the spirited revival meetings which were characteristic of the war-time life of the slaves; they read the Bible to the Negroes, prayed to them, instructed them in Sunday school, and listened with sympathy to their confessions of wrong-doing.

The efficacy of revival meetings in causing the Negroes to forget the turbulence and disorder of the world of realities which surrounded them, was noted with especial gratification. "Would Abolitionists, could they look upon that scene, fail to admit the blessings American 'slavery' had brought to the savage black man?" thought Mrs. Clement C. Clay as she sat in St. Catherine's Church on Beech Island, South Carolina, in 1864, watching several hundred blacks listening ecstatically to a discussion of heavenly problems, while, within a day's ride, an army bent upon revolutionizing the earthly status of these Negroes was marching.[43] During the same year the Federals in making a raid on Grove Hill, the plantation of the Breckinridge family in the Valley of Virginia, found only one Negro on the place who was touched by the event. The reason for this singular unconcern with such an important happening, a member of the Breckinridge family reveals in her diary, was that the servants were so absorbed in a revival that no thought could be given to other matters.[44]

Contemporary chronicles contain many other illustrations of the interest manifested by the white women in the religious enthusiasms of the Negroes. "Can I ever forget," wrote Mrs. Gilmer Breckinridge, "our Sabbath evening prayer meeting when my full heart ran over as their simple, earnest prayers ascended to our common Father to protect 'our dear master and bring him home safe again'?"[45] No less significant was the Sunday instruction imparted to the slaves by thousands of conscientious plantation mistresses throughout the South.[46] The moral precepts which usually accompanied such teaching frequently brought repentance of sins. "Amazed and bewildered," wrote Sarah Morgan at Baton Rouge after such a period of instruction, "I looked at the touching tableau before me of kissing and reconciliation, for Lucy can bear malice toward no one, and is ready to forgive before others repent. . . . Sometimes Lucy sings a wild hymn, 'Did you ever hear the heaven bells ring?' 'Come, my loving brothers,' 'When I put on my starry crown,' etc.; and after some such scenes as that just described, it is pleasant to hear them going out of the room saying, 'Goodnight, Miss Sarah!' 'God bless Miss Sarah!' and all that."[47]

Intensely religious as they were, the majority of the Southern women had the good judgment, however, to refrain from opposing certain peccadilloes for which the Negroes were notorious. This attitude was well illustrated in their tolerating the immoralities which were apparently inherent in the slave system. Although the rigid standards of morality which the women prescribed for themselves extended to the point of excluding the books of the more advanced women writers of the times from their shelves, no attempt was made to exclude lewd women servants from kitchens and bedrooms. "Bad books," wrote Mary Boykin Chesnut with a critical acumen rare among the women of the Confederacy, "are not allowed house room . . . but bad women, if they are not white, or serve in a menial capacity, may swarm the house unmolested; this ostrich game is thought a Christian act." The assumption of a less tolerant attitude toward the derelictions of the slave women would have been more in keeping with the much vaunted moral standards of the Southern white women, but this would have interfered with the smooth working of the slave system. "It is best to let the sinners alone, poor things," added Mrs. Chesnut apologetically. "If they are good servants otherwise, do not dismiss them; all that will come out straight as they grow older, and it does."[48]

Likewise, in spite of the sternness of legislators and the abjurations of moralists, the Negroes continued to enjoy throughout the war the numerous simple pleasures to which they had been accustomed. Among such pleasures were the Saturday night dances and 'possum hunts; also the singing of plantation melodies in which a dozen or more Negroes would indulge as they stood on the white sand of the plantation yard with the ladies of the household looking on silently from the colonnade. Another was the annual barbecue held in the plantation yard after the crops were "laid by" in July or August. The preparation of this feast created a weird scene on the night before the event as the Negroes, amid the ruddy glow of pine torches, "would be attending the roasting flesh, some with the swab, basting with the seasoning; some laughing loud enough to wake the sleeping echoes; some lazily stretched on the ground thinking of tomorrow's feast." When the morrow came, three or four large tables would be improvised in the shade of the grandest trees, weighted with the flesh of oxen, sheep and shoats, great pans of chicken pie, and large quantities of fruits, vegetables, light bread, and cakes made of bolted meal.[49] Nor was the desire of the race to appear in fine clothes on Sundays and holidays interrupted by the prevailing scarcity in wearing apparel. An Englishwoman traveling in Georgia was amazed at seeing "crowds of slaves in gayest attire . . . in dresses more expensive than many of their masters and mistresses, in those times of blockade and economy,"[50] and a traveler in Texas noted "innumerable negroes and negresses parading about the streets in the most outrageously grand costumes—silks, satins, crinolines, hats and feathers, lace, mantles, etc., forming an absurd contrast to the simple dresses of their mistresses."[51]

Although local masculine observers joined with the foreign travelers in characterizing "the airs and assumptions of dandified negroes" as "disgusting and offensive," the Southern women tolerated and even encouraged the sartorial and convivial extravagances of their slaves. This attitude is perhaps best illustrated by the part taken by the white women in Negro weddings. They often aided in the preparation of the wedding feast, decked the bride and her attendants with all the finery at their disposal, and witnessed the nuptial ceremonies, not in the slave cabins or meeting houses but in the spacious halls of their own residences. Such weddings were ostentatious affairs, even in war-torn Richmond. "I was sitting in a cool corner," remarked an astonished English guest at a hotel in that city, "when a great deal of rustling and giggling on the stairs in the hall attracted my attention; and looking up, beheld a troop of negro damsels all attired in white, profusely relieved by flowers and ribbons." It was a bridal party. One of the bride's attendants was arrayed in a gown "of white muslin, fancifully tucked to the waist, bouquets of white roses on the bodice and sleeves," white kid gloves, and "a wreath of white roses around her head of wavy, not wooly hair." She also wore gold bracelets, carried a gold watch and chain, and sported an embroidered pocket-handkerchief and a gaudy fan. Even more astounding to the English visitor than the magnificence of these costumes was the fact that they were largely provided by the women guests of the hotel.[52]

The plantation mistresses were not able to be as lavish as the dames of the Confederate capital in preparing for the weddings of their servants, but they showed the same zeal in these efforts. Representative accounts reveal them baking the wedding cakes, making the underclothing and bridal dresses, arranging the bridal wreaths on sable foreheads, witnessing the ceremony in the halls of plantation mansions, and standing on the verandas wreathed in smiles while the dusky company below ate the lavish feast prepared in the kitchen of the plantation house.[53] "On Friday E and I really worked," wrote a member of the Breckinridge family, "helping Matilda make cakes for her party. In the evening made a beautiful head-dress for Susan and carried it over to Aunt Sucky's. They begged E and I so hard to come to the wedding that we actually went. The bride looked very pretty, dressed in pink tarlatan. I arranged some ivy leaves for her."[54]

In giving their cast-off finery to the blacks and looking upon the entertainments of the slaves with approval, the women of the Confederacy assumed an attitude which was probably wiser than that of the stern critics of Negro amusements; for the indulgence of the race's instinct for pleasure created a degree of contentment which might not have been manifested had a policy of repression forced the thoughts of the Negroes into more serious channels. Dressing in fine clothes and taking long rides appeared, in the opinion of Catherine Cooper Hopley, to make the slaves into "merry, noisy, loquacious creatures, wholly unconscious of care or anxiety."[55]

OTHER METHODS OF MAINTAINING DISCIPLINE

Another potent factor in maintaining the loyalty of the slaves was the determination of the mistresses to continue as near as possible their traditional standards of living. A goodly portion of the cloth-making activity which has been described was for the benefit of the Negroes; and in trying to equip each slave with his customary heavy suit for winter and his customary two light suits for summer, many women showed a zeal comparable to that which they demonstrated in their efforts to equip the men absent in the army. Although the providing of the simple diet to which the blacks had been accustomed did not present such difficulties as those encountered in attempting to satisfy their clothing needs, the food problem nevertheless demanded careful attention and at times necessitated arduous sacrifices. To Negroes who did their own cooking, the plantation mistresses continued to apportion the provisions on Saturday night. Bacon and corn meal formed the basis of these rations, but sorghum, coffee substitutes, and the "Sunday cheer" of flour, lard, and butter were occasionally added. In the interest of economy, the food of the slaves was often cooked in the kitchen of the plantation house under the direct supervision of the mistress herself; and where the slaves were few and the provisions especially scarce, the same cooking utensils served for both races. Where sacrifices were necessary in order that the slaves might be adequately fed, the women were usually ready to make them. When meat was scarce, white households were known to have denied themselves bacon in order that the men working in the fields might have it.[56] The members of the Dabney family, fleeing from their plantation in Mississippi before the advance of Grant, willingly shared their limited rations with a little black servant, with the result that this servant was the only person in the party not hungry.[57] When a slave returned from a still in South Carolina, without the supply of whisky for which he had been sent by the mistress of a plantation in that state, saying that he had been beaten by armed men, she resolved that her slaves must have the whisky at any sacrifice. She secured it by riding to the still herself, despite the risks which such a trip involved.[58]

The women also sought to promote the good behavior of their slaves by fostering among them an attitude of suspicion or hostility toward the would-be deliverers from the North. The Federals were described to the Negroes as being destroyers of friendships, vandals, and robbers who would inflict their cruelties upon the blacks as readily as upon the whites. Some Negroes accepted this view, regarding the coming of the invaders with horror and the return of their masters and mistresses after the enemy had departed as a godsend. Servants were known to break into wild yells, as though they expected to be devoured by monsters, when they heard that the enemy was coming.[59]

As a matter of fact, the conduct of the enemy was in many cases of such character as to justify the suspicions which had thus been aroused. Although the Federals did not turn out to be the monsters which were expected, they frequently dispensed more harm to the Negroes than good. To follow the suggestions of freedom which they held out to the slaves, meant the breaking of social ties which were in many ways beneficial to the Negroes, the acceptance of new friends, and the assumption of untried ways of living. It meant the sacrifice of the care, the guidance, and the other protective advantages of the slave system, in favor of the unaccustomed necessity of providing for themselves. Furthermore, the Negroes had reason to believe that in many instances their so-called liberators were unsympathetic and even cruel. As was predicted by the women, the invaders often robbed the blacks as well as the whites. " 'Dey jes' tun ebry ting bottom side up, mam'!' " said one Negro in describing to his mistress the manner in which the invaders treated his hidden valuables. " 'De stockin' wid de chillum good luck money cum fuss,' " he added; and " 'Dey grab dat.' "[60] Likewise, the rank and file of the Federal army frequently showed contempt for the blacks. Although the Union guards placed around homes were capable of denouncing the Southern "nabobs" for their alleged disdain of manual labor, they were also capable of saying that their own wives were too proud to allow Negroes to enter their homes.[61] " 'Fight for the nigger!' " they were likely to exclaim in the presence of both whites and blacks in the invaded areas. " 'We'd see 'em in the bottom of the swamp before we'd fight for 'em.' "[62]

FORCEFUL MEASURES

When the measures of kindness and persuasion which have just been described failed to produce the required effect, the plantation mistresses did not hesitate to resort to more forceful methods of slave discipline. They ferreted out causes of incipient disloyalty, harangued the slaves on the wisdom of good conduct, led them out of reach of the invaders, confronted mobs of disorderly blacks, and threatened the insubordinates with the kind of vengeance which their masculine associates had been accustomed to inflict upon rebellious bondmen.

The methods used by plantation mistresses in ferreting out dissatisfaction were well illustrated by the conduct of Ida Dulany on her plantation near Upperville, Virginia. Discovering in 1862 that a group of Federals camped near by was trying to stir up discontent among her slaves by placing Unionists in some of her houses, she discreetly moved the Negroes to a section of the plantation which was unaffected by such influences. When she learned that some of her slaves were expressing dissatisfaction with their lot by refusing to work, she resolved to take decisive action. She sold some of them, hired others out, transported a third group to a safer area, whipped at least one, and then began to visit her fields personally to see that those whom she had allowed to remain were performing their allotted tasks. "This morning," she was able to report with satisfaction on June 28, 1862, "I walked towards the barn to see what the hands were doing. Sam and Ben were plowing and all five of the boys were at work. I gave each a separate task, telling them to come to me when they had finished."[63]

The success of a mistress in saving her slaves from the demoralizing influence of the Federals by removing them out of reach of the invaders, was evidenced in the case of Mrs. C. B. Howard of central Georgia. Hearing in April, 1865, that a party of Federals under General Wilson was about to invade her plantation, she resolved to transport the male members of her group of two hundred slaves to a thinly populated area south of her home. On the evening before the projected flight she summoned the slaves in question to her back porch and, under the light of flickering torches, revealed her plans to them. "I reminded them," she wrote later, "of their master's absence; how he had committed his wife and children to their care; how desirous was I to be able to tell him on his return that they deserved his confidence to the last." When she appeared early the next morning to lead the retreat, all but two of the slaves followed her.[64]

That it was possible for women of determination to cower insubordinate blacks when the latter manifested such tendencies during the last days of the Confederacy, was likewise demonstrated on numerous occasions. When a nineteen-year-old Florida girl heard a group of Negroes around her home singing "We'll hang Jeff Davis on a sour apple tree," she rushed into their midst and put them to flight with a carriage whip.[65] While visiting one of their plantations to demand the keys of their corn cribs, a South Carolina woman and her daughter found their carriage surrounded by a group of armed blacks demanding blood. The two women refused to retreat, however, and insisted in such a forceful manner upon having the keys that the desired articles were given them.[66] When a Columbia woman observed that one of her servants was disaffected by rumors that Sherman was coming, she brandished a pistol and warned the Negress so effectively that the latter showed no more signs of disaffection until after the enemy had arrived.[67] Noting that the Negroes were resorting to plunder after the passing of Sherman's army, Mrs. A. P. Aldrich of Barnwell, South Carolina, went among her slaves, told them that no law had been passed setting them free, and warned them that when they were free they could not be fed and clothed without work. To her great gratification they retired to their cabins and early the next morning resumed their accustomed duties.[68] Such tactics did not succeed in preventing the ultimate demoralization of slave discipline, it is true, for forces over which the women had no control shortly afterward decreed the permanent destruction of the South's "peculiar institution"; but it is likely that had the Union authorities not been in a position to disrupt completely the bonds between masters and slaves, the women of the Confederacy would have been a powerful factor in restoring the Negroes to the position which Southern whites thought proper for them.

✓ ✓ ✓ ✓

From what has been pointed out in this chapter, it is evident that the women of the Confederacy played an important part in maintaining slavery, an institution which they regarded as the corner stone of Southern society. Consciously and unconsciously they strove for its perpetuation through a variety of activities. Remaining among the blacks during the war, they promoted the bonds of affection which existed between the races; they endeavored to eradicate causes for servile discontent by furthering the religious, recreational, and physical well-being of their wards; and on occasions when such acts of kindness were not sufficient to insure the maintenance of slave discipline, they stood ready to supplement the efforts of the white men by resorting to more drastic measures. It would be an exaggeration to claim that the efforts of the women constituted the most important factor in maintaining the integrity of slavery until the end of the war; the inert temperament of the Negro and the nervous watchfulness of the Southern white men were factors which were doubtless of equal importance. Nevertheless, it is difficult to believe that the system could have survived as long as it did, in the face of the powerful factors which were fighting for its destruction, had not the women been active participants in the battle for its preservation. Nor was the final destruction of the "peculiar institution" due to any relenting on the part of the women; it was due to external forces over which they had no control.

CHAPTER XIII

GAYETY AND EXTRAVAGANCE

THE Confederate War accentuated the prominence of the Southern lady in the social gayeties to which she had long been accustomed. As the apex of a society which had long regarded itself as the reëmbodiment of medieval chivalry and for the preservation of which the war was being waged, she continued to demand and receive the fealty of gentlemen as a sort of natural right; and the fact that the men were frequently separated from her presence because of military duties endowed her with the romantic splendor of the distant and made her company on the rare occasion of the furlough a joy devoutly anticipated. In places where troops were concentrated she derived an additional social advantage from the fact that the men always outnumbered the women, and she was able under war conditions to engage in many novel activities from which she had formerly been restrained by a social system that emphasized the Victorian proprieties. For the first time in the history of the South she traveled without male escort, secured remunerative employment, was absorbed by political and military discussion, and on one occasion at least made a public address. Likewise, it should be noted that the Southern lady was not inclined to be unsympathetic toward the atmosphere of gayety which was created by the emotions of war time. Accustomed to spend her time in the gratification of feminine vanities and pleasures, she was capable of being charmed by the martial music, the patriotic oratory, the handsome men in uniform, and the other glamorous features of a country at war. When criticized, as was often the case, for indulging in excessive social pleasures and extravagant personal adornment, she could reply by ignoring the actualities of the war or by resorting to the convenient rationalization that the emergency demanded unusual conduct; and if, as befitted the tragedies and anxieties of the period, she wept frequently, the ability to follow tears with laughter was not to her an impossibility.

THE ELEGANCE OF CONFEDERATE SOCIETY

The Confederacy was inaugurated with a flare of social display in which the feminine element took a prominent part. From Charleston, Montgomery, and Richmond, the centers of activity where women of prominence gathered, came accounts of social events almost as conspicuous as the political and military events which occurred at those places. Some women, as has been suggested,[1] were so gay that they seem not to have realized that they were standing on the brink of a tragic war; others resolved to be as gay as possible in the short interval before the arrival of that actuality. There "could not be," said a witness of the "elegant *fête champêtre*" held in Charleston in honor of General Beauregard, "too much beauty to do honor to the occasion," and although few in civilian clothes were present, the thought of war did not cloud "the gayety of those who joined the brilliant throng that day."[2] "I was taken to drive and asked to tea," wrote Mary Boykin Chesnut in describing other phases of the social life in the South Carolina city. "There could not have been nicer suppers, more perfect of their kind than were to be found at the winding up of those festivities."[3]

In Montgomery the coming of Varina Howell Davis was an event as significant in the social sphere as had been the coming of her husband in the realm of politics. Before her arrival the ladies of the town converted the Presidential suite at the local hotel into a bower of roses. This "flowery kingdom" served to relieve the feeling of depression which the new President's wife had previously experienced, and she graciously assumed a position of leadership in the social life of the Confederate capital. An English visitor described her at this time as "a comely, sprightly woman, verging on matronhood, of good figure and manners, well dressed, ladylike, and clever," presiding without affectation of state or ceremony over receptions in a modest villa styled with some exaggeration the White House of the Confederacy.[4] Nearly every person of prominence in the South came under the influence of this woman and her coterie at these gatherings. Nor were the ladies of Montgomery to be outdone by the newly-arrived ladies of the official circle. "Such dinners at the Bibbs', such balls at the Pollards', and such receptions at Governor Moore's!" exclaimed Mrs. Louis D. Wigfall shortly after her arrival in the Alabama capital.[5]

The removal of the capital of the Confederacy from a small town to a city of some size naturally resulted in the enlargement of social functions. In fact, Richmond became such a center of gayety that to some the scene resembled a carnival rather than war. Crowds of women of various social classes thronged the hotels and boarding houses, rushing to the windows to wave handkerchiefs to favorite regiments and officers and taking advantage of abnormal conditions to express in many other ways emotions long suppressed. There were dances, receptions, and reviews. For the reviews ladies in fine carriages drove to the suburbs, there to admire and be admired by officers in bright uniforms mounted on mettlesome steeds. "What young girl's heart would not beat quicker in response to such experiences?" wrote

Mrs. Burton Harrison in recalling these events. "There were dinners cooked and served to us by our soldier lads, spread upon rough boards, and eaten out of tin plates and cups amid such a storm of rollicking gayety and high hope that war seemed a merry pastime."[6] On such occasions the wife of the President, in a landau drawn by spirited bays and surrounded by friends, was often the center of attraction.[7]

The initial clashes of arms seem to have in no way slackened the social pace of the Confederate capital. Rather did the actualities of war, as is often the case, serve to excite many women to fresh adventures. "With the knowledge that we were in a city which, more than any other, invited and defied the attacks of the enemy," wrote Mrs. Clement C. Clay, "a sense of danger spurred our spirits. Though the boom of the guns was not a distant sound, and the solemn carrying in of our wounded became increasingly frequent, few gave way to apprehensions and doubts."[8] Notwithstanding the fact that they often spent their mornings in dressing wounds, the ladies turned their evenings into entertainments for the heroes of civil and military life. Mrs. Davis was again the leader, assisted now by Mary Boykin Chesnut, Mrs. Louis D. Wigfall, Mrs. Joseph E. Johnston, Mrs. Stephen R. Mallory, Mrs. Clement C. Clay, and the wives of other prominent leaders.

For the use of the President and his family the city of Richmond purchased and furnished a residence designated the White House of the Confederacy. It was a handsome mansion with large, airy rooms, a stairway turning in graceful curves, mantels of Carrera marble, and furnishings in the elegant but restrained style of the Virginia aristocracy. There were terraced gardens and a magnificent view of the surrounding country. In describing the first reception held in this house, Judith W. McGuire wrote, "The rooms were crowded. The President looked weary and grave, but all was suavity and cordiality, and Mrs. Davis won all hearts by her usual unpretending kindness. I feel proud to have those dear rooms filled with the great, the noble, the *fair* of our land."[9] Another Virginia woman characterized the manners of the President's wife as "kind, graceful, easy and affable" and her receptions as attained by "the dignity and suavity which should very properly distinguish the drawing-room entertainments of the Chief Magistrate of a republic."[10]

The ladies of the Virginia aristocracy, although inclined at first to be somewhat suspicious of the newly-arrived women of the lower South, vied with Mrs. Davis in entertaining. Abiding in spacious houses set back from the streets in gardens, with magnolia trees guarding the portals, the Lees, the Ritchies, the Harrisons, the Cabells, the Randolphs, the Stanards, and other families with long pedigrees threw open their homes and dispensed the friendliest hospitality.[11] Deep gratitude to the battalions from the far South for coming to defend Virginia from a hated foe, lessened aristocratic reserve. "When asked into private homes," said Mrs. Burton Harrison in her reminiscences of Richmond, "we found tables laid, as of old, with shining silver and porcelain and snowy damask, although the bill of fare was unpretending."[12] Among those hostesses who were especially remembered was Martha Pierce Stanard, "who had such a charming house and gave such delicious teas, alluring such men as Soulé, Commodore Barrow, Henry Marshall, of Louisiana, and Butler King, and last, though not least, dear old Vice-President Stephens. She boasted that she had never read a book, and yet all these distinguished gentlemen gathered around her board and ate those hot muffins and broiled chicken with gusto!"[13]

Not even the great tragedies of America's bloodiest war were sufficient to destroy the craving of a considerable element of the feminine population of the Confederate capital for gayety and pleasure. In spite of Manassas, the fall of New Orleans and Vicksburg, the disasters at Chancellorsville and Gettysburg, and the numerous other engagements in which the flower of Southern manhood was sacrificed, the frivolities and joys of life continued. It is true that there were many women in Richmond who mourned the loss of friends and relatives, but it is also true that there were thousands of others who willingly subscribed to the widely-current belief that the surviving warriors who had won glories on the battlefields should, while on their furloughs, be paid for their toils with the smiles of the fair. "The younger and gayer people," wrote T. C. DeLeon in commenting upon the situation that prevailed in 1861, "indulged in 'danceable teas' . . . after their sewing circles. Imperceptibly the sewing was left for other times; and by Christmas there was a more constant—if less formal and general— round of gayety than had been known for years. This brought the citizens and strangers together, and naturally the result was a long season of more regular parties and unprecedented gayety."[14] A less friendly observer lamented that "the spirit of license tolerated in fashionable society elsewhere grew to be tolerated somewhat in Richmond," and noted that in the course of time the social set of the once conservative capital "was acknowledged 'fast enough for the fastest.' "[15]

Although the cities just described were doubtless the most important centers of Confederate society, they were by no means the only seats of elaborate social life. Mobile, for example, was said to have been so gay in 1863 that a stranger visiting the place would have concluded that a large portion of its inhabitants were "altogether unmindful of the distress and suffering that now pervades our once happy and prosperous country."[16] George Deas, who visited this city for a short time in 1864, reported that he attended sixteen weddings and twenty-seven tea parties,[17] while Sarah D. Eggleston afterwards recalled a continuous "round of receptions and parties and balls."[18] Nor was Columbia, South Carolina, without its happy hours. There were soldiers on furlough who wanted to dance and sing, and refugees who demanded amusement as well as shelter. The ladies of the Palmetto capital graciously heeded these desires, and the social life of the city was enlivened with concerts, balls, bazaars, and fairs.[19]

EXTRAVAGANT PERSONAL ADORNMENT

The spirited social activities of the Confederate lady called for the ostentation in dress which has been described in a previous chapter.[20] " 'We are going to war, Emily,' " said Mrs. Clement C. Clay to her colored maid as they were preparing to leave Washington for Richmond in 1861; " 'we shall have no need for velvets or jewels. We are going to nurse the sick; not dress and dance.' " But the maid, better understanding the requirements of the future, advised differently, and Mrs. Clay lived to feel gratified that she had followed her servant's advice. For she discovered that in the Confederate capital there were heroes to cheer and statesmen to dine and that such occasions demanded bright rather than somber costumes.[21] "We were young and in a garrisoned town, where officers and gold lace flourished," wrote another woman in explaining why fine clothes were considered necessary. "Ergo, it became us to look beautiful in their eyes, to put on goodly apparel, and, to the extent of our ability, we did."[22]

So great was the absorption of some women in this problem that they appeared to be more concerned with styles than over the fate of their country. It was said that the girls of Charleston were less interested in the outcome of the investment of that place than in newspaper announcements stating that the fashion writers of Europe had decreed that "no lady of tone will be seen promenading with trailing dresses or petticoats"; that "leather boots have high heels, colored, perhaps, and with strings and tassels of leather"; and that "to every dress for walking, modistes attach little rings, through which pass cords running through to the waist, which may be drawn up for the promenade, and dropped at home."[23] Mrs. Roger A. Pryor found that a group of Petersburg girls who visited her were more grieved over the shabby condition of their wardrobes than over the physical privations that the inhabitants of their besieged city were experiencing. " 'I really think,' " said one of the girls, " 'if we can only get along until we can wear white waists, we shall do very well. Every time a white waist is washed, it's made new—but these old flannel sacks—ugh!' " " 'Tell me about it,' " said Mrs. Pryor to another member of the group whose seraphic expression seemed to indicate that her lover had been promoted or at least granted a furlough. " 'It's just these gloves!' " replied the elated maiden. " 'I can't help it. They make me perfectly happy! They have just come through the blockade.' "[24] On returning to the South through the blockade, another observer found that the first question asked her by the women of Richmond was not, " 'How is our cause progressing in the North?' " but " 'What are the fashions?' "[25]

The craving for stylishness appears to have been so intense in certain circles that even those who tried were unable to overcome it. A woman of Bedford, Virginia, was indignant when she learned that her associates at the "sad little prayer meetings" were so frivolous as to adopt the idea of wearing "excrescences, of divers hues and contrivance, protruding from the back of ladies' heads." She resolved at first to ignore this crazy fashion, but upon finding herself made conspicuous one day as a result of her failure to conform to the prevailing style, she rushed home and added the much-prized convention to her bonnet.[26] There were even times when a woman who failed to heed the dictates of fashion ran the risk of being snubbed. A story that the aristocratic but plainly attired wife of General Lee was ordered out of one of the pews in a Richmond church by a fashionably dressed young woman, went the rounds of the Confederacy. This tale may be apocryphal, but it illustrated the attitude which many persons felt. "I have witnessed the like more than once in our Mobile churches," wrote Kate Cumming in commenting on the incident.[27]

The feminine love of ostentation created a lively trade in articles of personal adornment. When reduced to straitened circumstances by the capture of her husband, Mrs. Roger A. Pryor found little difficulty in selling her lace collars and handkerchiefs, her silk gowns, her opera cloak, and the other finery which she had accumulated in her Washington days. "There were," she disdainfully commented, "ladies in Richmond who could afford to buy, and the Confederate court offered opportunities for display."[28] Sallie A. Putnam doubted if such fine diamonds had ever been exhibited in the shops of Richmond before, and noted that many new stores were opened "in which there were splendid gems, fine watches, and other articles."[29] In certain sections the demand for feminine luxuries was so great that the importers, to the disgust of patriotic citizens, manifested a tendency to give these articles preference over war necessities. Governor Milton of Florida complained that the blockade runners took necessary wealth out of the South and returned with "barrels of oranges, bananas, ladies' shoes, fans, hats, parasols, cloaks, children's dolls, and picture books, etc."[80] The Confederate Congress eventually sought to check such extravagances by prohibiting, in February, 1864, the importation of a long list of articles, including furs, laces, antiques, metal ornaments, carriages, and precious stones.[81]

PROTESTS AND MISGIVINGS

The prevalence of excessive social gayety and the indulgence in extravagant personal adornment gave rise to vigorous protests. Such protests came from numerous quarters but especially from the old, the serious minded, and the practical patriots. The behavior of those who made merry was compared to Nero's fiddling while Rome burned and to the sound of revelry in Belgium's capital on the eve of the Battle of Waterloo. Judith W. McGuire, the patriotic and hard-working wife of a minister, voiced with emphasis the attitude of her class. "Some persons in this beleaguered city," she wrote at Richmond in January, 1865, "seem crazed on the subject of gayety. In the midst of the wounded and the dying, the low state of the commissariat, the anxiety of the whole country, the troubles of every kind with which we are surrounded, I am mortified to say that there are gay parties given in the city. . . . When returning from the hospital . . . with my heart full of the sorrows of hospital life, I passed a house where there was music and dancing. The revulsion of feeling was sickening. I thought of the gayety of Paris during the French Revolution . . . and felt shocked that our own Virginians, at such a time, should remind me of scenes we are wont to think only belonged to the lightness of foreign society."[82] Similar thoughts were expressed by many others. "Alas!" wrote Kate Cumming from the bedside of men ill in a Georgia hospital, "not all the recitals of the sufferings and more than human endurance of our brave martyrs have been able to deter us from the festal hall. The sound of the viol is heard as much, and even more, than it was before dread war held high carnival in every state of our beloved land. We forget that every step we take
'Gives back a coffin's hollow moan,'
and that every strain of music
'Wafts forth a dying soldier's groan.' "[83]

Ostentation in dress was subjected to criticism especially caustic. "The Confederacy is writhing in the throes of mighty agony," wrote a Mobile woman in 1864, "yet women can bow down to fashion's shrine and burn the most costly incense. . . . As long as they can buy glittering baubles, and throw their treasure in the extortioner's hand, so long will he press his iron heel upon the aching heart of the Sunny South."[34] Such general indictments were frequently supplemented by disdainful comments made upon individual offenders. " 'Honey,' " said a sage old Negress who was assisting Mrs. Roger A. Pryor in remodeling her old finery for the market, " 'don't you think, in these times of trouble, you might do better than to tempt po' lambs in Richmond to worship the golden calf and bow down to mammon? We prays not to be led into temptation, and you sho'ly is leadin' 'em into vanity.' "[35] This attitude was likewise expressed in higher quarters. "It is astonishing," wrote Julia LeGrand at New Orleans, "what latitude Miss N. Norcum allows herself. . . . Her father is not rich, but she dresses extravagantly, even in these times when wealthy women *generally* feel the cares and distress of the day too much to entertain a love of display."[36]

The most intense of all the criticisms, however, were those directed against Varina Howell Davis and the other ladies of the official set in Richmond. Although the entertainments at the Executive Mansion were carefully kept within the bounds of Victorian propriety, Mrs. Davis's genuine love of pleasure and social display was made the pretext for many unkind remarks from persons who disliked both her and the President. Her conduct was unfavorably contrasted with that of Mrs. Robert E. Lee, a serious-minded invalid who spent the entire period of the war in retirement knitting for the soldiers. The malicious Edward A. Pollard of the *Richmond Examiner* was exceptionally severe. He accused Mrs. Davis of attempting to create "an unrepublican court" by being snobbish, by aping royalty, by putting her servants in livery, and by reserving for herself the privilege of not returning calls.[37] Mrs. Roger A. Pryor was also critical of the "sort of court" that was maintained at the Confederate capital, in spite of the fact that she herself was by no means free from the charge of participating unduly in feminine vanities. "People here," she wrote from Richmond in 1863, "do not hesitate to say that our court ladies assume too much state for revolutionary times. They had better be careful. We won't guillotine them . . . but it would be lovelier if they could realize their fine opportunities. Think of Florence Nightingale!"[38]

That some of the "court ladies" did appreciate the gravity of the situation and feel certain compunctions of conscience over their behavior, is illustrated by several entries in the diary of Mary Boykin Chesnut. Although as gay, as worldly, and as self-indulgent as any woman in the Confederacy, this aristocratic South Carolinian was too thoughtful not to be self-critical. In 1862 her attention was attracted by the criticism directed against the members of her own social group in Columbia for "lolling back in their silks and satins, with tall foot-men in livery, driving up and down the streets while the poor soldiers' wives were on the sidewalks." Two years later she vainly tried to keep resolutions not to be gay, being impressed with her husband's vetoing of her social pleasures as "too risky" and as "hospitality run mad." At entertainments in the Confederate capital she noted that the ut-terances of her male associates were somber despite an exterior of frivolity. " 'My heart is heavy even here,' " said her host at a gay dinner party. " 'All seems too light, too careless, for these terrible times. It seems out of place in battle-scarred Richmond.' " Walking home from an amateur theatrical she said to her escort, " 'You have spent a jolly evening.' " " 'I do not know,' " he replied. " 'I have asked myself more than once tonight, "Are you the same man who stood gazing down on the faces of the dead on that awful battlefield? The soldiers lying there stare at you with their eyes wide open. Is this the same world? Here and there?" ' " It is not surprising that Mrs. Chesnut grew melancholy under such conditions. "What a blunder," she ex-claimed after a Columbia dance, "to bring us all together here!—a reunion of consumptives to dance and sing until one can almost hear the death-rattle."[39]

THE RATIONALIZATION OF SOCIAL PLEASURES

Neither protests nor misgivings were sufficient, however, to stop the social pleasures of the Confederacy. For one reason, many women, anticipating the views of the makers of later wars, sincerely believed that such activities were a necessary part of patriotism; that they were needed to sustain the morale of both the civil and military population, and that they served to provide a relief from the grinding anxieties and hardships of the times. The attitude of Varina Howell Davis affords the most notable example of this viewpoint. That she took pleasure in her social functions is without question, but she also considered them as moral obligations imposed upon her as the wife of the South's chief magistrate. And although she was no longer able to enjoy her receptions when, toward the end of the war, she learned from her husband the true significance of the movements of the armies of Grant and Sherman, she still continued to listen to the irrelevant chatter of these occasions because she felt that such was a part of her duties.[40] Among other women who manifested this same attitude was the mother of the Elmore sisters of South Carolina. Although the "croakers" in Columbia talked about "the sin and shame" of entertaining the soldiers and refugees when calamity might be so near, she "was of a different mind, and opened her hospitable doors to all the social calls of the situation."[41]

Another argument advanced in favor of social pleasures was that a somber disposition was not an indispensable accompaniment of the highest type of patriotism. "Gayety of manner," said a defense of the apparent levity of the ladies of Mobile, "is not necessarily a proof that the heart is not bleeding. In the whole South there were no truer women to the Confederate cause than those gay daughters of Mobile. If they did 'fiddle while Rome was burning,' they also 'fought the fire' as bravely as any of their sisters elsewhere."[42] It was also observed that the careless hearts who danced most gayly at night were often the stoutest hearts in the next day's battle. "The soldier danced with the lady of his love at night, and on the morrow danced the dance of death in the deadly trenches of the line," wrote Mrs. Roger A. Pryor in commenting upon the disposition of the soldiers at Petersburg to revel in times of suffering and danger;[43] while Mary Boykin Chesnut noted about the same time in Richmond that "many of the brave and gay spirits that we saw lately have taken flight, the only flight they know, and their bodies are left dead upon the battlefield."[44]

The young women who shared the pleasures of these heroes likewise shared their responsibilities without letting disaster and tragedy conquer their gay spirits. They waltzed with soldiers at night and on the next day bound up their wounds. While fulfilling the latter function three South Carolina girls whispered in the ears of the wounded men, " 'Hurry and get well. Mr. Bull is going to give your regiment a splendid fête champêtre at Accabee. Oh! we shall have a grand time of it if only we can just heal up these hurts quickly.' "[45] Nor did the fact that the Federal gunboats had ruined their homes bring dismay to a group of girls living on the banks of the Mississippi. "Everything looks bright to young eyes," wrote one of these girls in recalling the situation. "We danced, sang, and laughed away the hours." When they discovered on one occasion that their carriage had been destroyed, they tore off the top of an old hearse and went for a pleasure ride in the portion of that vehicle which remained, returning the mock sobs of the young men who followed them with outbursts of laughter.[46]

Such wholesome optimism was obviously an asset to a war-torn country; without it the life of the Confederacy would doubtless have been much shorter. Eternal seriousness would have been so depressing to many that there would have been left little room for hope and gallant enthusiasm. Moreover, the fact that the women had masculine support in these activities is indicated by numerous incidents. " 'In these days of hard fighting,' " said the uncle of a Florida girl, " 'it is your *duty* to do everything you can to add to the pleasures of these soldiers.' "[47] It was even observed that General Lee, whose judgment in all matters was regarded as supreme, came occasionally to the receptions at the Executive Mansion. There he engaged in pleasant raillery with the young ladies, and is reported to have said, " 'My boys must be entertained.' "[48]

FAILURE TO APPRECIATE THE ACTUALITIES OF WAR

Aside from the arguments advanced in favor of social pleasures, there were other factors which contributed to promote such activities. There were, as already indicated, many women in the South whose natural human craving for diversions was so great that they were unable to appreciate the real significance of the tragic struggle. Such women were thrown into a sort of ecstasy by the presence of men engaged in an undertaking so heroic as the conflict of the sixties. The war brought to them more adventure, more fun, more dancing, flirting, picnicking, singing, and even more churchgoing than they had ever contemplated in their dreams; more men and more lovers than they had ever read of in the extravagant romances of the period. "With what feelings of rapture did I hail these announcements!" wrote a young woman of this type in commenting upon her opportunity to visit the Confederate capital. "After three years' seclusion . . . suddenly to find myself transported to Richmond, the very capital of war! to see war! the pride and pomp, and the glorious circumstance of war!"[49]

Similar thoughts were also expressed by others. "One good thing the war has brought among many evils," wrote Eliza Frances Andrews of Georgia as she journeyed to a garrisoned town; "it has brought us in contact with many people we should never have known otherwise. I know it must be charming to have all those nice officers around."[50] Although it cost Malvina Gist a long and uncomfortable journey from South Carolina on one of the crowded and rickety trains of the Confederacy, she found in Richmond the opportunity to flirt with a character as handsome as any of those abounding in contemporary fiction. As described in her diary, he was tall, broad-shouldered, and possessed of "a tawny, flowing mustache and hair as bright as 'streaks from Aurora's fingers.'" Her reward for living in the besieged and congested capital was the opportunity to mingle with the "surging, intoxicating stream of brass buttons, epaulettes, and sword-belted manhood." "There is an air of military inspiration around us," she wrote shortly after her arrival in the city; "we exist in a tremor of ecstasy, or else foreboding. Our Richmond holds a little of everything save ennui—not a grain of that."[51]

Girls of this type were mystically romantic, manifesting an almost inevitable tendency to endow the Southern soldier with the heroic qualities found in such widely-read romances as *Thaddeus of Warsaw* and *The Days of Bruce*. "'Mamma, he was so beautiful that I was paralyzed! I never saw anyone so beautiful in all my life,'" exclaimed the youthful Elizabeth W. Allston regarding Poinsett Pringle when he left Charleston for the war;[52] while the eighteen-year-old Frances Westwood Ellzey wrote of a cousin in Mosby's command, "How proud I feel of him, his praise is on every tongue, gallantly, nobly he fought in the thickest of the battle; where the danger was nearest, there was his place, my gallant cousin."[53] Nor was it of great consequence to the average Southern girl that the Confederate soldier of reality was often a hungry and ragged rustic, for it was not held improper for men of inferior social position to take liberties with ladies so long as the former were in the uniforms of the Confederacy.[54] "One looks at a man so differently when we think he will be killed tomorrow," wrote a South Carolina girl in describing the soldiers that she met at a dance given within range of the enemy's guns at Fort Sumter. "Men whom up to that time I had thought dull and commonplace that night seemed charming."[55]

The men encouraged and returned these fine compliments. Although they appreciated the fiery patriotism, the hospital services, the relief work, and the other useful activities of the more practically-minded Confederate women, it was rather the delicate and sheltered feminine type that they adored—a being different from themselves, whom they could praise lavishly and for whom they could die gallantly. They looked, therefore, upon the conversations, the parties, and the rides which they had with these fair ones as favors conferred by superior creatures. "Give my love to your sunbeam of a sister," wrote the Secretary of the Navy to Mrs. Clement C. Clay in a typical outburst of Confederate gallantry. "If not one of the lost Pleiads, at least she is a heavenly body." When Mrs. Clay quoted these words to Lucius Quintus Cincinnatus Lamar, he felt called upon to elaborate the fustian.

" 'Mallory's compliments,' " said the Mississippi statesman, " 'grow languid in their impotence to do justice to that beautiful embodiment of all bright thoughts and ideal graces, your sister Celeste.' "[56] A gallant Virginia captain, writing to his mother, described a girl whom he had met as, "Pretty, modest, witty, beats all ballroom belles of whom she is not one. Idolized by her parents and returns it. . . . Thorough Virginian and such eyes—Deep as a well; truth lies at the bottom—they mirrour back to you pure thoughts and loving—I am at her feet. . . . Her colour comes and goes, and her eyes say a thousand things in a moment."[57] It mattered little to the women that such phrases were not always sincere, for flattery seldom provoked critical reactions.

Failure to appreciate the tragic actualities of the war was also caused by the fact that there were wide stretches in the Confederacy which, until near the end of the struggle, had no immediate contact with these realities. As late as March, 1865, a North Carolina woman referred to the conflict as but another illustration of Macaulay's dictum that in a great war a large portion of the population is not directly affected. "The ploughboy sings in the field," she wrote, "the wedding supper is provided, and the daily course of domestic life in general flows as smoothly as ever except immediately in the track of the armies."[58] The existence of such conditions made it possible for many women to pursue social pleasures approximately like those of peace times. "It was not like war times; dancing every night," wrote a Virginia girl after enjoying the pleasures of Montgomery White Sulphur Springs in 1863. "I should like to have spent a month there. One could almost forget a war was going on. We did not see a paper, and were happy in forgetting for a brief while the stormy world without."[59] Similar reports came from other watering places in Virginia. At Alleghany Springs, for instance, the social life "presented a brilliant and enjoyable spectacle," while "the bowling alley, the billiard room, and the ball room had a liberal patronage."[60]

The letters of certain Southern girls likewise reveal a little world of social pleasures as far removed, in many respects, from the battlefields of Virginia and Tennessee as it was from those of the war in progress at that time in Paraguay. Among such letters were those written by Lucy Massenburg of Salisbury, North Carolina. Small pleasures rather than war occupied her thoughts. "I went to a large picnic yesterday on the Yadkin River about six miles from here," she wrote in May, 1863. "There was quite a crowd. . . . I enjoyed it very much. . . . Last week I met with a great many of the doctors at their convention.

. . . I expect to go to Lexington tomorrow to spend three or four days. We will go to the commencement at Davidson the last of next month. Then . . . we will start on our trip to Pilot Mountain. . . . Salisbury is a large and pleasant place."[61] The letters of Maggie Pittman, another North Carolina girl, indicate that she was also absorbed in petty plans and pleasures. Although she had a brother in the war, she paid little attention to the fact; a report that he had been wounded being followed by what appears to have been regarded as the more important topic of how she entertained her company.[62]

The extent to which many young women were able to pursue their normal pleasures with a minimum of concern for the serious aspects of the great contemporary events is still further exemplified by extracts from the diary of Eliza Frances Andrews. During the fateful winter and spring months of 1865, this sensitive Georgia girl was occupied with such matters as admiring nature and clothes, horseback riding, dancing until late at night, listening to Negro spirituals, acting in amateur theatricals, calling on friends, and being bored by friends who stayed too long. In February she took a great interest in the coming of spring, observing the yellow jessamine buds showing their golden tips, the forget-me-nots peeping from under the wire grass, the somber swamps developing into huge mosaics of wild azaleas, atamasco lilies, and "a hundred other brilliant wild flowers." One of her greatest disappointments was caused by her inability to wear an elaborately prepared dress to a dinner party; not because of events connected with the war but on account of an unexpected rainstorm. She was able to wear the dress later, however, on which occasion she wrote, "I never enjoyed a party more. . . . My toilet was very much admired, and I had a great many compliments about it, and everybody turned to look as I passed, which put me in good spirits." Although the tenth of March had been designated as a day of fasting and prayer for the entire Confederacy, no thought was given to either of these worthy efforts in the Andrews home at Gopher Hill. "We had," confessed the young diarist, "late breakfast after our night's dissipation, and soon after, Mr. Baldwin and Mr. Bacon came over and played cards until dinner time." Still more remarkable was the fact that in her community the greatest excitement of the spring was apparently caused not by the surrender at Appomattox on April 9th but by the celebration of All Fools' Day on April 1st. "There was fooling and counter-fooling between Pine Bluff and Gum Pond all day," she wrote. "Jim Childs and Albert Bacon began it by sending us a beautiful bouquet over which they had sprinkled snuff. We returned the box which held the flowers,

filled with dead rats dressed up in capes and mob caps like old women."
Another feature of the revels of the day was the spreading of a false
report among the men that the enemy was coming. Then, after the
"laughing and yelping" of an old Negro had betrayed the fact that
the news was spurious, more fun was created by bombarding the male
visitors with hot biscuits and corn muffins. "I never enjoyed a day
more in my life," was Miss Andrews' conclusion after the festivities
of this April Fools' day were ended.[63]

THE LAST DAYS OF THE CONFEDERACY

Thus it was that neither stark tragedy nor the admonitions of the
serious-minded were able to stifle the spirit of gayety that prevailed
in the South during the war. In fact toward the end of the conflict,
many persons noted that this spirit was on the increase and ascribed
the fact to the acknowledgment that the fall of the Confederacy was
inevitable. Extravagance was encouraged by the realization that money
came easy, was growing less and less valuable, and would soon be
worthless. A careless air seemed to afford some protection against a
dark future, and a hectic fling was justified as a prelude to the hopeless
conditions which were supposed to be around the corner. "Hope and
fear are both gone, and it is distraction or death with us now," declared
Mary Boykin Chesnut on one occasion, while on another occasion she
wrote, "It is the winding up, but the old life as it begins to die will die
royally."[64] Let a civilization which was heroic and glorious, was the
feeling of others, die gallantly, leaving a splash of color on the pages
of history.[65]

From various sections of the South came reports of gay indulgences
during the last days of the Confederacy. "Wilson has been gay this
winter, more so than I have ever known it before," wrote a girl from
that North Carolina town in the January preceding Appomattox. "We
have had a number of parties, concerts, and tableaux."[66] The same
situation was observed in Alabama by Kate Cumming. "Mobile is gayer
than ever before," she wrote early in 1865 after receiving accounts of
the social life there; "I am told that there was as much visiting New
Year's Day as there usually is in peace time." A visit to the city three
weeks later only led to the confirmation of this opinion. "Not a night
passes," she wrote shortly after her arrival, "but some large party or
ball is given." Even after leaving the place the echoes of its extravagance grated on her ears. "I have heard," she wrote on March 9th,
"more about the dissipation of Mobile after leaving it than I did all the
time that I was there."[67] Likewise, the most extravagant entertainment

given in Columbia during the war was the bazaar held in the old state house a month before Sherman burned the town. It appears to have been of little consequence to the revelers who crowded the hall that critics compared the entertainment to Belshazzar's feast, and that the returns were in the worthless currency of an expiring government. There must be "youth, beauty, joyous laughter, fuss, feathers, and fun" before the curtain was rung down on the Confederacy.[68]

The gayety of the capital also continued to increase as the days of the Confederacy drew to a close. "Oh! the seduction, the novelty, the fascination of life in Richmond," wrote Malvina Gist in March, 1865. "If patriotism is its master-chord, pleasure is no less its dominant note, and while it is as indescribable as the sparkle of champagne, it is no less intoxicating." Instead of the "great and somber tragedies" which this South Carolina girl had anticipated, she found the streets crowded with "soldiers in uniform, officers gaily caparisoned, and beautiful women, beautifully dressed." The parlors were filled with visitors— "officers, privates, congressmen, senators, old friends, and new ones, from all parts of the country"—all paying their devoirs to the young and gay.[69] With reference to the same time and place, the daughter of Louis D. Wigfall wrote, "How the fiddle scraped and the music for 'the dancers dancing in tune'; while they shut their ears and would not hear the minor key that wailed the ruin of our hopes."[70] Still another observer noted that the women of Richmond took no account of the cost of luxuries during these last months. A trousseau which had formerly cost a hundred dollars, said Sallie A. Putnam, was now, without hesitation, purchased for several thousand dollars.[71]

The undercurrent of immorality, noted in the Confederate capital as early as 1861,[72] likewise flowed more freely during the last months of the war. The local press remarked that men were gambling more often and that sportive ladies were plying their trade more openly. As an illustration of the latter statement, one newspaper cited the case of a certain Mrs. Nathalia Dowell who, amid much drinking and noise, kept company with strange gentlemen all night. Complaints were also made regarding Ann Edwards, a girl from Culpeper claiming to be white and free, who harbored "females fair but frail" in her house, where they fiddled, danced, and caroused with men; and on another occasion regarding "a drunken man and woman, arms locked, reeling through the streets," while the woman, in loud tones, used the most violent and obscene language.[73] Richmond had not become a modern Babylon, for there is no evidence that such immoralities extended beyond the lower strata of the feminine population; yet the fact remains that a considerable portion of the city's inhabitants manifested a spirit of gayety which many persons thought improper in those tragic times.

✓   ✓   ✓   ✓

Such were the more extreme phases of the social life of the Confederacy. Having been accustomed to gay pleasures, many Southern women were not disposed to forego their enjoyment, and the excitement of the period led, in many other instances, to an extravagance in dress and conduct that was far out of keeping with the seriousness of the situation. Less extravagant, though no less intense, phases of the social life are described in the chapter which follows.

CHAPTER XIV

AMUSEMENTS AND SOCIAL DIVERSIONS

INTENSE as were the social activities of the women of the Confederacy, they were also varied. In addition to the gayeties and pleasures described in the preceding chapter, these women participated in numerous entertainments which the soldiers provided for them and in an equally numerous group of social functions which they arranged for the soldiers. Among the former diversions were visiting camps, witnessing parades, tournaments, and sham battles, riding out as guests of officers, taking part in picnics and pistol shootings, and most important of all, attending military balls; among the latter were improvised street receptions, formal receptions, promenades, picnics, balls, bazaars, and amateur theatricals. The crowning event of the social life of the Confederacy, however, was the war-time wedding and its attendant festivities.

ENTERTAINMENTS PROVIDED BY THE SOLDIERS

The visiting of camps, whether casual or planned, continued throughout the war to be attended with much of the same glamour that has already been described as characteristic of such activity during the early months of the conflict.[1] Whatever misgivings the ladies may have entertained at first regarding the propriety of these visits were soon dispelled by the soldiers' telling them that such trips were customary all over the South.[2] The pleasurable character of these events is revealed by numerous illustrations. "How delightful and proud the soldiers were to wait upon us," wrote the leader of a party of boarding school girls who spent the night in a camp near Centreville, Virginia. "They made up such a roaring fire, and brought blankets—new ones—and piled them on the baggage to make us comfortable seats. . . . Our supper consisted of excellent beefsteaks, fried potatoes, omelettes, hot rolls and bread, good butter, and hot coffee."[3] Another occasion equally enjoyable was that of a *déjeuner à la fourchette* given by General Wilcox to the ladies of Petersburg in return for the courtesies with which they had favored his command. Upon their arrival at the camp the visitors were ushered into a large tent garlanded with evergreens where, with hearty appetites, they sat down to a table of game, punch, and fruit cake made of dried apples and walnuts. After the completion of this repast the guests, joyously singing "The Bonnie Blue Flag," returned to the city in a gay procession of wagons provided by the host.[4]

Large numbers of women likewise continued to be exhilarated by witnessing military parades and reviews. "It was the sight of my life;

it thrilled and pulsated all through me," wrote Malvina Gist after observing the maneuvers of Gary's brigade of South Carolina troops at Richmond.[5] Perhaps the grandest of all these reviews was that of "Jeb" Stuart's cavalry held at Culpeper Court House immediately before the Gettysburg campaign. The fortunes of the Confederacy were then at high tide, Stuart was personally one of the most popular commanders in the South, and his troops were superbly drilled and in the highest of spirits. On the morning of this occasion the general and his staff made a gay and gallant appearance as, with plumes nodding and bugles sounding, they rode to their positions over a pathway strewn with flowers. The reviewing stand was surrounded with countless feminine devotees of the great cavalry leader, and the hearts of all those present swelled at the magnificent spectacle of thousands of splendidly mounted men sweeping before their beloved commander. The festivities were concluded with a ball. "As the night was fine," wrote a member of Stuart's staff, "we danced in the open air on a piece of turf near our headquarters, and by the light of the numerous wood fires, the ruddy glow of which upon the animated group of our assembly gave the whole scene a wild and romantic effect."[6]

Riding out as the guests of officers constituted another feminine diversion. These excursions were looked upon by the favored ladies as "some great event" for which toilettes must be elaborate and anticipations eager and long. "It was really a pretty sight," wrote Sarah Morgan in describing such an occurrence in Louisiana, "when Captain Morrison and I, who took the lead going, would reach the top of the steep hills and look down on the procession in the hollow below. . . . It was delightful to ride on the edge of the high bluff with the muddy Mississippi below, until you fancied what would be the possible sensation if the horse would plunge down into the waters."[7] Similar pleasure was experienced by Mrs. Roger A. Pryor when she and several other ladies were invited to ride with General Pemberton and a party of officers to Cooper's Point in Virginia. "We were a merry party, assembled in wagons on a frosty morning," she wrote, "and we enjoyed the drive with fleet horses through the keen air."[8] Another occasion of this type was a horseback ride which a party of ladies took with General Hardee and other officers to the top of a steep ridge near Chattanooga. The ladies were delighted with the company of the general and with the magnificent view—the river "as if peeping out from so many islands"; the foliage "beautiful with the gorgeous hues of autumn"; and the solemnity of the summit "which seemed like the 'felt presence of Deity.' "[9]

Still other entertainments which the soldiers arranged for visiting ladies were sham battles, tournaments, picnics, and pistol shootings. At the sham battles and tournaments the feminine visitors were passive but interested spectators. Each knight in a tournament championed the cause of some particular lady, and the lady of the victor was crowned queen of the festival. "We had a delightful day," wrote one of the participants in a tournament held in Orange County, Virginia, in the spring of 1864; "a large number of ladies were present as well as several general officers. . . . The band played at intervals, and the riding was really fine."[10] The pleasures derived from picnics and pistol shootings are likewise described in the accounts of participants. "We had the biggest kind of picnic at our Hd.Qrs.," wrote a young Virginia officer at Culpeper Court House in 1863. "Between thirty and forty ladies were present, and we had ice cream and cake. . . . We also had dancing, pistol shooting, etc."[11] The spirit which animated these informal gatherings is well illustrated by the events that occurred at General Lee's headquarters on the winter nights of 1861. "They wished no serious talk, these young warriors!" said Mrs. Roger A. Pryor. "They had a brief respite from fatigue and sorrow, and they intended to enjoy it. . . . With pretty Nellie at the piano, her blue eyes raised to heaven, and Jack Fleming accompanying her on the guitar, his eyes raised to Nellie, the effect was overwhelming." At times the tender and mournful strains of "Lorena" seemed to get possession of the singers, but soon the merriment would be restored by the singing of "Dixie," "The Bonnie Blue Flag," and by the telling of stories.[12]

The most delightful of all the social functions which the soldiers provided for the ladies were the dances held in camps and other improvised places. The equipment for these occasions was meager. The halls were usually without curtains and poorly supplied with furniture, while the lights consisted of feeble gas jets or dim tallow candles set in black bottles. Such inconveniences were of little consequence to the revelers, however; for nature furnished decorations of ivy and other evergreens, the dim lights hid the defects in the ladies' dresses, the musicians had not lost their cunning, and the existence of war created a spirit of gay abandon which could not have been duplicated in peace times. "For all that," said an English participant in referring to the inadequate appointments of a Fredericksburg ball, "we had as pleasant a party as could possible be, and we were very sorry when twelve o'clock came and put an end to the ball, as the next day was Sunday."[13] The greatest thrill of the young ladies of Charleston was said to be that of being rowed out to Fort Sumter during the investment of the city in order to dance with the officers of the garrison. "The strange charm of the situation," wrote Esther Alden, "wove a spell around me. There were cannon balls piled in every direction, sentinels pacing the ramparts, and within the casement pretty women and handsome well-bred men dancing as though unconscious that we were actually under the guns of the blockading fleet."[14]

The most spirited dances of the war were, in all probability, those given by "Jeb" Stuart under the direction of his chief of staff, Major J. H. Heros von Borcke. Stuart was handsome, picturesque in attire, rollicking, and melodramatic; von Borcke, a Prussian soldier of fortune, was almost a legendary figure, huge in stature, courtly in manners, but as rollicking as his chief. Wherever this minstrel-general rested in his wide rovings through the borderlands of the Confederacy, he would suggest a ball. "There was a great stir at headquarters on the morning of the 8th," wrote von Borcke in describing an event of this type which occurred during the invasion of Maryland in the summer of 1862. "Invitations to the ball were sent out to all the families of Urbana and its neighborhood and to the officers of the Hampton brigade. The large halls of the Academy were aired and swept and festooned with roses and battle flags borrowed from the different regiments. At seven in the evening all was complete, and already the broad avenues were filled with our fair guests according to their rank and fortune—some on foot, others in simple light 'rockaways,' others again in stately family coaches." Stuart and his staff won much applause as they entered the hall to begin the dance with a lively quadrille. "Louder and louder sounded the instruments, quicker and quicker moved the dancers," continued von Borcke, "and the whole crowded room, with its many exceedingly pretty women, and its martial figures of officers in their best uniforms, presented a striking spectacle of gayety and enjoyment." At one o'clock in the morning the enemy made an atttack, and the dance was stopped long enough to allow the men to repel this intrusion. When this had been accomplished, the revelry was resumed, lasting until dawn when the young belles of the ball were transformed into ministering angels to wait upon the victims of the night's fray.[15]

ENTERTAINMENTS ARRANGED FOR THE SOLDIERS

The pleasures furnished by the men were heartily returned by the ladies. The presence of officers and soldiers, convalescing or on furlough, in a town afforded an opportunity for social activity which the feminine inhabitants were not slow to grasp. The fact that carriages were shabby, scarce, and drawn by sorry nags, and that the men were often seedy and crippled, made little difference to many of the women of the Confederacy. The unsightly patch over the eye of a colonel might be considered "a badge of honor," as it was on one occasion, while the faded jacket of a captain, disfigured with a hole through which a minie ball had passed, served to give its wearer an added charm.[16]

For favorite generals the ladies often improvised street receptions. The liveliest of these occasions were inevitably those given in honor of "Jeb" Stuart. When this idol of the ladies arrived in a town, mobs of girls and women gathered around him, literally showering him with kisses, decking both him and his horse with flowers, and demanding locks from his hair and buttons from his clothing. "The general's uniform," said his chief of staff in referring to such an occasion at Shepherdstown in Virginia, "was in a few moments entirely shorn of buttons; and if he had given as many locks of hair as were asked for, our commander would have been entirely bald."[17] At Middleburg in the same state he was surrounded by ladies, "all eager to catch the words from his lips, and with tears in their eyes kissing the shirt of his uniform or the glove upon his hand." Soon an elderly woman threw her arms around him and gave him a resounding caress, after which, according to the informer just quoted, the kisses that the mob bestowed upon their idol "now popped in rapid succession like musketry."[18] Nor was Stuart the only commander who was favored with such receptions from the ladies. General Hardee was reported to have made it a practice to accept kisses from the wives and daughters of farmers in the country through which he passed;[19] while of an unnamed officer at Memphis, Mary Ann Loughborough wrote, "It is astonishing to see how the ladies do flock to see the old general, and all kiss him as a matter of course."[20]

The formal receptions with which aristocratic hostesses occasionally complimented the celebrated generals of the Confederacy were, as already indicated, occasions which best exemplified the dignity and splendor of the Old South as heightened by the thrill of war. For such an event held at Fredericksburg in the spring of 1862, in honor of General Ewell and his bride, assembled the flower of the aristocracy of that section of Virginia. Some ladies, with outriders of faithful slaves arrived from distant tidewater plantations. There were the Tayloes, the Braxtons, the Masons, the Carters, the Beverleys, the Dulanys, the Fitzhughs, and other representatives of the first families of the state. There were winsome maidens with flowers in their hair, adorned in lawns, muslins, and silks taken from old chests. "It was pretty," said one who was present, "to see the graceful girls in their tight basques and full skirts curtsying low to the old generals, gorgeous in gray and gold, dark curls bobbing as they did so, and gray head bent." What a supper for war times! added this writer. There were turkeys, home-cured hams, saddles of mutton, oysters in every style, chicken fried and roasted, stuffed mangoes, spiced pears, beaten biscuits, wines, and coffee. After this elaborate repast the young people retired to the porch. The air was quite cool, and the wind blew the candles out; but youth did not object to the dark, and mint juleps sent in great loving cups were fortifications against any breeze. The thoughts of impending danger enlivened the company; gayety was mixed with excitement; and there was much love making.[21]

Informal parties afforded a less elaborate but equally pleasurable source of amusement. When a friendly regiment or brigade was in a community, gatherings known as "soldiers' bees" were often arranged by the girls of the locality. Each girl was allowed to invite one lady friend and as many soldiers as she wished. The success of such functions, from the standpoint of the hostesses at least, was due to the excess of men present. "Four gentlemen were introduced to me at once," wrote a Virginia girl of a party given for the members of the Stonewall Brigade at Winchester in 1863.[22] More thrilling than the soldiers' bees were the parties given by the girls in response to the serenades of officers. It was not unusual for a group of such serenaders to burst into a parlor after midnight, there to demand and receive the presence of the girls of the household and whatever refreshments the housewife could afford. On one occasion of this type the revelers were so well pleased with the evening's entertainment that they returned on the following day at sunset, dressed this time in fantastic disguises. There were refreshments, and the talking and laughter lasted until a late hour, when the visitors, with a hearty goodnight, retired.[23]

Many of the young ladies were charmed by the dances which they gave for the soldiers. It appears to have made little difference to the hostesses if the rough camp shoes of their guests tore long rents in the carpets, and that the hands which clasped those of the maidens were often coarse and hard-fibered; for those who wrote of these occasions used only superlatives in describing them. "We had a glorious time—plenty of ice cream and cake and officers, the latter predominating," said a student at Mrs. Pegram's School in Richmond of a dance held in that city.[24] Others told of "the jingling of spurs and the clanging of sabres to the merry tune of the fiddle and the banjo"; of "old buildings reverberating to the soldiers' tread and the flying feet of Southern belles, in light dancing, often on summer nights"; and of flirting and love making as maidens skimmed about the ball room with the arms of handsome strangers around them.[25] The joyous character of these events is also revealed in the accounts of the masculine participants. "If there was no magnificent hall with the light showering down from a thousand wax candles on the brilliant toilettes of Europe," said a foreign guest at a Virginia dance, "there were many pretty faces and sparkling eyes to look into."[26] Of other dances in the same state, Captain Ham Chamberlayne wrote, "I doubt if the most splendid balls that ever were given came better up to the mark of all entertainments . . . than do these homely old Virginia frolics, that, sensibly, commence at dark, and foolishly, hardly end before light."[27]

Regardless of what has been said about the bountiful provender that characterized some of the entertainments of aristocratic Virginia, the majority of the Confederate hostesses experienced considerable difficulty in providing an appetizing repast for their parties and dances. If by good fortune ice cream and cake and "real" coffee could be secured, these refreshments were relished in a manner impossible for Southerners accustomed to the plenty of peace times to comprehend. In instances where it was impossible to procure even these simple comestibles, the soldiers were entertained at functions known as "starvation parties." At Richmond a group of young society women organized a Starvation Club, the principal rule of which was that there should be no refreshments at its entertainments. Since the male guests usually arranged for the music on these occasions, the only expense to the hostess was that of an extra fire in the parlor. Under such conditions, wrote Edward M. Alfriend, "the young people of Richmond and the young army officers assembled and danced as brightly and as happily as though a feast worthy of Lucullus awaited them. . . . No matter how peculiarly one might be attired, no matter how bad the music, no matter how limited the host's or hostess's ability to entertain, everybody laughed, danced, and was happy, although the reports of cannon often boomed in their ears."[28] Foreigners and other distinguished visitors at the Confederate capital were advised to attend the functions of the Starvation Club as a means of viewing the best society of the city, and membership in the organization was said to be highly prized and widely sought after.[29]

BAZAARS AND AMATEUR THEATRICALS

As noted in a previous chapter, bazaars were very popular among the Confederate women as a means of raising money for the extensive charities that were necessitated by the war.[30] These events may be included in the list of social diversions, since they served the ends of pleasure as well as those of benevolence and were sponsored by the frivolous as well as the serious. They were usually held in courthouses, schools, and other buildings of a public or semi-public character, and their booths were handsomely decorated with flags, bunting, flowers, and evergreens. Articles to be sold or raffled were secured by the ransacking of old chests, the sacrifice of family valuables, and by the ingenuity of the women in devising vendible items of food and wearing apparel. Little difficulty was encountered in effecting sales, for Confederate money was plentiful and goods were scarce.

Doubtless the most elaborate bazaar in the whole history of the Confederacy was the one held in the hall of representatives at the old state house in Columbia in January, 1865. "To give a just description of this royal festival, with its delightful accessories," said the effusive account of a local newspaper, "would require a pen dipped in the hues of a thousand rainbows, or the power to catch the fantastic shapes that live in the changing pictures of a kaleidoscope." For several weeks previous to the event the ladies of the South Carolina capital, both the residents and refugees, racked their heads, toiled with their fingers, and persuaded with their tongues in order to make ready for the enterprise. Contributions were levied on all sides; many articles were bought, begged, or manufactured; and gold subscribed by Southern sympathizers in England was converted into curiosities, ornaments, and other necessities which could not be purchased in the Confederacy. From domestic sources came blankets, yards of calico and flannel, shoes, home-knit socks and stockings, shawls, silverware, dolls, cakes, bread, and even a live calf; from abroad came penknives, pins, hairpins, Parisian bonnets, ostrich plumes, sugarplums, almonds, and other rarities. In front of the speaker's desk was placed a huge booth garlanded with evergreens and Spanish moss, and surmounted by a banner emblazoned in letters of gold with "A Tribute to Our Sick and Wounded Soldiers." On either side of this structure were semicircles of other booths, each marked with the shield of one of the Confederate states and managed by representatives of these respective commonwealths. For days gay throngs crowded around the booths, nonchalantly paying fabulous prices for whatever articles might strike their fancy and wondering how so much finery and luxury could be gathered among a people whose resources were supposed to be so limited.[31]

Amateur theatricals likewise served the double purpose of raising money and affording amusement. Night after night young women congregated in the parlors of mansions and in courthouses and other public buildings for the rehearsals of these events, and large and enthusiastic audiences usually crowded the halls to witness the final productions.[32] If they were given near a camp or garrison, military men were always present both as actors and as spectators. One of the most favored performances was that of a tableau representing the various states of the Confederacy. "The whole bright galaxy was there," wrote a Virginia woman in describing a production of this character. "South Carolina in scarlet, restless and fiery; Virginia, grave and dignified, yet bright with hope, seemed beckoning Kentucky on, who stood beyond the threshold, her eyes cast down with shame and suffering; Maryland was at the threshold, but held back by a strong hand; all the rest of the fair sisters were there in their appropriate places, forming a beautiful picture."[33] Musical entertainments were also popular. They were usually given by local talent, although sometimes assisted by stranded professionals or amateurs from neighboring towns. A program given at Decatur, Georgia, which may be regarded as typical of these performances, consisted of an opening chorus, piano duets, vocal solos of patriotic and sentimental airs, and selections for the violin.[34]

Still another type of dramatic entertainment was afforded by producing the classics of the English stage. The most notable efforts along this line occurred at Richmond in the homes of the wives of Cabinet members and Virginia gentlemen. The principal rôles were played by the belles and grand dames of the capital, while the minor parts were taken by such gallants of the town and army as were available. The audiences included many of the high officials of the government, even President Davis at times. A performance of *The Rivals* in the winter of 1862, at the home of Cora Semmes Ives, has been adjudged the most ambitious social venture of the Confederacy, the fame of this entertainment spreading so far that a daring officer of McClellan's command is said to have planned to attend it disguised as a Confederate. Constance Cary, a beauty of the Fairfax family attired in a rich costume which "had been worn by distinguished ancestors in the days of the Old Dominion's glory," captured all hearts as the languishing Lydia, and Mrs. Clement C. Clay, in a rich brocaded gown, antique lace and jewels, high puffed hair, and nodding plumes which added expression to her moving utterances, played Mrs. Malaprop.[35] T. C. DeLeon asserted that there were many among the Confederate actors and actresses who would have taken high rank in any dramatic circle;

but he added that the audiences were composed of friends of these amateurs who would have been pleased regardless of the quality of the performances.[36]

CONFEDERATE WEDDINGS

Public opinion professed to condemn marriages during the war, at least those with which the critics had no immediate concern. "I think it indiscreet for anyone to fall in love much less to marry in such times as these," was a typical masculine judgement regarding the matter;[37] while a typical feminine opinion was expressed in the words, "I do not expect to marry until the war is over, if then, for I think it is much better to remain single than to marry a man in the army who is exposed to danger."[38] Such positive statements must be accepted with certain reservations, however, for if we are to believe the accounts of the surprised chroniclers of the times, marriages were even more frequent during the war than before. "I believe that neither war, pestilence, nor famine," wrote Judith W. McGuire, "could put an end to the marrying and giving in marriage which is constantly going on. Strange that these sons of Mars can so assiduously devote themselves to Cupid and Hymen; but every respite, every furlough, must be thus employed."[39]

The frequency of marriage was ascribed to a variety of causes. The excitement and social contacts of war, according to a Richmond man, had a tendency to stimulate love-making. "The soldiers," he wrote, "do more courting here in a day than they would do at home, without war, in ten years." This view was also shared by Mary Boykin Chesnut, who reported that the men who had to go to the front made love desperately and had a unique way of courting. "Since I saw you—last year—standing by the turnpike gate, you know," this diarist quoted a warrior-lover as saying to his sweetheart, "my battle-cry has been: 'God, my Country and you.' "[40] Paradoxical as it may seem the very reason why so many persons objected to marriages—that is, the uncertain character of the times—often had the opposite effect. The brief furloughs, the certainty of separation, and the possibility of death in battle appeared to quicken the romantic inclinations of many young persons and to result in weddings which in normal times would have been deferred. Edward M. Alfriend believed that the contacts of the hospital led to love and marriages. "I know," he wrote afterwards, "of several wives and mothers in the South who lost their hearts and won their soldier-husbands in this way."[41] Furthermore, the inability of a prospective bridegroom to support a wife, usually a bar to marriage, did not operate in war times. "Jeb" Stuart, who had the reputation of a matchmaker, was reported to have told his officers that war was the time for marrying, since "they could marry without any questions being asked as to how they could support their wives, who would naturally remain at their parents' homes and be taken care of."[42] This story may be apocryphal, but it illustrates an actual condition. Confederate officers and soldiers were not expected to support or shelter their brides; their manner of living and their meager wages stood in the way.

Efforts were made to surround these war marriages with the glamour and ceremony which are characteristic of such events in normal times. Since no Confederate bride was willing to be without a trousseau, trunks were ransacked for wedding garments and other finery which mothers and aunts had stored away in the days of their youth. White slippers were mended and chalked, old muslins were renovated, linen table and bed coverings were made into soft fabrics.[43] The bridal costumes which resulted from such efforts were often described as triumphs. When Della Allston married Arnoldus Vander Horst at Charleston in June, 1863, she wore "a full plain dress of Brussels' net, beautiful material, over a splendid white silk, with a beautiful real lace veil falling almost to the ground; a wreath of wild hyacinths and a bouquet of the same."[44] When Betty Bierne was married to William Porcher Miles, a few months later, she appeared "in white satin and point d'Alençon," the dress of a sister widowed by the war.[45] Those not so fortunate as to have relatives with stores of finery in reserve resorted to homespun. In the creation of such trousseaus the ingenuity of the Confederate women was at its best, and the result was often evidenced in garments of which their friends were justly proud.[46]

To provide settings for weddings in the best tradition of the Old South was not so difficult. With the exception of certain localities the churches were all intact, and save for the absence of rugs and curtains there were numerous mansions which remained much as they had been before the war. Likewise, the woods still supplied their bounties of flowers and garlands for decorative purposes. At Della Allston's wedding the beautiful oval drawing room of one of the Charleston mansions was used. "It had," said a sister of the bride, "a very high ceiling and was papered in white with small sprigs of golden flowers scattered over it. There were four large windows on the south, opening on an iron balcony. . . . There was a high mantelpiece of white wood carved with exquisite figures of women dancing and holding aloof garlands of flowers."[47] The guests which assembled on such occasions, especially in the large centers of population, formed a company more brilliant than could ordinarily have been gathered in more prosaic times. The uniforms of the groom and his attendants added a martial touch to the events, and heroic emotions stirred the company if, as frequently happened, the ceremony was performed within the sound of the enemy's guns. "In spite of war," wrote a Louisiana bride, "I had a big home wedding—ten attendants. General Sterling Price and his staff were there in full uniform, as well as all the other officers. Our plantation was ten miles in Yankee lines, and there was some fear that the Yankees might come and capture the officers, so we had sentinels out."[48]

The providing of the traditional wedding supper was no easy task, but such feats were not altogether impossible. "We all exercized our taste in arranging the table," said Judith W. McGuire in describing a wedding repast at Berryville, Virginia, "which, with its ices, jellies, and the usual etceteras of an elegant bridal supper, made us forget that we were in a blockaded country.[49] A less sumptuous wedding feast, also held in Virginia, consisted of roast fowl, dessert of dried apple pies, a course of cracked walnuts, and coffee made of a clever mixture of okra seed and sweet potatoes.[50]

*   *   *   *

In this and the foregoing chapter the social diversions in which the women of the Confederacy participated have been described, as well as the circumstances which made such events possible. These events were varied, widespread, and intense, but, as stated at the beginning of the preceding chapter, they represent only a part of the activities of Confederate women. Many of these women were intolerant of pleasures and did not participate in them, while others who made merry at one moment were weeping for the sorrows of the land at another. It is entirely probable that in many cases the gay manners of the Confederate women served only to conceal hearts that were bleeding, and that the cheerfulness which many of them displayed was assumed largely for the benefit of the soldiers; for, as will be demonstrated in the next chapter, the trials of these women were many and their anxieties and griefs profound.

CHAPTER XV

ANGUISH AND TEARS

IN spite of their sanguine hopes for the success of the Southern cause, the women of the Confederacy were confronted, from the very beginning of the hostilities, with the realization that their friends and relatives were constantly exposed to the perils of imprisonment, illness, wounds, and death. The harrowing suspense that resulted from this condition gnawed unceasingly at the hearts of thousands of women and was more devastating to them in many ways than the physical hardships that accompanied the invasion and the blockade. Indeed there was for many women no relief from this anxiety as long as the war lasted, except the grief which came when seemingly all hope had been shattered by the death of one or more relatives in camp, in battle, or in prison.

APPREHENSION AND SUSPENSE

"Only those who have felt this anxiety know what it is," said a Confederate wife in describing the feelings of those who had husbands in active service.[1] These women often felt that they had only one great fact before them, that any moment might record their supreme sorrow and loss. Under such conditions levity, even if possible, was considered an unintended mockery. "I scarcely laugh now," wrote a Virginia woman, "and when I do so the sound of my voice startles me and I immediately reproach myself for having forgotten for a moment the weight which hangs over my spirit."[2] In other instances a feeling of utter gloom prevailed. "Do you think a few words can give an idea of our agony and despair?" wrote the leader of a group of Louisiana girls who were separated from their soldier-relatives. "I can't stand it much longer. I'll give away presently, and I know my heart will break."[3]

The thought that battles, with their long lists of casualties, were likely to take place led many women into fervent if vain protests against those inevitable features of war. "Oh, I trust that a battle is not at hand! I feel unnerved, as if I could not stand the suspense of another engagement," wrote Judith W. McGuire in voicing the feelings of hundreds of Southern women when they heard in July, 1863, that Lee and Meade were approaching each other. The belief that, in the event of an engagement, the Confederates would be victorious in no way lessened this anxiety. "But the dread casualties!" added Mrs. McGuire. "The fearful list of killed and wounded, when so many of our nearest and dearest are engaged, is too full of anguish to anticipate without a sinking of heart."[4] With pathetic eagerness the women often looked forward to the coming of bad weather as a possible check upon the martial inclinations of the men. "I would welcome two feet of snow," wrote a Virginia woman in December, 1861, "for I would be sure there would be no fighting under such circumstances. My spirits always rise when I think the weather too bad for military operations."[5]

The realization that a battle was actually impending caused the drooping hearts of the women to sink still lower. The anxiety for news from the front was mingled with the dread of receiving such information, for there was always the fear that friends and relatives would be numbered among the casualties.[6] The only refuge in such an emergency was to put faith in the Lord or to write pathetic but often futile letters of advice to kinsmen on how to avoid the dangers of battle. "My heart has been full of anxiety and trouble about the many reports of a battle at York Town," wrote a Virginia mother to her son. "I can only pray and put my trust in the Lord. May God send home my dear son and grandson unharmed and full of honour."[7] A Tennessee woman who was a refugee in Georgia, wrote to her husband on the eve of the Battle of Dalton, "I feel very anxious just now. O *do take care* and keep out of the way of the *shells* and *Yankees*."[8]

The knowledge that kinsmen were really participating in battles often threw women into spasms of fright. The intensity of this feeling is graphically illustrated in a letter written by a Lynchburg woman to her husband during the Battle of First Manassas. "Oh! my precious husband," she wrote, "I am miserable about you this evening! . . . I pray God to spare you, but at this moment I may be a widow. I shall die and join you very soon if you are gone. I cannot live without you."[9] In describing the effect of another battle upon a young North Carolina woman who had a husband in the engagement, Catherine Ann Edmonston wrote, "Poor Patty seems to suffer intensely. All day long her moans and cries sound in my ears. Poor thing, it is tearing open her wounds afresh."[10]

Dramatic intensity was given to these spasms of excitement when the women could hear the sound of the guns in the battles in which their relatives were taking part. Such noises, said a South Carolina woman, "seemed to smite like a sword within our breasts." There was nothing left to do, she added, but to pace the floor in suspense or else to sit in despair with folded hands and blanched faces.[11] Among the countless hundreds of women who experienced this harrowing anxiety were six who, in 1863, sat at a window on a plantation at Linwood, Louisiana, and watched, in the faint starlight, the flashes from the guns of the attack on Baton Rouge, wondering with hopeless uncertainty who among friends and relatives would be included in the list of the slain. These women were able to suppress their cries, said one of their number, but they could not keep their teeth from chattering.[12] Among others in the same difficulty were two boarding school girls who sat at a window of the Baptist college in Warrenton, Virginia, to hear, in the stillness of the autumn air, the dreadful cannonading which incoherently told that kinsmen were in peril on the bloody field of Leesburg, thirty miles away. "The poor children," said one of their teachers, "were ashamed to display signs of fear; yet the pale faces and compressed lips plainly told of the inward terror they suffered in behalf of their homes and parents."[13] Still others of this type included the women of Richmond who sat holding each other's hands in terror as they heard the sound of the guns at Seven Pines. "The sudden boom of the cannon," said one of these unhappy creatures, "broke in upon us, and we would start and shiver as if it had shot *us,* and sometimes the tears would come."[14] When servants told Margaret Junkin Preston at Lexington, Virginia, in May, 1862, that they heard cannonading in the distance, she cried in bitter anguish, "Oh! my husband! Could I but know that he was safe! I wonder at myself that I do not lose my senses. My God! help me to stay my heart on thee!"[15]

The suspense induced by a battle was often not relieved until long after the engagement was over. It is true that the women were usually informed promptly as to whether there had been a victory or a defeat, and given some idea concerning the approximate number of the killed, wounded, and missing; but the inadequate news service of the times often failed to list the names of those unfortunates. In many instances the only newspaper available to a circle of women would merely inform them that their relatives' regiment went into battle with a certain number of men and came out with half that number. A burning question which then arose was, "Who were among the lost?" And if, after days of waiting, it was discovered that kinsmen were in this class, a more tantalizing question then arose, "Were the relatives dead or in a Northern prison or hospital?" The solution of the latter question often required months; in some cases years. Captivity was naturally preferred to death, for life, even in a Northern prison, still held hope; but only too often the reward for this agonizing speculation was the final discovery that the missing kinsmen had died on the field of battle.

Outstanding among those who were forced to endure the suspense and anxiety that followed a great battle were the mothers of Lexington, Virginia, after the bloody engagement at Chancellorsville. On May

5, 1863, they were informed that a great victory had been won, but since this news was not accompanied by particulars it afforded little relief to those who had sons among the regiments involved. "Not one mother," wrote Margaret Junkin Preston, "lays her head on her pillow this night, sure that her son is not slain. . . . God pity the tortured hearts that will pant through this night!" Nor was the situation improved four days later when the same observer again noted, "No relief still from the tormenting suspense which is hanging over almost every household. Not a letter yet from the army." When finally, on the fifth day after the battle, mail containing the coveted details did arrive, the excitement was so great that the church services which were in progress were broken up.[16] Similar conditions existed in Halifax County, North Carolina, when, during the spring fighting around Richmond in 1864, no news came from the front for seventeen days. "The state of suspense in which we live is fearful," wrote Catherine Ann Edmonston in commenting upon the situation that prevailed in her community.[17]

Perhaps the most pathetic figures in the entire Confederacy were those women who wandered about looking for missing soldier-relatives, not knowing whether the objects of their quest were dead or alive. Some of these unfortunates went from one hospital to another, searching for husbands and sons who had probably been killed but whom they hoped to find among the wounded. Others rushed to the scenes where great battles had been recently fought, hoping to find traces of those who had been missing since these engagements. Still others gathered at Richmond and other points along the frontier of the Confederacy, seeking to find their kinsmen among paroled or exchanged prisoners, or trying to secure some information which would prove that the missing ones were alive in Northern prisons. Among the women of this type were two mothers from the far South whom Judith W. McGuire observed searching the hospitals of Richmond for their lost sons; and an old friend whom this Virginia diarist met in 1863, miserable because she could get no clues of a son reported "missing" and of another reported "wounded."[18] Another pathetic case was that of a South Carolina woman who, for seventeen months after a great battle, searched for her husband when his friends had given him up for dead. Finally she received a letter, written in a tremulous hand, urging her to come to Savannah. There, in one of the hospitals, she found a man with one eye eaten out and a form so attenuated that he seemed a living skeleton. He faintly called her name, and she recognized him as her husband. She carried him home, but two days after arriving there he died.[19] In Capitol Square at Richmond in March, 1865, Mary Boykin Chesnut noticed a pitiful woman going in and out of a crowd of returned prisoners, carrying a basket of provisions for a son whom she believed had been captured at Gettysburg, twenty months before. "She was utterly unconscious of the crowd. The anxious dread, expectation, hurry, and hope which led her on showed in her face."[20]

THE PRICE OF SOUTHERN LAURELS

The anxieties of the women of the Confederacy over the fate of their kinsmen were, as already suggested, only too frequently justified by the consequences of the great engagements. These women were in fact the victims of one of the most sanguinary conflicts in modern history—a war which caused, in thousands of instances, the deaths of those who were nearest and dearest to them. Sometimes the men died in the charge of battle, and the women were immediately but tactfully notified. At other times the news came rudely and suddenly, crushing the hopes of mothers and wives. Not infrequently the information came from distant hospitals, where death had come to the sick or wounded soldier without the presence of friends or relatives to give comfort to his last hours or Christian cheer to his expiring spirit. Still others, as already indicated, died anonymously on battlefields or in prisons, leaving their kin to learn of their fate after long weeks of waiting or searching. Regardless of how the death notices came, however, these sad features, and not the heroism and romance of the conflict, gradually became the central fact of the war to thousands of women. Feminine tears were many, feminine grief was loud, and feminine black became the symbol of hearts seemingly crushed beyond repair.

Even the celebrations of great victories were often accompanied, beneath the show of pleasure, by an undercurrent of anguish; for victories were always won at the price of many killed and wounded. The women felt this burden most keenly and as a result seldom participated whole-heartedly in the rejoicing. This fact is well illustrated by the manner in which they received the news from Manassas, the first great victory of the war. "What a variety of expressions were to be seen among the women!" wrote an English observer at Richmond. "Between kindred love and patriotism, what a tumult of feeling seemed panting for utterance!" Those who had no relatives in the battle did not disguise their exultation, but hundreds of others rent the air with cries of "Oh, my only son!" "My husband!" or "My brother!" as they rushed about feverishly seeking for news from the front. A constant tide of fresh information brought relief to some but alarm and consternation to others, and the horrors of the many who were uncertain were mingled with the griefs of those to whom sad losses were suddenly revealed.[21]

If a victory at the outset of the war should have caused so much anguish and suspense, it was inevitable that these emotions should be intensified when the women learned, through bitter experience, the price they had to pay for the laurels of the Confederacy. "The clouds were lifted and the skies brightened upon political prospects, but death held high carnival in our city," said Sallie A. Putnam in describing the conditions that prevailed in Richmond after the Confederate victory at Seven Pines. Instead of making merry over this triumph, many mothers nervously watched for persons who might bring news of their sons, and wives clasped their children to their bosoms as, in their frightful agony, they imagined themselves widows; others grew pale when horsemen drew up at their doors, unable to nerve themselves to the point of listening to the tidings which the riders brought.[22] "The feeling of personal anxiety keeps us humble during the flush of victory," wrote Judith W. McGuire upon receiving, in a Richmond hospital, the announcement of Jackson's successes in the Valley of Virginia. "What news may each mail bring to us of those who are dear to our heart's blood? Each telegram that is brought into the hospital makes me blind with apprehension, until it passes on, and other countenances denote the same anxiety." Several weeks later this same chronicler remarked that the hearts of the people of Richmond were filled with joy and gladness because McClellan was retreating from the Peninsula, but she felt impelled to note also that "the city is sad because of the dead and dying."[23] Another chronicler wrote that, after receiving the news of the victory in the Wilderness, the Confederate capital "was wild with joy and with woe as well;" and that from Petersburg, twenty miles from the scene of this terrible engagement, "came the sound of mourning. Rachel weeping for her children and refusing to be comforted because they were not."[24]

A feature of additional sadness was presented in the death notices of this, as of most wars, by the contrast between actual tragedy and past hopes; for, as is well known, the harvest of war is generally gathered from among the young and the able, those strong in mind, body, and courage. "The hope, the pride, almost the idol of the family, thus suddenly cut down," wrote Judith W. McGuire in recording the death of "that young Christian hero," Randolph Fairfax. She and her friends "had watched his boyhood and youth, the gradual development of that brilliant mind and lofty character," and they "mourned him dead, as we had loved and admired him living." Sixteen months later the same diarist was called upon to record the death of Washington Stuart, the youngest and dearest son of another family with whom she was intimately acquainted. "Sad tidings are brought to our cottage this morning," she wrote on this melancholy occasion. "The mother and sisters are overwhelmed, while our whole household is shrouded in sorrow. He was young, brave, and a Christian. He fell while nobly fighting with his company."[25]

Similar stories were repeated by hundreds of others. Mrs. Clement C. Clay told of a young cousin who had been shot down at Malvern Hill as he bore the banner which he had thought would carry him to victory. "His blood-stained cap, marked by a bullet hole," concluded this writer, "was all that returned of our fair young soldier boy."[26] When Mary Boykin Chesnut heard of the death of Cheves McCord, the only son of a close friend, she wrote, "He is barely twenty-one—is married—his wife a beautiful girl. Unfortunate and miserable and wretched is it all."[27] Upon receiving the news of the death of Johnson Pettigrew, a brilliant young writer and soldier, a member of his family wrote, "Our brightest hope is gone. It is so dreadful. Alas for the young; all hope for the future of this frail life is put out. . . . Surely we are broken up."[28] There was need of mighty courage under such conditions, for the very seed corn of the race was being sacrificed. No wonder that Catherine Ann Edmonston, in chronicling the deaths of the sons of six intimate friends, ruefully remarked, "How long can this continue? Our country is drained of her best and dearest. Our mothers are bereaved, our wives widowed, and still the tale of blood goes on."[29]

GRIEF AND MOURNING

The grief of the bereaved ones had both a practical and a sentimental basis. These unfortunate women were as dependent as any women in history upon their men for support and counsel, and their love for these men was as tender and as romantic as that of any other women in the world. Consequently, when tragic fate had shattered the sources of their protection and destroyed the objects of their devotion, they often felt themselves justified in believing that all hope had passed from their lives. "Were these the same people—these haggard, wrinkled women, bowed down with trouble and care and unusual toil?" asked a woman in contemplating the hardships of those who, in 1863, had lost relatives in the war. "These tame, pale, tearless girls from whose soft flesh the witching dimples have long since departed or were drawn down in furrows—were they the school girls of '61? Oh! that silent and terrible battlefield where the women of the South fought so bravely and so patiently! There were mail days when letters brought news of father, son, husband, lover, and friend, who had been 'taken prisoner,' 'shot through the heart,' 'died in prison,' or 'died on the road home,' or worst than all 'missing.' Oh, God! how did we stand to fight this battle and still live?"[30]

The fact that the fatal news often came in startling and unexpected forms served to intensify the grief of many of those bereft by the war. One day at Richmond a young bride, seeing a body being carried into a near-by house, retired from the porch of her own home to inform her mother that a neighbor's son had been killed. Upon hastening to the front door the mother found that a mistake had been made, that the pallbearers were retracing their steps and bringing the body into her house. Understanding what had happened, she caught the fainting daughter in her arms and laid her, now a widow, on the same spot where a few months before she had stood as a bride.[31] In another Virginia town a young woman with a baby in her arms was observed weeping and with an expression of the wildest grief on her face. The cause of her anguish was the fact that her father, who had gone to Danville to bring her husband home from a hospital, had returned from that city with the intelligence that the wounded man was already buried.[32] The same observer who reported this case also told of an officer who had died of severe wounds in a Richmond hospital. After he was interred the nurses thought they would hear no more of him, but "in the dead of night came hurriedly a single carriage to the gate of the hospital. A lone woman, tall, straight, and dressed in deep mourning, got quickly out, and moved rapidly up the steps into the large hall, where, meeting the guard, she asked anxiously, 'Where's Captain T?' " When told that he had been buried, she fell in a swoon as one dead, and upon being revived made the whole building ring with the sound of her lamentations.[33] At a Chattanooga hospital Kate Cumming said that such scenes were with her "a daily occurrence." Of one of them, that of a wife who found her husband dead, this matron wrote, "The shock nearly made her lose her reason. Poor thing! My heart aches for her."[34]

The dead of night seems to have been no unusual time for tragic information to arrive from the front. One night on a South Carolina plantation two girls were awakened by the barking of a dog to hear the manservant of a soldier-relative tell the following tale to the mother of his master: " 'Oh! miss, Marse Frank is done for. When dem cannon 'gin to bellow and roar fore the Battle of Seven Pines, he come to me and say, "Here Bip, if I fall today carry my Bible and watch to my mother; goodbye." And he choke like and walk off quick, looking so fine and grand in dem shiny clothes. "My God," I say, "Marse Frank, lemme go too." But the drum beat and de music start, and our mens get wild, dey fight like tigers, but I ain't see Marse Frank no more. Late that evenin' . . . Marse Shelton Moore gallop by me, en he wipe he eye and say, "Bip, Frank is killed. . . . Go home and tell his mother." So, miss, I come, but my heart is broke for the young master I left behind.' "[35]

Some of those who received death notices were so unrestrained in the expression of their grief that fears were entertained for their sanity. " 'Oh, God! God, they have not slain my boy?' " screamed one woman as, with pallid cheeks and glaring eyes, she stretched forth her hands to those who told her of the death of her son.[36] Another woman, when informed of the death of her husband by a servant, uttered the most piercing shrieks for nearly an hour and then fell into a swoon which indicated strong symptoms of an unbalanced mind.[37] Of the demonstrations of a niece who had lost two relatives in the war, Catherine Ann Edmonston wrote, "Her grief is fearful! In the most heart rending accents she would call on her husband! on her brother! Exclaim that they were her all! until one's heart and brain reeled at the presence of such sorrow."[38] " 'This,' " said a half-demented woman in Richmond as she pointed to blood stains on the floor of her parlor, " 'this will always be here; it is part of my boy's body, and I am glad the floor was bare when they brought him home; this, and a lock of hair clotted with blood, is all I have left, and they will never be far from me.' "[39] Equally strident were the expressions of grief uttered by groups of women who stood near the battlefields as the victims were brought to the rear. "The screams of the women of Vicksburg were the saddest I have ever heard," said a resident of that city during the siege. "The wailings over the dead seemed full of heart-sick agony. I cannot attempt to describe the thrill of pity, mingled with fear, that pierced my soul, as suddenly vibrating through the air would come these sorrowful shrieks."[40]

" 'Death deserts the army and takes fancy shots of the most eccentric kind nearer home,' " said a quaint old uncle of Mary Boykin Chesnut; while the South Carolina diarist herself declared that "Grief and constant anxiety killed nearly as many women at home as men are killed on the battlefield." Although the latter assertion was most certainly an exaggeration, it is undoubtedly true that hundreds of women did actually die of grief during the conflict. "Hearts do break in silence, without a word or a sigh," wrote Mrs. Chesnut in 1864. "Mrs. Means and Mary Barnwell made no moan—simply turned their faces to the wall and died. How many more that we know not of!" In another portion of her diary, this observer wrote of a woman who was told that her son had been killed; then told that the news was false. In the midst of her wild delight over the second report, however, a hearse drove up to her gate with the body. The sudden changes from grief to joy and from joy to grief again were more than this afflicted mother could bear.[41]

Added to the private griefs of the women was the grief caused by the great public disasters which overtook the Confederacy. The loss of great battles brought gloom, equalled in extent only by that occasioned by the deaths of popular heroes. "I found myself weeping, not for my changed life, not for my own sorrows, but for the dear city," said Mrs. Roger A. Pryor of the time when the sound of the enemy's guns told her that Richmond was being attacked; "the dear, doomed city, so loved! so loved!" "The news from Gettysburg," wrote this same chronicler, "plunged our state into mourning and lamentation," only to be followed by the news from Vicksburg, which brought the realization to many that "surely and swiftly the coil was tightening around us."[42] The death of Stonewall Jackson doubtless caused more grief among the women generally than any other single event of the war. "How can I record the sorrow which has befallen our country? . . . The good, the great, the glorious Stonewall Jackson is numbered with the dead!" wrote Judith W. McGuire in expressing the sentiments of the women of Virginia.[43] Mrs. Louis D. Wigfall expressed the thoughts of the women of the lower South when she wrote, "We are all saddened to the heart tonight by hearing of the death of our hero Jackson! . . . It will cause mourning all over the land and each person seems to feel as if he had lost a relative."[44] Sorrowful women decked his funeral car with wreaths and crosses, and as his body lay in state in the capitol at Richmond, they covered it with lilies of the valley and other spring flowers; for to thousands of the women of the South this Christian warrior was an instrument whom God had produced to champion their cause. Had they not believed that the same God who gave him would raise up other champions, they might have believed that his death would seal the doom of the Confederacy.

It was inevitable that women who manifested so much grief should attempt to give it some outward symbol. Out of the scant supplies of cloth which the blockaded Confederacy afforded, they consequently devised garments of the darkest mourning. "It is melancholy," wrote Judith W. McGuire in commenting upon the clerks who were associated with her in a government bureau, "to see how many wear mourning for brothers and other relatives, the victims of war."[45] The churches of Atlanta, said a local newspaper, were "filled with gentle women dressed in black," and during the last months of the war, according to one commentator, it was unusual to see women, anywhere in the Confederacy, not clad in that somber color.[46]

*   *   *   *

The incidents described in the preceding pages serve to illustrate the manner in which a considerable portion of the women of the Confederacy reacted to the countless series of tragedies and anticipations of tragedy of which a great war made them the helpless victims. For four long years they were forced to endure the suspense of knowing that many of those near and dear to them were exposed to the perils of camp and battlefield, hospital and prison; and they could, in numerous instances, see no hope for the future when dire apprehensions had been realized in the loss of friends and relatives. To maintain that the Southern women completely, or even largely, gave themselves over to tears and despair would be to contradict the many evidences of serious hopefulness and sane achievement, as well as the frequent references to gayety and frivolity which have been presented elsewhere in this book; but the fact remains that to thousands of these women the war was a sordid reality whose flashes of brightness were illusory. Anxiety and tragedy cut deep into their hearts, with a result that was disastrous to the morale of the Confederacy.

CHAPTER XVI

DEFEATISM AND DEMORALIZATION

THE constant strain of direful expectations, followed only too often by the realization of such apprehensions, inevitably affected the thoughts and emotions of the women of the Confederacy. The pessimistic forebodings which some had entertained since the beginning of the struggle were confirmed; the sanguine dreams which others had cherished regarding their heroes' winning easy victories in a glorious war were supplanted by discouragement, war weariness, and despondency. The enthusiasm to make sacrifices upon the altar of patriotism gave way in thousands of instances to a more elemental emotion, the desire to preserve self and kinsmen at all costs. The Southern women were made of the same clay as other women, and it was but natural that their stamina should have weakened under the terrible burden of anguish and suspense that was imposed upon them. It is true that some women showed greater powers of sustaining themselves under this burden than did others, and perhaps within the souls of a majority, patriotic emotions struggled valiantly to maintain themselves against the emotions of fright and despair; but the cumulative forces of the great disasters cut deeply into the morale of the women as well as into that of everyone else in the Confederacy. That the women did not become completely demoralized before the curtain was lowered at Appomattox in the final act of the great tragedy is indeed a high tribute to their heroic perseverance.

DESPONDENCY AND GLOOM

As previously indicated,[1] there were some women who, at the very outset of the war, expressed thoughts which contained the seeds of future demoralization. In fact this category included some of the most resolute of Southern patriots. "Poor fellows," wrote Mrs. Louis D. Wigfall on June 14, 1861, after a drive among the men in camp at Richmond, "how many will ever return to their homes!"[2] Nor was Judith W. McGuire able to enjoy the celebration that followed the victory at First Manassas. Two days after that event she expressed the fear that although the Northerners had been driven from the land, they were a people of such indomitable perseverance that they would return to butcher the young men of the South.[3] There was little cause for the abatement of such anxieties, for, as these women had predicted, many of the soldiers did not return to their homes and the Northerners most certainly did return to Virginia.

As the struggle progressed, a growing current of sadness crept into the writings of Southern women. "Never had so sad a Christmas dawned upon us," wrote Sallie A. Putnam in describing the manner in which the women of Richmond passed the great Southern holiday season in 1861. "Our religious services were not remitted, and the Christmas was plenteous as of old; but in nothing further did it remind us of the days gone by. We had neither the heart nor the inclination to make the week merry with joyfulness when such a sad calamity hovered over us."[4] The same state of mind was manifested by Julia LeGrand in commenting upon the New Year's at New Orleans. "We are so lonely-hearted," she wrote, "so wasted by early affliction; anxious, nervous fears and desolating losses, that we have nothing of feeling or interest to exchange with anyone."[5] A few months later the results of the spring battles increased the gloom. "Darkness seems gathering over the Southern land," wrote Margaret Junkin Preston on April 3, 1862; "disaster follows disaster; where will it all end? My very soul is sick of carnage. I loathe the word—war."[6] The next month a North Carolina woman expressed a willingness to be deprived of everything in order to conquer the enemy. "But," she added, "it is a gloomy time with us; everything seems to favor the Yankees."[7]

There was little in the events of the last months of 1862, nor in the two years which followed, to lift the spell of despondency that was gradually settling over the minds of the women; in fact there was much to increase it. If the Christmas of 1861 had been sad, that of 1862 was sadder. In many households there were no celebrations of any kind because of deaths. "How different the scene our house presents tonight and this time last year," wrote the head of such a household on December 25, 1862. "The sadness forbids any recognition of Christmas; we are scattered to our separate rooms to mourn over the contrast, and the library is in darkness."[8] Two years later the prevalence of want, disaster, and death had in numerous instances banished even the most wistful reflections regarding the celebration of what had once been the most joyous season on the Southern calendar. "Our thoughts, whether we will or no," wrote an Alabama woman on Christmas Day, 1864, "wander to where our armies are struggling to maintain our rights against fearful odds. Alas! when will this strife and bloodshed cease? When will we have peace? Sweet peace is in her grave!"[9]

With the passing of these weary months, cries for peace and predictions of defeat were mingled with increasing frequency in the chronicles of disaster which many women wrote. As early as September, 1862, there were some who quite inconsistently mixed their counsels of resistance to the bitter end with predictions of catastrophe if a speedy peace were not agreed upon. "If I dared hoped that next summer would bring us peace!" wrote a Louisiana girl at that time. "I always prophesy it just six months off; but do I believe it? Indeed, I don't know what will become of us if it is delayed much longer."[10] By 1863 a considerable number of women had learned to recognize the true significance of the growing series of disasters which was overtaking the Southern cause. "I feel depressed tonight," wrote Judith W. McGuire on May 20 of that year, in the prelude to a twelve months' narrative of suffering and defeat.[11] Other writings were equally despondent, abounding in numerous cases with predictions of inevitable doom. "One by one our towns and villages were depopulated and those who cannot leave have to bear the tyranny of the invader," wrote Kate Mason Rowland in Virginia on Easter Sunday, 1863. "Little by little is our beloved state slipping away from us until, like Ireland in the days of Cromwell, it will be ruled by a foreign power, a mercenary soldiery."[12] A Texas woman, predicting starvation as a result of Federal victories and the impressment of the slaves, wrote in January, 1864, "I wish the war will end and I reckon it will soon, but not in our favor I am afraid."[13] Regarding the attitude of the women of Alabama some months later, Parthenia Antoinette Hague wrote, "Day by day the newspapers brought us news of defeat after defeat; day by day they told us of the inexorable advance of the Federal troops; day by day the conviction strengthened with us that, struggle as we would, we were on the losing side, and ours was to go down in history as 'the lost cause.' "[14] By August, 1864, the conviction that further struggle was not worth the price was gaining adherents among the women of Richmond. "There is a strong feeling among the people I meet," wrote a friend of Mrs. Roger A. Pryor in that city, " that the hour has come when we should consider the lives of the few men left us. Why let the enemy wipe us off the face of the earth. . . . *I* am for a tidal wave of peace—and I am not alone."[15]

Although the women who entertained such thoughts as those which have just been described were unable to bring about the much-coveted peace, they sought by various means to achieve the same ends as those for the accomplishment of which the cessation of hostilities was desired. In large numbers they followed their soldier-relatives to the scenes of action, hoping to protect them in cases of danger or to aid them in cases of actual or anticipated distress. In still larger numbers they used their influence to dissuade relatives from entering or remaining in the army, a type of disloyalty which was manifested with ever-increasing frequency as the tragedies and hardships of the war mounted.

RAMBLING OVER THE CONFEDERACY

The frequency with which distressed women traveled about in the wake of husbands and sons was a notable feature of the life of the Confederacy. In fact there was never a time in the history of the South, until the coming of the automobile, when women moved about as freely and as widely as they did in those hectic years which followed the tragic news from Manassas. They journeyed in every direction—to Richmond, to Mobile, to Memphis, to Charleston, to hospitals, to battlefields, and to various other places where soldiers were concentrated, adding to the confusion already caused by the movement of troops and refugees. Wives of the humblest backwoodsmen, distressed over the strange circumstances which had taken their husbands from them, as well as the wives of rich planters, joined in this unprecedented migration. Richmond, the center of Confederate activities, became so crowded with refugees and feminine migrants of this type that, as has been noted elsewhere,[16] the problem of food and housing became extremely acute. There and to other places, however, the women continued to travel, patiently enduring the discomforts of high prices, scarcity and overcrowding in order to secure news from or catch glimpses of those who had left them to enter the army.

The men, knowing the perils of Confederate travel and the hardships of living in the congested areas of the South, strenuously urged the women to remain at home. When, for example, Ella King Newsom, the well-known hospital matron, announced to General Hardee that it was her purpose to go from Tennessee to Arkansas in order to visit her distressed parents, he advised her that the railroads were crowded, that she would find no boats or vehicles to carry her between the terminals of these lines at Memphis, that there was no food on which she could subsist en route, and no friends to whom she could apply for shelter.[17] Charles L. Blackford wrote to his wife, upon hearing that she was planning to visit his camp at Centreville, Virginia, "I do not think it safe for you to come down here, even if the other ladies do. You will suffer perfect torment, for every day or two I am off on some scout duty when I do not come home until late at night and you would be terribly uneasy and suffer as much as if I had been really killed."[18] Likewise, when Mary Boykin Chesnut offered to assist the wife of a relative in going from South Carolina to Richmond in order that the latter might be with her wounded husband, the father of the wife declared that in no case would he permit her to go and advised Mrs. Chesnut that it would be the better part of wisdom for her not to encourage his daughter in the projected trip.[19] A North Carolina woman who expressed a desire to visit her husband in the army was warned by a male relative that she would be "making the greatest mistake to leave home at this time,"[20] while a Tennessee husband threatened his bride with divorce if she persisted in her intention to follow him into North Carolina.[21]

In spite of the forcefulness with which it was asserted, however, masculine advice to the women regarding the wisdom of staying at home in war times was no more readily heeded by the women of the South than is masculine advice concerning feminine whims in normal times; for Confederate women flung considerations of prudence to the winds in order to gratify the over-mastering impulse to go to the aid of kinsmen in distress. Both Mrs. Newsom and Mrs. Blackford made the journeys against which they were advised, and, since there is no evidence to the contrary, it may be assumed that the other women mentioned in the preceding paragraph did likewise. The motives which impelled these women to make such trips are easily inferred from the accounts of contemporaries. "Sister Mag has made up her mind to go to the front where she can be at hand if Brother Amos is wounded," wrote a Florida girl in 1862. "This dreadful waiting, waiting, has almost broken her heart."[22] A Virginia woman was described as being "almost crazy" until she learned that she could join her husband in camp.[23] Many wives, especially those of prominent officers, considered the establishment of themselves and their families in their husbands' camps as in no sense incongruous or detrimental to military discipline. Among this group was Mrs. Roger A. Pryor who, with the aid of the army cooks and foragers, lived very happily in General Pryor's encampment on Blackwater River in Virginia.[24]

In their zeal to follow their relatives in the rapid movements often necessitated by the exigencies of military life, some wives and mothers rambled over the Confederacy with startling agility. Neither domestic obligations of the most important character nor warnings concerning the difficulties of travel on the Confederate railroads could keep such women at home. An example of this type of migrant was Mrs. S. E. D. Smith, a boarding-house keeper of Memphis, with a husband and one son in the army. When she learned on one occasion that these two relatives were ill in Mississippi, she boarded an over-crowded train, in spite of the protests of the crew, and rushed first to the scene of her son's distress. Putting him on another over-crowded train, again over the protests of the guards, she then went to her husband's rescue. After nursing the two men back to health she became a hospital matron, but her memoirs indicate that her zeal in the discharge of the duties of this profession did not prevent her from going on other excursions when she fancied that her son or her husband stood in need of her presence.[25] Sarah D. Eggleston was another woman of this type. "I performed an unusual amount of traveling during the war," she wrote in her memoirs, "for whenever the place where my husband was stationed was threatened by the enemy he would send me away and recall me again after the danger had passed." In the pursuit of this plan she moved back and forth several times between Mobile and her Mississippi plantation at one end of the Confederacy and Norfolk, Raleigh, and Richmond at the other extreme.[26] "I resolved to disregard my husband's express injunction never to leave home for any point within the lines without permission being obtained from him," confessed a third woman of this type in describing a foolhardy trip which she made with her baby and two servants from Bedford, Virginia, to Richmond in the hot and crowded cars during the summer of 1862. Arriving at her destination after many difficulties, she discovered that her husband had simultaneously gone to Bedford. She returned to that place, ill as a result of her experience, but, far from letting matters rest, she forced her husband to abandon a proposed trip to Louisiana in order to establish himself with her at a mountain resort.[27]

COMPLAINTS AGAINST MILITARY SERVICE

Far more detrimental to the cause of the Confederacy than the desire of the women to be near the soldiers were the efforts of a considerable element of the feminine population of the South to keep their men out of the army, or to induce those who had entered that organization to withdraw therefrom. Many of those who were otherwise patriotic expressed delight when they had no relatives undergoing the perils of camp and battlefield; others adjured their men to seek positions as far away from the enemy as possible. Even in the breasts of the most devoted women of the Confederacy there was a struggle between the exalted emotions of patriotism and the naturally human desire to have the lives of kinsmen saved at all cost, the latter emotion often triumphing over the former and expressing itself in strong complaints against the obligations of military service.

The letters and diaries of the period reveal many women belonging to the highest circles of Southern society who, although loyal to the Confederacy in many respects, were unwilling to tolerate the idea of their relatives being in active service. Notable among this group was Betty Herndon Maury, the daughter of the illustrious oceanographer, who complained bitterly against her father's taking part in a naval expedition which might endanger his life. She felt that his death would be an everlasting stain upon the reputation of the Confederate government, and that he should go to France or Russia where he would be out of danger and where his abilities would be best appreciated. She also objected strenuously when her husband expressed an intention to abandon the civil service of the Confederacy in order to enter the army. Military life, she affirmed, would be repugnant to his inclinations. "If he goes," she added with vindictive sourness, "he will make a greater sacrifice of tastes and feelings and worldly prospects than anybody I know."[28] Susan Bradford, the daughter of a Florida planter, confessed that her mother was bitterly opposed to her father's joining the army, an objection in which she herself heartily concurred; that her sister was "not a bit patriotic," since the latter was "almost broken-hearted" when her husband enlisted; and that an aunt was so confirmed in her opposition to military service that she refused her son permission to volunteer.[29] Margaret Junkin Preston was another who sought to prevent her husband's entering the armed forces. "I do not conceive that the indications of Providence point him to go," she wrote with passionate earnestness in 1862 when he was planning to enlist in Jackson's command; "and I have perhaps gone beyond a wife's privilege in my *strenuous* arguments to induce him to think so too. Oh! if we might only be permitted to withdraw from the turmoil of horrid strife —if it were only to a log cabin on some mountain side!"[30]

Instances of this sort might be multiplied almost indefinitely. Even Mary Boykin Chesnut protested mildly against her husband's facing the perils of a military career, feeling, on the eve of the Battle of First Manassas, that he ought to give up his "amateur aideship" and return to his "regular duties" as a Confederate Senator. On hearing it suggested that he could be of greater service to his country in a civil rather than in a military capacity, she wrote, "I do not say to the contrary; I dare not throw my influence on the army side, for if anything happened!"[31] One of the most striking cases of this type, however, was that of Catherine Ann Edmonston. She was wealthy, with no reason to fear physical want in the absence of male support, and she was passionately devoted to the cause of the Confederacy. Likewise, her husband was within age of service and, as a graduate of West Point, was presumably well fitted for a military career. Notwithstanding these facts, however, there are spacious records in her diary which demonstrate that she was delighted when circumstances prevented his entering the active service. When she heard that he had been unsuccessful in his efforts to obtain a commission in the Confederate army, she wrote, "I feel more settled than I have for months, and were it not for the extension of the conscript age to all under forty-five . . . I think I could sit down content with my husband at home." After receiving further assurance that he was not to be taken from her, she wrote a few months later, "As I listened to Mr. E's regular breathing by my side, my heart melted in grateful thankfulness that he was not exposed to the dangers and hardships of the battlefield and that I was spared the torture of uncertainty and anxiety as to his fate which now agonizes the hearts of thousands of wives and mothers in this Confederacy. God, I thank Thee!"[32]

The expedients to which some women could resort in their efforts to influence relatives to abandon the military service are well illustrated in the letters of Anne Perkins of Forkland, Cumberland County, Virginia. Although the possession of ample means and the presence of other male relatives at home forestalled the pleas of inadequate support and insufficient protection, her fears for his safety caused her to use every other conceivable argument to induce her husband, the captain of a troop stationed at Yorktown, to resign his commission and return to her. He should come home, she argued, because her father's mind was failing; because she and her children were ill; because he was not strong enough to withstand the hardships of camp life; because exposure to the enemy's bullets endangered his life; because he could resign his commission without dishonor upon himself and his country; and, most important of all from her standpoint, because his absence was breaking her heart. When told that the colonel of his regiment had praised him highly, she was full of disappointment. "I do not doubt," she wrote upon this occasion, "but that the high praise given by Col. Johnson was *well deserved,* and yet, darling, so little ambition and so much selfishness have I, that I would rather his speech were reversed if by that means you would come home." Over and over again she wrote such plaintive notes as, "I long for rest, either in your home, or if that cannot be, then I pray for the rest of the grave. . . . I am too miserable to give comfort to anyone on earth." As in the case of other women already mentioned, the news that her husband might take part in a battle threw her into wild panics. "O! my darling husband," she wrote on receiving such information, "if you should not succeed in getting your resignation accepted before you should go into battle, I feel as if my last hope will be taken from me. I never cease to pray that God will remove every obstacle in the way of its speedy acceptance and soon restore to us our only earthly protector."[33] Less

THE ARRIVAL OF THE INVADERS
(From Harper's Weekly)

pointed but of a similar character were the letters of Harriet Perry of Marshall, Texas. "Sometimes for days," said one of her gloomy epistles to her soldier-husband, "I have the most oppressive feelings. I feel there is a weight of tons and tons upon my breast and without any will of my own. I sigh and groan all the time. Oh, husband, I feel as if I should die here all alone. I can't take any interest in anything in the world, hardly my baby, and I don't think anything could arouse me but your presence."[84]

THE ENCOURAGEMENT OF DESERTION

If complaints of this character should have come from the women of the higher economic levels of Confederate society, it was only natural that they should be duplicated in the thoughts and actions of the less fortunate classes of white women. The women of the latter classes shared with their aristocratic associates the same anxieties concerning the safety of their kinsmen on the battlefield; they felt more acutely the economic problems created by the absence of husbands and sons; and, moreover, their stake in the Confederacy is generally considered to have been less than that of those who had extensive holdings of land and slaves to protect. Consequently, they wrote thousands of plaintive and disgruntled letters to their relatives in the army, the inevitable result of which was discontent among the soldiers, followed in countless numbers of instances by the worst of all military crimes, desertion.[85]

"I have always been proud of you, and since your connection with the Confederate army I have been prouder of you than ever before," ran a typical letter of this class. "I would not have you do anything wrong for the world; but before God, Edward, unless you come home we must die! Last night I was aroused by little Eddie's crying. . . . He said, 'Oh, mamma, I'm so hungry!' And Lucy, Edward, your darling Lucy, she never complains, but she is growing thinner and thinner every day."[86] Other letters from home were couched in similarly unpatriotic terms. A hospital matron in Richmond asserted that practically all of those received by the more humble of her patients contained complaints of hardships and expressed a desire for the stronger heart and frame to return and assist in the burden of supporting the family.[87] The letters received by the men of a certain North Carolina regiment, according to its commander, Colonel Lee M. M'Afee, were filled "with repinings and cowardly forebodings." A sister wrote to a member of this regiment, "Father and George think you had better go to the enemy. Billy and mother and Jane want you to try and get home. If a big crowd comes, you come too—that is my advice." Another member of this organization was advised by his wife, "I am glad to hear from you, and that you are coming home. . . . If you are coming, I want you to start right now. Start right now, and don't fire another gun for the rebels."[38]

One of the most extensive sources of information regarding the efforts of the women of the humbler classes to free their relatives from the army is found in the correspondence of Governor Zebulon B. Vance of North Carolina. The reputation of this official as a friend of the common people and as an enemy of the conscription policies of the Confederate government led discontented women to pour their complaints into his ears. In letter after letter, pathetic and semi-illiterate, they informed him of their sorrows, their hardships, and their desires to have husbands and sons at home. "He is the only man I haf that is able to work," wrote one woman in protesting against the recall of a son to military service after he had been released. "I has won small son that is sickly and is not able to work. All the way that I has to git my living is to keep up my farm and I am not able to tend my farm without help."[39] Another letter asked for the return of a conscript from whom nothing had been heard since he entered the army. "If he does not return shortly," said his wife, "nothing but starvation, devastation & final ruin to his family will be the consequence. . . . I have to break up housekeeping in a short time if he dont return."[40] Others based their complaints on somewhat different grounds. One wife expressed the belief that her husband ought to be left at home because of his valuable services to the community. "My husband," she wrote, "is a cooper by trade and is considered a very good won and has bin very bisey since the war. . . . I have bin very uneasy fer fere he would haft to go in the army."[41] Still another wife wanted her conscripted husband released because she believed that he had been illegally taken. "I parted with him," wrote this woman, "with all possible fortitude, nowinge it was a duty he owed to his country but hav learned since that he and others were taken without any lawful orders. If that be the case, I umbly intreat you to release him that he may return to the bosum of his family."[42]

Although the Confederate government, especially after the great losses in the battles of 1863, made strenuous efforts to enforce its conscription laws, the discontented elements made efforts equally as strenuous to evade the officers who were charged with this duty. Many draft evaders and deserters hid in the woods and in caves especially constructed for this purpose, a practice in which they were often given active assistance by their women folk. In many instances, wives fed the fugitives on food grown with their own hands and in some cases devised ingenuous methods of forestalling the vigilance of the conscription officers. Sometimes a certain bed quilt hung on the fence by a woman signified danger to a hiding man, while a quilt of another pattern meant safety. At other times a slight change in the method of calling hogs would inform a deserter a mile away that he could approach his home with impunity.[43]

Regardless of whether the complaints of the women against their relatives' serving in the armed forces were justified by the prevailing mental anguish and physical distress, such activity caused irreparable injury to the Confederate cause. Many men were thereby deterred from entering the ever-thinning ranks of the Southern armies, and others, when forced into these ranks by conscription, were induced to desert. "It is my deliberate conviction," wrote Major Robert Stiles, a man intimately acquainted with conditions in the Confederate Army, "that the Southern soldier who remained faithful under the unspeakable pressure of letters and messages revealing suffering, starvation, and despair at home displayed more than human heroism."[44] A memorial from western North Carolina asserted that the most of the desertions in that section were caused by the knowledge that families were suffering,[45] while a Florida editor declared in 1863 that "The murmuring from suffering families at home is going up to the camps, and is doing more to dishearten our brave defenders than the balls and bayonets of the enemy."[46]

✓   ✓   ✓   ✓

The courage of the women of the Confederacy was not superhuman; although generally long-suffering and possessed of a noble fortitude, they gradually weakened under the fearful trials and tragedies which were forced upon them. The result was disillusion and war-weariness; the feeling that the independence of the Confederacy was impossible to attain or not worth the cost which experience demonstrated it would entail; and a recoil from the thought of having relatives subjected to the perils of the many bloody battles which characterized the great conflict between the sections—defeatism and demoralization, as fatal to the cause of the South as were the great losses suffered on the battlefield.

CHAPTER XVII

THE DESTRUCTION OF THE CONFEDERACY

BECAUSE of the destructive character of the invasions which marked the last year of the war, the hardships suffered by the women of the Confederacy during that year were more severe than they had been during the first three years of the great conflict. As already suggested, the troubles of the women during the earlier period had been mitigated by the ability of the Confederate armies to limit the areas of invasion and by the tendency of the Federal commanders to enforce the restraints of civilized warfare. During the last twelve months of the war this situation changed, for Federal soldiers now penetrated into the very heart of the Confederacy, disrupted the bonds between master and slave, and wrought disaster and pillage upon a grander scale than ever before. The women of the invaded areas were not exempted from these outrages. They were robbed, their property was destroyed, their slaves were taken from them, and they were subjected to many other indignities and humiliations; for it was the opinion of many of the conquerors that these women should be punished for the large share they personally had in bringing on and keeping up the war.

THE APPROACH OF DISASTER

Exasperated by the tenacity with which the South, in spite of its inferior resources and numbers, held on to what the North considered an unholy cause, the Federal commanders became convinced in 1864 that the speediest and most effective means of bringing the Confederacy to its knees was the adoption of a policy of wholesale destruction. Sheridan was accordingly dispatched to ravage the Valley of Virginia, a task which he accomplished with such thoroughness as to render the region unfit for Confederate military operations in the future; and in the same year Sherman began at Atlanta his famous March to the Sea, the object of which was to bring the war, in all of its frightfulness and ruin, home to the inhabitants of the lower South and to destroy the granary that was feeding Lee's armies. Having reached and occupied Savannah, Sherman then began, early in 1865, his equally well-known march northward across the Carolinas, the conduct of his troops being characterized by systematic destruction, pillage, and general lawlessness, in which the culminating event was the burning of Columbia. In the meantime Grant was stubbornly battling his way toward Richmond.

As these commanders proceeded with the execution of their plans, disconcerting rumors regarding the possible conduct of their armies began to circulate with increasing frequency among the women of the areas about to be occupied. On every hand appeared "countless stories of the deeds of violence and brutality" which might be expected from the marching Northerners.[1] It was said that in territories already invaded by these armies, "Women are insulted—outraged. Household property—furniture of all descriptions—totally destroyed, provisions destroyed, negroes carried off; the whole land left a desert waste."[2] These rumors were doubtless exaggerated in certain instances, but that they were not without considerable foundation is demonstrated by well-known utterances of the Federal commanders themselves. "If the enemy has left Maryland, as I suppose he has," wrote Grant of what was expected of Sheridan in the Valley, "he should have upon his heels veterans, militiamen, men on horseback, and everything that can be got to follow to eat out Virginia clear and clean as far as they can go, so that crows flying over it for the balance of this season will have to carry their provender with them."[3] On the eve of his expedition to the sea, Sherman declared, "Until we can repopulate Georgia, it is useless to occupy it, but the utter destruction of its roads, houses, and people will cripple their [the Confederates'] military resources. . . . I can make the march and make Georgia howl."[4] In contemplating the northward march from Savannah, the same commander wrote, "The truth is, the whole army is burning with an insatiable desire to wreak vengeance upon South Carolina. I almost tremble for her fate, but feel that she deserves all that seems in store for her."[5]

The anticipation of such conduct naturally produced a morbid fright among the women. " 'What! leave us?' " cried one group of these distressed creatures after a detachment of Confederates who were retreating. " 'Leave us in the hands of the dreadful foe? Then God have mercy upon us poor, helpless, deserted women.' "[6] Susan R. Jervey experienced "an age of terror" on her lonely plantation in South Carolina,[7] and Catherine Ann Edmonston, similarly situated in North Carolina, reported, "The state of mind is pitiable! Such terrible uncertainty!"[8] After the protectors had gone, and the sounds of the oncoming foe were heard, these fears were intensified. Seeing the sky arched with fires caused by the destructiveness of the enemy alarmed the women of Columbia "like a winnowing of chaos,"[9] while the hearts of the women of Richmond "almost ceased to beat" when they heard the artillery of the advancing Federals roaring in the distance.[10] In describing the confusion which often prevailed under such circumstances, a Georgia woman wrote, "Women cried and prayed, babies yelled . . . and went off to sleep with a sob, dogs howled and yelped, mules brayed, negro drivers swore, while negro girls giggled, more from excitement and fright than from any mirth-provoking cause."[11] Although hopes that the invaders would not be totally devoid of common American civility were occasionally expressed, such suggestions "failed to remove the anxiety which sat upon the faces of all."[12]

The nervous apprehension thus created led to flights even more disorderly than those which had taken place during the earlier years of the war. "Oh! the wild confusion, the headlong haste," said a graphic description of the scene presented at a railroad station in Columbia during the hurried exodus from that city in February, 1865. "Many, who had not thought of leaving their homes, caught the contagious panic, and, at the eleventh hour, determined to flee. . . . What a crowd was there, shoving, pushing, cursing, swearing, trying to find room on the train for their worldly goods."[13] In many instances the crowds who endeavored to attach themselves in some fashion to the flimsy cars of the Confederate railway service were so great that "the aisles and platform down to the last steps were full of people clinging on like bees swarming around the door of a hive."[14] Those who had the doubtful good fortune of getting away on these trains were still confronted with the likely possibility of having their journey brought to a sudden end in some wilderness by reason of the worn-out tracks completely collapsing or being broken by raids of the enemy. On such occasions the passengers, "amid the wildest scenes of pushing, pressing, jostling, rushing, struggling, cursing, and praying," would make their exits, hoping to board other trains ahead of the broken rails or to find refuge in some farmhouse along the way.[15]

Even worse than the physical discomforts of these hasty departures were the anxious forebodings in the minds of those who fled concerning the lot of those who were left behind. "My God! How terrible if true!" exclaimed Malvina Gist when, pausing in her flight at Charlotte, she heard of the burning of Columbia. "What has been the fate of my parents and Johnnie! . . . Why was I ever persuaded to leave my home and dear ones in this time of danger!"[16] Another South Carolina woman, looking back from Kingville to see "a great red glare" in the direction of the ill-fated capital, stood in dismay and "felt a horror at the thought of Sherman and his cruel army being there."[17]

AWAITING THE ENEMY

Despite the existence of the fears which have been mentioned, there was a considerable number of women in the South who neither succumbed to them nor fled when the conquerors approached. Inured by three years of experience to the hardships and dangers of war, these women resolved to face the invaders with the fortitude they had exhibited on other occasions. They devised plans to evade the wrath of the enemy, secreted their valuables as best they could, and hoped that a foe not wholly barbarian would respect the conventions of civilized warfare.

The stratagems by which it was hoped to escape the wrath of the enemy were similar to those used in the earlier years of the war. Some women, rallying from the depression caused by contemplating the possible deeds of "a cruel and vindictive foe," hid pistols and daggers in the folds of their garments and comforted themselves with the belief that through the use of these weapons they could emerge safely from encounters with the invaders.[18] Others remained behind bolted doors, hoping to avoid obtrusiveness by keeping out of sight. When in the lion's grip, according to one of this class, motives both of honor and of expediency prompted a dignified silence rather than "a warm and open expression of feelings."[19] One of the shrewdest of the artifices employed by the women was that of placing their best food in the most conspicuous places, arraying themselves in their best clothing, and assuming their best manners, the theory being that such calculated courtesy would arouse the better instincts of would-be marauders.[20]

Both experience and apprehension impelled the hiding of valuables on a large scale during the last months of the war. These tasks were frequently performed by the women themselves, usually in the dead of night after the Negroes had gone to bed. "In doing this work," said a North Carolina observer, "ladies who had never in their lives left the house, even in the daytime, without an escort, wielded other tool than the riding whip or lifted heavier weight than the tea urn, bore heavy burdens unaided to the woods at midnight and plied the grubbing hoe and the spade."[21] The assistance of the slaves was not usually asked, since it was feared that they, willingly or under compulsion, might later reveal the hiding places to the Federals; and in those instances where such aid was secured the persons so employed were often sent away before the enemy arrived.[22]

The usual method of concealing valuables was that of burying them, a process which was effected in a variety of ways. Some, fearing thefts, buried their treasures under steps, under piles of wood, and under stones in their yards, or in freshly plowed fields near their houses. Holes dug in the woods and covered with leaves or pine straw, however, proved to be safer places of refuge from the inquiring bayonets and spades of the Federal plunderers. Sometimes, to make assurance doubly sure, a small watercourse would be dammed, the treasure, rendered as waterproof as possible, would be buried in the bed of the stream, and then the water allowed to resume its former channel. A less difficult process than burying was that of placing valuables under overhanging rocks, in hollow logs, or in the tops of trees, but hiding places above the ground were always attended with the danger that the articles might become the prey of the weather, of prying dogs, or of Negroes in search of rabbits and 'possums. Perhaps the most convenient but also the most risky expedient was that of secreting the valuables under loose planks in floors or in obscure corners of lofts.[23]

Such expedients are illustrated by many concrete instances found in the accounts of the times. Cherishing fondly their supply of Madeira, the ladies of the Allston plantation in South Carolina placed this precious store in a piano box and late at night lowered it into the bottom of a mill pond.[24] A family in Camden County, North Carolina, saved its chickens by driving them through a hole into the loft over their dining room. Although horses were usually placed out of sight of the invaders by being driven into swamps or other wooded places, a woman of Bainbridge, Georgia, directed a servant to hide a favorite animal in the loft of her house, where it remained safely while the enemy stole every other horse on the plantation. A South Carolina woman concealed a parcel of valuables under a setting hen, and another woman in the same state hung her meats on bent saplings which were then allowed to reassume their upright positions. This latter stratagem was employed on the theory that "creatures who steal from women and helpless children never dare look up." Others saved their meats by sprinkling flour on them and then informing all comers that the harmless substance was poison placed there by rough soldiers.[25]

Many women encumbered their persons with their most precious possessions; for, in spite of alarming tales, they believed that the invaders would not put their hands upon the persons of Southern white women. Long pockets of the stoutest homespun were made, filled with valuables, and hung to specially made waistbands beneath the folds of the ample skirts of the period. In such manner a woman was capable of storing "provisions for an indefinite period, besides spoons and forks by the dozen, tea, coffee, and so on."[23] Valuable dresses were often concealed by wearing several of them underneath a costume of ordinary material. The cumbersomeness of such habiliments often appealed to a sense of the grotesque on the part of those who beheld them. How suddenly fat one's acquaintances had become! was a remark frequently accompanied by laughter. "Our kind and generous neighbor," wrote Elizabeth W. Allston Pringle in describing an experience at Society Hill, South Carolina, "was a very, very thin, tall woman, but when I ran over to see her during these days of anxiety and she came out into the piazza to meet me, I could not believe my eyes. She seemed to be an enormously stout woman!"[27] How suddenly the lithe had become ungainly! was another observation often made. "A near neighbor came to see us in these times of peril," said a Georgia woman, "and in consequence of having arrayed herself in dresses over dresses, she found it impossible to ascend our flight of steps from the weight of her garments. Being conducted to a back entrance near the ground, she entered, but then discovered she could not sit down."[28]

THE ARRIVAL OF THE INVADERS

The appearance of the enemy in Southern communities was often attended, during the last years of the war, by circumstances well calculated to demoralize the women. From behind shuttered windows the feminine inhabitants of Columbia looked upon "a terrible army with banners, clad in blue, burnished blades and well polished guns, an endless stream of soldiers—infantry, cavalry, and artillery;"[29] while the glare of Sheridan's camp fires at Charlottesville, according to a woman of that place, caused "the impression of our besieged and forlorn condition to come yet more forcibly upon us."[30] The fires and detonations which heralded the fall of Charleston were said to have "reddened the sky and lit up the whole of the upper portion of the city" and to have stricken "even the bravest hearts with awe."[31] The gunboats *Charleston, Chicora,* and *Palmetto State* were blown up at their wharves on February 17th, followed on the next day by the demolition of the Northeastern Railroad Depot, a disaster which involved the death of about one hundred and fifty persons, the wounding of two hundred more, and the destruction of the northern part of the town. The flames raged down the entire length of Alexander Street, exuding a smoke which "darkened the sun as its hideous folds curled skyward." Then came sad farewells to the last Confederate column and the closing of shutters as the triumphant columns of the enemy, with bands playing and banners flying, took possession of the city where the first ordinance of secession had been passed.[32]

The fall of the capital of the Confederacy was attended by circumstances equally awe-inspiring. "All that evening," wrote Constance Cary of the hours immediately preceding the occupation of Richmond by the Federals, "the air was full of farewells as of the dead. Hardly anybody went to bed. We walked the streets like lost spirits until nearly daybreak."[33] On the next day, said another contemporary, there was "an accumulation of terrors and griefs that I humbly pray I shall never witness or share again."[34] First among these terrors was the explosion of the Confederate rams on the James, the impact of which shattered windows two miles away and created the impression that the city was being bombarded. Then came the firing of tobacco warehouses, their flames spreading rapidly to other buildings while bands of plunderers rushed about looting shops and lapping up liquor from the gutters into which it had been thrown. In the midst of this confusion, cries of "The Yankees! The Yankees are coming!" echoed up and down the streets as the invaders made their appearance at the edge of the city. Although the Federals performed the very useful function of checking the fire, their presence awakened bitter thoughts in the minds of the women. There was the Negro cavalry, brandishing swords, singing "John Brown's Body," and uttering savage yells which were replied to by the shouts of their own color among the civilian population. There was the hissing and crackling of the flames, the sounds of martial music, the rude cheers of the white soldiers, the neighing of horses, and the shroud of smoke through which the sun shone like a ball of fire. The tragic change was symbolized with dramatic intensity in Capitol Square where, amid the strains of "The Star Spangled Banner," the colors of the United States were raised over the building which the day before had been the capitol of the Confederacy.[35]

As reported by their feminine victims, the conduct of the invaders on these occasions was usually such as to fulfill the direful anticipations which had been entertained on the eve of the conquest. Such conduct took the form of threatening or abusive language, looting, burning, and in some cases acts of personal violence. "They delight in making terrible threats and they gloat over our misery," said a typical comment upon the language of the soldiers. When the author of this comment told a Federal captain that the South was only fighting for its existence, he is alleged to have replied, " 'We won't let you have it. . . . We'll starve you out! Not in one place that we have visited have we left three meals.' "[36] When a Georgia woman protested to a soldier who for the third time had seized the breakfast which she had placed upon her table, he looked savagely at her, according to her account, and said, " 'D--n you, I don't care if you all starve; get out o' my way or I'll push you out the door.' "[37] To a group of women at Aiken, South Carolina, who complained of the befouling of their rice, the only food supply which the invaders had not carried away, one of the soldiers is said to have answered, " 'Oh, when we are gone you all can pick up and wash it and while eating it think of the friends who gave you something to fill up your time.' "[38] A Tallahassee, Florida, girl applied to the general in command of that town for a pass to go to Memphis, whereupon he demanded a kiss in payment for the favor. To her indignant rejection of the suggestion, she records his reply as " 'Heigh-ho, little Rebel, you'll get some of this knocked out of you before you get to Memphis.' "[39]

Accounts of looting and vandalism occupy a large space in the feminine narratives of the conquest. "I ran to the front door and down the steps," wrote Mrs. C. P. Poppenheim in describing her experiences with Sherman's army at Liberty Hill, South Carolina; "saw them halt, then pass and seize a negro boy, take his horse and make him lead them to the lot. In a few minutes, a band of ruffians, a wild, savage looking set, dashed in the house, into the dining room, and swept all the silver from the table, that was set for dinner; ran upstairs, broke doors, locks and drawers, and the utmost confusion prevailed; the hammering sounded like a dozen carpenters were at work, and soon all the floors were covered with scattered papers, in their search for money and valuables." The next day brought a repetition of the same experience. "Thousands of Yankees coming on; one command after another in quick succession; all robbing and plundering; poor Mrs. Brown is robbed of provisions, silver and almost everything; they go down in the cellar and pour kerosine oil, molasses and feathers all together, and stir them up with bayonets." Nor had the vandalism ceased four days later, when the same narrator wrote, "The wicked Yankees! How they torment the people! The brutal wretches! How they insult helpless women! They take every morsel of food that is being cooked in the kitchen. . . . A foraging party led by a lieutenant, and a squad led by a captain, plunder every corner of the house that has not already been searched."[40]

Among others who reported similar experiences was a Georgia woman who saw soldiers, with hateful leers in their eyes, walk up her back steps and, with savage delight, cut her hams and shoulders into pieces. Then, according to her account, they brought out the sugar, flour, lard, salt, and syrup which had been hidden in a cellar under the house of one of her Negroes, indicating by a significant nod, which she recognized as plainly as though they had spoken, " 'You see, you can't hide anything from Yankees.' "[41] Still another account of this type was that narrated by a woman of Dunlord, Virginia. "It was terrific," she wrote, "for two days to be brought in contact with the ruffians who swarmed through our house polluting the air we breathed with their profanity and brutality." These marauders took a watch from the pocket of her mother and stole five hundred pounds of bacon, ten barrels of flour, two barrels of sugar, seventeen horses, and eleven saddles, in addition to large quantities of silver, jewelry, clothing, and house linen. Scarcely anything was left, concluded the victim of this vandalism, "except the hard tallow and leather."[42]

A typical experience with Federal incendiaries was that recorded by Mrs. A. P. Aldrich of Barnwell District, South Carolina. Sherman's men fired her house or threatened it with fire eight times, and her corn crib was saved from destruction only by the efforts of faithful servants and the appeals which she made to the more humane among the invading contingents.[43] Feminine accounts of the march through North Carolina indicate that arson and incendiarism were also prevalent in that state. "Not a farm-house in the country but was visited and wantonly robbed," wrote Cornelia Phillips Spencer of events occurring around Goldsboro. "Many were burned, and very many, together with outhouses, were pulled down and hauled into camp for use."[44]

ACTS OF VIOLENCE

The accounts of the women assert with emphatic reiteration that they were at times subjected to acts of physical violence on the part of the invaders. It was reported that an old woman of Lancaster, South Carolina, while engaged in prayer early one morning in February, 1865, was set upon by members of Sherman's command, who tore her spectacles from her face, rifled her pockets, and cried, " 'Get up, old woman; praying will do you no good now, for Sherman's bummers are upon you.' "[45] In a similar story it was alleged that certain members of General Potter's command at Manning, South Carolina, unwilling to believe the assertion of an old woman that she had no brandy hidden, forced her out of bed and, while she was in a faint as a result of the excitement, stepped over her prostrate form in a vain search for the mythical liquor.[46] Still a third tale of this type was related of a young woman at Berryville, Virginia. While attempting to escape from her house with a quantity of jewels, she was, according to the account which has been preserved, "seized by two ruffians on the stair-steps, held by the arms by one, while the other forcibly took the jewels; they then . . . lifted her over the banister and let her drop into the passage below." Among other experiences alleged to have been encountered by the same young woman on this occasion were those of having a fire set below her while she was attempting to remove some valuables from a perch and having a sentinel inform her in brutal language, after her house was in flames, that she could not enter the burning edifice to rescue her baby.[47]

Numerous instances are likewise related in which the Federal commanders failed to check the persecutions which the women experienced at the hands of the common soldiers. When the woman who was described in the preceding paragraph as having had her spectacles torn from her face at Lancaster, South Carolina, appealed to an officer to stop the violence of his men, he is said to have replied, " 'I can promise nothing. Every restraint is removed from our men in South Carolina.' "[48] In response to a similar appeal at Orangeburg in the same state, an officer is reported to have exclaimed, " 'The ladies be d--d! If it hadn't been for them encouraging and egging on the men to fight, the war would have been squelched long ago.' "[49] Perhaps the most extreme illustration of this type of behavior is found in an incident which is alleged to have occurred near Fayetteville, North Carolina, when a group of soldiers burst into the room of a girl who was dying of typhoid fever, while an officer, in spite of frantic supplications for his intervention being made by the women of the house, casually remarked, " 'Go ahead, boys; do all the mischief you can.' "[50]

The women further affirm that the conquerors occasionally subjected them to physical torture and other species of unjustified cruelty. According to one tale of this type, a group of soldiers in February, 1864, thrust the leg of a woman into hot coals near Clarksville, Arkansas, when she refused to reveal the supposed hiding place of her money, and upon receiving a second refusal, cooked her leg "until the flesh fell off from the knee to the toe."[51] There were likewise certain instances in which it is alleged that heinous crimes were committed. Mary Boykin Chesnut recorded the case of a handsome young girl who, failing to heed the suggestions of friends that she get out of the way of the armies, was raped and murdered by an independent band of several Federals before the very eyes of her mother.[52]

Although there is little evidence to support the belief that Negro troops were more ruthless than others who wore the Federal uniform, the women of the South dreaded the appearance of the black soldiers more than they did that of the white invaders. This situation was due largely to the fact that Southerners regarded the Negro as an anomaly in any capacity save that of a menial and also feared the demoralizing effect which his presence in arms often produced among those of the race who still remained in slavery. "Those dreadful negro wretches, whose very looks betokened their brutal natures," according to a typical feminine observation, "caused an indefinable thrill of horror and loathing."[53] Another chronicler described the appearance of the black regiments on Southern premises as attended by "shrieks and screams, mingled with curses and demoniac laughter."[54] Likewise, as in the case of the white invaders, the arrival of the Negro soldiers was often followed by noisy plundering and coarse familiarities. "They broke open the smokehouse, store-rooms, and barns," said an account of their conduct on a plantation in South Carolina, "and threw out to the negroes all the provisions and things that they could find. At last several of them ran up the back steps and . . . went into the house and began throwing things about, cursing and swearing, lashing long carriage whips about our heads and saying 'Damned rebels' very often; also kicking open doors, thrusting their bayonets into closets and wardrobes, tearing off the desk doors and evidently looking for wine and silver."[55] Among the various familiarities which they are alleged to have committed on such occasions were asking white maidens for kisses and forcing the servants to prepare feasts for them at the white man's table.[56]

Perhaps the most bitterly resented act of violence that was committed against the women of the Confederacy was the sack and burning of Columbia. A place of refuge for many women from the lower portion of the state as well as from Georgia because of its supposed safety from invasion, the beautiful capital of South Carolina became, on the night of February 17, 1865, a holocaust of destruction amid a mixture of wails and coarse laughter. The wails came from the women who had been left behind by the Confederates to share the consequences of the latter's defeat; the laughter came from the invaders who were jubilant over the opportunity to gratify their personal craving for loot and their patriotic desire to humble the capital of a state which they held responsible for originating a tragic war. Soon after nightfall flames burst out in many parts of the city, and the streets became crowded with helpless women and children, some of them in night clothes; agonized mothers seeking their frightened children rushed from houses about to be given to the flames, while invalids lay in the thoroughfares exposed to the perils of fire and smoke. In the meantime, soldiers moved from house to house, emptying them of their valuables and then firing them; Negroes carried off piles of booty, grinning and exulting over the good chance which had come their way; and officers and men reveled in the liquors and wines which had been brought from their hiding places.[57] "A wave of that corrupted mass, inflamed by liquor and every other excess," and led by a tall Negro with a whip in one hand and a torch in the other, was the impression which was stamped upon the memory of one woman by the invaders of her home;[58] while to another whose home was entered, the intruders appeared as a mass of "drunken dancing, shouting, cursing wretches," who took food and trinkets, tore up blankets, and arrayed themselves in ladies' finery.[59] The crowning act of vandalism was the destruction of the Ursuline Convent School. Before that edifice was ignited, wrote one of the nuns in a letter to the Congregation of Paris, some of the soldiers who had been detailed to guard it opened the piano and played and danced; others, with hatchets and crowbars, broke open rooms and trunks and rifled their contents, while one burly trooper entered the students' dormitory, carrying a holy water font which he insultingly shook in the face of a nun whom he encountered.[60] By morning the flames had spent their course, and the sun rose on "groups of crouching, weeping, helpless women and children" left in despair amid the ruins of what had the day before been their homes.[61] "Oh! the utter desolation of a city in ashes and its people wanderers!" wrote one of these victims. "Even the very landmarks were lost, and you stood a stranger on your own threshold. Nothing was left but smokeless chimneys, keeping ward over widespread ruin."[62]

Such stories as those which have been related in the preceding paragraphs are without doubt exaggerated by their impassioned narrators, but the fact that they exist in such great numbers prevents their being ignored by the critical reader. They are likewise substantiated in many instances by contemporary chronicles and accounts from the pens of Federal officers and other observers who accompanied the Union army in the South. In describing the methods of domestic plunder which were practiced by this army in Georgia, a newspaper writer attached to Sherman's command asserted that "every inch of ground in the vicinity of dwellings was poked by ramrods, pierced with sabres, or upturned with spades. . . . If the soldiers 'struck a vein' a spade was immediately put in requisition, and the coveted wealth was speedily unearthed."[63] Even worse conduct was mentioned in the dispatches of certain Federal commanders. Among a number of "the most outrageous robberies" reported as having been observed in South Carolina, General O. O. Howard listed those of a soldier violently striking a woman and then taking her watch from her, and of other soldiers' forcibly stripping the rings from a woman's fingers in the presence of an officer;[64] and General Francis P. Blair asserted that as the army was leaving that state, "every house on his line of march today was pillaged, trunks broken open, jewelry, silver, etc., taken."[65] Although Sherman is said to have instructed his men to deal moderately with the inhabitants of North Carolina, the vicious habits acquired in Georgia and South Carolina were too profitable to be suddenly abandoned upon the crossing of a state line. Three weeks after the army had entered North Carolina, one of the commanders of the Fifteenth Corps reported, "There are still a large number of mounted men from this corps; they are stripping the people of everything that can sustain life. I saw families of women, children, and negroes who had absolutely nothing to eat, and their houses and quarters stripped of everything— cooking utensils, bedding, crockery, etc. Some rascals are beginning to set fire to deserted houses of those who have fled to Goldsborough— also burning fences."[66] Similar outrages were also mentioned by one of General Schofield's subordinates as having been committed in the vicinity of Wilmington, where the population was terrorized by "stragglers, deserters from either army, marauders, bummers, and strolling vagabonds, negroes and whites." "To say nothing of insults and plundering," added this informer, "there have been three cases of rape and one of murder, to say nothing of rumors of others."[67]

MITIGATING CIRCUMSTANCES

Despite all the misery and destruction wrought by those who effected the final overthrow of the Confederacy, the historian must admit that there were mitigating circumstances which partly explain the harsh conduct of these conquerors. Much of the evil that occurred was nothing more than the inevitable consequence of the hard law of military necessity. The Federal commanders believed, as already pointed out, that the speediest and most effective means of securing victory and peace was by devastating the heart of the Confederacy; and the effects of the destruction which they wrought proved that their belief was correct. Moreover, the hardships which were inflicted upon the women could have been worse and more extensive. Individual Northerners, according to the testimony of the women themselves, often performed deeds of kindness for the victims of the bad conduct of their associates, and that the invaders were usually under some restraint is demonstrated by the fact that they generally respected the persons of the feminine inhabitants of the areas which they occupied. Likewise, it is scarcely just to assert that the conquerors were motivated solely by a spirit of ruthlessness in their treatment of the South. That such was not the case is well illustrated by the different fates accorded to certain Southern cities.

Savannah was not fired, and Charleston and Richmond were saved from the flames lit by retreating Confederates, the explanation being that these three cities were so located as to make possible their occupation by the Federal armies and the appropriation of their resources for Federal purposes. Atlanta and Columbia, on the other hand, were destroyed because their locations, at distances from Federal bases, made their occupation hazardous and the appropriation of their resources inconvenient. In other words, the discrimination made between the treatment of these two types of cities demonstrates that neither motives of humanity nor of inhumanity controlled the Southern policy of the Federal government; but rather the motive of military expediency, working at times for the alleviation of human misery and at other times for its promotion. And finally, it should be noted that, as will be illustrated more fully in a later chapter, the Federal commanders, as soon as they were satisfied that they had the South at their mercy, became conscious of the suffering they had caused and strove with commendable energy to relieve the physical distress that prevailed among the women and children of the defeated section.[68]

In recording the kindnesses which they received at the hands of individual Northerners during the last months of the war, the women of the Confederacy often displayed a generosity no less intense than was the asperity with which they recorded on other pages the injuries which they received. Tales of horror were followed in many instances by stories of rescues by Federal officers or by the more humane among the common soldiers. Among stories of this type was one from South Carolina, in which a New Haven trooper is said to have cared for a sick woman, whose home had been ransacked by a group of soldiers, "as tenderly as if he were her son and was ashamed of the conduct of his fellows";[69] also two stories from Georgia, one in which a soldier rescued a girl from another soldier who was trying to prevent her from leaving a room, and another in which two soldiers saved a woman from a ruffian who was attempting to seize her watch.[70] Still other stories of the same type came from Virginia, representative ones from this state including an instance in which an officer, with a wave of his sword, cleared a home of raiders, and the case of two young Philadelphians who, saying it was their custom to guard houses in areas occupied by their army, sat with the ladies of this same home all day, driving off marauders who might otherwise have wrought much destruction.[71] There were likewise many stories of soldiers' showing restraint in their treatment of Southern women. Those who pillaged her home in Columbia were described by Mrs. St. Julian Ravenel as being "in a way curiously civil and abstaining from personal insult," calling the women "ladies" and expressing sympathy for them,[72] while those who ransacked another house in the same city were said to have refrained from entering one of the rooms when informed that it contained an ill woman and her new-born baby.[73] It was even admitted that the dreaded Negro troops would scarcely dare to take the lives of non-combatants, and that when firmly addressed by women they frequently showed signs of civility.[74]

It should also be noted that the Federals were not the only persons who were guilty of reprehensible conduct toward the Southern women during the last months of the war; for numerous complaints were made against the behavior of the Confederates. Outstanding as an example of the rudeness of which Southern soldiers were said to be capable was the conduct of a detachment of cavalrymen when they were given a meal on the porch rather than in the dining room of the home of Eliza Frances Andrews at Washington, Georgia. "They were so incensed at not being invited into the house," wrote this diarist, "that mammy says they cursed her and said that Judge Andrews was a d--d old aristocrat who deserved to have his house burned."[75] The peculations and thefts committed by Confederate foragers were especially annoying to the women. Regarding the conditions which prevailed in north Georgia during January, 1864, Kate Cumming wrote, "Our cavalry behave very badly, taking everything they can lay their hands on,"[76] and another commentator, writing of the same region a few months later, asserted that "our army, while falling back from Dalton, was even more dreaded by the inhabitants than was the army of Sherman."[77] Doubtless the worst offenders of this type were Wheeler's troopers on their retreat through the Carolinas before Sherman. They were accused of stealing horses and cattle, chickens and ducks, furniture and various other kinds of property from the inhabitants of the regions through which they passed.[78] "I am sorry to say," wrote Charlotte St. Julian Ravenel in protesting against this conduct, "that Wheeler's men have done us more damage than the Yankees. . . . I do blame them very much for their wanton destruction of property they ought to protect."[79]

In addition to the complaints made against the depredations of organized Confederates, there were also many complaints regarding the conduct of unorganized detachments, deserters, and paroled prisoners. These men were reported to be "adoing a heap of mischief" in Texas during the early part of 1865;[80] while Kate Cumming wrote in Georgia, a month after Lee's surrender, "Scarcely a day passes without our hearing of some outrage committed by men calling themselves returned Confederates." Among such outrages was that of a man entering a house in search of gold and hanging the wife of the householder until the latter yielded the desired treasure, and that of two men leading a party of women to demand the surrender of commissary stores.[81] Although the depredations of organized and unorganized bands of Confederates were in no sense as extensive as those of the Federals, they cannot be disregarded as a cause of the hardships which were suffered by the women of the South.

*   *   *   *

After making due allowances for the inevitable exaggerations which are found in the feminine accounts of the behavior of the invaders, and for the fact that a considerable portion of the destruction was wrought by the Confederates themselves, the conclusion still remains that the mental and physical suffering of the women of the South during the last year of the war was painful and humiliating. The appearance of armies bent upon plunder and ruin in the heart of the Confederacy struck terror in the hearts of many, and the fall of a government of which so much had been expected caused many others to feel that hope was dead. Bad as such conditions were, however, they could have been worse; for, as will be demonstrated in the chapters which follow, the conduct of the conquerors was not so ruthless as it might have been, and the women proved able to adjust themselves, in a surprising manner, to the changed situation which followed the destruction of the Confederacy.

CHAPTER XVIII

THE MISERY OF DEFEAT

THE destruction of the Confederacy imposed upon the women of the South a formidable array of discomforts and disappointments. Among the distressing factors which contributed to the plight of these women after the surrender were poverty and physical suffering, the demoralizing anguish of a great defeat, the presence of the hated "Yankees" in their midst, grave apprehensions concerning the fate which these conquerors were supposed to have in store for them, and the pangs and hardships which attended the shattering of their traditional system of domestic economy. So depressing were these conditions that there arose among many of the feminine inhabitants of the vanquished area a belief that the failure of the Confederacy was a disaster from which there could be no recovery; that the surrender at Appomattox marked the end of an ideal and noble way of life, the memory of which could only invoke the bitterest regrets.

POVERTY AND PHYSICAL SUFFERING

The most pressing of the difficulties which confronted the women during the months immediately following the surrender was the physical suffering caused by the ravages of the Federal armies. "We are starving here," wrote a woman from South Carolina; "have nothing left to eat but sorghum molasses and black shorts bread. Sherman's army has left no living thing on their route; nothing but blackened chimneys and smoking ruins."[1] Other victims of Sherman's wrath had no food except small quantities of corn which they gathered from the deserted corrals of the enemy's horses.[2] The "heart-rending" destitution which prevailed in Atlanta in March, 1865, made it necessary for some women to walk sixteen miles to get the food which stood between them and starvation.[3] Two months later the lack of currency and stores in the same city was about to cause "the most absolute distress," and the terrible want in Macon and Augusta was provoking bread riots in which the women and children took active parts.[4]

Similar reports came from many other sections of the conquered area. At Holly Hill, once the center of a prosperous agricultural region in southwestern Tennessee, two thousand old men, women, and children had been reduced to poverty by the passage of the armies. There was not a store left in the town, not a fenced field in the surrounding country, and food could only be had by purchasing it at enormous prices and hauling it fifty miles over the almost impassable roads from Memphis.[5] In that portion of North Carolina which had been devastated by Schofield's army, "not a living animal, not a morsel of food of any description" were left. The women of this region were forced to subsist upon parched corn, peas boiled without salt, and scraps of meat picked up around the enemy's camps. "It was most heart-rending," wrote Cornelia Phillips Spencer, "to see daily crowds of country people, from three score and ten down to the unconscious infant carried in its mother's arms, coming into town to beg for food and shelter, to ask alms from those who had despoiled them;"[6] while a correspondent of the *New York Herald* observed "the gaunt figures of these wasted women," congregating at the railroad stations and "moving like clothed skeletons around the cars to gather up any corn which perchance may escape from the sack, or to scrape up the infusion of sugar and filth which crusted on the floor of a car where the saccharine casks had been."[7] In the Valley of Virginia women were observed leaving home, on foot or behind sorry nags, to beg the means of subsistence. "Here a tired woman, with a babe in one arm and a little toddler clinging to her skirts, appeared with a homemade basket to carry away her treasures of flour and meal," said a description of such a group. "There a twelve-year-old boy, dragging a wooden cart of his own construction. . . . Aged women, hobbling along, accompanied by tow-headed grandchildren. . . . Shy young girls, with basket and bag, blushing under the impudent leers and coarse jests of the loafing soldiery."[8] Even in aristocratic Richmond, during the weeks immediately following the fall of that city, the fare of the best families was said to consist of bread and water, with a joint of meat once a week as a great luxury.[9]

Scarcely less pressing than the lack of food was the absence of the physical equipment necessary for housekeeping. Many women were completely homeless, and others were frequently without adequate funiture and domestic utensils. A Columbia woman returning to her home after Sherman's departure from the city discovered "not a lock, bolt or bar on door or window—not a chair." One old bedstead "so mean as to escape the destructive clutches of the plunderers," and one bench with a foot off, constituted her furniture.[10] A similar fate had overtaken the household supplies of many other South Carolinians whose homes were in the path of Sherman's army. In Virginia Mrs. Roger A. Pryor, returning to the country place she had occupied before Lee's retreat from Petersburg, found her grass and flowers destroyed and the carcasses of six cows polluting her yard. Her house was littered with old cans and bottles, molasses drippings, flies, and other types of filth too nauseating to mention. Picture frames were empty, the only chair was bottomless, and the one surviving bed was a wreck fastened together with bayonets.[11]

The realization that the Confederacy was lost beyond all recovery caused the Southern women even sharper anguish than did the physical difficulties just described. This was in part due to the fact that the news from Appomattox came as a shock, a sudden substitute for the almost mystical faith that the Confederacy would ultimately triumph; for notwithstanding the approach of disaster in the early months of 1865 many women had continued to be hopeful of the success of the Southern cause. "Though everything looks dark at present," wrote Kate Cumming in January, "that is nothing. The sun is often obscured by clouds, only to shine out more resplendent than ever." Two months later the same writer asserted, "Though not one ray of light gleams from any quarter, the failure of the cause is impossible because of its justice."[12] Even after the fall of Richmond and the surrender of Lee there were women who failed to realize that the day of the Confederacy was in fact over. They took refuge in phantasy. There were rumors of delivery by a French fleet, the recognition of the Confederacy by the great powers of Europe, an armistice, the defeat of Grant after Appomattox, and the invincibility of the Southern soldiers on the basis of guerrilla warfare.[13] When relentless reality had brushed these rumors aside, some took refuge in religious faith. "I don't believe the God of battle will forsake us," wrote one representing this view. "He will bring us through this trouble, and many more perhaps, before He thinks fit to give us our freedom."[14] In fact there were a few women in the South as late as the summer of 1865 still under the delusion that the Confederacy would be resurrected.[15]

It was inevitable, therefore, that to women of such faith the news of the final failure should come "like a thunderbolt from a clear sky."[16] Many could not believe it at first; that Lee should have surrendered was beyond their powers of comprehension. "I seem as tho' in a dream!" wrote Catherine Ann Edmonston upon receiving the startling intelligence at her plantation in North Carolina. "I go about in a kind of *drowsy dream*. I sleep—sleep—sleep endlessly. I sit in my chair for ten minutes—I doze—I think of it but cannot grasp it or its future consequences! I sit benumbed! It is to me like the idea of eternity." The arrival of the tragic information at Richmond on the night of April 9th brought dullness and heaviness to the hearts of the anxious women who had remained there. "I cannot even now shake it off," wrote Judith W. McGuire on the following day. "We passed the night, I cannot tell how—I know not how to live at all."[18] Margaret Junkin Preston was "struck dumb with astonishment" at Lexington,[19] and Varina Howell Davis wrote to her husband, "The fearful news that I hear fills me with horror. . . . I do not believe it all, yet enough is thrust upon my unwilling credence to *weight me down to earth.*"[20]

When all doubts had been removed by confirmation of the early announcements, grief was unrestrained. "Oh, the bitter, crushing disappointment that has fallen on us," wrote a Virginia woman. "Oh, I wish I were dead, or if that is wicked, I wish I had a heart of stone that I could not feel love and hope, joy and sorrow."[21] The doleful second thought of the women was that four years of cruel sacrifice had been in vain; "that all the suffering, all the spilt blood, all the poverty, all the desolation of the South was *for naught;*" that the very fidelity, heroism, and fortitude of the section had wrought its undoing.[22] "Why all these four years of suffering—of separation—of horror—of blood— of havoc—of awful bereavement?" asked Margaret Junkin Preston. "Why these ruined homes—these broken family circles—these scenes of terror that must scathe the brains of those who witnessed them until their dying day? Why is our dear Willy in his uncoffined grave? Why is poor Frank to go through life with one arm? Is it wholly and forever in vain?"[23] Some few even took the attitude that God had deserted them. Cornelia Phillips Spencer said that she had lost an incentive to prayer,[24] and Betty Herndon Maury wrote, "My faith and trust are weak. I feel as if God had hidden His face from us as a nation and as individuals."[25]

Added to the feelings of disappointment were grave apprehensions concerning the terrible vengeance which the victors were suspected of planning to execute. There was talk among the women of being "sent to a country far away," and of life in "any desert spot" being preferable to living under "Yankee tyranny" and the sort of Union which the Northerners were expected to restore.[26] "We see before us humiliation, privation, and a life of continued toil," soberly reflected a well-informed North Carolina woman. "This Southern land is ruined for this and coming generations."[27]

BITTERNESS AND ANIMOSITY

The griefs and disappointments of the women were supplemented by what seemed to be an undying hatred for those who were considered the authors of their woes. Feminine curses and imprecations were said to have sounded above the steady tramp and martial music of the legions of victorious conquerors as they marched through Southern settlements.[28] Federal generals were characterized as "princes of high-way robbers," their men as "vermin" and "hoardes of dastardly ruffi-ans," and the desire was not infrequently expressed "to put a rope around the neck of every red-handed devil of a Yankee" in the South.[29] Women in occupied towns frequently refused to attend church services because they did not wish "to sit in God's house with Yankees" and to hear ministers pray for "that infamous scoundrel," the President of the United States;[30] and a drawing room of Richmond ladies, when told that a Southern editor had whipped a representative of the *New York Times,* "clapped their hands with joy that the 'miserable Yankee' should have been so well thrashed."[31] As already suggested, there were many women who went so far as to feel that exile would be better than the rule of the hated Federals. "If they try to play the masters," wrote Mary Boykin Chesnut, "anywhere upon the habitable globe will I go, never to see a Yankee, and if I die in that, so much the better."[32]

Observers noted that a distinct difference existed between the atti-tudes of the two sexes in the South toward their conquerors in the months immediately following the overthrow of the Confederacy. In many instances the men prudently showed a tendency to adjust them-selves to the changed circumstances, but the women, beyond recognizing the reality of the defeat, made few gestures in the direction of recon-ciliation. "In Richmond, Atlanta, Charleston and elsewhere," wrote T. C. DeLeon, the Southern women were "bitter and unforgiving." Every blind was closed and every curtain drawn in many cities and towns, giving an appearance as if a plague had entered. Federal officers often gave receptions, displayed their trappings, and sought to hold fine reviews in honor of the ladies, but the women of the defeated Confederacy were usually inclined to regard such advances with a haughty disdain.[33] The color of blue was often ignored completely. Compromising fathers and husbands dared not suggest to the feminine members of their households that they receive the Federals into their homes, for they knew what domestic hurricanes such suggestions would raise.[34]

The depth of the hatred felt by these women for the nation which had defeated them is strikingly revealed in the attitudes which were expressed in regard to the assassination of Lincoln. To thousands of Southern women the great Unionist was the instigator of a cruel and aggressive war, a conspirator against the integrity of their social order, the motive behind the legions of Grant, Sherman, and Sheridan; and his death was interpreted by them as the judgment of a righteous God. "It is said and believed," wrote Judith W. McGuire, "that Lincoln is dead, and Seward much injured. I trust that, if true, it may not be by the hand of an assassin, though it would seem to fulfill the warning of Scripture. His efforts to carry out his abolition theories have caused the shedding of oceans of Southern blood, and by man it seems that now his blood is shed."[35] A minister presiding over a congregation of women in western South Carolina spoke of the murder "as if a benefit had been conferred," and his audience applauded the deed as "a happy event."[36] A plantation mistress in the same state received the news as "very cheering,"[37] and a New York newspaper correspondent reported that women in Charleston "actually fell on their knees and thanked God for it as 'a crowning mercy.' "[38] That such expressions were not even more numerous was doubtless due less to feelings of regret over the deed than to the belief that Lincoln's successor in the Presidency was a worse evil than the Emancipator himself, for Johnson was regarded by the majority of Southern women as "the drunken tailor," a plebeian who was planning vengeance upon his native section.[39] "Lincoln the oppressor is dead!" wrote Catherine Ann Edmonston. "But if Booth intended to turn assassin why, O why, did he delay it for so long? Andy Johnson, the vulgar renegade, now President of the United States!"[40]

The grievances which the women nourished against the Federals were accentuated, in the months following the surrender, by many acts of the victors. This fact is most conveniently illustrated by the journal of Eliza Frances Andrews, a spirited record of events in a Georgia community, which affords perhaps the fullest available account of Southern feminine thoughts immediately after the war. To the initial objections of this diarist to "a vulgar plebeian like Andy Johnson," "a lot of miserable oppressors like Stanton and Thad Stevens," and the other members of "the gang that are swooping down upon us like buzzards on a battlefield," was added bitterness caused by the conduct of the Federal garrison in her town. There were "the gorgeous Yankee officers flaunting their smart new uniforms in the face of our poor, shabby Rebs"; "the old brute," General Wilds, who "actually seemed to glory in his brutal work" of turning Mrs. Robert Toombs out of her home; and the case of an aunt who had to purchase safety from a guard who had threatened to burn her house "by having this plebeian of a Yankee sit at the table." "I was so angry," said the young diarist in commenting upon the last named incident, "that I felt as if I would like to run a knitting needle into the rascal, who sat lolling at ease in an armchair on the piazza, looking as insolent as if he were the master of the house." When to her great regret this high-spirited girl learned that her father had taken part in a movement for coöperation between the conquerors and the conquered, she disdainfully admitted the necessity of coming to terms with "the pirate crew;" but she did not fail to add, "It has always been my doctrine that if we have to go to the devil, it would be better to go fighting, and so keep your self-respect."[41]

The treatment accorded Jefferson Davis by the Federal authorities caused the anguish of the Southern women to burst forth in a fresh passion of invective and hate. Although previously admired by few women, the President of the former Confederacy became a hero and a martyr when he was manacled in prison, and to the feminine population of the South his persecutors and jailers appeared as cruel and malicious villains for whom there was no pardon in the sight of God. The animosity of the Northern press toward him stunned the women's powers of thought, the distorted pictures of his reported attempt to escape in female attire causing some to remove their slippers and use them to beat the detested journals in their senseless wrath; and President Johnson's offer of rewards for the arrest of Davis and others on the charge that they were implicated in the assassination of Lincoln was declared to be the hardest of the burdens yet put upon the South.[42] "His treatment by the United States Government," said one, expressing a representative feminine reaction to the humiliations imposed upon the ex-Confederate leader in Fortress Monroe, "is a disgrace to the nation which can never be wiped out. What a record of crime is treasured up against the North! 'Vengeance is mine, I will repay,' saith the Lord."[43]

THE NEW STATUS OF THE NEGRO

Doubtless the most irritating of all the conditions which the failure of the Confederacy imposed upon the feminine population of the South were those which accompanied the new status of the Negro. The resentment against black regiments which had been manifested throughout the war was intensified when, after the surrender, these regiments began to assume a large share in the work of occupying the conquered areas. In the opinion of Eliza Frances Andrews, the Stars and Stripes in the hands of such troops was "a hateful old striped rag" which she wished the wind would "tear to flinders and roll it in the dirt until it was black all over as the colors of such a crew ought to be." The efforts of Northern missionaries to instruct the blacks in the rights acquired by emancipation was also a source of deep resentment. One of these emissaries was described by the Georgia diarist just quoted as "a whang-nosed fanatic . . . of the sleek unctious kind that tries to cover his rascality under the cloak of religion;" she wished that he would catch "a cough that would stop that pestiferous windpipe of his and follow him to—his last resting place." As illustrations of the "insolence and crime" which he had fostered among the former slaves, she cited the "ridiculous travesty" of Negro girls' flirting with colored troops; the "horrid blasphemy" of the belief that the missionaries had done more for the Negroes "than Jesus Christ ever did;" and the impudence of the Andrews maid, who came to wait upon the family table with her face whitened with flour which she had pilfered from the family bin. This writer felt that much trouble would be caused by the policy of "elevating the negro by putting into his ignorant, savage head notions impossible to gratify," and that the perfect interracial harmony which, in her opinion, had previously existed would be supplanted by a war of races, the outcome of which would be the extermination of the blacks. Obviously there was little room in the minds of such women for compromises with new ideas on the race question.[44]

Still another source of discomfort to the Southern women was the disruption of the bonds which had bound the slaves to their masters and mistresses. These women often failed to realize that this change had to come as an inevitable consequence of the triumph of the Northern armies; many received it as "astonishing information." "I could not understand it; it seemed inexplicable to me and suicidal to the last degree," wrote Catherine Ann Edmonston in describing her state of mind upon hearing that her husband and father were freeing the family bondmen.[45] Others predicted that freedom would inaugurate "the terrible days," and that "the sweet ties that bound old family servants to us will be broken and replaced by envy and ill-will."[46] The poignant occasions upon which such predictions were often realized brought additional sadness and gloom. A Louisiana girl, making her way to the Negro quarters with the expectation of receiving the usual greeting from her servants, found only one slave left. "When I got to the big gate which led to the fields," she wrote, "I looked through expecting to see fields white with cotton, and the cotton pickers with their baskets. But there were no negroes, and there were no cotton fields lying snowy in the sunshine. Not a single soul was in sight, and the fields were bare and brown."[47] Still others felt utterly helpless when the declaration of freedom had been followed by the flight of the freedmen. "Just imagine," wrote a Virginia woman of herself and her husband when they were suddenly abandoned by their entire household staff, "two forlorn beings as we are, neither of us able to help ourselves, left without a soul to do anything for us."[58]

Painful and distressing as were the conditions which have just been described, they did not suffice, however, to effect a complete demoralization of the women of the South; for, as will be shown in the following chapter, these women succeeded to a surprising degree, as the months passed, in making certain adjustments to the changed circumstances with which they found themselves surrounded.

CHAPTER XIX

ADJUSTMENT AND RECOVERY

ALTHOUGH it is often difficult for feminine hearts to forgive injuries readily and forget vanished glories easily, women—including those of the South—can be practical. The women of the defeated Confederacy soon recognized that all was not gloom in the post-bellum scene, and that adjustments to the exigencies of the times were both necessary and possible. They gradually learned the futility of resisting many of the demands of the conquerors, and at the same time learned that these conquerors were not as vindictive as they had imagined, that the Federal commanders were in fact capable of numerous acts of kindness and charity to a defeated people. In addition to this, the women undertook the task of physical and moral rehabilitation in their communities with something of the same alacrity as that with which they had, four years earlier, assumed the burden of assisting in the prosecution of the war. And finally, they recovered their pride, which had been severely shattered by the humiliation of a great defeat, by fostering and promoting the conviction that the Confederacy had not failed because of a want of valor among its soldiers or a lack of merit in its cause, but that the South had been overwhelmed by the superior numbers and the unfair tactics of its adversaries. As a result of their efforts in this direction, the events of the war were destined, in the years to come, to assume the proportions of the heroic, to live in the minds of the Southern women as a memory no less glorious than that of the civilization which the Southern soldiers had fought to sustain.

A NEW VIEW OF THE CONQUERORS

As time passed, allowing the violent passions of the war period to subside, some of the bitterness and hatred with which the Southern women had previously regarded the conquerors began to disappear. Many women were forced to acknowledge that they had underestimated the fighting qualities of the Northerners, and others admitted, to a surprising degree, the necessity of their masculine associates' taking the oath of allegiance to the United States.[1] "Our consolation is that it is the will of the Almighty," wrote a Virginia woman in justification of the latter attitude. "Mysterious as the Providence is to us, we must *bow* into submission, and remember 'The Lord of the whole earth must do right.' "[2] These acts of adjustment were soon supplemented by women all over the South visiting the Federal commissaries to apply for food. "We said we *would* not do it—we could not do it," wrote one; but when acute distress had forced the problem, they did do it, swarming the rations offices to get their allotted portions of codfish, fat pork, and yellow meal.[3] Nor did the fact that these supplies were distributed by men who wore a uniform which the women had long learned to hate prevent the manifestation of grateful sentiments by those who were the recipients of such favors.[4]

Acts of kindness and generosity on the part of the Federal commanders, which were frequently shown to the inhabitants of the South when once it became evident that additional blows would not be necessary in order to effect the conquest of the region, were often acknowledged by the women with a readiness resembling that with which they had previously condemned the acts of these officers. Women who had been filled with deep indignation and resentment over the Federal occupation of Richmond admitted that General Ord, the officer in command of the city, was "polite and gentlemanly, and seems to do everything in his power to lessen the horrors of this dreadful calamity," and that feminine residents of the city who visited his headquarters "were treated with perfect courtesy and consideration."[5] General Cox, the officer in command at Greensboro, North Carolina, was characterized by a woman of that place as "a Christian gentleman and Presbyterian elder" who ruled "wisely and well,"[6] while the officer stationed at Chapel Hill in the same state was described by a local woman as being a gentleman who "deplored the inevitable accompaniments of war."[7]

Doubtless the most highly appreciated of all these courtesies was the scrupulous regard shown by the Federal authorities in Richmond for the feelings of Mrs. Robert E. Lee, who was an aged invalid confined to her home. The replacement of a colored guard in front of her house by a white guard evoked the gratitude of women throughout the entire South.[8] Nor did the women fail to appreciate the readiness with which the Federal commanders often responded to their complaints in regard to the quality of rations which were furnished to them at the government commissaries.[9] Even the fiery Eliza Frances Andrews found some good in Federal officers. Of a captain who had apologized for a raid upon the Robert Toombs home, she wrote, "He really seems to have the instincts of a gentleman, and I am afraid I shall be obliged to respect him in spite of his uniform." She also expressed pleasure when another Federal captain was invited to a barbecue given by several of her masculine friends, because he too "behaved like a gentleman," not associating with Negroes any more than he could help.[10]

ECONOMIC AND SOCIAL REHABILITATION

Without the emotional conflicts which troubled their relations with the conquerors, the women strove heroically to lift themselves out of the physical distress in which they had been left by the war. Various devices were utilized in satisfying the most pressing needs. Some made their first acquaintance after the surrender with United States pennies and dimes by selling cigars, pies, and other small articles to the Federal soldiers, and others secured enough food for themselves and their families by collecting scraps of meat from abandoned camps or by making journeys in makeshift vehicles behind improvised teams to distant plantations.[11] In Columbia the supply of beef left behind by Sherman's army was carefully conserved and apportioned; salt was secured by digging into the ruins of stores; cloth was fished out of wells; old bottles were made into drinking cups; the necessity of cutting hair was forestalled by having one comb serve a large group; and looking-glasses were provided by distributing the fragments of a large mirror.[12] Another effective means of securing necessities was that of exchanging old finery—veils, laces, gloves, parasols, and other articles of feminine adornment—with the Negroes in return for the products of their gardens and chicken yards. "I daily part with my raiment for food," wrote Mary Boykin Chesnut at Lincolnton, North Carolina. "We find no one who will exchange eatables for Confederate money; so we are devouring our clothes."[13]

The women also assumed with vigor the unaccustomed labors that were created by the dislocation of their domestic economy. "They cooked, swept, and scrubbed," said a report of their activities during the months following the emancipation of the slaves; "they split wood, fed horses, milked and watered the cattle, and took upon themselves the duties of not only the servants of the family, but . . . those of the men of the household as well."[14] And although such chores were difficult for hands unfamiliar with toil, they were often performed without complete gloom. "Sister and I do most of the house work now," wrote Eliza Frances Andrews in August, 1865. "Sister attended to the bedrooms this morning, while Mett and I cleaned down stairs and mother washed the dishes. It is very different from having a servant always at hand to attend to your smallest need, but I can't say that I altogether regret the change; in fact, I had a merry time over my work."[15] Even the washing of clothes, the *bête noire* of Southern white women, was undertaken without total despair. "As no one came to take out the clothes last Monday," wrote a South Carolina woman, "Marianne and I went to work very bravely. I went to the tub and she drew the water and hung out the clothes. I have scrubbed and rubbed until my poor hands are skinned, and my only consolation is the clothes ought to look very white and clean."[16]

Nor was the normally masculine problem of agricultural rehabilitation completely neglected. A Georgia woman, returning to the home from which she had fled during the war, put her house and farm in order before her husband could return from the army in Virginia. "She toiled in the kitchen, the garden, and perhaps in the open field," said an account of her activities, and when her husband arrived he found "the nucleus of a new start in life glorified by a woman's courage and fidelity under the most trying ordeal." A similar case was that of a woman in Duplin County, North Carolina. With the aid of two female helpers she began planting corn early in the spring of 1865, digging the holes, dropping the seed by hand, and covering it with a hoe. This example of industry had the desired effect of inducing the idle colored men of the neighborhood to enter into working agreements, and when the master of the farm returned from the army early in the summer, the season's crop was well under way.[17]

A spirit of determination and self-sacrifice was also manifested by the women in their efforts to rebuild the disordered foundations of Southern community life. "I don't mind being poor myself, I know I am ready and willing to give up all self-indulgences," wrote a Virginia woman in contemplating the ruin and desolation which surrounded her;[18] while of a South Carolina woman similarly situated it was said, " 'You see, she doesn't howl; she doesn't cry; she never, never tells anybody about what she is used to at home, and what she has lost.' "[19] This attitude was perhaps best and most concretely revealed in the numerous acts which were designed to revive the despondent spirits of the returning soldiers. As the footsore and penniless veterans of Lee's army straggled homeward, thousands of women, suppressing their tears, emerged from their houses to bestow food, clothing, and comforting words upon these discouraged creatures. "I ran out to speak to them in every instance," recorded Cornelia Phillips Spencer; "to shake hands and say a kind word, and to offer them something to eat."[20] "Dear mother always knows just what is best to do and say," wrote a Florida girl in describing the part played by the feminine members of her family in healing the physical and emotional sores of the former Confederates in their community.[21] Of such women, George Cary Eggleston afterwards wrote, "They kept their spirits up through it all, and improvised a new social system in which absolute poverty, cheerfully borne, was the badge of respectability. The want of means became a jest, and nobody mourned over it. The men came home moody, worn out, discouraged, and but for the influence of woman's cheerfulness,

ACCEPTING AID FROM THE U. S. COMMISSARY AT SAVANNAH

(From *Frank Leslie's Illustrated Newspaper*)

the Southern States might have fallen into a lethargy from which they could not have recovered for generations."[22]

Some observers were shocked at the promptness with which the Southern women resumed their social activities after the war. In 1865 Mary Boykin Chesnut noted with amazement that the young people of Winnsboro, South Carolina, "had a May-day celebration amid the smoking ruins;"[23] and Catherine Ann Edmonston was horrified that her neighbors in Halifax County, North Carolina, spent their time in "feasting, dancing, fishing, and merrymaking," a procedure which she characterized as "almost like dancing over their husbands' and brothers' and sons' graves" and portending a future without honor for the South.[24] Such gloomy interpretations of the frivolities of the times were scarcely justified, however, for the resumption of gayety was a hopeful indication of the recovery of the shattered morale of the women and a necessary factor in reviving the despondent spirits of the returned soldiers. "These are serious days and there is much food for thought," said a typical reply to the critics of post-bellum social diversions; "but we cannot always be sad and wear a long face. We must cheer the soldiers of the Confederacy who have so many battles ahead of them. A hand to hand fight with poverty is no joke, and that is what is staring us Southerners starkly in the face in the near future. Even so we will be merry while we may."[25]

THE BLESSINGS OF PEACE

Although the perverse character of the ending of the war caused the women much grief, the mere fact that some end had been brought to the horrible struggle was not without its compensations. The return of peace afforded a relief from the discomforts and inconveniences of the war-time economy. No longer did the women have to give a large portion of the products of their labor for the use of the army; no longer have to be without the aid of male relatives in solving the problems of physical existence; and no longer were they confronted with the necessity of making with their own hands the many articles which before the war they had purchased from the merchants. A North Carolina woman expressed pleasure that the time would soon be at hand when the stores would be open and she could substitute prints and muslins for war-time homespuns.[26]

The most satisfying relief that accompanied the cessation of hostilities, however, was of an emotional rather than a physical character. Instead of the terrible suspense of knowing that any hour might bring news of the death or disappearance of the men whom they loved, there was now an opportunity for the women to rejoice at the return of long absent husbands, sons, and lovers. These men were defeated and often hungry, ragged, and vermin-infested, but they were forever safe from hostile bullets, and they were heroes whose rags and disappointments but gave additional cause for love and admiration. "Your general lives. My colonel lives. What words can express our gratitude?" wrote a friend to Mrs. Roger A. Pryor.[27] "The sense of duty done, and the knowledge of God's providence overruling all things," said a South Carolina woman in summarizing the attitude of those whose relatives had returned safely, "filled us with joy and peace, and we exclaimed, 'The Lord is good.'"[28]

Another compensation for the anguish and disappointment which accompanied the surrender was a widespread belief on the part of the women that the defeat of the Confederacy was accomplished only through the use of superior numbers and unfair tactics by its adversaries. "They could not with equal numbers and fair fighting succeed over us," said a feminine estimate of the achievements of the Federals. "And we feel thankful that we were not whipped, but overpowered." This writer asserted that the numerical superiority of the Northerners was "at least twenty to one."[29] Among the unfair tactics ascribed to the enemy, the blockade and the use of Negroes and "foreign soldiers" evoked the most severe condemnation. The blockade was denounced as a dastardly trick which brought success to the North through the exhaustion of Southern resources rather than as a result of victories on the battlefield. "Had one port been left open—only one, by which we could have secured food and clothing," affirmed Judith W. McGuire, "Richmond would not now be in their hands; our men starved into submission."[30] With regard to the character and personnel of the Federal armies, another patriotic Southern woman asserted, "The North found that they could gain nothing by fighting themselves, so they hired foreigners, and at last had to take the *darky,* and Sambo boasts that the *rebels* could not be conquered until he took the field."[31]

The conviction that the Confederacy was overwhelmed by physical exhaustion, superior numbers, and the introduction of men who should never have been involved in the struggle inevitably led to the belief that the problem of the war was not to understand why the South was defeated but why it held out so long.[32] Such a belief naturally produced the feeling that the ultimate verdict of history would be on the Southern side. Although the Federals might spread their "false tales" for the present, it was confidently expected that some day a Motley or a Macaulay and a Walter Scott would arise to tell the truth and weave the halo of romance. Eliza Frances Andrews was positive that the heroes of these writers would all be Confederates, for "the bare idea of a full-blown Yankee hero or heroine" was to her mind preposterous. The Northerners, in her opinion, "made no sacrifices, they suffered no loss," and there was "nothing on their side to call up scenes of pathos and heroism."[33]

✓   ✓   ✓   ✓

The efforts at recovery which have formed the theme of this chapter were but the initial phases of a lengthy battle for the restoration of the ante-bellum civilization of the South. The course of this battle, the successes and failures of its participants, and the final settlement of the issues involved lie beyond the province of the present work. If the shadow of the great defeat continued for an indefinite period to envelop the thoughts and actions of thousands of Southern women, if it was ultimately realized by those who hoped to restore the cherished glories of a vanished civilization that this civilization was dead beyond the power of resurrection, and if there were many elements of the counterfeit in the attempted reconstruction of Southern society—these features do not obscure the fact that out of the ruins of the defeated Confederacy there arose many hopeful and forward-looking women who were destined to have a vital part in creating the civilization of the New South.

CHAPTER XX
RETREAT FROM GLORY

THE events of the War for Southern Independence made such a lasting impression upon the women of the South as to be for several generations the dominant influence in their lives. As is usually true of periods characterized by civic disorder and social dislocation, the most easily remembered of these events were the unpleasant ones. In spite of numerous cases of individual reconciliation, the hatred of Northerners to which frequent references have been made in these pages continued to glow in the feminine heart long after the veterans of the Blue and the Gray were bridging "the bloody chasm" through demonstrations of intersectional fraternity. Thousands of the women of the post-bellum South never tired of instilling into their young the vivid tales of bygone cruelties and wrongs, and in their estimates of the past there was no room for the saving graces of tolerance and good humor. The traditional softness of their natures was subordinated to their seemingly undying recollections of past grievances; they found no room in their hearts for even a simulated politeness to the Northerner who in any way exhibited his sectional principles. To them the great conflict of the sixties was a subject neither for debate nor for qualifying adjectives; both the rational and the irrational emotions which it evoked forced all conclusions into the simple categories of the right and the wrong, in which the South was always adjudged to be in the right and the North always in the wrong. Even well into the twentieth century, when in most fields of social and economic thinking the attitudes of the Old South had given way to those of the New, the number of Southern women sufficiently anachronistic in their thought to resent the Stars and Stripes flying in public places was by no means negligible.

Added to the women's heritage of hate was a nostalgia which tended to prevent an energetic grasping of contemporary opportunities. Too frequently the Southern women of the post-bellum period seemed only aware of such irritating conditions as poverty, "Yankee rule," Negro insubordination, and the rise of the lower classes of Southern whites to political power; they failed to appreciate such developments on the brighter side of Southern life as economic progress, interracial coöperation, democracy in education, the softening of the Northern attitude toward the section of the country which had been defeated, and the liberal share allowed the South in the life of the nation. Rather did they tend to become obsessed with the memories of a glorious past—a romantic figment dominated by slave baronies, ladies who were always gracious and beautiful, and gentlemen who were always brave and courteous. This was stark pessimism, for, unlike most heavenly visions, it was recognized that this past was dead and could never be resurrected. In keeping with such an attitude it is significant that the principal collective activity of the women of the South for thirty or forty years after the war was the decorating of the graves of dead heroes and the building of "those pathetic monuments which adorn the courthouse and capitol lawns" of every Southern state from Maryland to Texas.[1]

To believe, however, that the Southern women gained no benefits from the great struggle of the sixties would be to subscribe to the inaccurate generalization that suffering and sorrow have no compensations. Actually the war left the women a heritage which in some respects was both physically and emotionally helpful. "Heaven forbid," wrote a thoughtful North Carolina woman, "that we should forget the good the war has brought us amid such incalculable evils." Among the benefits enumerated by this writer were faith and courage, lessons in patience, charity, and ingenuity, and the bringing of all classes together in a unity inspired by a common purpose and by the splendid gallantry of the soldiers.[2] Similar meditations led another thoughtful Southern woman to write, "I am glad to have lived through a period like this, and believe that what there was in me of womanliness and strength of character and endurance is greatly due to the lessons of self-sacrifice and helpfulness taught me during the war."[3] In addition to these features, there was the heritage of glory sobered by disaster. The women had the proud privilege "of treasuring up the buttons, and the stars, and the dear gray coats, faded and worn as they are, with the soiled and tattered banner, which had no dishonoring blot, the untarnished sword, and other arms, though defeated, still crowned with glory."[4] Such reminiscences often brought grief and pessimism, but in a certain sense the melancholy of these women was uplifting. If they shed tears in visiting their many cemeteries and in listening to their orators and rimesters recount the pathos of the Lost Cause, these tears were proud.

And finally, there were many women who had the satisfaction of enjoying the afterglow of what they had considered a great civilization. They retained the roomy old mansions and the tangled gardens of the ante-bellum period, and in these homes and gardens they were privileged to associate with the men who had survived the great conflict. The Confederate veteran might be poor and disappointed, often maimed, and sometimes a worthless idler; but he charmed his feminine listeners with tales as stirring as any his country affords, and these listeners enveloped him with the aura of the heroic.

NOTES

CHAPTER I

CHAMPIONS OF THE SOUTHERN CAUSE

1. "Diary of Susan Bradford," in Susan Bradford Eppes, *Through Some Eventful Years* (Macon, Ga., 1926), p. 119.

2. Parthenia A. Hague, *A Blockaded Family: Life in Southern Alabama During the Civil War* (New York, 1888), p. 5. Cf. Susan L. Blackford, *Memoirs of Life In and Out of the Army in Virginia During the War Between the States* (Lynchburg, 1894), I, 5.

3. Unsigned letter from a niece of James L. Petigru to Minnie Pettigrew, Magnolia, S. C., Apr. 13, 1861, Pettigrew Letters.

4. Helen J. Backus to Anne H. Jewett, Wilmington, N. C., Apr. 29, 1861, in Martha G. and Mary A. Waring, eds., "Some Observations of the Years 1860 and 1861 as Revealed by a Packet of Old Letters," *Georgia Historical Quarterly*, XV (September, 1931), 275.

5. Mrs. Clement C. Clay, *A Belle of the Fifties* (New York, 1905), pp. 149-50.

6. *A Rebel's Recollections* (New York, 1905), pp. 62-3.

7. Helen J. Backus to Anne H. Jewett, Wilmington, N. C., June 4, 1861, in Waring, eds., *op. cit.*, p. 289; Kate Cumming, *Journal of Hospital Life in the Confederate Army of the Tennessee* (Louisville, Ky., 1866). p. 25.

8. "War Diary of a Union Woman in the South," in George W. Cable, ed., *Famous Adventures and Prison Escapes of the Civil War* (New York, 1893), p. 7.

9. *A Diary from Dixie* (New York, 1929), p. 170.

10. "Diary of Susan Bradford," p. 121.

11. *Ibid.*, pp. 135-6.

12. Chesnut, *op. cit.*, pp. 60, 150.

13. Catherine A. Edmonston, Diary, Sept., 1861.

14. Judith W. McGuire, *Diary of a Southern Refugee During the War* (Richmond, 1889), p. 94.

15. Kate Mason Rowland, Diary, Aug. 5, 1861.

16. See William S. Jenkins, *Pro-Slavery Thought in the Old South* (Chapel Hill, 1935), for a convenient and scholarly analysis of this theory.

17. *Journal of Julia LeGrand* (Richmond, 1911), p. 101.

18. Edmonston, Diary, Nov. 25, 1860. This argument was of course not originated by the women of the Confederacy, having been developed at an earlier period in such writings as E. N. Elliott, ed., *Cotton is King and Pro-Slavery Arguments* (Augusta, Ga., 1860), Josiah C. Nott, *Types of Mankind* (Philadelphia, 1854), and George Fitzhugh, *Sociology for the South* (Richmond, 1854).

19. W. W. Malet, *An Errand to the South in the Summer of 1862* (London, 1863), p. 156.

20. Rowland, Diary, Aug. 5, 1861.

21. Clay, *op. cit.*, p. 167; Rowland, Diary, May 10, 1861; Caroline Pettigrew to her mother, Magnolia, S. C., Mar. 19, 1861, Pettigrew Letters.

22. *Journal of Julia LeGrand*, p. 297.

23. Unidentified member of the Pettigrew family to her mother, Bonava, N. C., May 9, 1861, Pettigrew Letters.

24. Edmonston, Diary, June 27, 1861, May 16, 1862.

25. Blackford, *op. cit.*, I, 108.

26. McGuire, *op. cit.*, p. 13.

27. Edmonston, Diary, Apr. 24, 1861.

28. Catherine C. Hopley, *Life in the South . . . from the Spring of 1860 to August, 1862* (London, 1863), I, 330.

29. *Infra*, pp. 33-36.

30. Mrs. Thomas Taylor, *et al.* eds., *South Carolina Women in the Confederacy* (Columbia, 1903), I, 157.

31. Maria —— to a cousin, Dinwiddie County, Va., Apr. 26, 1861, Gilliam Letters.

32. Rowland, Diary, June 22, 1861.

33. *Ibid.*, Aug. 5, 1861.

34. *Life in the South,* I, 284-5.

35. S. P. Day, *Down South: or an Englishman's Experiences at the Seat of the American War* (London, 1862), I, 194, 208. Cf. "War Diary of a Union Woman in the South," pp. 7-8.

36. Mrs. Burton Harrison, *Recollections Grave and Gay* (New York, 1912), pp. 56-7.

37. Francis W. Dawson, ed., *Our Women in the War. The Lives They Lived; the Deaths They Died* (Charleston, 1885), p. 382.

38. M. E. to Mollie Hawkins, Waverly, S. C., May 21, 1861, Pettigrew Letters.

39. Eron Rowland, *Varina Howell, Wife of Jefferson Davis* (New York, 1931), II; 14-15, 128-9.

40. *A Diary from Dixie,* p. 33.

41. *Ibid.,* p. 3.

42. "Diary of a Young Girl . . . at the Nashville Female Academy When the Famous First Tennessee Regiment Went Marching to War," in C. Irvine Walker, comp., *The Women of the Southern Confederacy* (Charleston, 1908), n.p.

43. Hague, *op. cit.,* p. 4.

44. Mrs. Roger A. Pryor, *Reminiscences of Peace and War* (New York, 1904), pp. 98, 113; Chesnut, *op. cit.,* pp. 16-20; Clay, *op. cit.,* pp. 142-7.

45. *South Carolina Women in the Confederacy,* I, 156.

46. *Our Women in the War.* p. 11.

47. Edmonston, Diary, Jan., 1861.

48. Chesnut, *op. cit.,* pp. 35-7; Mrs. N. R. Middleton to Louisa Marston, Charleston, Apr. 12, 1861, in Alicia Hopton Middleton, ed., *Life in Carolina and New England* (Providence, R. I., 1929), pp. 115-6; Mary to Cary Pettigrew, Charleston, Apr. 13, 1861, Pettigrew Letters.

49. Anna to Cary Pettigrew, Charleston, Apr. 16, 1861, Pettigrew Letters.

50. *A Diary from Dixie,* p. 40.

51. W. H. Russell, *My Diary North and South* (London, 1862), I, 197.

52. *Our Women in the War,* p. 169.

53. Virginius Dabney to Lucy P. Chamberlayne, Richmond, Feb. 20, 1861, in C. G. Chamberlayne, ed., *Ham Chamberlayne—Virginian* (Richmond, 1932), p. 15.

54. *Diary of a Southern Refugee,* pp. 16-7. See Henry T. Shanks, *The Secession Movement in Virginia* (Richmond, 1934), pp. 158-90, for an account of the secession convention.

55. Maria —— to a cousin, Dinwiddie County, Va., Apr. 26, 1861, Gilliam Letters.

56. *A Diary from Dixie,* pp. 58-9.

57. Diary, Feb. 18 and 19, 1861.

58. Member of the Bryan family to an unidentified brother, North Carolina, 1861, Pettigrew Letters.

59. See J. G. deR. Hamilton, *Reconstruction in North Carolina* (New York, 1914), pp. 10-36, for an account of the struggle over secession in that state.

60. Edmonston, Diary, May 22, 1861.

61. Russell, *op. cit.,* I, 229.

62. Cited in Eppes, *Through Some Eventful Years,* p. 151.

63. Chesnut, *op. cit.,* pp. 49-50; W. L. Fleming, *Civil War and Reconstruction in Alabama* (New York, 1905), p. 230.

64. Mrs. Frances Hall, *Major Hall's Wife* (Syracuse, 1884), p. 7; "War Diary of a Union Woman in the South," pp. 4-5.

65. "War Diary of a Union Woman in the South." pp. 18-9.

66. *Confederate Veteran,* XXXIV (January, 1926), 45.

67. Rowland, Diary, June 16, 1861; Harrison, *op. cit.,* pp. 56-8.

68. *War of the Rebellion, Official Records of the Union and Confederate Armies* (Washington, 1880-1901), Ser. II, Vol. II, 561-77, 1315-21, 1346-51. (Hereinafter cited as *O.R.*) These exploits are also described in dramatic fashion by Rose O'Neal Greenhow in *My Imprisonment* (London, 1863), pp. 1-130.

CHAPTER II

THE CREATION AND EQUIPMENT OF ARMIES

1. J. L. Underwood, ed., *The Women of the Confederacy* (New York, 1906), p. 186.
2. Sarah Morgan Dawson, *A Confederate Girl's Diary* (New York, 1913), pp. 138-9.
3. Anna to Mrs. Cary Pettigrew, Charleston, Apr. 16, 1861, Pettigrew Letters.
4. *Our Women in the War*, p. 71.
5. *Ibid.*, p. 25. These "Home Guards," or local defense organizations which were exempted from the Confederate service by the governors of certain states, created a troublesome problem for the Confederate conscription authorities as well as for the Southern women. See A. B. Moore, *Conscription and Conflict in the Confederacy* (New York, 1924), pp. 57-8, 249-50, and Frank L. Owsley, "Local Defense and the Overthrow of the Confederacy," *Mississippi Valley Historical Review,* XI (March, 1925), 500-19, for further information on this problem.
6. Lieutenant Colonel [Arthur J. L.] Fremantle, *Three Months in the Southern States* (New York, 1864), pp. 173-4.
7. *South Carolina Women in the Confederacy,* II, 137.
8. *Ibid.*, II, 181.
9. Chesnut, *A Diary from Dixie,* p. 146.
10. "War Diary of a Union Woman in the South," p. 56.
11. *Infra,* pp. 222-27.
12. Betty Herndon Maury, Diary, June 3, 1861.
13. *Ibid.*, Oct. 6, 1861.
14. Sallie A. Putnam, *Richmond During the War: Four Years of Personal Observations by a Richmond Lady* (New York, 1867), p. 45.
15. Blackford, *Memoirs,* I, 116; Charlotte R. Holmes, ed., *The Burckmyer Letters* (Columbia, S. C., 1926), p. 56.
16. Dawson, *A Confederate Girl's Diary,* p. 139.
17. Pryor, *Reminiscences of Peace and War,* pp. 129-30.
18. McGuire, *Diary of a Southern Refugee,* p. 39.
19. *Ibid.*, pp. 99-100.
20. Lucy London Anderson, *North Carolina Women of the Confederacy* (Fayetteville, N. C., 1926), pp. 123-31. This record is perhaps unusual. Out of a total white population of 629,942, North Carolina contributed 125,000 troops to the Confederate service, proportionally more than any other Southern state and more men than there were legal voters in the state. See J. G. deR. Hamilton, *North Carolina Since 1860* (Chicago, 1919), pp. 7-12, and Thomas L. Livermore, *Numbers and Losses During the American Civil War* (New York, 1900), pp. 62-76.
21. *Wilmington Journal,* Nov. 26, 1863.
22. *Richmond Sentinel,* Oct. 13, 1863.
23. J. H. Heros von Borcke, *Memoirs of the Confederate War for Independence* (London, 1866), I, 179.
24. Fremantle, *op. cit.,* p. 147.
25. The work of the slaves under the supervision of the women must of course be taken into account. For a discussion of this phase of the activity of the Confederate women see, *infra,* pp. 160-75.
26. Fleming, *Civil War and Reconstruction in Alabama,* pp. 232, 246.
27. Blackford, *op. cit.,* I, 17.
28. Pryor, *op. cit.,* p. 133; T. C. DeLeon, *Four Years in Rebel Capitals* (Mobile, 1890), p. 198; *Our Women in the War,* p. 122; Putnam, *op. cit.,* pp. 39-40.
29. *Our Women in the War,* p. 301.
30. *South Carolina Women in the Confederacy,* I, 196.
31. *Ibid.*, I, 100-1.
32. Edmonston, Diary, Dec. 25, 1861.
33. Maury, Diary, Jan. 26, 1861.
34. Diary, Oct. 24, 1862.
35. Harriet to Theophilus Perry, Marshall, Tex., Feb. 19, 1862, Person Papers.
36. Martha Lee to Zebulon B. Vance, Eagle Rock, Wake County, N. C., Nov. 16, 1864, Executive Papers of North Carolina, Vance.

37. *South Carolina Women in the Confederacy*, II, 29-30.

38. *Ibid.*, II, 129-30.

39. Clyde Olin Fisher, "Relief of Soldiers' Families in North Carolina During the Civil War," *South Atlantic Quarterly*, XVI (January, 1917), 71.

40. Underwood, ed., *op. cit.,* pp. 97-8.

41. Fleming, *op. cit.*, p. 244.

42. *South Carolina Women in the Confederacy*, II, 20-5.

43. *Ibid.*, II, 39-40.

44. Mary A. V. Carroll to Zebulon B. Vance, Feb. 6, 1863, Executive Papers of North Carolina, Vance.

45. *South Carolina Women in the Confederacy*, II, 17.

46. Edmonston, Diary, Jan. 31, 1862.

47. *Infra*, pp. 82-85.

48. *Ocala Home Journal*, cited in Underwood, ed., *op. cit.*, pp. 78-9.

49. *Charleston Mercury*, Jan. 3, 1861.

50. Fleming, *op. cit.*, p. 244.

51. *South Carolina Women in the Confederacy*, II, 22-3.

52. *Ibid.*, II, 90.

53. Pattie W. Hedges in Walker, comp., *Women of the Southern Confederacy*, n.p.

54. Day, *Down South*, I, 127.

55. Daniel Hackney to Zebulon B. Vance, Chatham County, N. C., Nov. 29, 1862, in J. G. deR. Hamilton, ed., *Correspondence of Jonathan Worth* (Raleigh, 1909), I, 202.

✓ ✓ ✓

CHAPTER III

MARTIAL ENTHUSIASM AND RELIGIOUS FAITH

1. Dawson, *A Confederate Girl's Diary*, p. 5.

2. Hall, *Major Hall's Wife*, pp. 7-8.

3. *South Carolina Women in the Confederacy*, I, 172.

4. Edmonston, Diary, Oct. 30, 1860.

5. Mrs. Blake L. Woodson, *et al.*, eds., *Reminiscences of the Women of Missouri in the Sixties* (Jefferson City, [1916]), pp. 10-13; "Diary of a Young Girl . . . at the Nashville Female Academy," in Walker, comp., *Women of the Southern Confederacy*, n.p.; "Diary of Susan Bradford," p. 151.

6. Hall, *op. cit.*, p. 8.

7. *Our Women in the War*, p. 435.

8. *A Southern Woman's War-Time Reminiscences* (Memphis, 1905), p. 28.

9. *Infra*, pp. 217-27.

10. McGuire, *Diary of a Southern Refugee*, pp. 102-3.

11. *Our Women in the War*, pp. 70-1.

12. Kate V. C. Logan, *My Confederate Girlhood* (Richmond, 1932), pp. 50-1.

13. Baxter Smith in Walker, comp., *op. cit.*, n.p.

14. Dawson, *A Confederate Girl's Diary*, pp. 219-20.

15. "Diary of Susan Bradford," p. 202.

16. *Southern Soldier Stories* (New York, 1911), p. 204.

17. *Our Women in the War*, p. 220.

18. *A Diary from Dixie*, p. 155.

19. Diary, Feb. 17, 1862.

20. *Our Women in the War*, p. 404; Pryor, *Reminiscences of Peace and War*, p. 261; Edmonston, Diary, Mar. 15, 1865.

21. *Journal of Hospital Life*, p. 139.

22. Eggleston, *A Rebel's Recollections*, p. 68.

23. *Diary of a Southern Refugee*, p. 341.

24. *Ibid.*, p. 341.

25. Fleming, *Civil War and Reconstruction in Alabama*, pp. 245-6.

26. *Our Women in the War*, p. 42; McGuire, *op. cit.*, pp. 197-8.

27. *Journal of Hospital Life*, p. 115.

28. *A Confederate Girl's Diary,* p. 325.
29. Cumming, *op. cit.,* p. 159.
30. Fremantle, *Three Months in the Southern States,* pp. 143-4.
31. *Four Years in Rebel Capitals,* p. 192.
32. Chamberlayne, ed., *Ham Chamberlayne—Virginian,* p. 275.
33. *A Rebel's Recollections,* p. 71.
34. *Infra,* pp. 217-27.
35. Mary to John Iverson, Mitchell County, Ga., July 20, 1863, in Underwood, ed., *Women of the Confederacy,* p. 62.
36. Mollie to M. B. DeWitt, Henderson, Ga., Apr. 30, May 7, and May 11, 1864, DeWitt Letters.
37. Eliza F. Andrews, *War-Time Journal of a Georgia Girl* (New York, 1908), p. 87.
38. Putnam, *Richmond During the War,* p. 169.
39. Mary A. Loughborough, *My Cave Life in Vicksburg* (New York, 1864), p. 43.
40. Chesnut, *op. cit.,* p. 189.
41. *Journal of Julia LeGrand,* p. 40.
42. Mrs. W. W. Lord, Journal of the Siege of Vicksburg, July 3, 1863.
43. Edmonston, Diary, Feb. 28, 1864.
44. Mrs. M. H. Maury to Mrs. M. F. Maury, Charlottesville, Va., Mar. 15, 1865, Maury Papers.
45. Chesnut, *op. cit.,* p. 120.
46. Edmonston, Diary, Apr. 6, 1865.
47. *Our Women in the War,* p. 163; Rowland, Diary, July 22, 1862.
48. *Journal of Julia LeGrand,* p. 169.
49. Edmonston, Diary, Apr. 1, July 11, 1863.
50. *Journal of Julia LeGrand,* p. 235.
51. Nannie M. Corbin, to an unidentified cousin, Fredericksburg, Va., Feb. 12, 1863, Maury Papers.
52. Rowland, Diary, May 14, 1862.
53. *Burckmyer Letters,* pp. 133, 413, 440.
54. *Charleston Mercury,* Jan. 24, 1865.
55. McGuire, *op. cit.,* p. 108.
56. Edmonston, Diary, May 1, 1863, Mar. 20, Aug. 16, and Oct. 18, 1864.
57. Myrta L. Avary, ed., *A Virginia Girl in the Civil War* (New York, 1903), p. 356.
58. *Our Women in the War,* p. 154.
59. *Ibid.,* p. 275.
60. Mary K. Williams to Mrs. W. H. Polk, Warrenton, N. C., July 1, 1863, Polk Papers.
61. *Burckmyer Letters,* p. 126.
62. Mrs. E. L. Perkins to W. A. Perkins, Cumberland County, Va., Aug. 4, 1861, Perkins Letters.
63. *Diary of a Southern Refugee,* p. 31.
64. Diary, May 19, 1864.
65. Mrs. G. N. Stinson in Walker comp., *op. cit.,* n.p.
66. *Our Women in the War,* pp. 404-5.
67. Marietta M. Andrews, *Scraps of Paper* (New York, 1929), p. 217.
68. Mollie to M. D. DeWitt, Henderson, Ga., Sept. 10, 1864, DeWitt Letters.
69. Chesnut, *op. cit.,* p. 331.
70. Cornie Beckwith to Mary Pettigrew, Petersburg, Va., June 27, 1862, Pettigrew Letters.
71. Bettie to Tempie Person, Pleasant Grove, N. C., Nov. 10, 1863, Person Papers.
72. *Diary of a Southern Refugee,* p. 179.
73. Tempie to Bettie Person, Louisburg, N. C., Nov. 14, 1863, Person Papers.
74. Caroline to Charles Pettigrew, Hillsboro, N. C., Mar. 19, 1862, Pettigrew Letters.
75. McGuire, *op. cit.,* p. 266.
76. Mollie to M. B. DeWitt, Henderson, Ga., Apr. 29, 1864, DeWitt Letters.

77. Cited in J. Fraise Richard, *The Florence Nightingale of the Southern Army* (New York, 1914), p. 22.

78. *South Carolina Women in the Confederacy,* II, 29.

79. Mrs. M. F. Maury to J. H. Maury, Old Mansion, Va., Feb. 8, 1863, Maury Papers.

80. Mrs. E. L. Perkins to W. A. Perkins, Cumberland County, Va., Aug. 4, 1861, Perkins Letters.

81. Mollie to M. B. DeWitt, Henderson, Ga., May 5, 1864, DeWitt Letters.

82. Cumming, *op. cit.,* p. 52.

83. *Blackwood's Magazine,* cited in Mrs. D. Giraud Wright, *A Southern Girl in '61* (New York, 1905), p. 79. Cf. McGuire, *op. cit.,* pp. 142-3.

84. Diary, June 24, 1862.

85. Phoebe Yates Pember, *A Southern Woman's Story* (New York, 1879), p. 125.

86. *Our Women in the War,* p. 467.

87. *Reminiscences of the Women of Missouri,* pp. 258-63.

88. *Journal of Julia LeGrand,* p. 163.

89. Anna A. Stork, to an unidentified member of the Davis family, Barhamville, S. C., Aug. 5, 1863, R. Means Davis Papers.

90. Richard, *op. cit.,* p. 59.

✓   ✓   ✓

CHAPTER IV

RECEPTION OF THE INVADERS

1. The number of skulkers, peace advocates, and other disaffected persons who sought to evade the Confederate service was by no means negligible. See Ella Lonn, *Desertion During the Civil War* (New York, 1928); Georgia L. Tatum, *Disloyalty in the Confederacy* (Chapel Hill, 1934); and A. B. Moore, *Conscription and Conflict in the Confederacy* for an extended account of these classes; for their relations with the women of the Confederacy, see *infra,* pp. 225-27.

2. See *infra,* pp. 100-10, for a discussion of the refugees.

3. Fremantle, *Three Months in the Southern States,* p. 140.

4. Hopley, *Life in the South,* I, 306.

5. Unidentified writer, Oxford, Miss., June 5, 1862, Somers Papers; *Burckmyer Letters,* p. 205; Russell, *My Diary North and South,* I, 326.

6. Andrews, *War-Time Journal of a Georgia Girl,* p. 67.

7. W. C. Corson, *Two Months in the Confederate States* (London, 1863), p. 30.

8. McGuire, *Diary of a Southern Refugee,* p. 46. Cf. Edmonston, Diary, July, 1861; Maury, Diary, July 20, 1861; and A. M. to T. E. Cabell, Green Hill, Va., July 23, 1861, Perkins Letters.

9. Matthew P. Andrews, ed., *The Women of the South in War Times* (Baltimore, 1924), p. 45.

10. Edmonston, Diary, June 22, 1863; *Burckmyer Letters,* p. 291.

11. *Journal of Hospital Life,* p. 136.

12. *Burckmyer Letters,* pp. 66, 441; Edmonston, Diary, June 6, June 28, and Oct. 6, 1862; Cumming, *op. cit.,* p. 191.

13. Cited in Chesnut, *A Diary from Dixie,* p. 175.

14. Joel Cook, *The Siege of Richmond* (Philadelphia, 1863), p. 154.

15. Cited in *Journal of Julia LeGrand,* p. 299.

16. Cited in W. W. Davis, *Civil War and Reconstruction in Florida* (New York, 1913), p. 160.

17. Dawson, *A Confederate Girl's Diary,* p. 79.

18. Edmonston, Diary, Apr. 9, Nov. 14, Nov. 21, Dec. 31, 1862; May 23, 1863; Jan. 11, 1864.

19. Cumming, *op. cit.,* p. 68; *Journal of Julia LeGrand,* p. 247; "War Diary of a Union Woman in the South," p. 13.

20. Rowland, *Varina Howell,* II, 115.

21. Edmonston, Diary, June 1, 1861.

22. *A Confederate Girl's Diary,* p. 335.

23. Cited in McGuire, *op. cit.*, p. 192.

24. Cited in Edmonston, Diary, Nov. 9, 1862.

25. Caroline R. Searles in Walker, comp., *Women of the Southern Confederacy*, n.p.

26. *Our Women in the War*, p. 18.

27. Cited in Dawson, *A Confederate Girl's Diary*, pp. 191-2.

28. See John McElroy, *The Struggle for Missouri* (Washington, 1909); E. C. Smith, *The Borderland in the Civil War* (New York, 1927); and A. W. Bishop, *Loyalty on the Frontier* (St. Louis, 1863) for extended accounts of the situation in Missouri.

29. The outrages of these marauders are described in a dramatic but greatly exaggerated manner in James W. Evans and A. Wendell Keith, eds., *Autobiography of Samuel S. Hildebrand* (Jefferson City, Mo., 1870).

30. *Reminiscences of the Women of Missouri*, p. 216.

31. *Ibid.*, p. 32.

32. *Ibid.*, pp. 35-7.

33. Cited in Rowland, Diary, June 26, 1861.

34. *Our Women in the War*, p. 338.

35. Eggleston, *A Rebel's Recollections*, p. 63.

36. *Ibid.*, p. 64.

37. Rowland, Diary, June 7, 1861.

38. McGuire, *op. cit.*, pp. 51-3.

39. *Our Women in the War*, p. 19.

40. *Reminiscences of the Women of Missouri*, p. 275.

41. Clara D. Maclean, "The Last Raid," *Southern Historical Society Papers*, XIII (1885), 468-72.

42. Mary Hunt McCaleb in Walker, comp., *op. cit.*, n.p.

43. *Richmond Enquirer*, Mar. 30, 1865.

44. W. F. Forbes in Walker, comp., *op. cit.*, n.p.

45. Lucy London Anderson in *Fayetteville* (N. C.) *Observer*, Oct. 9, 1923, *Confederate Clippings*, University of North Carolina Library.

46. *Our Women in the War*, p. 92.

47. Sue L. James in Walker, comp., *op. cit.*, n.p.

48. Mrs. F. L. Sutton in *ibid.*, n.p.

49. Mrs. J. B. Crump in *ibid.*, n.p.

50. *Richmond Enquirer*, Apr. 7, 1864.

51. B. L. Ridley in Walker, comp., *op. cit.*, n.p.

✓   ✓   ✓

CHAPTER V

RELATIONS WITH THE ENEMY

1. *Our Women in the War*, p. 267.

2. *Diary of a Southern Refugee*, p. 213.

3. Cited in *ibid.*, pp. 142-3.

4. "The Journal of Ida Dulany," in Andrews, *Scraps of Paper*, pp. 66-7.

5. Anne to Emmie ——, Raymond, Miss., June 17, 1863, in Walker, comp., *Women of the Southern Confederacy*, n.p.

6. *Our Women in the War*, p. 378.

7. *Journal of Julia LeGrand*, p. 66.

8. *Our Women in the War*, p. 397.

9. Dawson, *A Confederate Girl's Diary*, p. 308.

10. Clay, *A Belle of the Fifties*, p. 184.

11. Rowland, Diary, June 16, 1861.

12. Dawson, *A Confederate Girl's Diary*, p. 160.

13. *Supra*, p. 12.

14. Day, *Down South*, II, 268-9.

15. Andrews, ed., *Women of the South in War Times*, p. 41.

16. *Richmond Enquirer*, Feb. 26, 1864.

17. *Reminiscences of the Women of Missouri*, pp. 78-82.

18. *Our Women in the War*, pp. 397-9.

19. Dawson, *A Confederate Girl's Diary*, p. 388.

20. *Reminiscences of the Women of Missouri*, p. 236.

21. Diary, May 11, 1862.

22. *Journal of Julia LeGrand*, p. 113.

23. *A Confederate Girl's Diary*, p. 397.

24. *Journal of Julia LeGrand*, p. 167.

25. *Our Women in the War*, p. 465.

26. Diary, May 17, 1862.

27. *Ibid.*, May 22, 1862.

28. *War-Time Journal of a Georgia Girl*, p. 290.

29. *Journal of Julia LeGrand*, p. 61.

30. Mary A. H. Gay, *Life in Dixie During the War* (Atlanta, 1894), p. 162.

31. *Journal of Julia LeGrand*, p. 180.

32. Kate Powell to George Carter, Upperville, Va., 1863, in Andrews, *Scraps of Paper*, p. 214.

33. *A Confederate Girl's Diary*, p. 61.

34. *Ibid.*, p. 69.

35. *Ibid.*, p. 71.

36. *General Butler in New Orleans* (New York, 1864), pp. 324-5.

37. *A Confederate Girl's Diary*, p. 78.

38. Parton, *op. cit.*, pp. 325-7.

39. Carl Russell Fish, "Benjamin Franklin Butler," *Dictionary of American Biography* (New York, 1929), III, 358.

40. Parton, *op. cit.*, pp. 331-41.

41. "The Diary of Harriette Cary," *Tyler's Quarterly*, IX (October, 1927), 104, and XII (January, 1930), 172.

42. McGuire, *op. cit.*, p. 165.

43. Cited in Rowland, Diary, June 7, 1861.

44. Andrews, ed., *Women of the South in War Times*, p. 211.

45. "The Journal of Ida Dulany," pp. 23-5.

46. *Confederate Veteran*, XIV (February, 1906), 72-3.

47. Anne to Emmie ——, Raymond, Miss., June 17, 1863, in Walker, comp., *op. cit.*, n.p.

48. Cited in McGuire, *op. cit.*, p. 279.

49. *A Confederate Girl's Diary*, p. 29.

50. Avary, ed., *A Virginia Girl in the Civil War*, p. 214.

51. Diary, May 11, 1862.

52. *A Confederate Girl's Diary*, pp. 73-4.

53. Cumming, *Journal of Hospital Life*, p. 92; Dawson, *A Confederate Girl's Diary*, pp. 32.

54. *Infra*, pp.

55. *Diary of a Southern Refugee*, p. 70.

56. *Ibid.*, p. 225.

57. *Our Women in the War*, pp. 67-9; Dawson, *A Confederate Girl's Diary*, pp. 383-93.

58. *Women of the Debatable Land* (Washington, 1912), p. 116.

59. Avary, ed., *op. cit.*, p. 89.

60. *Journal of Julia LeGrand*, p. 60.

61. Maggie Pittman to Rosa G. C. Burnette, Marley's Mill, N. C., July 26, 1864, Gilliam Letters.

62. For example, Marion Harland's *Sunnybrook* (New York, 1866).

63. Nashville was occupied by the Federal forces on February 22, 1862, and, although desperate efforts were made at Murfreesboro on December 31, 1862, and during Hood's campaign in the latter part of 1864, the Confederates were never able to rescue Middle Tennessee from Union control. It should also be kept in mind that the Union sentiment was very strong in Tennessee, the secession of the state having been effected with great difficulty. See James W. Patton, *Unionism and Reconstruction in Tennessee* (Chapel Hill, 1934), pp. 3-75, for an account of secession and the Civil War in that state.

64. Anson and Fannie Nelson, *Memorials of Sarah Childress Polk* (New York, 1892), pp. 170-3.

65. Mrs. Andrew McGregor to General L. H. Rousseau, Nashville, Jan. 27, 1864, in Walker, comp., *op. cit.*, n.p.

66. Maria to Tom ——, Nashville, Jan. 29, 1865, in *ibid.*, n.p.

67. Naomi Hayes to Mrs. W. H. Polk, Columbia, Tenn., Aug. 10, 1863, Polk Papers.

68. *Ibid.*, Oct. 10, 1863.

69. Mollie to M. B. DeWitt, Henderson, Ga., Dec. 26, 1864, DeWitt Letters.

70. For an account of the Civil War in East Tennessee see William G. Brownlow, *Sketches of the Rise, Progress, and Decline of Secession* (Philadelphia, 1862); Thomas W. Humes, *The Loyal Mountaineers of Tennessee* (Knoxville, 1888); and Oliver P. Temple, *East Tennessee and the Civil War* (Cincinnati, 1899).

71. A. G. Graham to Jefferson Davis, Jonesborough, Tenn., Nov. 12, 1861, *O.R.*, Ser. I, Vol. IV, 239.

72. Major T. J. Cannon to Colonel W. B. Wood, Loudon, Tenn., Nov. 10, 1861, *ibid.*, p. 233.

73. William B. Carter to General George H. Thomas, Kingston, Tenn., Oct. 27, 1861, *ibid.*, p. 320.

74. Memorial of Nathaniel G. Taylor in Edward Everett, *Account of the Fund for the Relief of East Tennessee* (Boston, 1864), p. 6.

75. *Supra*, p. 54.

76. David P. Conyngham, *Sherman's March Through the South* (New York, 1865), p. 328.

77. George W. Nichols, *The Story of the Great March; from the Diary of a Staff Officer* (New York, 1865), pp. 208-9.

78. James G. Gibbes, *Who Burnt Columbia?* (Newberry, S. C., 1902), pp. 20-2.

79. *South Carolina Women in the Confederacy*, I, 259.

80. *Augusta Chronicle*, Sept. 18, 1927, reprinting an undated obituary article by D. A. Dickert of Newberry, S. C. The subsequent career of Mary Boozer, according to this authority, was even more glamorous than her war-time activities, and doubtless without parallel in the annals of the women of South Carolina. When she reached Washington, a bill was rushed through Congress granting her $10,000.00 for the services she had rendered to Federal prisoners and the losses she had consequently sustained. She became a reigning beauty at the capital and married James Beecher, a wealthy resident of New York City, who gave her $100,000.00 as a wedding present. But he growing jealous and she tired of his commonplaceness, they were divorced. Armed with letters of introduction from prominent officials at Washington, she then went to Europe where, with the notorious Cora Pearl as her companion, she gained admission to the highest circles of society. At St. Petersburg a Russian grand duke fell in love with her and in his infatuation made her a present of his grandmother's jewels, worth a prince's ransom. She had the effrontery to wear these heirlooms of royalty to a court ball, and Czar Alexander II was so outraged that he ordered her out of his domains never to return on pain of death. Going thence to Paris, she met and married the French ambassador to Japan, receiving magnificent gifts from the Empress Eugenie. She continued her daring adventures in Japan, whither she and her husband soon sailed, her charms ensnaring a number of important officials in the Mikado's government. Divorced by the French ambassador, she married the Japanese prime minister, who, finally wearying of her continued indiscretions, had her thrown into prison and beheaded. For another account of the experiences of this adventuress, even more sensational than the one just cited, see *A Checkered Life: Being a Brief History of the Countess Pourtales, Formerly Miss Marie* [sic] *Boozer, of Columbia, S. C. Compiled by "One Who Knows"* (Columbia, 1878).

81. *Our Women in the War*, p. 106.

82. Cumming, *op. cit.*, p. 14.

83. Andrews, *War-Time Journal of a Georgia Girl*, p. 131.

84. *Diary of a Southern Refugee*, p. 296.

85. *Journal of Hospital Life*, p. 140.

86. *A Confederate Girl's Diary*, p. 135.

87. Underwood, ed., *Women of the Confederacy*, p. 119.

88. Pryor, *Reminiscences of Peace and War*, p. 298.

89. *South Carolina Women in the Confederacy*, I, 58.

90. *War-Time Journal of a Georgia Girl*, p. 59.

91. *Journal of Hospital Life*, p. 139.

92. *War-Time Journal of a Georgia Girl*, p. 64.

93. *War Pictures from the South* (London, 1863), pp. 166-70.

94. *A Confederate Girl's Diary*, pp. 74, 78-81.

95. Space does not here permit an examination of the merits of this contention, the authors being concerned only with the fact that such a war psychosis was prevalent among the Southern women. The opposite belief was entertained with equal vehemence in the North, both during the war and, as illustrated by the enormous amount of prison literature published and read, for a long time afterward. For a scholarly treatment of this controversial subject see William B. Hesseltine, *Civil War Prisons* (Columbus, Ohio, 1930), pp. 34-69, 114-72, 247-58.

96. *Journal of Hospital Life*, p. 186.

97. This feeling was also widely held in the North, and the criticism which it aroused there was an important factor in forcing the Federal government to agree to the cartel of July 22, 1862, providing for a general exchange of prisoners. See Hesseltine, *op. cit.*, pp. 7-34, 69-113, for a discussion of Lincoln's policy regarding exchanges and for an account of the technical questions growing out of the execution of the cartel.

98. *Journal of Hospital Life*, p. 147.

↗   ↗   ↗

CHAPTER VI

INSTANCES OF HEROISM

1. *Reminiscences of Peace and War*, pp. 280, 297.

2. *Our Women in the War*, p. 252.

3. "The Journal of Ida Dulany," p. 53.

4. *A Diary from Dixie*, p. 293.

5. *Diary of a Southern Refugee*, p. 124.

6. *Southern Soldier Stories*, p. 72.

7. *South Carolina Women in the Confederacy*, I, 163.

8. Underwood, ed., *Women of the Confederacy*, p. 194.

9. *Ibid.*, pp. 228-30.

10. Walker, comp., *Women of the Southern Confederacy*, n.p.

11. Hobart Aisquith, "A Confederate Mother," *Confederate Veteran*, XXXV (February, 1927), 75.

12. *Reminiscences of the Women of Missouri*, p. 103.

13. *Southern Historical Society Papers*, XXIII (1895), 328.

14. " 'Woman's Devotion'—A Winchester Heroine," in *ibid.*, VI (1878), 218.

15. *My Cave Life in Vicksburg*, p. 72.

16. Lord, Journal of the Siege of Vicksburg, June 28, 1863.

17. Loughborough, *op. cit.*, p. 61.

18. Walker, comp., *op. cit.*, n.p.

19. *My Cave Life in Vicksburg*, pp. 79-80, 91-2.

20. "War Diary of a Union Woman in the South," p. 73.

21. For a more detailed description of this diet see Loughborough, *op. cit.*, pp. 60, 105; Lord, *op. cit.*, June 28, 1863; and Ellen Martin in Walker, comp., *op. cit.*, n.p.

22. Loughborough, *op. cit.*, p. 114.

23. Lord, *op. cit.*, June 1, 1863.

24. *Journal of Julia LeGrand*, p. 52.

25. *A Confederate Girl's Diary*, p. 24.

26. Fannie A. Beers, *Memories: A Record of Personal Experience and Adventure During Four Years of War* (Philadelphia, 1888), pp. 217-20.

27. Andrews, ed., *Women of the South in War Times*, pp. 112-5.

28. Bradley T. Johnson, "Memoir of Jane Claudia Johnson," *Southern Historical Society Papers*, XXIX (1901), 33-4.

29. Cited in *Wilmington Journal*, Dec. 1, 1864.

30. Eggleston, *A Rebel's Recollections*, p. 66.

31. Andrews, ed., *Women of the South in War Times*, pp. 278-83.

32. Hunter, *Women of the Debatable Land*, pp. 51-5.

33. Walker, comp., *op. cit.*, n.p.

34. Blackford, *Memoirs*, I, 111.

35. Hunter, *op. cit.*, pp. 51-5.

36. Day, *Down South*, II, 76-7.

37. Rowland, Diary, Dec. 25, 1861.

38. Francis T. Miller, ed., *Photographic History of the Civil War* (New York, 1911), VIII, 287.

39. Lucy London Anderson in *Fayetteville* (N. C.) *Observer*, Oct. 9, 1923, *Confederate Clippings*, University of North Carolina Library.

40. Eggleston, *Southern Soldier Stories*, pp. 82-3.

41. L. C. Baker, *History of the United States Secret Service* (Philadelphia, 1867), pp. 170-3, That Miss Ford's information led to the capture of Stoughton was afterward denied by Mosby. See John J. Williamson, *Mosby's Rangers: A Record . . . of the Forty-Third Battalion Virginia Cavalry* (New York, 1896), p. 46.

42. *Supra*, p. 12.

43. *O. R.*, Ser. II, Vol. II, 561-77; Greenhow, *My Imprisonment*, pp. 16-39, 323; Harrison, *Recollections Grave and Gay*, p. 54; Carrol Dulany, "Mrs. Greenhow, Confederate Spy," *Confederate Veteran*, XL (May, 1923), 187.

44. *O. R.*, Ser. II, Vol. IV, 309-10, 349, 461.

45. The story of Belle Boyd's achievements for the South rests largely upon her own none too trustworthy account, *Belle Boyd in Camp and Prison*, 2 vols. (London, 1865). Marie A. Kasten, "Belle Boyd," *Dictionary of American Biography*, II (1929), 524-5, briefly appraises her career, and Joseph Hergesheimer, *Swords and Roses* (New York, 1929), pp. 235-64, weaves it into an engaging story. Hardinge died soon after their marriage, and she went on the English stage, making her debut as Pauline in *The Lady of Lyons* at Manchester in 1866. Success encouraged her to try the same career in America, where she made her first appearance at St. Louis, followed by a starring tour in the South and Southwest. In 1868 she appeared at New York in *The Honeymoon* and subsequently played in stock companies in Cincinnati, Houston, and Galveston. She was married in 1869 to John Hammond, a former officer in the British army, and in 1885 to Nathaniel High of Toledo, Ohio. In 1886 she presented a dramatic narrative of her exploits as a Confederate spy in Toledo, continuing this type of lecture until her sudden death from a heart attack at Kilbourne, Wisconsin, whither she had gone to speak, on June 11, 1900. Dion Boucicault's play, *Belle Lamar*, is said to have been based upon her experiences during the Civil War.

46. Avary, ed., *A Virginia Girl in the Civil War*, pp. 52-8.

47. Lucy London Anderson in *Fayetteville* (N. C.) *Observer*, Oct. 9, 1923, *Confederate Clippings*, University of North Carolina Library.

48. *Jackson Mississippian*, Dec. 30, 1862, cited in H. W. R. Jackson, *The Southern Women of the Second American Revolution* (Atlanta, 1863), p. 7.

49. *Three Months in the Southern States*, p. 173.

50. *A Visit to the Cities and Camps of the Confederate States* (London, 1863), p. 132.

51. These adventures, many of which are doubtless apocryphal, are described at great length in C. G. Worthington, ed., *The Woman in Battle: A Narrative of the Exploits, Adventures, and Travels of Madame Loreta Janeta Velasquez* (New York, 1890), pp. 40-226.

52. Charles M. Blackford to Susan L. Blackford, Fairfax Court House, Va., July 10, 1861, in Blackford, *Memoirs*, I, 57.

✓   ✓   ✓

CHAPTER VII

TREATMENT OF THE SICK AND WOUNDED

1. See the report of a Congressional investigating committee, Jan. 29, 1862, *Journal of the Confederate Congress* (Washington, 1904), I, 724-6.

2. Maury, *Diary*, June 21, 1861.

3. *South Carolina Women in the Confederacy*, II, 98-9.

4. *Life in the South*, I, 102.

5. Putnam, *Richmond During the War*, p. 68.

6. Day, *Down South*, II, 104.

7. *Diary of a Southern Refugee*, p. 29.

8. *Ibid.*, p. 163; *Our Women in the War*, pp. 338-9. For accounts of similar liberality in two Georgia towns see *Our Women in the War*, pp. 115-6, and Cumming, *Journal of Hospital Life*, p. 142.

9. *Supra*, pp. 18-24.

10. *Infra*, pp. 135-36.

11. Hopley, *op. cit.*, I, 415.

12. Mrs. S. E. D. Smith, *The Soldier's Friend . . . Four Years' Experience and Observation in the Hospitals of the South* (Memphis, 1867), pp. 34-52; Louise Benton Graham, *et al.*, eds., *History of the Confederated Memorial Associations of the South* (New Orleans, 1904), pp. 262-3.

13. *Our Women in the War*, pp. 258-60.

14. Mrs. Fielding Lewis Taylor, "Captain Sallie Tompkins," *Confederate Veteran*, XXIV (November, 1916), 521; Andrews, ed., *Women of the South in War Times*, pp. 127-9; Wyndham B. Blanton, *Medicine in Virginia in the Nineteenth Century* (Richmond, 1933), p. 303.

15. Richard, *The Florence Nightingale of the Southern Army*, pp. 13-88.

16. *O. R.*, Ser. IV, Vol. II, 199-200.

17. *The Soldier's Friend*, pp. 181-4.

18. Jessie Melville Fraser, "Louisa C. McCord," *Bulletin of the University of South Carolina*, XCI (October, 1920), 35-6.

19. List compiled from T. C. DeLeon, *Belles, Beaux, and Brains of the 60's* (New York, 1907), pp. 380-93.

20. *A Diary from Dixie*, p. 317.

21. Pember, *A Southern Woman's Story*, p. 112.

22. Hopley, *op. cit.*, I, 402.

23. Cumming, *op. cit.*, p. 53.

24. Pember, *op. cit.*, pp. 46-54.

25. *South Carolina Women in the Confederacy*, II, 215; Blackford, *Memoirs*, I, 45; Margaret to Cary Pettigrew, Abbeville District, S. C., May 1, 1862, Pettigrew Letters.

26. Augusta J. Evans to Ella King Newsom, Mobile, Oct. 28, 1863, in Richard, *op. cit.*, p. 93.

27. *Journal of Hospital Life*, p. 115.

28. Putnam, *op. cit.*, p. 318; Pember, *op. cit.*, pp. 15-6; Blackford, *op. cit.*, I, 179.

29. *urnal of Hospital Life*, p. 88.

30. *d.*, p. 78.

31. *Ibid.*, pp. 88, 95, 120.

32. *Diary*, Sept. 5, 1862.

33. *A Southern Woman's Story*, pp. 13, 157.

34. Cumming, *op. cit.*, pp. 13-4.

35. Harrison, *Recollections Grave and Gay*, pp. 182-3.

36. Pember, *op. cit.*, pp. 98-104.

37. *Journal of Hospital Life*, pp. 44-5.

38. *Ibid.*, p. 115.

39. *Ibid.*, pp. 46, 48, 53-4, 106.

40. *Our Women in the War*, p. 150.

41. *A Southern Woman's Story*, p. 101.

42. *Ibid.*, pp. 33, 55-7; Cumming, *op. cit.*, pp. 26, 31-2, 35.

43. J. W. Jones, *Christ in Camp* (Richmond, 1888), p. 199.

44. *Journal of Hospital Life*, p. 12.

45. Day, *Down South*, II, 104.

46. *Our Women in the War*, p. 227.

47. Andrews, ed., *Women of the South in War Times*, p. 136.

48. Cited in Loughborough, *My Cave Life in Vicksburg*, p. 171.

49. Pember, *op. cit.*, pp. 138-9.

50. Cumming, *op. cit.*, p. 106.

51. Cited in Smith, *op. cit.*, p. 226.

52. For more detailed and extensive information on the activities of the Catholic sisterhoods see George Barton, *Angels of the Battlefields* (Philadelphia, 1897), and Ellen Ryan Jolly, *Nuns of the Battlefield* (Providence, R. I., 1927).

53. Chesnut, *op. cit.*, pp. 205-6; *Our Women in the War*, pp. 2-4.

54. *South Carolina Women in the Confederacy*, I, 94.

55. Cumming, *op. cit.*, p. 150.

56. Mrs. J. S. Welborn, "A Wayside Hospital," *Confederate Veteran*, XXXVIII (March, 1930), 95-6.

57. Underwood, ed., *Women of the Confederacy*, pp. 108-9.

58. *South Carolina Women in the Confederacy*, I, 364.

59. *Diary of a Southern Refugee*, p. 176.

60. *South Carolina Women in the Confederacy*, I, 147-8.

61. Putnam, *op. cit.*, p. 135; Maury, Diary, July 20, 1862; Eggleston, *A Rebel's Recollections*, p. 67.

62. Andrews, ed., *Women of the South in War Times*, p. 233.

63. *Charleston Mercury*, Aug. 20, 1862.

64. *Four Years in Rebel Capitals*, p. 198.

65. *A Rebel's Recollections*, p. 69.

66. *Our Women in the War*, pp. 306-7.

67. Cumming, *op. cit.*, pp. 30, 33.

68. *Our Women in the War*, p. 274.

69. J. B. Polley, *A Soldier's Letters to Charming Nellie* (New York, 1908), p. 270.

✓   ✓   ✓

CHAPTER VIII

THE REFUGEES

1. Dawson, *A Confederate Girl's Diary*, pp. 37-8, 220; *Our Women in the War*, p. 213.

2. McGuire, *Diary of a Southern Refugee*, p. 68.

3. *From Flag to Flag: A Woman's Adventures and Experiences in the South During the War* (New York, 1889), pp. 34-9.

4. Dawson, *A Confederate Girl's Diary*, pp. 40-1; McGuire, *op. cit.*, p. 222; *Our Women in the War*, p. 302.

5. Pember, *A Southern Woman's Story*, pp. 142-9.

6. *Our Women in the War*, p. 165.

7. Pember, *op. cit.*, p. 152.

8. Cumming, *Journal of Hospital Life*, p. 36.

9. Clay, *A Belle of the Fifties*, p. 192.

10. *A Southern Woman's Story*, p. 151.

11. *War-Time Journal of a Georgia Girl*, p. 46.

12. Dawson, *A Confederate Girl's Diary*, p. 372.

13. *Diary of a Southern Refugee*, pp. 168-9.

14. *Reminiscences of Peace and War*, pp. 251-2.

15. Wright, *A Southern Girl in '61*, p. 175.

16. *Our Women in the War*, pp. 86, 438.

17. *Diary of a Southern Refugee*, p. 88.

18. Putnam, *Richmond During the War*, pp. 252, 320; Avary, ed., *A Virginia Girl in the Civil War*, pp. 349-53.

19. Cited in John B. McMaster, *History of the United States During Lincoln's Administration* (New York, 1927), p. 338.

20. *Diary of a Southern Refugee*, p. 247.

21. *Ibid.*, p. 324.

22. Putnam, *op. cit.*, p. 252; *Our Women in the War*, p. 99.

23. *Four Years in Rebel Capitals*, p. 234.

24. *South Carolina Women in the Confederacy*, I, 279, 281.

25. Putnam, *op. cit.*, p. 253.

26. *Our Women in the War*, p. 400.
27. *Diary of a Southern Refugee*, pp. 327-8.
28. *Ibid.*, p. 252.
29. *Journal of Hospital Life*, p. 91.
30. Dec. 22, 1864.
31. *Journal of Hospital Life*, p. 103.
32. *South Carolina Women in the Confederacy*, I, 174-5.
33. *Diary of a Southern Refugee*, p. 89.
34. Mrs. F. C. Roberts, *Historical Incidents* (Beaufort, N. C., 1909), p. 6.
35. McGuire, *op. cit.*, p. 325.
36. *South Carolina Women in the Confederacy*, I, 99-100.
37. *Journal of Julia LeGrand*, p. 158.
38. *War-Time Journal of a Georgia Girl*, p. 40.
39. *South Carolina Women in the Confederacy*, II, 187-8.
40. *Ibid.*, I, 313-7.
41. McGuire, *op. cit.*, pp. 168, 240.
42. Roberts, *op. cit.*, p. 6.
43. *Our Women in the War*, p. 438.
44. *South Carolina Women in the Confederacy*, II, 187.
45. *Our Women in the War*, p. 128.
46. *South Carolina Women in the Confederacy*, I, 285.
47. *Our Women in the War*, pp. 86, 283, 439.
48. *Infra*, pp. 194-205.
49. *Our Women in the War*, p. 63.

✓ ✓ ✓

CHAPTER IX

THE PROBLEM OF SELF-SUPPORT

1. *Infra*, pp. 160-75.
2. *Our Women in the War*, p. 7.
3. Elizabeth W. Allston Pringle, *Chronicles of Chicora Wood* (New York, 1922), p. 212.
4. Caroline to William Pettigrew, Cherry Hill, S. C., June 27, 1862, Pettigrew Letters.
5. "The Journal of Ida Dulany, pp. 15 *et seq.*
6. *Supra*, pp. 19-21.
7. *South Carolina Women in the Confederacy*, I, 223.
8. Mildred Maury Humphreys to Colonel B. G. Humphreys, Ittabena, Miss., Feb. 20, 1863, in Walker, comp., *Women of the Southern Confederacy*, n.p.
9. *South Carolina Women in the Confederacy*, I, 189-206.
10. "The Journal of Ida Dulany," pp. 18-78.
11. *O. R.*, Ser. IV, Vol. II, 211-2, 469-71, 559-61.
12. *Ibid.*, pp. 404-5, 863-4, 875-7, 943-4, 973-5; Tatum, *Disloyalty in the Confederacy*, pp. 17-9; Nathaniel W. Stephenson, *The Day of the Confederacy* (New York, 1920), pp. 80, 90-1.
13. Mrs. D. A. Puryear to the governor, Mecklenburg County, Va., Mar. 6, 1865, Executive Papers of the Governors of Virginia, 1865.
14. *O. R.*, Ser. IV, Vol. II, 521-2; Tatum, *op. cit.*, pp. 19-20; Stephenson, *op. cit.*, pp. 80-1, 91-2; J. C. Schwab, *The Confederate States of America* (New York, 1901), pp. 220-5.
15. Malet, *An Errand to the South*, p. 36.
16. *Columbia Baptist*, cited in *South Carolina Women in the Confederacy*, II, 14.
17. Mrs. F. L. Sutton, Mrs. M. C. Hines, and Mrs. J. B. Crump in Walker, comp., *op. cit.*, n.pp.
18. E. E. Collier in *ibid.*, n.p.
19. Day, *Down South*, II, 200.
20. Aug. 19, 1863.
21. Richard to Mrs. M. F. Maury, Camp Barton, Va., Nov. 15, 1863, Maury Papers.

22. David Dodge, pseud., "Domestic Economy in the Confederacy," *Atlantic Monthly*, LVIII (August, 1886), 259.

23. *Our Women in the War*, pp. 444-5.

24. *Diary of a Southern Refugee*, pp. 238-9.

25. For example, Miss C. C. Ball to Governor William Smith, Columbia, S. C., May 27, 1864, Letters and Miscellaneous Papers of the Governors of Virginia, 1864.

26. Putnam, *Richmond During the War*, pp. 173-5.

27. McGuire, *op. cit.*, p. 298.

28. Fisher, "Relief of Soldiers' Families in North Carolina During the Civil War," *loc. cit.*, pp. 69-71; E. A. Volger to Zebulon B. Vance, Salem, N. C., Feb. 7, 1863, Executive Papers of North Carolina, Vance.

29. *Wilmington Journal*, Apr. 30, 1864.

30. Gainesville (Fla.) *Cotton Plant*, cited in *ibid.*, Dec. 3, 1863.

31. *Our Women in the War*, p. 276.

32. Diary, Dec., 1861, Oct. 17 and 18, 1862, June 17, 1864.

33. Underwood, ed., *Women of the Confederacy*, p. 115.

34. Cumming, *Journal of Hospital Life*, p. 122.

35. Fleming, *Civil War and Reconstruction in Alabama*, p. 198.

36. *Charleston Mercury*, Nov. 19, 1862, Sept. 9, 1863.

37. Fisher, *op. cit.*, pp. 60-73; Davis, *Civil War and Reconstruction in Florida*, pp. 188-9; Fleming, *op. cit.*, pp. 196-205.

38. Feb. 29, 1864.

39. G. H. White to Zebulon B. Vance, Statesville, N. C., Nov. 4, 1864, Executive Papers of North Carolina, Vance.

40. Fisher, *op. cit.*, p. 68.

41. *The Last Ninety Days of the War in North Carolina* (New York, 1866), p. 20.

42. Davis, *op. cit.*, pp. 188-9.

43. Fleming, *op. cit.*, pp. 196-201.

44. *Richmond During the War*, p. 343.

45. *Journal of Hospital Life*, p. 160.

46. Nancy P. Richardson to Zebulon B. Vance, Eagle Rock, N. C., Nov. 1, 1864, Executive Papers of North Carolina, Vance.

47. *Our Women in the War*, p. 276.

48. *Journal of Julia LeGrand*, pp. 37-8.

49. *From Flag to Flag*, p. 67.

50. *Three Months in the Southern States*, p. 102.

51. Nichols, *Story of the Great March*, p. 158.

52. Marie Morton to William Smith, Keysville, Va., 1865, Executive Papers of the Governors of Virginia, 1865.

53. Rebecca to William Johnson, Boykins Depot, Va., Jan. 25, 1863, *ibid.*, 1863.

54. Martha W. Banford to William Smith, Rice's Depot, Va., 1864, Miscellaneous Papers and Letters of the Governors of Virginia, 1864.

55. Margaret Smith and others to Zebulon B. Vance, Wayne County, N. C., Feb. 9, 1863, Executive Papers of North Carolina, Vance.

56. Susan C. Walker to Zebulon B. Vance, Hillsdale, N. C., Apr. 3, 1864, *ibid.*

57. Sally Fitzgerald to Zebulon B. Vance, Summerfield, N. C., Apr. 3, 1864, *ibid.*

58. *Charlotte Bulletin*, Mar. 19, 1863, in *Confederate Clippings*, University of North Carolina Library; Tatum, *op. cit.*, p. 22.

59. J. W. Ellis and others to Zebulon B. Vance, Columbus, N. C., Apr. 13, 1864, Executive Papers of North Carolina, Vance.

60. *Our Women in the War*, p. 168.

61. *Richmond Examiner*, Apr. 3, 4, 6, 14, 1863; McGuire, *op. cit.*, pp. 203-4; Putnam, *op. cit.*, pp. 208-10.

62. Edmonston, Diary, Apr. 10, 1863; McGuire, *op. cit.*, p. 203; Putnam, *op. cit.*, p. 210; *Richmond Whig*, cited in (Raleigh) *North Carolina Standard*, Apr. 15, 1863.

63. Pryor, *Reminiscences of Peace and War*, p. 238.

CHAPTER X

INFLATION, THE BLOCKADE, AND SMUGGLING

1. *Supra*, pp. 114-15.
2. Stephenson, *The Day of the Confederacy*, pp. 48-50.
3. McGuire, *Diary of a Southern Refugee*, p. 173.
4. *A Diary from Dixie*, p. 139.
5. Cumming, *Journal of Hospital Life*, pp. 52-3, 108; Sue F. to her brother, Glenfern, Va., Nov. 24, 1861, Gilliam Letters.
6. Margaret Junkin Preston, "A Journal of War Times," in Elizabeth Preston Allan, *The Life and Letters of Margaret Junkin Preston* (New York, 1903), p. 134.
7. Edmonston, Diary, Dec. 13, 1863.
8. *A Diary from Dixie*, p. 294.
9. *Diary of a Southern Refugee*, p. 292. For other comments on the high prices of the period see, *South Carolina Women in the Confederacy*, I, 172-3, and *Our Women in the War*, pp. 356, 437.
10. Edmonston, Diary, Sept. 19, 1864.
11. *South Carolina Women in the Confederacy*, I, 362.
12. Quoted in Stephenson, *op. cit.*, p. 158.
13. Dodge, pseud., "Domestic Economy in the Confederacy," *loc. cit.*, pp. 240-1.
14. Corson, *Two Months in the Confederate States*, p. 100.
15. Hopley, *Life in the South*, II, 335.
16. *A Confederate Girl's Diary*, pp. 212-3.
17. Hopley, *op. cit.*, II, 185.
18. *Sketches of the Rise, Progress, and Decline of Secession*, pp. 422-3. Other accounts of shopping difficulties may be found in Eppes, *Through Some Eventful Years*, p. 190, and Edmonston, Diary, Apr. 8, 1862.
19. *South Carolina Women in the Confederacy*, II, 181.
20. *Our Women in the War*, p. 35.
21. *Ibid.*, p. 439.
22. *Richmond During the War*, p. 303.
23. Harrison, *Recollections Grave and Gay*, p. 191.
24. *Our Women in the War*, p. 164.
25. *A Belle of the Fifties*, pp. 185-6.
26. *Life in the South*, II, 222.
27. *Journal of Hospital Life*, p. 125.
28. *Ibid.*, p. 169.
29. Andrews, *War-Time Journal of a Georgia Girl*, p. 209.
30. J. M. Lucey in Walker, comp., *Women of the Southern Confederacy*, n.p.
31. Annie E. Hill in *ibid.*, n.p.
32. "War Diary of a Union Woman in the South," p. 48.
33. *Reminiscences of Peace and War*, p. 223.
34. Andrews, ed., *Women of the South in War Times*, pp. 116-9.
35. McGuire, *op. cit.*, p. 184.
36. *A Diary from Dixie*, p. 117.
37. *Journal of Julia LeGrand*, p. 118.
38. Baker, *History of the United States Secret Service*, p. 115.
39. Andrews, ed., *Women of the South in War Times*, p. 119.

✐   ✐   ✐

CHAPTER XI

THE ECONOMY OF SCARCITY

1. Hague, *A Blockaded Family*, pp. 32-3, 46-7. See also Eppes, *Through Some Eventful Years*, pp. 177-8, and Mrs. M. P. Handy, "Confederate Make-Shifts," *Harpers Magazine*, LII (March, 1876), 578.
2. Hague, *op. cit.*, p. 33.
3. *Ibid.*, p. 47.
4. *Our Women in the War*, p. 276.

5. Hague, *op. cit.,* pp. 33, 47. For further discussion of the substitutes for drugs and medicines see *Our Women in the War,* p. 428, and Fleming, *Civil War and Reconstruction in Alabama,* pp. 240-1.

6. *Our Women in the War,* p. 245.

7. Hague, *op. cit.,* p. 102.

8. *Reminiscences of Peace and War,* p. 252.

9. *Our Women in the War,* p. 383.

10. Cited in Dodge, pseud., "Domestic Economy in the Confederacy," *loc. cit.,* p. 234.

11. McHatton-Ripley, *From Flag to Flag,* p. 101.

12. Mary J. Welsh, "Makeshifts of the War Between the States," *Publications of the Mississippi Historical Society,* VII (1903), 102.

13. Dodge, pseud., *op. cit.,* p. 235.

14. *From Flag to Flag,* p. 101.

15. *Our Women in the War,* p. 383.

16. *Ibid.,* p. 44.

17. "Domestic Economy in the Confederacy," *loc. cit.,* p. 235.

18. *A Blockaded Family,* p. 31. For other comments on sugar substitutes see Fleming, *op. cit.,* p. 235; Welsh, *op. cit.,* p. 103; and Handy, *op. cit.,* p. 577.

19. *South Carolina Women in the Confederacy,* I, 161-2; Hague, *op. cit.,* pp. 47-8; Welsh, *op. cit.,* p. 104.

20. Corson, *Two Months in the Confederate States,* p. 66.

21. For a comprehensive discussion of the importance of this preservative see Ella Lonn, *Salt as a Factor in the Confederacy* (New York, 1933).

22. Clay, *A Belle of the Fifties,* p. 223; *South Carolina Women in the Confederacy,* I, 142; Dodge, pseud., *op. cit.,* pp. 230-2; Welsh, *op. cit.,* pp. 104-5; Handy, *op. cit.,* pp. 576-7.

23. *A Belle of the Fifties,* p. 235.

24. *South Carolina Women in the Confederacy,* I, 162; *Our Women in the War,* p. 12; McHatton-Ripley, *op. cit.,* p. 100; Hague, *op. cit.,* p. 25; Welsh, *op. cit.,* p. 104.

25. *Our Women in the War,* p. 12.

26. *Ibid.,* p. 429.

27. McHatton-Ripley, *op. cit.,* p. 97.

28. "War Diary of a Union Woman in the South," p. 25.

29. McHatton-Ripley, *op. cit.,* pp. 98-9.

30. Hague, *op. cit.,* pp. 48, 61; Fleming, *op. cit.,* p. 234; Welsh, *op. cit.,* pp. 110-1.

31. *A Blockaded Family,* p. 105.

32. June 19, 1862.

33. Edmonston, Diary, Nov. 17, 1863; Handy, *op. cit.,* pp. 557-8; Welsh, *op. cit.,* p. 104; Mary K. Williams to Mrs. W. H. Polk, Warrenton, N. C., Mar. 23, 1863, Polk Papers.

34. Putnam, *Richmond During the War,* p. 190; Dodge, pseud., *op. cit.,* p. 236; *South Carolina Women in the Confederacy,* I, 363; *Our Women in the War,* p. 455.

35. Cumming, *Journal of Hospital Life,* p. 160.

36. *Our Women in the War,* p. 275.

37. *A Blockaded Family,* p. 41.

38. Elaborate descriptions of these dyeing processes are given in *Our Women in the War,* p. 401; Hague, *op. cit.,* pp. 40, 45-6, 50-1; Fleming, *op. cit.,* p. 238; Putnam, *op. cit.,* p. 251; Handy, *op. cit.,* p. 576; Edmonston, Diary, Feb. 12, 1865; and *Wilmington Journal,* Oct. 27, 1864.

39. Hague, *op. cit.,* pp. 62-4, 118-9.

40. *Ibid.,* p. 37.

41. *South Carolina Women in the Confederacy,* I, 363.

42. Wright, *A Southern Girl in '61,* pp. 197-8; Welsh, *op. cit.,* pp. 109-10; *Our Women in the War,* pp. 27-8.

43. Hague, *op. cit.,* p. 115.

44. *Journal of Hospital Life,* p. 160.

45. *Our Women in the War,* pp. 426-7.

46. Fleming, *op. cit.,* p. 239; *Our Women in the War,* p. 383.

47. *Our Women in the War,* p. 13.

48. "War Diary of a Union Woman in the South," p. 51.

49. Mrs. M. E. Hawkins to Mrs. W. H. Polk, Waverly, N. C., Mar. 20, 1862, Polk Papers.

50. Maury, Diary, Aug. 18, 1862.

51. Harriet to Theophilus Perry, Marshall, Tex., Dec. 6, 1863, Person Papers.

52. *Ibid.*, Sept. 24, 1862.

53. *Richmond During the War*, p. 251.

54. Hague, *op. cit.*, pp. 95-6.

55. *Ibid.*, p. 90.

56. Lib to Nannie ——, Virginia, Feb., 1862, Perkins Letters; unidentified writer to Caroline Caldwell, Newberry, S. C., Feb. 15, 1864, Confederate Mail Bag.

57. Mrs. S. F. Williams, "In the Days of Homespun Dresses," *Confederate Veteran,* XXXIV (April, 1926), 132.

58. Blackford, *Memoirs*, I, 108.

59. Fleming, *op. cit.*, pp. 236-7; Hague, *op. cit.*, pp. 39-40.

60. *Supra,* pp. 18-19.

61. Gay, *Life in Dixie During the War*, p. 29.

62. *Richmond During the War*, p. 88.

63. Edmonston, Diary, Nov. 29, 1862.

64. Hague, *op. cit.*, pp. 49-52; Fleming, *op. cit.*, p. 238; Welsh, *op. cit.*, p. 107.

65. *Our Women in the War*, p. 12.

66. *Ibid.*, p. 340.

67. *Ibid.*, p. 62.

68. McGuire, *Diary of a Southern Refugee*, p. 196.

69. *Our Women in the War*, p. 275.

70. Hague, *op. cit.*, pp. 57-60.

71. *Reminiscences of Peace and War*, pp. 264-5.

72. *Ibid.*, pp. 316-7.

73. Hague, *op. cit.*, p. 52.

74. Handy, *op. cit.*, p. 579; Dodge, pseud., *op. cit.*, pp. 232-3; Welsh, *op. cit.*, pp. 107-8; Fleming, *op. cit.*, p. 234.

75. *South Carolina Women in the Confederacy*, I, 362.

76. *A Blockaded Family*, p. 54.

77. *South Carolina Women in the Confederacy*, I, 73.

78. *Our Women in the War*, p. 384.

79. *Diary of a Southern Refugee*, p. 185.

80. *Our Women in the War*, p. 312.

81. *Ibid.*, p. 356.

82. McGuire, *op. cit.*, pp. 186, 197.

83. *Charleston Mercury*, Oct. 9, 1863.

84. *Our Women in the War*, p. 32.

85. *South Carolina Women in the Confederacy*, I, 364.

86. *Our Women in the War*, p. 32.

87. Andrews, *War-Time Journal of a Georgia Girl*, p. 54.

88. "War Diary of a Union Woman in the South," p. 45.

89. *Our Women in the War*, p. 62.

90. Naomi Hayes to Mrs. W. H. Polk, Shelbyville, Tenn., May 15, 1863, Polk Papers.

91. Andrews, *War-Time Journal of a Georgia Girl*, p. 87.

92. *A Blockaded Family*, p. 91.

93. *Recollections Grave and Gay*, p. 135.

94. *A Southern Woman's Story*, p. 184.

✦   ✦   ✦

CHAPTER XII

RELATIONS WITH THE SLAVES

1. *Journal of Julia LeGrand*, p. 168.

2. *A Diary from Dixie*, p. 38.

3. *Our Women in the War*, p. 340.

4. Davis, *Civil War and Reconstruction in Florida,* pp. 220-4.

5. Rowland, *Varina Howell,* II, 311-2.

6. *A Diary from Dixie,* p. 275.

7. Kate Powell to George Carter, Upperville, Va., 1863, in Andrews, *Scraps of Paper,* p. 209.

8. Hopley, *Life in the South,* II, 227.

9. Anne to W. A. Perkins, Cumberland County, Va., Oct. 2, 1861, Perkins Letters.

10. Edmonston, Diary, Mar. 31, 1862.

11. Margaret to Charles Pettigrew, Badwell, S. C., June 19, 1862, Pettigrew Letters.

12. Caroline to Charles Pettigrew, Cherry Hill, S. C., Oct. 22, 1862, and Mar 27, 1863, *ibid.*

13. Unidentified member of the Pettigrew family to Charles Pettigrew, Abbeville District, S. C., 1863, *ibid.*

14. *Our Women in the War,* pp. 109, 117, 294.

15. McGuire, *Diary of a Southern Refugee,* p. 278.

16. Malet, *An Errand to the South,* pp. 43-4.

17. "A Journal of War Times," pp. 136-7.

18. Diary, Oct. 6, 1862, Feb. 27, 1865.

19. *A Southern Planter* (New York, 1890), p. 196.

20. *Our Women in the War,* p. 455.

21. *Ibid.,* pp. 187, 277.

22. Loughborough, *My Cave Life in Vicksburg,* pp. 135, 144.

23. Smith, *The Soldier's Friend,* p. 122.

24. Dawson, *A Confederate Girl's Diary,* p. 193.

25. Andrews, *War-Time Journal of a Georgia Girl,* p. 242.

26. *South Carolina Women in the Confederacy,* II, 12, 18.

27. Dawson, *A Confederate Girl's Diary,* p. 46.

28. *South Carolina Women in the Confederacy,* I, 208.

29. Edmonston, Diary, Sept. 28, 1863.

30. *Ibid.,* Dec. 6, 1863.

31. Dawson, *A Confederate Girl's Diary,* p. 277.

32. *South Carolina Women in the Confederacy,* I, 73.

33. Cited in Malet, *op. cit.,* p. 265.

34. *Ibid.,* p. 123.

35. *A Blockaded Family,* p. 121.

36. Diary, Mar. 4, 11, Aug. 26, Nov. 13, 1862; June 27, 1863.

37. *Burckmyer Letters,* p. 182.

38. Hopley, *op. cit.,* II, 266.

39. *War-Time Journal of a Georgia Girl,* p. 122.

40. Elizabeth Collins, *Memories of the Southern States* (Taunton, England, 1865), pp. 30-3.

41. Susie Gentry, Williamson County, Tenn., in Walker, comp., *Women of the Southern Confederacy,* n. p.

42. *Our Women in the War,* p. 369.

43. *A Belle of the Fifties,* p. 219.

44. *Our Women in the War,* p. 389.

45. *Ibid.,* p. 389.

46. Roberts, *Historical Incidents,* p. 13; "The Journal of Ida Dulany," p. 18.

47. *A Confederate Girl's Diary,* p. 89.

48. *A Diary from Dixie,* p. 46.

49. Hague, *op. cit.,* pp. 122-4; Edmonston, Diary, Jan. 9, 1865; "Diary of Susan Bradford," pp. 155, 168, 183.

50. Hopley, *op. cit.,* II, 336.

51. Fremantle, *Three Months in the Southern States,* p. 75.

52. Hopley, *op. cit.,* II, 53-5.

53. *Reminiscences of the Women of Missouri,* p. 193; Hague, *op. cit.,* p. 89.

54. *Our Women in the War,* p. 386.

55. *Life in the South,* II, 336.

56. Hague, *op. cit.,* p. 119; Fleming, *Civil War and Reconstruction in Alabama,* p. 244.

57. Smedes, *A Southern Planter*, pp. 212-3.
58. *Our Women in the War*, p. 357.
59. *Ibid.*, pp. 362, 417, 431.
60. *Ibid.*, p. 403.
61. *Ibid.*, pp. 386-7.
62. *Ibid.*, p. 392.
63. "The Journal of Ida Dulany," pp. 20-69.
64. *Our Women in the War*, pp. 186-8.
65. Eppes, *Through Some Eventful Years*, pp. 279-80.
66. Pringle, *Chronicles of Chicora Wood*, pp. 269-75.
67. *Our Women in the War.*, p. 85.
68. *Ibid.*, p. 205.

✓   ✓   ✓

CHAPTER XIII

GAYETY AND EXTRAVAGANCE

1. *Supra*, pp. 4-6.
2. *South Carolina Women in the Confederacy*, I, 171.
3. *A Diary from Dixie*, pp. 166-7.
4. Russell, *My Diary North and South*, I, 255.
5. Rowland, *Varina Howell*, II, 99.
6. *Recollections Grave and Gay*, p. 47.
7. Rowland, *Varina Howell*, II, 153-5.
8. *A Belle of the Fifties*, p. 173.
9. *Diary of a Southern Refugee*, p. 96.
10. Putnam, *Richmond During the War.* p. 38.
11. DeLeon, *Belles, Beaux, and Brains of the 60's*, p. 199.
12. *Recollections Grave and Gay*, p. 94.
13. Clay, *op. cit.*, p. 173.
14. *Four Years in Rebel Capitals*, p. 148.
15. Putnam, *op. cit.*, p. 81.
16. Diary of Travels in the Confederate States, 1863 (anonymous manuscript in New York Public Library).
17. Chesnut, *op. cit.*, p. 298.
18. *Our Women in the War*, p. 167.
19. *South Carolina Women in the Confederacy*, I, 200-1.
20. *Supra*, pp. 155-58.
21. *A Belle of the Fifties*, p. 169.
22. *Our Women in the War*, p. 427.
23. *Charleston Mercury*, Apr. 17, Oct. 9, 1863.
24. *Reminiscences of Peace and War*, p. 265.
25. Cited in Cumming, *Journal of Hospital Life*, p. 191.
26. *Our Women in the War*, p. 234.
27. *Journal of Hospital Life*, p. 184.
28. *Reminiscences of Peace and War*, pp. 313-6.
29. *Richmond During the War*, p. 193.
30. Davis, *Civil War and Reconstruction in Florida*, pp. 199-200.
31. *O. R.*, Ser. IV, Vol. III, 78-80.
32. *Diary of a Southern Refugee*, pp. 328-9.
33. *Journal of Hospital Life*, p. 86.
34. Cited in *Wilmington Journal*, Feb. 4, 1864.
35. Pryor, *op. cit.*, p. 315.
36. *Journal of Julia LeGrand*, p. 173.
37. Rowland, *Varina Howell*, II, 305-10.
38. *Reminiscences of Peace and War*, p. 235.
39. *A Diary from Dixie*, pp. 155, 248, 269, 276, 286, 314.
40. Rowland, *Varina Howell*, II, 374.
41. *South Carolina Women in the Confederacy*, I, 200.
42. *Our Women in the War*, p. 167.

43. *Reminiscences of Peace and War*, p. 326.
44. *A Diary from Dixie*, p. 306.
45. *Our Women in the War*, p. 32.
46. *Ibid.*, p. 325.
47. Eppes, *Through Some Eventful Years*, p. 228.
48. Rowland, *Varina Howell*, II, 283-4.
49. *Our Women in the War*, p. 315.
50. *War-Time Journal of a Georgia Girl*, p. 92.
51. *South Carolina Women in the Confederacy*, I, 278-81.
52. Pringle, *Chronicles of Chicora Wood*, p. 190.
53. Andrews, *Scraps of Paper*, p. 219.
54. Dawson, *A Confederate Girl's Diary*, p. 233.
55. *Our Women in the War*, p. 355.
56. Clay, *op. cit.*, p. 195.
57. Chamberlayne, ed., *Ham Chamberlayne—Virginia*, pp. 299-300.
58. Cornelia Phillips Spencer, Diary, Mar., 1865.
59. Rowland, Diary, July 23, 1863.
60. *Our Women in the War*, p. 304.
61. Lucy Massenburg to an unidentified cousin, Salisbury, N. C., May 29, 1864, Person Papers.
62. Maggie Pittman to Rosa G. C. Burnette, Marley's Mill, N. C., June 15, 1864, Gilliam Letters. See also Mary to Mrs. M. F. Maury, Richmond, Nov. 23, 1863, Maury Papers; and Virginia Baxton Page to Mrs. Reed, Lexington, Va., May 19, 1865, Miscellaneous Confederate Letters, University of Virginia Library.
63. *War-Time Journal of a Georgia Girl*, pp. 71-127, 133-4.
64. *A Diary from Dixie*, pp. 276, 330.
65. Andrews, *War-Time Journal of a Georgia Girl*, p. 61.
66. Sallie E. Blount to Tempie Person, Wilson, N. C., Jan. 4, 1865, Person Papers.
67. *Journal of Hospital Life*, pp. 159, 165, 168.
68. *South Carolina Women in the Confederacy*, I, 253.
69. *Ibid.*, I, 277-9.
70. Wright, *A Southern Girl in '61*, p. 241.
71. *Richmond During the War*, p. 345
72. Day, *Down South*, I, 98-9.
73. *Richmond Examiner*, Feb. 15, Mar. 22, 24, 27, 1865.

❡   ❡   ❡

CHAPTER XIV

AMUSEMENTS AND SOCIAL DIVERSIONS

1. See *supra*, pp. 25-26.
2. Dawson, *A Confederate Girl's Diary*, p. 281; Sue Hart Maury to Mrs. M. F. Maury, Wood Grove, Va., Nov. 12, 1863, Maury Papers.
3. Hopley, *Life in the South*, II, 154-5.
4. Pryor, *Reminiscences of Peace and War*, pp. 324-6.
5. *South Carolina Women in the Confederacy*, I, 280.
6. Von Borcke, *Memoirs of the Confederate War for Independence*, II, 264-7.
7. *A Confederate Girl's Diary*, pp. 245-6.
8. *Reminiscences of Peace and War*, p. 163.
9. Cumming, *Journal of Hospital Life*, p. 51.
10. J. H. Lane, "Glimpses of Army Life in 1864," *Southern Historical Society Papers*, XVIII (1890), 410.
11. Charles Minnegerode, Jr., to Mrs. Charles Minnegerode, Culpeper Court House, Va., May 30, 1863, in Andrews, *Scraps of Paper*, p. 118.
12. *Reminiscences of Peace and War*, pp. 196-7.
13. Ross, *A Visit to the Cities and Camps of the Confederate States*, pp. 223-4.
14. *Our Women in the War*, p. 355.
15. *Memoirs of the Confederate War for Independence*, I, 191-8.
16. Wright, *A Southern Girl in '61*, pp. 149-50, 194.

17. Von Borcke, *op. cit.*, I, 276-81.

18. *Ibid.*, II, 15-6.

19. Fremantle, *Three Months in the Southern States,* pp. 138-9; Naomi Hayes to Mrs. W. H. Polk, Shelbyville, Tenn., June 6, 1863, Polk Papers.

20. *My Cave Life in Vicksburg,* p. 154.

21. Andrews, *Scraps of Paper,* pp. 109-12.

22. Kate Powell to George Carter, Upperville, Va., 1863, in *ibid,* p. 207.

23. Dawson, *A Confederate Girl's Diary,* p. 306.

24. Wright, *op. cit.,* p. 119.

25. *Ibid.*, p. 136; *Our Women in the War,* p. 63; Dawson, *A Confederate Girl's Diary,* p. 314.

26. Von Borcke, *op. cit.,* II, 88.

27. Chamberlayne, ed., *Ham Chamberlayne—Virginian,* p. 156.

28. "Social Life in Richmond During the War," *Southern Historical Society Papers,* XIX (1891), 381.

29. Harrison, *Recollections Grave and Gay,* p. 150; Putnam, *Richmond During the War,* p. 270.

30. *Supra,* p. 28.

31. *Columbia Carolinian,* cited in *New York Herald,* Jan. 29, 1865; *South Carolina Women in the Confederacy,* I, 217-8, 243.

32. Andrews, *War-Time Journal of a Georgia Girl,* pp. 83-4; Harriet Perry to Sallie M. Person, Marshall, Tex., Feb. 18, 1863, Person Papers.

33. McGuire, *Diary of a Southern Refugee,* p. 217.

34. Gay, *Life in Dixie During the War,* pp. 24-8.

35. Clay, *A Belle of the Fifties,* pp. 174-7; Chesnut, *A Diary from Dixie,* pp. 272-4; Harrison, *op. cit.,* pp. 128-30; DeLeon, *Belles, Beaux, and Brains of the 60's,* pp. 216-30.

36. *Four Years in Rebel Capitals,* p. 149.

37. Thad E. Pittman to Rosa G. C. Burnette, Taylorsville, Va., Sept. 16, 1863, Gilliam Letters.

38. Mollie to W. D. Somers, Statesville, N. C., June 1, 1864, Somers Papers.

39. *Diary of a Southern Refugee,* pp. 243-4.

40. *A Diary from Dixie,* pp. 288-9.

41. "Social Life in Richmond During the War," *loc. cit.,* p. 382.

42. Ross, *op. cit.,* p. 251.

43. *Our Women in the War,* p. 428.

44. Pringle, *Chronicles of Chicora Wood,* p. 188.

45. Chesnut, *op. cit.,* p. 235.

46. Hague, *A Blockaded Family,* pp. 137-9.

47. Pringle, *op. cit.,* pp. 187-8.

48. *Reminiscences of the Women of Missouri,* p. 194.

49. *Diary of a Southern Refugee,* p. 54.

50. *Our Women in the War,* p. 126.

✓   ✓   ✓

CHAPTER XV

ANGUISH AND TEARS

1. *Our Women in the War,* p. 262.

2. Blackford, *Memoirs,* I, 104.

3. Dawson, *A Confederate Girl's Diary,* p. 63.

4. *Diary of a Southern Refugee,* p. 234.

5. Blackford, *op. cit.,* I, 121.

6. Mollie to W. D. Somers, Statesville, N. C., June 1, 1864, Somers Papers; Harriet Perry to Sallie M. Person, Marshall, Tex., Feb. 18, 1863, Person Papers; *Our Women in the War,* p. 414.

7. E. L. to W. A. Perkins, Green Hill, Va., 1861, Perkins Letters.

8. Mollie to M. B. DeWitt, Henderson, Ga., Apr. 29, 1864, DeWitt Letters.

9. Blackford, *op. cit.,* I, 68.

10. Diary, May 8, 1864.
11. *Our Women in the War*, p. 414.
12. Dawson, *A Confederate Girl's Diary*, pp. 337-8.
13. Hopley, *Life in the South*, I, 136.
14. Avary, ed., *A Virginia Girl in the Civil War*, pp. 40-1.
15. "A Journal of War Times," p. 139.
16. *Ibid.*, pp. 163-4.
17. Diary, May 18, 1864.
18. *Diary of a Southern Refugee*, p. 231.
19. *Our Women in the War*, pp. 8-10.
20. *A Diary from Dixie*, p. 301.
21. Hopley, *op. cit.*, II, 6-7.
22. *Richmond During the War*, pp. 150-1.
23. *Diary of a Southern Refugee*, pp. 120, 126.
24. Avary, ed., *op. cit.*, p. 228.
25. *Diary of a Southern Refugee*, pp. 179, 211.
26. *A Belle of the Fifties*, p. 190.
27. Mary Boykin Chesnut to Mrs. Louis D. Wigfall, Richmond, June, 1861, in Wright, *A Southern Girl in '61*, p. 84.
28. Minnie Pettigrew to Mrs. Philip I. Porcher, Badwell, S. C., July 21, 1863, Pettigrew Papers.
29. Diary, May 25, 1864.
30. *Our Women in the War*, pp. 437-8.
31. *Reminiscences of the Women of Missouri*, pp. 88-9.
32. McGuire, *op. cit.*, p. 129.
33. *Ibid.*, p. 312.
34. *Journal of Hospital Life*, p. 50.
35. *South Carolina Women in the Confederacy*, II, 153-4.
36. *Our Women in the War*, p. 452.
37. Mrs. Mollie Iredell to Mrs. A. L. Bryan, Raleigh, N. C., July 17, 1863, Pettigrew Letters.
38. Diary, Sept. 3, 1864.
39. *Our Women in the War*, p. 307.
40. Loughborough, *My Cave Life in Vicksburg*, p. 131.
41. *A Diary from Dixie*, pp. 129, 178, 316.
42. *Reminiscences of Peace and War*, pp. 178, 248-50.
43. *Diary of a Southern Refugee*, pp. 211-12.
44. Quoted in Wright, *op. cit.*, p. 126.
45. *Diary of a Southern Refugee*, p. 251.
46. *South Carolina Women in the Confederacy*, II, 15.

✓   ✓   ✓

CHAPTER XVI

DEFEATISM AND DEMORALIZATION

1. *Supra*, pp. 7-8.
2. Cited in Wright, *A Southern Girl in '61*, p. 56.
3. *Diary of a Southern Refugee*, pp. 43-4.
4. *Richmond During the War*, p. 89.
5. *Journal of Julia LeGrand*, p. 38.
6. "A Journal of War Times," p. 134.
7. Tempie to Jessie Person, Louisburg, N. C., May 9, 1862, Person Papers.
8. Preston, "A Journal of War Times," p. 157.
9. Cumming, *Journal of Hospital Lfe*, p. 158.
10. Dawson, *A Confederate Girl's Diary*, p. 210.
11. *Diary of a Southern Refugee*, p. 216.
12. Diary, Apr. 20, 1863.
13. Harriet to Theophilus Perry, Spring Hill, Tex., Jan. 18, 1864, Person Papers.
14. *A Blockaded Family*, p. 142.
15. Pryor, *Reminiscences of Peace and War*, p. 293.

16. *Supra,* pp. 104-6.

17. Richard, *The Florence Nightingale of the Southern Army,* pp. 23-4.

18. Blackford, *Memoirs,* I, 51.

19. *A Diary from Dixie,* pp. 311-12.

20. Charles Pettigrew to an unidentified relative, Hillsboro, N. C., May 9, 1862, Pettigrew Letters.

21. Naomi Hayes Moore to Mrs. W. H. Polk, Augusta, Ga., Feb. 15, 1865, Polk Papers.

22. "Diary of Susan Bradford," p. 180.

23. Maria —— to a cousin, Dinwiddie County, Va., Apr. 26, 1861, Gilliam Letters.

24. *Reminiscences of Peace and War,* pp. 217-9.

25. Smith, *The Soldier's Friend,* pp. 56-82.

26. *Our Women in the War,* p. 164.

27. *Ibid.,* pp. 235-7.

28. Diary, June 20, 1861, Feb. 14, Apr. 23, 1862.

29. "Diary of Susan Bradford," pp. 150, 157-8, 181-2.

30. "A Journal of War Times," p. 137.

31. *A Diary from Dixie,* pp. 86, 106.

32. Diary, Sept. 2, Dec. 14, 1862. Other sentiments of the same character are manifested in the entries of May 23, June 27, July 4 and 9, 1862; May 19, 1864; and Feb. 25, 1865.

33. Anne to W. A. Perkins, Cumberland County, Va., Sept. 5, Nov. 7, 24, Dec. 1, 1861; Feb. 6, 12, Mar. 6, 1862, Perkins Letters.

34. Harriet to Theophilus Perry, Marshall, Tex., Sept. 23, 1864, Person Papers.

35. It has been estimated that, of the 850,000 men who enlisted at one time or another in the Confederate service, 100,000, or more, deserted. See Moore, *Conscription and Conflict in the Confederacy,* p. 359.

36. Cited in Underwood, ed., *Women of the Confederacy,* p. 170.

37. Pember, *A Southern Woman's Story,* p. 64.

38. *New York Herald,* Mar. 26, 1865.

39. Martha E. Curtis to Zebulon B. Vance, Hominy Creek, Buncombe County, N. C., Feb. 15, 1863, Executive Papers of North Carolina, Vance.

40. Margaret Perry to Zebulon B. Vance, Stanly County, N. C., Feb. 7, 1864, *ibid.*

41. Catherine Hunt to Zebulon B. Vance, Randolph County, N. C., Jan. 15, 1863, *ibid.*

42. Mrs. E. L. McCallum to Zebulon B. Vance, Moore County, N. C., Feb. 1, 1863, *ibid.*

43. David Dodge, pseud., "Cave-Dwellers of the Confederacy," *Atlantic Monthly,* LXVIII (October, 1891), 518-9; *O. R.,* Ser. IV, Vol. II, 772-4; Tatum, *Disloyalty in the Confederacy,* pp. 138-9, 151.

44. *Four Years Under Marse Robert* (New York, 1903), p. 349.

45. *O. R.,* Ser. IV, Vol. II, 247.

46. Gainesville *Cotton Plant,* cited in *Wilmington Journal,* Dec. 3, 1863.

✓ ✓ ✓

CHAPTER XVII

THE DESTRUCTION OF THE CONFEDERACY

1. *Our Women in the War,* p. 154.

2. Spencer, Diary, Mar. 20, 1865.

3. Grant to Halleck, City Point, Va., July 14, 1864, *O. R.,* Ser. I, Vol. XXXVII, Pt. II, 300-1.

4. Sherman to Grant, Allatoona, Ga., Oct. 9, 1864, *ibid.,* Ser. I, Vol. XXXIX, Pt. III, 162.

5. Sherman to Halleck, Savannah, Ga., Dec. 24, 1864, *ibid.,* Ser. I, XLIV, 799.

6. *Our Women in the War,* p. 253.

7. *Two Diaries from Middle St. John's, Berkeley, South Carolina* ([Pinopolis, S. C.], 1921), p. 4.

8. Diary, Mar. 14, 1865.

9. *South Carolina Women in the Confederacy*, I, 274.
10. *Our Women in the War*, p. 100.
11. *Ibid.*, p. 441.
12. *Ibid.*, p. 130.
13. *South Carolina Women in the Confederacy*, I, 219.
14. Andrews, *War-Time Journal of a Georgia Girl*, pp. 149-50.
15. *Our Women in the War*, pp. 246-7; Wright, *A Southern Girl in '61*, pp. 201-2.
16. *South Carolina Women in the Confederacy*, I, 276.
17. *Ibid.*, I, 255.
18. *Our Women in the War*, pp. 109, 131; McGuire, *Diary of a Southern Refugee*, p. 290.
19. Cumming, *Journal of Hospital Life*, p. 172.
20. *South Carolina Women in the Confederacy*, I, 166; *Our Women in the War*, p. 240; Mrs. S. H. Last in Walker, comp., *Women of the Southern Confederacy*, n.p.; Mrs. M. H. Maury to Mrs. M. F. Maury, Charlottesville, Virginia, Mar. 14, 1865, Maury Papers.
21. David Dodge, pseud., "Home Scenes at the Fall of the Confederacy," *Atlantic Monthly*, LXIX (May, 1892), 666.
22. *Our Women in the War*, p. 403.
23. Dodge, pseud., "Home Scenes at the Fall of the Confederacy," *loc. cit.*, pp. 664-5.
24. Pringle, *Chronicles of Chicora Wood*, p. 222.
25. *Our Women in the War*, pp. 311, 336, 403.
26. *Ibid.*, p. 358.
27. *Chronicles of Chicora Wood*, p. 224.
28. *Our Women in the War*, p. 108.
29. *South Carolina Women in the Confederacy*, I, 298.
30. *Our Women in the War*, p. 109.
31. *Ibid.*, p. 51.
32. *South Carolina Women in the Confederacy*, I, 164-8; *Charleston Daily Courier*, Feb. 20, 1865.
33. Harrison, *Recollections Grave and Gay*, p. 210.
34. Sue Hart Maury to Mrs. M. F. Maury, Richmond, Apr. 23, 1865, Maury Papers.
35. Putnam, *Richmond During the War*, pp. 366-9; Pryor, *Reminiscences of Peace and War*, pp. 354-7; *New York Herald*, Mar. 13, 1891.
36. *Our Women in the War*, p. 360.
37. *Ibid.*, p. 135.
38. *Ibid.*, p. 434.
39. "Diary of Susan Bradford," p. 274.
40. *South Carolina Women in the Confederacy*, I, 259, 261.
41. *Our Women in the War*, p. 195.
42. Mrs. S. F. Dabney to Mrs. M. F. Maury, Dunlord, Va., Mar. 27, 1865, Maury Papers.
43. *Our Women in the War*, pp. 199-200.
44. *The Last Ninety Days of the War in North Carolina*, p. 95.
45. *Our Women in the War*, p. 327.
46. *Ibid.*, p. 294.
47. McGuire, *op. cit.*, pp. 294-5.
48. *Our Women in the War*, p. 328.
49. *Ibid.*, p. 156.
50. Andrews, ed., *Women of the South in War Times*, p. 227.
51. Sallie E. Jordan in Walker, comp., *op. cit.*, n.p.
52. *A Diary from Dixie*, pp. 359-60.
53. *Our Women in the War*, p. 73.
54. *Ibid.*, p. 215.
55. Elizabeth A. Coxe, *Memories of a South Carolina Plantation* (Philadelphia, 1912), p. 44.
56. *Our Women in the War*, pp. 72, 216.
57. Conyngham, *Sherman's March Through the South*, p. 331.
58. *South Carolina Women in the Confederacy*, I, 266.
59. *Ibid.*, I, 325.

60. *Ibid.*, I, 295-6.

61. Conyngham, *op. cit.*, p. 333.

62. *South Carolina Women in the Confederacy,* I, 331.

63. Nichols, *Story of the Great March,* p. 111.

64. Howard to Logan and Blair, Rice Creek Springs, S. C., Feb. 20, 1865, *O. R.,* Ser. I, Vol. XLVII, Pt. II, 505.

65. Blair to Howard, Beaver Dam Creek, S. C., Mar. 7, 1865, *ibid.,* Ser. I, Vol. XLXII, Pt. II, 717.

66. John M. Oliver to Gordon Lofland, Goldsborough, N. C., Mar. 28, 1865, *ibid.,* Ser. I, Vol. XLVII, Pt. III, 46.

67. Joseph Hawley to J. A. Campbell, Wilmington, N. C., Apr. 1, 1865, *ibid.,* Ser. I, Vol. XLVII, Pt. III, 79.

68. See *infra,* pp. 253-55.

69. *South Carolina Women in the Confederacy,* I, 222.

70. *Our Women in the War,* pp. 137-8.

71. *Ibid.,* pp. 241-3.

72. *South Carolina Women in the Confederacy,* I, 326.

73. *Our Women in the War,* p. 254.

74. *Two Diaries from Middle St. John's, Berkeley, South Carolina,* pp. 31-2; Coxe, *op. cit.,* p. 57.

75. *War-Time Journal of a Georgia Girl,* pp. 199-200.

76. *Journal of Hospital Life,* p. 121.

77. *Wilmington Journal,* Sept. 22, 1864.

78. *Charleston Daily Courier,* Jan. 13, 1865; Reminiscences of Sarah Eloise Ruff, R. Means Davis Papers.

79. *Two Diaries from Middle St. John's, Berkeley, South Carolina.* p. 42.

80. Mrs. H. B. Fraser to H. B. Fraser, Harrison County, Tex., Feb. 14, 1865, Person Papers.

81. *Journal of Hospital Life,* p. 185.

✓   ✓   ✓

CHAPTER XVIII

THE MISERY OF DEFEAT

1. *South Carolina Women in the Confederacy,* I, 260.

2. *Our Women in the War,* p. 196.

3. *Richmond Whig,* Mar. 24, 1865.

4. *New York Herald,* May 20, 21, 1865.

5. *Our Women in the War,* pp. 73-4.

6. *The Last Ninety Days of the War in North Carolina,* pp. 95-6.

7. *New York Herald,* July 16, 1865.

8. *Our Women in the War,* p. 142.

9. *New York Herald,* May 29, 1865.

10. *Our Women in the War,* p. 118.

11. *Reminiscences of Peace and War,* p. 383.

12. *Journal of Hospital Life,* pp. 163, 171. Similar platitudes and expressions of vain optimism are found in Lily Logan to Gen. T. M. Logan, Columbia, S. C., Mar. 2, 1865, in Logan, *My Confederate Girlhood,* p. 80; Naomi Hayes Moore to Mrs. W. H. Polk, Greensboro, Ga., Feb. 25, 1865, Polk Papers; and Edmonston, Diary, Mar. 21, 1865.

13. Cumming, *op. cit.,* p. 176; Edmonston, Diary, Apr. 11, 1865; Alice to Ebbie Leigh, Hood Grove, Miss., Apr. 15, 1865, in *Confederate Veteran,* XXXVI (September, 1928), 355.

14. *Burckmyer Letters,* pp. 471-2.

15. Catherine V. Baxley, Diary and Note Book, June 15, 1865; *New York Herald,* July 14, 1865.

16. Smith, *The Soldier's Friend,* p. 168.

17. Diary, Apr. 16, 1865.

18. *Diary of a Southern Refugee,* p. 352.

19. "A Journal of War Times," p. 207.

20. Rowland, *Varina Howell*, II, 404.

21. Mary H. Maury to M. F. Maury, Charlottesville, Va., May 20, 1865, Maury Papers.

22. Pryor, *op. cit.*, p. 372.

23. "A Journal of War Times," pp. 207-8.

24. Diary, May 5, 1865.

25. Betty H. Maury to Mrs. M. F. Maury, Richmond, Apr. 24, 1865, Maury Papers.

26. Mary Rowe, "A Southern Girl's Diary," *Confederate Veteran*, XL (August, 1932), 301; Dawson, *A Confederate Girl's Diary*, pp. 445-6.

27. Spencer, Diary, May 5, 1865.

28. *South Carolina Women in the Confederacy*, I, 331.

29. *Our Women in the War*, p. 429; Andrews, *War-Time Journal of a Georgia Girl*, pp. 32-3.

30. Rowe, *op. cit.*, pp. 301-2.

31. Francis W. Dawson, *Reminiscences of Confederate Service* (Charleston, 1882), p. 156.

32. *A Diary from Dixie*, p. 353.

33. Cited in Underwood, ed., *Women of the Confederacy*, p. 103.

34. Cumming, *op. cit.*, p. 198; *New York Herald*, May 23, 1865; Andrews, *War-Time Journal of a Georgia Girl*, pp. 227-8; Sidney Andrews, *The South Since the War* (Boston, 1866), pp. 12-16.

35. *Diary of a Southern Refugee*, pp. 355-6.

36. *Our Women in the War*, p. 218.

37. *Two Diaries from Middle St. John's, Berkeley, South Carolina*, p. 45.

38. *New York Herald*, May 6, 1865.

39. Chesnut, *op. cit.*, p. 390; Baxley, Diary and Note Book, June, 1865.

40. Diary, Apr. 23, 1865.

41. *War-Time Journal of a Georgia Girl*, pp. 223-364, *passim*.

42. *Ibid.*, pp. 237-8, 371; Clay, *A Belle of the Fifties*, p. 270.

43. Susan P. Quarles to John R. Thompson, Inglewood, Va., July 2, 1865, Miscellaneous Confederate Letters, University of Virginia Library.

44. *War-Time Journal of a Georgia Girl*, pp. 315-60, *passim*.

45. Diary, May 8, 1865.

46. Andrews, *War-Time Journal of a Georgia Girl*, p. 347.

47. Quoted in Lyle Saxon, *Old Louisiana* (New York, 1929), p. 288.

48. Mrs. J. E. to Irene White, Smithfield, Va., May 13, 1865, Miscellaneous Confederate Letters, University of Virginia Library.

❧   ❧   ❧

CHAPTER XIX

ADJUSTMENT AND RECOVERY

1. Andrews, *The South Since the War*, p. 29; Andrews, *War-Time Journal of a Georgia Girl*, p. 365; Charles A. Dana to E. M. Stanton, Richmond, Apr. 10, 1865, Stanton Papers.

2. Mary H. Maury to Trevina Maury, Charlottesville, Va., May 21, 1865, Maury Papers.

3. Avary, ed., *A Virginia Girl in the Civil War*, p. 369; *Our Women in the War*, pp. 104-5.

4. Putnam, *Richmond During the War*, p. 373.

5. McGuire, *Diary of a Southern Refugee*, p. 349; Harrison, *Recollections Grave and Gay*, p. 212; Pember, *A Southern Woman's Story*, p. 176.

6. Andrews, ed., *Women of the South in War Times*, p. 235.

7. Spencer, Diary, May 4, 1865.

8. *New York Herald*, Apr. 13, 1865.

9. Pryor, *Reminscences of Peace and War*, pp. 376-80.

10. *War-Time Journal of a Georgia Girl*, pp. 224, 356-7, 362.

11. Pryor, *op. cit.*, p. 368; *Our Women in the War*, p. 107.

12. *Our Women in the War*, pp. 119-21.

13. *A Diary from Dixie*, p. 253.

14. *South Carolina Women in the Confederacy*, I, 167.

15. *War-Time Journal of a Georgia Girl*, p. 373.

16. *Our Women in the War*, p. 217.

17. Andrews, ed., *Women of the South in War Times*, pp. 241-5.

18. Sue Hart Maury to Mrs. M. F. Maury, Richmond, Apr. 23, 1865, Maury Papers.

19. Chesnut, *op. cit.*, p. 363.

20. Diary, May 5, 1865.

21. "Diary of Susan Bradford," p. 276.

22. *A Rebel's Recollections*, p. 73.

23. *A Diary from Dixie*, p. 385.

24. Diary, May 7, 1865.

25. "Diary of Susan Bradford," p. 298.

26. *New York Herald*, May 8, 1865.

27. Quoted in Pryor, *op. cit.*, p. 354.

28. *South Carolina Women in the Confederacy*, II, 160.

29. Smith, *The Soldier's Friend*, p. 159.

30. *Diary of a Southern Refugee*, p. 355.

31. Cumming, *Journal of Hospital Life*, p. 198.

32. Putnam, *op. cit.*, p. 386.

33. *War-Time Journal of a Georgia Girl*, pp. 289-90.

✝ ✝ ✝

CHAPTER XX

RETREAT FROM GLORY

1. Graham, *et al.*, eds., *History of the Confederated Memorial Associations of the South*, pp. 29-31; Charles W. Ramsdell, "The Southern Heritage," in W. T. Couch, ed., *Culture in the South* (Chapel Hill, 1934), p. 15; Marjorie S. Mendenhall, "Southern Women of a 'Lost Generation,'" *South Atlantic Quarterly*, XXXIII (October, 1934), 334-53.

2. Spencer, *The Last Ninety Days of the War in North Carolina*, p. 265.

3. *South Carolina Women in the Confederacy*, I, 371.

4. McGuire, *Diary of a Southern Refugee*, p. 360.

BIBLIOGRAPHY

PRIMARY SOURCES

I. Manuscripts

Among unpublished materials used in the preparation of this volume the most extensive single item is Catherine Ann (Devereaux) Edmonston, Diary, 1860-1866 (North Carolina Historical Commission), an outspoken and profuse record kept by the intensely pro-Southern daughter of a wealthy planter in Halifax County, North Carolina. Similar in character but less voluminous are Kate Mason Rowland, Diary, 1861-1865 (Confederate Museum, Richmond), and Betty Herndon Maury, Diary, June, 1861-February, 1865 (Library of Congress). More restricted are Ella Saunders McFarland, Journal, Courtland, Alabama, 1862-1864 (Tennessee State Library) ; Mrs. W. W. Lord, Journal Kept During the Siege of Vicksburg, May-July, 1863 (Library of Congress) ; Catherine Virginia Baxley, Diary and Note Book . . . While a Prisoner in Old Capitol Prison, Washington, April-August, 1865 (New York Public Library) ; and Cornelia Phillips Spencer, Diary, Chapel Hill, North Carolina, 1865 (University of North Carolina Library). Of slight value are Mrs. T. D. Trapier, Memoirs (University of North Carolina Library), and Hanson Hard, Account of a Journey from Paducah, Kentucky . . . to Mobile (Library of Congress).

The largest collection of unpublished correspondence examined is the Pettigrew Letters (University of North Carolina Library), containing hundreds of letters which elaborately disclose the thoughts and problems of the feminine members of a family that was prominent in the two Carolinas. Other collections, less extensive but equally informing, are Miscellaneous Confederate Letters (University of Virginia Library) ; Gilliam Letters (in the possession of Mrs. Martha Cox Wheeler, Burnt Quarter, Dinwiddie County, Virginia) ; the Matthew F. Maury Letters (Library of Congress) ; Person Papers (Duke University Library) ; Somers Papers (Duke University Library) ; and the William H. Polk Papers and Letters (North Carolina Historical Commission and University of North Carolina Library). A few letters of this type are also contained in the W. H. S. Burgwyn Papers (North Carolina Historical Commission) ; Pettigrew Papers (North Carolina Historical Commission) ; the Edwin M. Stanton Papers (Library of Congress) ; the R. Means Davis Papers (in the possession of Professor Henry C. Davis, Columbia, South Carolina) ; and Confederate Mail Bag, Newberry, South Carolina, 1864 (New York Public Library). The William A. Perkins Letters (University of Virginia Library) and the M. B. DeWitt Letters (in the possession of Judge John H. DeWitt, Nashville, Tennessee) intimately reveal relations between Confederate wives and their soldier-husbands. The feelings and problems of the women of the poorer classes are profusely set forth in the Zebulon B. Vance Papers and the Executive Papers of North Carolina, Vance (North Carolina Historical Commission) ; and to a lesser extent in Letters and Miscellaneous Papers of the Governors of Virginia, 1861-1865, and Executive Papers of the Governors of Virginia, 1861-1865 (State Archives, Richmond).

II. Printed Sources

1. Official Documents

The Confederate Statutes at Large, 8 vols. (Richmond, 1861-1864), and the Journals of the Congress of the Confederate States, 8 vols. (Washington, 1904), contain a few scattered references to the work of Southern women among the sick and wounded of the Confederate armies. The voluminous War of the Rebellion, Official Records of the Union and Confederate Armies, 130 vols. (Washington, 1880-1901), is only slightly concerned with the problems of Confederate women.

2. Diaries and Contemporary Correspondence

Mary Boykin Chesnut, A Diary from Dixie, edited by Isabella D. Martin and Myrta L. Avary (New York, 1929), is a fascinating and brilliantly written work, covering the entire period of the war and giving a thorough, critical, and confessional insight into the thoughts of the women of the Confederate aristocracy. Less extensively known but equally enlightening are Kate Cumming, Journal of Hospital Life in the Confederate Army of the Tennessee from the Battle of Shiloh . . . (Louisville, 1866), and Judith W. McGuire, Diary of a Southern Refugee During the War (Richmond, 1889). Approximating these three works in scope and detail are Sarah Morgan Dawson, A Confederate Girl's Diary, edited by Warrington Dawson (New York, 1913); Journal of Julia LeGrand, edited by Kate Mason Rowland and Mrs. Morris LeGrand Croxall (Richmond, 1911); Eliza Frances Andrews, War-Time Journal of a Georgia Girl (New York, 1908); and the diary of Susan Bradford in Susan Bradford Eppes, Through Some Eventful Years (Macon, Ga., 1926). Less elaborate diaries of Southern women are Margaret Junkin Preston, "A Journal of War Times," in Elizabeth Preston Allan, Life and Letters of Margaret Junkin Preston (New York, 1903); "The Journal of Ida Dulany," in Marietta Minnigerode Andrews, Scraps of Paper (New York, 1929); "War Diary of a Union Woman in the South," in George W. Cable, ed., Famous Adventures and Prison Escapes of the Civil War (New York, 1893); "The Diary of Harriette Cary," Tyler's Quarterly Historical and Genealogical Magazine, IX (October, 1927), 105-115, and XII (January, 1930), 160-173; [Susan R. Jervey and Charlotte St. Julian Ravenel], Two Diaries from Middle St. John's, Berkeley, South Carolina ([Pinopolis, S. C.], 1921); Frances H. Fearn, ed., Diary of a Refugee (New York, 1910); Dolly Sumner Lunt Burge, A Woman's Wartime Journal: an Account of the Passage Over a Georgia Plantation of Sherman's Army on the March to the Sea, edited by Julian Street (New York, 1927); and Cornelia McDonald, Diary with Reminiscences of the War and Refugee Life in the Shenandoah Valley, edited by Hunter McDonald (Nashville, 1935). John B. Jones, A Rebel War Clerk's Diary at the Confederate States Capital, 2 vols. (Philadelphia, 1866), and M. A. De Wolfe Howe, ed., Marching with Sherman: Passages from the Letters and Campaign Diaries of Henry Hitchcock (New Haven, 1927), give some attention to feminine problems in the South.

Important collections of contemporary correspondence are Charlotte R. Holmes, ed., The Burckmyer Letters (Columbia S. C., 1926), vividly portraying the thoughts of a Charleston woman living in France; and Susan Leigh Colston

Blackford, *Memoirs of Life In and Out of the Army in Virginia During the War Between the States,* 2 vols. (35 copies privately printed, Lynchburg, 1894), containing many intimate letters from a wife to a soldier-husband. Other collections, containing occasional references to feminine affairs, are C. G. Chamberlayne, ed., *Ham Chamberlayne—Virginian: Letters and Papers of an Artillery Officer in the War for Southern Independence* (Richmond, 1932) ; J. G. deRoulhac Hamilton, ed., *Correspondence of Jonathan Worth,* 2 vols. (Raleigh, 1909) ; Martha G. and Mary A. Waring, eds., "Some Observations of the Years 1860 and 1861 as Revealed by a Packet of Old Letters," *Georgia Historical Quarterly,* XV (September, 1931), 272-292; Alicia Hopton Middleton, ed., *Life in Carolina and New England During the Nineteenth Century as Illustrated by Reminiscences and Letters of the Middleton Family of Charleston, South Carolina, and of the De Wolfe Family of Bristol, Rhode Island* (Providence, R. I., 1929) ; and J. B. Polley, *A Soldier's Letters to Charming Nellie* (New York, 1908).

3. Travelers' Accounts

The most informing treatment of living conditions among Confederate women by a foreign traveler is Catherine Cooper Hopley, *Life in the South . . . from the Spring of 1860 to August, 1862,* 2 vols. (London, 1863), the record of an English schoolmistress who was employed in Virginia and Florida. William Wyndham Malet, *An Errand to the South in the Summer of 1862* (London, 1863), and Elizabeth Collins, *Memories of the Southern States* (Taunton, England, 1865), briefly describe the experiences of two English people on the same South Carolina plantation. Frequent references to living conditions are also found in Samuel Phillips Day, *Down South; or an Englishman's Experiences at the Seat of the American War,* 2 vols. (London, 1862) ; Sarah L. Jones, *Life in the South* (London, 1863) ; Fitzgerald Ross, *A Visit to the Cities and Camps of the Confederate States* (London, 1865) ; and W. C. Corson, *Two Months in the Confederate States, Including a Visit to New Orleans Under th Domination of General Butler* (London, 1863). Eliza McHatton-Ripley, *From Flag to Flag: a Woman's Adventures and Experiences in the South During the War, in Mexico, and in Cuba* (New York, 1889), portrays a journey through Louisiana and Texas, with lively attention to the more active phases of feminine life. Vivid descriptions of war-time social life are given in J. H. Heros von Borcke, *Memoirs of the Confederate War for Independence,* 2 vols. (London, 1866), a sprightly narrative by the Prussian companion of "Jeb" Stuart. The better known works of foreign travelers, William Howard Russell, *My Diary North and South,* 2 vols. (London, 1862), and Lieutenant Colonel [Arthur J. L.] Fremantle, *Three Months in the Southern States* (New York, 1864), are too preoccupied with public matters to give more than passing attention to feminine problems. This is also true of "An English Officer" [Garnet Wolseley], "A Month's Visit to the Confederate Headquarters," *Blackwood's Magazine,* XCIII (January, 1863), 1-29. Bela Estvan, *War Pictures from the South* (London, 1863), is an unreliable account by a foreign adventurer who claims to have served in the Confederate army.

The numerous accounts by Northern travelers in the South are as a general rule little concerned with conditions among the women. The following works, however, reveal fugitive information on this subject: Joel Cook, *The Siege of*

Richmond (Philadelphia, 1863) ; L. C. Baker, *History of the United States Secret Service* (Philadelphia, 1867) ; David P. Conyngham, *Sherman's March Through the South* (New York, 1867) ; George Ward Nichols, *The Story of the Great March; from the Diary of a Staff Officer* (New York, 1865) ; and Sidney Andrews, *The South Since the War as Shown by Fourteen Weeks of Observation in Georgia and the Carolinas* (Boston, 1866).

4. Memoirs and Reminiscences

Sources of this type are extensive and contain much valuable information scattered through much that is trivial and unreliable. Francis W. Dawson, ed., *Our Women in the War. The Lives They Lived; the Deaths They Died* (Charleston, 1885), is a voluminous and informing compilation, containing seventy-nine recollections and diaries by women from most of the states of the former Confederacy, written in many instances with lively passion and naïve frankness. Similar compilations, devoted to individual states, are Mrs. Thomas Taylor, *et al.*, eds., *South Carolina Women in the Confederacy*, 2 vols. (Columbia, 1903 and 1907) ; Mrs. Blake L. Woodson, *et al.*, eds., *Reminiscences of the Women of Missouri in the Sixties* (Jefferson City, [1916]) ; and J. M. Lucey, *et al.*, eds., *Confederate Women of Arkansas in the Civil War* (Little Rock, 1907). Mrs. Roger A. Pryor, *Reminiscences of Peace and War* (New York, 1904) ; Mrs. Clement C. Clay, *A Belle of the Fifties* (New York, 1905) ; Mrs. Burton Harrison, *Recollections Grave and Gay* (New York, 1912) ; and Mrs. D. Giraud Wright, *A Southern Girl in '61: War-Time Memories of a Confederate Senator's Daughter* (New York, 1905), are standard recollections of Confederate women who moved in official circles. More realistic and critical but less extensively known are Phoebe Yates Pember, *A Southern Woman's Story* (New York, 1879) ; Sallie A. Brock Putnam, *Richmond During the War: Four Years of Personal Observations by a Richmond Lady* (New York, 1867) ; and Myrta L. Avary, ed., *A Virginia Girl in the Civil War, Being the Record of the Actual Experiences of the Wife of a Confederate Officer* (New York, 1903). Susan Dabney Smedes, *A Southern Planter* (New York, 1890) ; Elizabeth W. Allston Pringle, *Chronicles of Chicora Wood* (New York, 1922) ; and Rebecca Latimer Felton, *Country Life in Georgia in the Days of My Youth* (Atlanta, 1919), devote chapters to war-time domestic problems. Especially difficult hardships are described in Mary Ann Webster Loughborough, *My Cave Life in Vicksburg* (New York, 1864), and Cornelia Phillips Spencer, *The Last Ninety Days of the War in North Carolina* (New York, 1886). Parthenia Antoinette Hague, *A Blockaded Family: Life in Southern Alabama During the Civil War* (New York, 1888), is a work of particular merit, discussing household problems intimately and thoroughly. The voluminous apologia of Varina Howell Davis, *Jefferson Davis, ex-President of the Confederacy; A Memoir by His Wife*, 2 vols. (New York, 1890), is distinctly disappointing from the feminine point of view.

The following recollections are of some importance and are arranged in the order of their value to the present study: Mrs. S. E. D. Smith, *The Soldier's Friend . . . Four Years' Experience and Observation in the Hospitals of the South* (Memphis, 1867) ; Fannie A. Beers, *Memories: A Record of Personal Experience and Adventure During Four Years of War* (Philadelphia, 1888) ;

Elizabeth Allen Coxe, *Memories of a South Carolina Plantation During the War* (Privately printed, Philadelphia, 1912) ; Mary A. H. Gay, *Life in Dixie During the War* (Atlanta, 1894) ; Elizabeth Lyle Saxon, *A Southern Woman's War-Time Reminiscences* (Memphis, 1905) ; Sallie Chapman Law, *Reminiscences of the War of the Sixties Between the North and South* (Memphis, 1892) ; Kate Virginia Cox Logan, *My Confederate Girlhood*, edited by Lily Logan Morrill (Richmond, 1932) ; Mrs. Frances Hall, *Major Hall's Wife: a Thrilling Story of the Life of a Southern Wife and Mother While a Refugee* (Syracuse, 1884) ; La Salle Corbell Pickett, *What Happened to Me* (New York, 1917) ; Mary Branch Polk, *Memoirs of a Southern Woman Within the Lines* (Chicago, 1912) ; Rose Harlow Warren, *A Southern Home in War Times* (New York, 1914) ; Caroline E. Merrick, *Old Times in Dixie Land: A Southern Matron's Memories* (New York, 1901) ; and Mrs. F. C. Roberts, *Historical Incidents: What "Our Women in the War" Did and Suffered* (Beaufort, N. C., 1909).

The following works of adventure are of slight value and of doubtful authenticity: Belle Boyd, *Belle Boyd in Camp and Prison*, 2 vols. (London, 1865) ; Rose O'Neal Greenhow, *My Imprisonment and the First Year of Abolition Rule in Washington* (London, 1863) ; and C. G. Worthington, ed., *The Woman in Battle: a Narrative of the Exploits, Adventures, and Travels of Madame Loreta Janeta Velasquez* (New York, 1890).

The extensive memoirs of the Southern men of the period usually contain little information on domestic and feminine problems. Among the few works which are exceptions to this rule are: Thomas Cooper DeLeon, *Four Years in Rebel Capitals* (Mobile, 1892) and *Belles, Beaux and Brains of the 60's* (New York, 1907), giving intimate descriptions of the social life of Richmond and other Southern cities; George Cary Eggleston, *A Rebel's Recollections* (New York, 1905) and *Southern Soldier Stories* (New York, 1911), books rich in anecdotes; and Francis W. Dawson, *Reminiscences of Confederate Service* (Privately printed, Charleston, 1882), a slender volume which touches upon social life in the Confederate capital. William G. Brownlow, *Sketches of the Rise, Progress and Decline of Secession, with a Narrative of Personal Adventures Among the Rebels* (Philadelphia, 1862), and James W. Evans and A. Wendell Keith, eds., *Autobiography of Samuel S. Hildebrand* (Jefferson City, Mo., 1870), give some attention to conditions among the women of the border states; and Robert Stiles, *Four Years Under Marse Robert* (New York, 1903), has brief comments upon the significance of domestic hardships as a cause of desertion among the Confederate soldiers.

Miscellaneous memoirs and personal accounts of some slight value are contained in H. W. R. Jackson, *The Southern Women of the Second American Revolution* (Atlanta, 1863) ; A. W. Bishop, *Loyalty on the Frontier* (St. Louis, 1863) ; Edward Everett, *Account of the Fund for the Relief of East Tennessee* (Boston, 1864) ; J. W. Jones, *Christ in Camp; or Religion in Lee's Army* (Richmond, 1888) ; John J. Williamson, *Mosby's Rangers: A Record of the Operations of the Forty-Third Battalion Virginia Cavalry from its Organization to the Surrender* (New York, 1896) ; and James G. Gibbes, *Who Burnt Columbia?* (Newberry, S. C., 1902).

III. Newspapers, Scrapbooks, and Periodicals

Representative among the newspapers which have been consulted are the *Charleston Mercury* and *Charleston Courier;* the *Richmond Enquirer, Richmond Examiner,* and *Richmond Sentinel;* the *Wilmington* (N. C.) *Journal* and the (Raleigh) *North Carolina Standard.* Scattered through the files of these journals are references to feminine problems taken from newspapers in every section of the Confederacy. *The Southern Illustrated News,* published at Richmond, carried a housewife's department in which Confederate recipes and other items pertaining to the domestic economy of war times were frequently printed. The *New York Herald* and the *New York Times* are valuable for the reports of their Southern correspondents.

C. Irvine Walker, comp., *The Women of the Southern Confederacy During the War . . . Original Historical Incidents of Their Heroism, Suffering, and Devotion Published in "Our Women in the War" Supplements to Leading Newspapers . . . Clipped from Original Publications,* 2 vols. (Printed title pages, Charleston, 1908), is a huge scrapbook in the possession of the Charleston Library Society, containing many reminiscences of Confederate women, some letters, and a few diaries. A less extensive collection of the same character is preserved in *Confederate Clippings,* a file in the Library of the University of North Carolina.

The *Southern Historical Society Papers,* 47 vols. (Richmond, 1873-1930), and the *Confederate Veteran,* 40 vols. (Nashville, 1893-1932), also contain frequent references to the experiences of Confederate women. *The Southern Magazine* (Wytheville, Va., 1934-) promises to have similar material.

SECONDARY WORKS

J. L. Underwood, ed., *The Women of the Confederacy . . . With Accounts of Their Trials During the War and the Period of Reconstruction* (New York, 1906), and Matthew Page Andrews, ed., *The Women of the South in War Times* (Baltimore, 1924), are widely known general treatments, but they are little else than compilations of some of the more obvious sources with much irrelevant material added. The most elaborate biography of a Confederate woman is Eron Rowland, *Varina Howell, Wife of Jefferson Davis,* 2 vols. (New York, 1927 and 1931). Other biographical works are Anson and Fannie Nelson, *Memorials of Sarah Childress Polk* (New York, 1892) ; Hope S. Chamberlain, *Old Days in Chapel Hill, Being the Life and Letters of Cornelia Phillips Spencer* (Chapel Hill, 1926) ; J. Fraise Richard, *The Florence Nightingale of the Southern Army: Experiences of Ella King Newsom* (New York, 1914) ; Bradley T. Johnson, "Memoir of Jane Claudia Johnson," *Southern Historical Society Papers,* XXIX (1901), 33-45; and Jessie Melville Fraser, "Louisa C. McCord," *Bulletin of the University of South Carolina,* XCI (October, 1920), 3-42. A few sketches of Confederate women are included in Allen Johnson and Dumas Malone, eds., *Dictionary of American Biography* (New York, 1928-). Joseph Hergesheimer, *Swords and Roses* (New York, 1929) ; Allen Tate, *Jefferson Davis: His Rise and Fall* (New York, 1929) ; and Lyle Saxon, *Old Louisiana* (New York, 1929), contain brilliant characterizations of Confederate women; and *A Checkered Life: Being a Brief History of the*

*Countess Pourtales, Formerly Miss Marie Boozer of Columbia, S. C. . . .
Compiled by "One Who Knows"* (Columbia, 1878), gives a glamorous but unreliable account of the career of a Confederate adventuress. The work of Roman Catholic religious orders among the sick and wounded is effectively described in George Barton, *Angels of the Battlefields: A History of the Catholic Sisterhoods in the Late Civil War* (Philadelphia, 1897), and Ellen Ryan Jolly, *Nuns of the Battlefield* (Providence, R. I., 1927).

Authoritative treatments of various phases of domestic life in the Confederacy are found in Walter L. Fleming, *Civil War and Reconstruction in Alabama* (New York, 1905) ; William Watson Davis, *Civil War and Reconstruction in Florida* (New York, 1913) ; Ella Lonn, *Desertion During the Civil War* (New York, 1928) and *Salt as a Factor in the Confederacy* (New York, 1933) ; David Dodge, pseud. [O. W. Blacknall], "Domestic Economy in the Confederacy," *Atlantic Monthly*, LVIII (August, 1886), 229-242, "Cave Dwellers of the Confederacy," *Atlantic Monthly*, LXVIII (October, 1891), 514-521, and "Home Scenes at the Fall of the Confederacy," *Atlantic Monthly*, LXIX (May, 1892), 661-670; Mrs. M. P. Handy, "Confederate Make-Shifts," *Harpers Magazine*, LII (March, 1876), 576-580; Mary J. Welsh, "Makeshifts of the War Between the States," *Publications of the Mississippi Historical Society*, VII (1903), 101-113; and Clyde Olin Fisher, "Relief of Soldiers' Families in North Carolina During the Civil War," *South Atlantic Quarterly*, XVI (January, 1917), 60-73. Georgia Lee Tatum, *Disloyalty in the Confederacy* (Chapel Hill, 1934) ; Albert B. Moore, *Conscription and Conflict in the Confederacy* (New York, 1924) ; and Frank L. Owsley, "Local Defense and the Overthrow of the Confederacy," *Mississippi Valley Historical Review*, XI (March, 1925), 490-525, are also authoritative treatises but throw little light on feminine problems.

Various features of feminine activity are discussed in Lucy London Anderson, *North Carolina Women of the Confederacy* (Fayetteville, N. C., 1926), a compilation containing important facts; Alexander Hunter, *Women of the Debatable Land* (Washington, 1912) ; James Parton, *General Butler in New Orleans* (New York, 1864) ; Louise Benton Graham, *et al.*, eds., *History of the Confederated Memorial Associations of the South* (New Orleans, 1904) ; Wyndham B. Blanton, *Medicine in Virginia in the Nineteenth Century* (Richmond, 1933) ; Virginia Gearhart Gray, "Activities of Southern Women, 1840-1860," *South Atlantic Quarterly*, XXVII (July, 1928), 264-279; and Marjorie S. Mendenhall, "Southern Women of a 'Lost Generation,'" *South Atlantic Quarterly*, XXXIII (October, 1934), 334-353.

The following are standard treatments whose value to the present work is obvious: John B. McMaster, *A History of the United States During Lincoln's Administration* (New York, 1927) ; Francis T. Miller, ed., *Photographic History of the Civil War*, 10 vols. (New York, 1911) ; Nathaniel Wright Stephenson, *The Day of the Confederacy, A Chronicle of the Embattled South* (New York, 1920) ; William Best Hesseltine, *Civil War Prisons, a Study in War Psychosis* (Columbus, Ohio, 1930) ; Thomas L. Livermore, *Numbers and Losses During the American Civil War* (New York, 1900) ; J. C. Schwab, *The Confederate States of America* (New York, 1901) ; Henry T. Shanks, *The Secession Movement in Virginia* (Richmond, 1934) ; J. G. deRoulhac Hamilton, *Reconstruction in North Carolina* (New York, 1914) and *North Carolina Since*

1860 (Chicago, 1919) ; James Welch Patton, *Unionism and Reconstruction in Tennessee* (Chapel Hill, 1934) ; Oliver P. Temple, *East Tennessee and the Civil War* (Cincinnati, 1899) ; Thomas W. Humes, *The Loyal Mountaineers of Tennessee* (Knoxville, 1888) ; E. C. Smith, *The Borderland in the Civil War* (New York, 1927) ; and John McElroy, *The Struggle for Missouri* (Washington, 1909).

INDEX

Abbeville District, S. C., 162.
Aberdeen, Miss., 48.
Abolitionists, 1-2, 162-3.
Alabama, soldiers' relief in, 22, 23; relief of soldiers' families, 120, 122-3, 124; shortage of clothing, 148.
Alabama, women of, 76, 140, 167, 218, 219; encouraging martial activity, 17; support hospital at Montgomery, 85; destitution among, 120, 124; make substitutes for drugs, 138; cloth-making, 150.
Alachua County, Fla., 120.
Alden, Esther, 197.
Aldrich, Mrs. A. P., maintains discipline among slaves, 175; experience with Federal incendiaries, 236.
Aldrich sisters, journey across South Carolina, 108.
Alexandria, Va., 46.
Alfriend, Edward M., quoted, 200, 203.
Alleghany Springs, Va., 189.
Allston, Della, wedding of, 204.
Allston, Elizabeth W., 188.
Allston, Mrs. Robert F. W., manages plantation, 112.
Amateur theatricals, 201-3.
Amusements, 194-203; among Negroes, 170-2.
Anderson, S. C., 96.
Andersonville Prison, 66, 68.
Andrews, Eliza F., 103, 259; avoids Federals, 55; on treatment of Federal prisoners, 65, 66; experiences as a refugee, 108; protests against whipping a slave, 168; defends social pleasures, 187; social activities, 190-1; experience with Federal soldiers, 242; on conduct of the conquerors, 249-50, 254; on new status of the Negro, 250; does housework, 255.
Appomattox, surrender at, 190, 246-7.
Arkansas, women of, encourage secession, 11; experience with Federal marauders, 34-5, 48-9; manage farms, 116; smugglers, 135.
Ashland, Va., 96-7.
Atlanta, 248; extravagance in, 26; mourning in, 216; destitution in, 244.
Augusta, Ga., 244.

Bainbridge, Ga., 232.
Balls Bluff, battle of, 81.
Balls, military, 196-7, 199-200.
Barbecues, 170, 254.
Barnwell, Mary, 215.
Barnwell, S. C., 175, 236.
Barrington, Mat, 48-9.
Baton Rouge, La., 52, 56, 60, 67, 101, 165, 169, 208.
Baxley, Catherine V., 12.

Bazaars, 192, 200-1.
Bedford, Va., 182, 222.
Beech Island, S. C., 169.
Beers, Fannie A., 88.
Benton, Ark., 48.
Berryville, Va., 46-7, 205, 236-7.
Bible-reading, encouragement of, 36-7; to the slaves, 167.
Bierne, Betty, wedding of, 204.
Black Creek, Ala., 76.
Blackford, Mrs. Charles L., 220.
Blacknall, O. W., see Dodge, David.
Black Oak Soldiers' Relief Association, 65.
Bladenboro, N. C., 127.
Blair, Gen. Francis P., 239-40.
Blalock, Mrs. L. M., 80.
Blockade, effects of, 131-5.
Boon Hill, N. C., 127.
Boozer, Mary, adventures of, 63-4, 271.
Border states, women of, 11-12.
Bovina, Miss., 59.
Bowling Green, Ky., 86.
Boyd, Belle, exploits of, 79-80, 273.
Bradford, Mary, 71-2.
Bradford, Susan, 223.
Bragg, Gen. Braxton, 31.
Bread riots, 126-8.
Breckinridge, Mrs. Gilmer, 6; experience with Federal intruders, 46; on coffee substitutes, 140; on tea substitutes, 141.
Brockenbrough, Mrs. W. S. R., 37-8.
Brown, Mrs. D. W., 20.
Brown, John, reaction to raid of, 1.
Brown, Madge, 117.
Brownlow, W. G., 132-3.
Buford, Lieut. Harry T., see Velasquez, Loreta J.
Buie, Mary Ann, 21.
Burial of soldiers, 37-8.
Bushwhackers, 45, 47.
Butler, Gen. B. F., at Norfolk, 53; at New Orleans, 57-8.
Buttons, manufacture of, 155.

Camden, S. C., 2-3.
Camden County, N. C., 232.
Camp-followers, 75.
Candles, substitutes for, 145.
Carter, William B., 63.
Cary, Constance, see Harrison, Mrs. Burton.
Cary, Harriette, 58-9.
Cary, Jennie and Hetty, 12.
Catholic sisterhoods, nursing work of, 94-5.
Cave-life, in Vicksburg, 72-4; in North Carolina, 226-7.
Censorship, Confederate, use of, 34.
Centreville, Va., 194, 220.
Chamberlayne, Capt. Ham, 30, 200.